ZIONISM: THE CRUCIAL PHASE

ZIONISM:
THE
CRUCIAL PHASE

DAVID VITAL

CLARENDON PRESS · OXFORD

1987

Oxford University Press, Walton Street, Oxford OX2 6DP
Oxford New York Toronto
Delhi Bombay Calcutta Madras Karachi
Petaling Jaya Singapore Hong Kong Tokyo
Nairobi Dar es Salaam Cape Town
Melbourne Auckland

and associated companies in
Beirut Berlin Ibadan Nicosia

Oxford is a trade mark of Oxford University Press

British Library Cataloguing in Publication Data
Vital, David
Zionism: the crucial phase.
1. Zionism – History
I. Title
956.94'001   DS149
ISBN 0-19-821932-6

Library of Congress Cataloging in Publication Data
Vital, David
Zionism: the crucial phase.
Bibliography: p.
Includes index.
1. Zionism – History. I. Title.
DS149.V515 1987   956.94'001
ISBN 0-19-821932-6

Set by Pentacor Ltd, High Wycombe, Bucks.
Printed in Great Britain
at the University Press, Oxford
By David Stanford
Printer to the University

Our captivity within the incomprehensible logic of accident is the only logic of the universe.

Joseph Conrad

Preface

This is the concluding volume of what has become—but was not originally intended to be—a series of three. Each was conceived and written in turn as an independent book, dealing with a specific period and with a distinct theme. In the first case,[1] it was with the circumstances in which a radically new national movement emerged in Jewry in the years 1881–97. In the second,[2] it was with the process by which the movement took on its more or less definitive character in the years 1898–1906 and with the essential features of that character. But together, the three books do nevertheless represent an attempt to treat a larger subject, the re-entry of the Jewish people into the world political arena, through a more extended period. And it is with the precise circumstances in which the threshold of that arena was attained and entry finally gained that the present volume deals. While the three books do not depend on each other, and overlapping and cross-references have been cut down to a minimum, it is the author's hope that the links between them will, none the less, be apparent.

All three books, but the present volume especially, are offered as a contribution to the *political* history of the Jewish people—and this is natural enough. It was of the essence of the matter of Zionism that its adepts called—often uncertainly, it is true, and at times, in their heart of hearts, doubtfully—for a grand effort to make of the Jews an independent, self-governing, and therefore political nation once more. By having raised the flag of autonomy publicly and by the inner logic of their own internal procedures and institutions, it was they, ultimately, who did accomplish that truly revolutionary change, transforming not only the structure of Jewry, its condition among the nations, and the play of conflicting religious and secular beliefs and ideologies within it, but much else in the world besides. A history of Zionism is therefore necessarily first and foremost a political history.

---

[1] *The Origins of Zionism* (Oxford, 1975, repr. 1980).
[2] *Zionism: The Formative Years* (Oxford, 1982).

There is another sense in which this concluding study could not be other than, for the most part, an examination of political forces, processes, and decisions. The Zionists were of course devoid of any of the classic sources and instruments of power. They controlled no territory, they had no fighting formations, they possessed no economic leverage, they lacked even the means to impose discipline upon their own adherents. Within Jewry itself they were a minoritarian movement subject to powerful opposition. In the years immediately preceding the Great War, their movement was in decline. Thus their admittance into the world political arena could not but owe a great deal less to their own intrinsic political weight than to the contingency of a change in the structure of world forces and a conscious decision in their favour by the gate-keepers to that arena—Great Britain being chief among them at the time in question.

But then one of the central characteristic of politics, *a fortiori* of international politics, is, of course, that it is a matter of contending and co-operating forces, and that an understanding of the affairs and progress (or regress) of one protagonist cannot be achieved without a very close look being paid to the other(s). When the Zionists at last plunged fully and irreversibly into the world of politics—as they had always to do if they were to advance at all—their history ceased to be essentially, let alone exclusively, internal and, as it were, private. The history of Zionism, and in significant respects the history of the entire Jewish people, became interwoven with certain, admittedly limited, aspects of the political, diplomatic, and strategic history of Great Britain, and so it would remain for a generation and more.

One salient and immediate effect of this intermingling of purposes—and, of course, of persons—was to put unprecedented influence, not to say power, in the hands of those who were accepted by the British as the effective managers of the Zionists' business. Since the consequences of the transactions the two sides then entered into could not fail to be capital for the structure and quality of the movement as a whole, this is equally the point at which the external politics of Zionism become inseparable both in fact and in retrospective analysis from the internal.

It is as an attempt to draw these various threads together that the present book may, perhaps, best be seen.

D.V.

Acknowledgements

My first debt is to the directors and staffs of the archives to which I had recourse, often over extended periods, while this book was in preparation. I recall with gratitude the courtesy and assistance extended to me at (in order of the alphabet, not, I fear, of the burden imposed on remarkably patient people in each case): the Bibliothèque Nationale, Paris; the archives of the Board of Deputies of British Jews, London; the Bodleian Library, Oxford; the British Library (Department of Manuscripts), Bloomsbury; the Brynmor Jones Library, University of Hull; the Central Archives for the History of the Jewish People, Jerusalem; the Central Zionist Archives, Jerusalem; the House of Lords Record Office, Westminster; the India Office Library and Records, London; the Israel State Archives, Jerusalem; the Jabotinsky Archives, Tel-Aviv; the Kressel Library, Oxford Centre for Postgraduate Hebrew Studies, Yarnton; the Archives diplomatiques, at the Ministère des Relations Extérieures, Paris; the Mocatta Library, University College, London; the Public Record Office, Kew; the Scottish Record Office, Edinburgh; the archives of the Service Historique de l'Armée de Terre, Château de Vincennes, Paris; the Sterling Library, Yale University; and the Weizmann Archives, Reḥovot, Israel.

I am also very grateful to Professor Eugene Black, Professor Ben Halpern, Dr Michael Heymann, Professor Jacob M. Landau, Dr Mark Levene, and Mr Joseph Wenkert for expert advice at certain points, and to Shemu'el Cohen, Mrs Bracha Freundlich, Nussi Schneider, and Mrs Stella Shossberger for their valuable assistance at various stages of the book's preparation.

This is an opportunity to express my thanks, once again, to the staff of the Oxford University Press and, most particularly, to my editor, Ivon Asquith, for his unfailing courtesy over a long period and for the encouragement and good advice he has always given me.

Mrs Ruth Nijk typed and retyped the whole of this book with extraordinary devotion and care for which—and for saving me from many errors—I cannot thank her enough.

Finally, I should like to record that the late Max Rowe, a valued friend, was, in his way, a discreet participant in my attempt to write a general history of the Zionist movement from the inception of the project over a decade and a half ago. His death last year has deprived me of the anticipated pleasure of presenting him with a copy of the present volume upon its publication. But I shall hold his memory dear.

November 1986

Contents

List of Illustrations   xii

A Note on Transliteration, Translation, and Nomenclature   xiii

List of Abbreviations   xv

PART ONE. DECLINE

1. *The Turkish Wall*   3
2. *Drift*   35

PART TWO. THE WAR

3. *The New Setting*   89
4. *Disarray*   120

PART THREE. DECISIONS

5. *A Plan Aborted*   169
6. *The Terms of the Final Equation*   207
7. *The Solomonic Judgement*   271

PART FOUR. INTO THE ARENA

8. *London, Petrograd, Jerusalem*   297
9. *On the Threshold*   324
10. *The End of the Beginning*   358

Select Bibliography   377

Index   385

List of Illustrations

PLATES

Plates appear between pages 192 and 193

1. David Wolffsohn

2. Otto Warburg

3. Yeḥiel Tchlenov

4. Naḥum Sokolov

5. Arthur Ruppin

6. Victor Jacobson

7. Yosef Trumpeldor

8. Ze'ev Jabotinsky

9. Herbert Samuel

10. Sir Mark Sykes

11. Lucien Wolf

12. Sylvain Lévi

13. Arthur James Balfour

14. Chaim Weizmann

Illustrations 1–9 and 11–13 by courtesy of the Central Zionist Archives, Jerusalem; illustrations 10 and 14 by courtesy of the Weizmann Archives, Reḥovot.

MAPS

1. The de Bunsen Committee, June 1915: two schemes
   of annexation.   99
2. The Sykes-Picot Agreement, May 1916.   200

A Note on Transliteration, Translation, and Nomenclature

The rules adopted for transliteration (especially from the Hebrew), for place names (for which different forms exist), for the spelling of surnames (where variations abound), and for dates (Julian, Gregorian, or Jewish), are those employed in the first two volumes of the series and set out within them in full.[1] But, briefly, the aim has been to be as accurate and as suggestive of contemporary usage as may be compatible with an avoidance of pedantry.

Responsibility for translations of source material into English is my own, unless otherwise indicated.

There remains the question of the name of the Land. One or two critics have questioned my use of the term 'Erez-Israel' (literally: 'Land of Israel') to denote a country that a great many people do indeed think of as 'Palestine'. The difficulty is that for centuries, until the British took it over at the end of the Great War, it was an exceedingly loose geographical expression at best; and no political or administrative unit of that name, or covering that territory even approximately, existed. The Jews, who are, after all, the subject of this book, tended strongly to continue to think of it in their own traditional terms, one of which was 'Erez-Israel'. They most certainly did so in the particular context of the modern Jewish revival and of thoughts about a Return, although 'Palestine' did creep in to speech and writing, especially when not conducted in their own languages and in discourse with non-Jews. On the other hand, few non-Jews used the term except, perhaps, in flights of Biblical fancy. I have therefore thought it right to use the term 'Palestine' when the context or the documents required it and 'Erez-Israel' when it seemed the more appropriate.

If the result may not be entirely satisfactory, all alternatives seem to me to be less so. They fail to convey the far from insignificant

---

[1] *Origins*, pp. xv–xvi; *Formative Years*, pp. xv–xvi.

datum that, whatever others may have thought of them and their claims, those Jews who identified themselves with Zionism in this, its crucial phase, did see the country as their own and tended very strongly to refer to it accordingly.

Abbreviations

AE	Archives diplomatiques, Ministère des Relations Extérieures.
AIU	Alliance Israélite Universelle.
BD	Archives of the Board of Deputies of British Jews.
BL	British Library.
CAHJP	Central Archives for the History of the Jewish People.
CFC	Conjoint Foreign Committee.
CUP	Committee of Union and Progress.
CZA	Central Zionist Archives.
DBFP	*Documents on British Foreign Policy.*
Durham	Sudan Archive, Durham University.
EAC	Engeres Aktions-Comité (Smaller Actions Committee).
EEF	Egyptian Expeditionary Force.
Formative Years	*Zionism: The Formative Years* (Oxford, 1982).
GAC	Grosses Aktions-Comité (Greater Actions Committee).
GAC Minutes	*Ha-protokolim shel ha-vaʿad ha-poʿel ha-ẓioni* [Minutes of the Zionist General Council or Actions Committee], edited by Y. Freundlich and G. Yogev (Tel-Aviv, 1975).
HLRO	House of Lords Record Office.
Hull SP	Sykes Papers, Hull University Library.
ICA	Jewish Colonization Association.
Igrot AH	*Igrot Aḥad Ha-ʿAm* [*The Letters of Aḥad Ha-ʿAm*], second edition, edited by A. [L.] Simon and Y. Pograbinsky (Tel-Aviv, 1956–60).
IOLR	India Office Library and Records.

ISA	Israel State Archives.
ITO	Jewish Territorial Organization.
JA	Jabotinsky Archives.
LIGP	Lloyd George Papers, House of Lords Record Office.
MFA	Ministry for Foreign Affairs.
ML	Mocatta Library.
OFMA	Ottoman Foreign Ministry Archives.
Origins	*The Origins of Zionism* (Oxford, 1975).
PRO	Public Record Office.
Protokoll I, II, III, etc.	*Stenographisches Protokoll der Verhandlungen des I. [II., III., etc.] Zionisten-Kongresses* (verbatim reports of debates at the First, Second, Third, etc., Zionist Congresses).
SHAT	Service Historique de l'Armée de Terre.
SRO	Scottish Record Office.
TP	Moritz Tarschis Papers.
WA	Weizmann Archives.
Weizmann Letters	*The Letters and Papers of Chaim Weizmann, Series A, Letters*, 23 vols., general editors M. W. Weisgal and B. Litvinoff (London and Jerusalem, 1968–80).
Yale, WP	Wiseman Papers, Yale University.

PART ONE

Decline

1

The Turkish Wall

i

A pervading feature of the life of the Jews in their Exile has been their weakness: a permanent and notorious inability ever (and anywhere) to match strength for strength, pressure for pressure, or even benevolence for benevolence. Weakness was at the very foundation of their relations with the people among whom they lived and the alien rulers to whom they were subject. Nothing of consequence in the history of those relations can be explained without reference to it. Nowhere were they masters, not even—in the final analysis—in their own homes.

The weakness of the Jews derived ultimately from the fact of Exile. And exile and weakness fed on, and helped to perpetuate, each other. True, neither in this respect nor in respect of any other single characteristic were the Jews wholly unique among the peoples of Europe and the Levant. There have been and there are other submerged or subject peoples, other nations without access to the instrumentalities of power, force, and coercion, other groups, sects, and churches set apart from their surroundings and at odds with all by reason of their history, or religious beliefs, or notion of their own cosmic role (as opposed to that of all other peoples). There have been other castes and classes who were not merely prevented from participating openly and as such in the general political society of nations, but whose participation—where so much as hinted at, let alone attempted—was regarded as impermissible and illegitimate. But in no other group or nation were these deprivations manifest at such intensity and with such profound and lasting consequences. And therefore if there was one great issue on which the conduct and thinking of the Jews turned in the early years of the twentieth century it was on whether it was right and politic—but above all whether it still was necessary—to acquiesce in their condition. It was under this cloud of political impotence that the Zionists—pledged to disperse it—had somehow to evolve and operate. In this sense there was an element of (necessary) truth in the charge made against Herzl by his critics that he sought to reverse the course of Jewish history—in effect, to overcome the tremendous disparity between the splendid aims of Zionism and the pitiful means available to it—by something like a sleight of hand. In practice, the history of post-Herzlian Zionism is one of continuous adjustment of such ends to such means, now justified by hard political calculation, now rationalized by ideological casuistry.

Besides, to rebel against the Jewish condition, as against any long-established *status quo*, was to incur resistance. The more radical the intent and the more effective the means to implement it, the greater the resistance. Thus within Jewry; thus without. Change required a mobilization of human and material resources, defined purposes, organization—in short, a venture into politics and, sooner or later, a drive for power. But every settled thing in Jewry militated against a radical approach to its ills: habit of mind, precedent, the Tradition itself in its most explicit forms, the invertebrate, powerless (and partly voluntary) structure of the nation, and the private views and purposes of a majority—if indeed a diminishing majority—of the Jews themselves. Moreover, those who favoured rebellion and sought radical change were themselves divided on the question of the Exile. Some thought that a way could be found to assure the Jews equality of treatment and status without displacing them from the lands of their present settlement. The socialists, most notably, believed that by altering the terms on which all society was founded and governed the millennium could be ushered in for the Jews along with their neighbours. But the true radicals were the Zionists, for they thought quite otherwise: here and there some partial, necessarily temporary and uncertain amelioration could perhaps be engineered; but it was the very condition of exile that was at the root of the Jews' troubles and afflictions, and it was that in the end that had to be wound up. Thus, at all events, for those upon whom the material afflictions weighed most heavily and for those for whom the national-cultural condition of Jewry was a matter of central concern.

On this all varieties of Zionists were agreed: 'politicals' as well as 'practicals', the religiously observant as well as the secularists and atheists, 'Palestinophiles' as well as 'territorialists', 'cultural' or 'spiritual' Zionists as well as socialists, and, with strongest of all reasons, the rank-and-file supporters of the movement in eastern Europe. Agreement on such a basis for action (however loose) and on the need for action itself (whatever argument there might be about detail) was an extraordinary, an unprecedented achievement in itself in a people prey as never before to a thousand centrifugal forces. And indeed the Zionists had rapidly made their mark. None the less, in the fallow years between the death of the movement's founder and the outbreak of the Great War the movement was manifestly in decline.

In the last year of Herzl's life and in the years immediately following his death virtually all doubts and ambivalence about the *locus* of the national revival had been swept away. The reduction of the Exile had come to be indissolubly linked to the return of the Jews to their ancestral land, Erez-Israel. The Land of the Jews was of course virtually identical—fatally so, it might be said—with geographical and historical Palestine as understood by Christian Europeans and with the *mutasarrıflık* of Jerusalem and the two southern *sanjaks* of the *vilayet* of Beirut as understood and governed by the Muslim Turks. But at any rate, so far as the Zionists were concerned, the great internal quarrel which had erupted in 1903 upon the knowledge that Herzl was considering a British Government proposal to set up a semi-autonomous Jewish territory in East Africa had settled that great question once and for all. It had fixed the movement in a frame of mind that looked to the Tradition almost as strongly as it looked forward to breaking out of it.[1] It had committed the Zionists, as a matter of top priority, to a bolstering of the existing Jewish presence in Erez-Israel/Palestine: the nation's bridgehead, as they saw it, that which would herald and facilitate the greater Return that they believed lay in the future. But if the ideological air was largely cleared by 1906 or thereabouts, there were important ways in which the results for the movement were grievous.

To the great mass of eastern European Jewry whose present misery and doubtful prospects were at the heart of the *raison d'être* of Zionism, the movement could now offer little more than an ever

---

[1] See *Formative Years*, Part Three.

vaguer outline of an alternative set in an ever more remote future.[2]
Small wonder that the numbers of paid-up members had gone into
decline after Herzl's death, that nothing the Zionists did or said had
any effect on the great, continuous migration to the west out of
Russia, Poland, and Romania, and that in desperation minds were
turning increasingly to political action on the spot in Europe after
all. That in itself seemed to spell erosion of the movement, and
threaten ultimate collapse. Certainly in the interim it produced
uncertainty, confusion, and frustration at all levels, as we shall see.
For from the decision to reject all non-Palestinian or 'territorialist'
solutions—even explicitly temporary ones—it followed that the
progress of Zionism was now wholly conditional on Ottoman
acquiescence or, at the very least, indifference. And that way led
Zionism, as it had always led it, to a monumental stone wall.

It is true that the Turks had from the first accepted Zionism as a
fair and by no means illegitimate embodiment of the national
tendency in Jewry.[3] For the Zionists the achievement of recognition
in Constantinople, so far as it went, was a minor (in fact, an easy)
triumph. But it came to be borne in upon them that whatever they
might do or say in Turkey or elsewhere it did not seem to the Turks,
for their part, that they were under any compulsion to deviate from
their own set policy on local national autonomy within their Empire.
They had their own views on what the proper place and role of the
Jews in the Empire might be. They hardly saw the matter as a fit
subject for real (as opposed to simulated) negotiations with other
Powers—least of all, perhaps, with the Jews themselves. In their
view—a view characteristic of all Islamic states—Jews were
properly objects, not subjects of policy. Thus the decision of the
Zionists to concern themselves exclusively with Erez-Israel had led
the movement into a trap, one from which their affairs in the decade
leading up to the Great War amounted to little more than a
protracted effort to struggle free.

ii

The Zionists never succeeded in penetrating the Ottoman arcana.[4]
They never learned to cope with the kaleidoscopic, shifting faces of

---

[2] On the material condition of, especially, Russo-Polish Jewry at the turn of the
century, see *Formative Years*, pp. 165–81. For the subsequent decade, see below, pp.
36–43.

[3] *Origins*, pp. 296–8.

[4] Least of all Herzl. See e.g. *Formative Years*, Chapter 4.

government in Constantinople: the Islamic face, the Ottoman-imperial face, the Turkish-nationalist, the pro-western progressive, the anti-western traditionalist, the anti-western loyalist face. They never learned to deal effectively, let alone confidently, with the men who ruled in Constantinople, or with those who had access to or influence over those who ruled. One or two enormously patient and inquisitive individuals apart, none of the Zionist leaders and functionaries who sought to do the movement's business with the Ottoman officials, or win them over to the movement's cause, or argue the advantages that a massive resettlement of Jews in Palestine would bring to the Empire in general and to Palestine in particular, were mentally and culturally equipped to cope with the sloth, distrust, xenophobic hatred, preference for intrigue, and common venality that confronted them at every turn, often in impenetrable and soul-destroying combination.

It is certainly the case, that the Turks, for their part, by and large, were less hostile to Jews and Jewry than society and government tended to be in Christian Europe. They were also well aware that they had nothing to fear and, possibly, something to gain from the commercial and industrial initiative of Ottoman Jewry. They were, as they repeatedly told the Zionists, far from averse to a fresh influx of Jews into the Empire. What they were not prepared to countenance was some sort of actual or potential alignment of the Jews with the European forces seeking to penetrate the Empire and deliberately or otherwise accelerate its decomposition. Nor were they prepared to countenance the appearance of the Jews on the internal political stage as yet another self-conscious, dissatisfied, and potentially rebellious national minority. Accordingly, they were not only utterly opposed to the idea of a national state in Erez-Israel or to political autonomy, however attenuated, for the Jews: their faces were set against the very entry of the Jews into the country and against any attempt by them to establish themselves there effectively and permanently. Immigration into Palestine was therefore prohibited, as was the purchase of land for the building of homes and for cultivation. These prohibitions, in force for a generation, were applicable specifically and uniquely to Jews.

The history of the relations between the Zionists and the Ottoman Government had thus from the beginning been one of a sort of interplay between, on the one side, a mixture of ill-founded hopes for change and irritable despondency and, on the other, the Ottoman side, set opposition, hostility, and suspicion—rays of goodwill and generosity breaking through occasionally in both directions. Thus it had been in the very early years of Ḥibbat Ẓion; thus too, as Herzl had finally been forced to perceive, in the years in which the Zionist movement proper had taken shape.[5] Turkish policy was set; nothing the Zionists had ever attempted had ever softened official Turkey's refusal to be interested. There had been hints from time to time and winks and whispers of a change, but nothing had ever materialized. If one did not abandon hope entirely, or turn (as Zangwill and his Territorialists were doing[6]) to other lands controlled by other governments, one could only resign oneself to waiting for the crumbling structure of Ottoman imperial rule in the Levant finally to disintegrate. And, in the meantime, one could seek to take advantage of every crevice in the wall of anti-Zionist regulations the Turks had erected and every incompetent or venal official on the ground in Palestine itself to (as the phrase went) 'infiltrate' the country and build up the Jewish presence family by family, brick by brick, *dunam* by *dunam*[7] in quiet defiance of the Government. But could one be sure that the Empire would collapse? Did one know what would replace it? And was this not precisely the infinitely slow, absurdly modest, unimaginative, somewhat dishonourable, certainly undignified, and above all—having regard to the scale and intensity of the plight of the Jews of eastern Europe—well-nigh useless policy which Herzl had sought to sweep away and replace by something larger, swifter, and much more radical? But that the movement had now come full circle none, not even his old opponents, wished to admit. His heirs, for their part, continued to profess their belief that, the problem being political in essence, was amenable only to a political solution. But what form that solution might take they had ever greater difficulty in saying.

iii

One of the legacies of the great quarrel over the East Africa project had been the broad division of the movement into two schools: the 'politicals' (Herzl's institutional and ideological heirs) and the

---

[5] See *Formative Years*, pp. 48–60, 106–28.

[6] See ibid., pp. 435–43.

[7] The common measure of land: 1,000 square metres (roughly a quarter of an acre).

'practicals' (who corresponded, more or less, to the opposition to Herzl and to his heirs). The questions what the 'political' approach might or should be in practice and what 'practical' alternative, if there was one, could and should replace it had long been the central issue for debate within the movement, deepening and sharpening argument and conflict on all other matters, not least the matter of the leadership and management of the movement itself. Thus in Herzl's lifetime; all the more so after his death. When the Eighth Congress of Zionists convened in The Hague in mid-August 1907,[8] once again it was these questions and the invariably uncertain answers to them that were chiefly tossed back and forth in the course of its sessions. Accordingly, very little of what was said during the Congress was in any important respect new.

Nordau duly restated the Zionist creed (in its Herzlian form) with a clarity no one else could equal and an eloquence that had come to be taken for granted. Zionism was not a philanthropic or benevolent movement, he sought to remind the delegates. To the Jewish people it could *give* nothing. All it could do was muster and direct the resources they needed if they were ever to emerge out of their 'two-thousand-year-old dull submission' and work out their salvation on their own soil. For the Jews were now faced with a dilemma from which there was no escape. They had no choice but finally to decide whether they wished to remain a nation or not. If they did not, then they should proceed to assimilate as rapidly as conditions allowed them. But if they wished to remain a nation, as indeed the long isolation to which they had clung for so many centuries did certainly suggest, then they must now make the necessary effort to attain full and equal status as one nation among all others. For what purpose could there be in merely maintaining themselves as a distinct but distrusted minority in the Diaspora? What future, what fate awaited

---

[8] This was a departure from the usual practice of meeting at Basel. Until now there had been only one exception: the Fourth Congress was held in London in 1900 in the hope of drawing attention to the movement in the capital of the nation by which Herzl set greatest store. The Hague was chosen because in 1907 it was the scene of the great gathering for the international Peace Conference. Wolffsohn, having in mind as always what he thought Herzl might have done in his place, thought the Congress might make an impression on the assembled dignitaries. Nordau warned him that it would be a waste of time and effort: there was not the slightest hope that the Peace Conference would take notice of the Zionists, least of all official notice. (Nordau to Wolffsohn, 12 June 1907. CZA, W961.) Wolffsohn had his way. Nordau's irritable prediction proved correct.

them if they persisted? ⌈The alternatives facing the Jews were therefore clear: they were 'Zionism or national liquidation'.⌉[9] Nordau was cheered—ritually, it might be said—and the Congress then got down to business, the heart of which was yet another confrontation between the opposing schools.

The opposition, in which the delegates from Russia, as always, were preponderant, proceeded to press the line laid down at their own Helsingfors conference at the end of the previous year, duly reinforced and restated at the caucus of Russian delegates held just before the Congress formally assembled. This argued for a 'synthesis' of political and practical Zionism, one to reinforce the other, neither to be pursued exclusively.[10] On the face of it, it was a formula which implied no more than compromise and concentration by all schools on the immediate and the achievable. But it carried with it a corollary that was distinctly controversial and which laid the basic formula open to very serious question. This was the argument that much greater attention be paid to such 'current tasks' as the movement could perform here and now in the Diaspora itself. 'Current tasks' (*Gegenwartsarbeit* in the jargon of the movement) was a loose term which could be understood as covering anything from educational-cultural work, the better to intensify and focus national consciousness, to the very much bolder idea of direct participation in general political activity in the lands of the Jewish dispersion, especially in Austria and Russia, in the *local* Jewish national interest. This in turn meant no less than a Zionist *party* competing in Austrian parliamentary elections and, in Russia, activity of a semi-revolutionary—at the very least anti-government—nature. Such ideas cut clearly against the grain of all thinking in the opposing Herzlian-political camp, where it was the co-operation of the Powers and other forces of *status quo* that had always been sought. The 'politicals' had also always feared that such forms of political and social activity risked diverting the attention of the Zionists themselves from what they, the 'politicals', had always seen as the central aim of achieving political autonomy in Erez-Israel (rather than in the Diaspora). There was the further risk that it would divert

---

[9] *Protokoll VIII*, pp. 21–5.

[10] On the conferance of Russian Zionists held in Helsingfors in December 1906 and the idea of a 'synthetic' Zionist policy, originally put by Idelson, see *Formative years*, pp. 467–75.

attention away from the immediate but huge and daunting task of rescuing and rehabilitating impoverished, persecuted eastern European *Jewry* to the admittedly worthy but less urgent one of promoting a general, modernist *aggiornamento* of *Judaism*. ('When the people are hungry,' one delegate rebuked a leading 'cultural' Zionist, 'its mind is not on literature, but before all else on how to quell hunger.'[11]) And there was the real fear that it would bring (in fact, the knowledge that it had already brought) the movement into conflict with a whole array of external forces both within and outside Jewry. These, in the first instance, were the orthodox, who resented and resisted the sort of modernist, Hebrew-language, essentially secular culture that the majority of Zionists favoured and which some of them were vigorously propagating.

Hardly less worrying was the resentment engendered in powerful external forces: the Imperial Russian Government wanted no non-Russian nationalist activity, by Jews or others, anywhere in its domain; the Polish nationalists in both Austrian Galicia and in Russian-ruled 'Congress Poland' wanted no competition from other ethnic groups—so much so, indeed, that in the interest of the Jews being counted as Poles and so swelling their numbers at election-time, they were prepared for once to swallow a great deal of their own anti-Semitic bile. But even devoid of corollaries, the main theme of 'synthesis', presented and re-presented both at the Russian caucus and at the Congress by one speaker after another (Tchlenov, Adolf Friedemann, Daniel Pasmanik, Adolf Böhm, Menaḥem Sheinkin, Adolf Stand, and Weizmann, among others[12]) as a *compromise* was in fact nothing of the kind.

It was fundamental to the 'political' approach that the small-

---

[11] Pasmanik attacking Ehrenpreis. *Protokoll VIII*, p. 90. Returning to the subject later in the Congress, Ehrenpreis retorted that it was not the misery of the stomach that concerned him so much as the misery of the soul. 'These past few years,' he told the Congress, 'we have suffered a pogrom of the spirit which in its range and consequences has been no less significant and far-reaching than the material pogrom.' Ibid., p. 265.

[12] Tchlenov, *Die Welt*, 6 September 1907, p. 15; Adolf Friedemann, *Protokoll VIII*, pp. 67 8; Daniel Pasmanik, ibid., p. 91; Adolf Böhm, ibid., p. 238; Menaḥem Sheinkin, ibid., p. 273; Adolf Stand, ibid., p. 278; and Weizmann, ibid., p. 301. Weizmann's statement was the strongest and clearest of the series and, as his reputation grew in later years, the one he and his followers tended to regard as the speech by which he had first made a real mark in the movement at large. That said, his own account of it in his autobiography is inaccurate.

scale 'infiltration' into the Land constantly advocated and promoted by the 'practical' Zionists was provocative to the Turks,[13] dangerous in itself because all small achievements were liable to be swept away at will by the hostile sovereign power, useless as a solution, even a partial solution, to the immense problem of eastern Jewry, and meaningless in terms of the central goal of inducing change in the *status* of the Jews not only in Erez-Israel in particular, but among the 'nations' in general. Of course, it might be the case, as Leo Motzkin told the Congress, that the cause was hopeless, that the Jews were insufficiently interested in a national revival to gather under the Zionist flag. In that case, while the Zionists were right in principle, their movement would fail in practice. For it was now undeniable that unless the full strength of the Jewish people was mobilized, nothing could be achieved. Therein lay one of the great dilemmas facing the movement: nothing but a goal of the very first order would ultimately move the Jews, in their numbers, to give of their strength to a great national cause. Small-scale settlement of Jews in Erez-Israel did not constitute such a goal; nor did small-scale settlement necessarily lead to large-scale settlement; nor was it the case that a community of Jews in the country was a pre-condition of a Charter establishing their special status and rights there being granted. Motzkin, one of the first of the proto-Zionists to rally to Herzl upon the founding of the movement, had nothing against small-scale settlement in itself. He could well understand, he affirmed, the attraction a return to the Land held for those who undertook it. But such settlement, such 'practical' labour, was not a means to a true political end, the end to which Zionism aspired; and the poor resources of the movement should not be squandered in penny-packets to support it.

The work in Palestine is for each one of us an enchanting task—there can be no doubt of that—but it is in no sense a national movement. . . . I can tell you, that when I was in Palestine, I felt tremendous joy to be in the Land . . . and for years my wanting to live there preoccupied me. But shall I therefore go to the Jewish people and say, this is the solution to the Jewish Problem? . . . It is a kind of poetical aspect to our efforts . . . but it is not Zionist *work*, not yet. Zionism must strive to realize the old principle of territorial gathering and concentration of the Jews in Palestine, and that alone.[14]

---

[13] Ottoman officials, especially in Palestine, were well aware of the systematic effort to circumvent the rules they were supposed to enforce. See *Formative Years*, p. 55.

[14] *Protokoll VIII*, p. 289. Emphasis in original. On Motzkin see *Formative Years*, pp. 194–7.

In the minds of most delegates, it was the 'practicals' none the less who had the better arguments. What they asked for seemed at least to be within the realm of the feasible, and the sentimental attraction of the new farming communities, as Motzkin had recognized, could not be denied. In contrast, the 'politicals', so long as they had made the running, had achieved nothing that was in any sense lasting and concrete, not even under their late leader. The upshot was that while no serious attempt was made to shackle the EAC in its day-to-day work, the opposition had no difficulty getting the Congress to resolve that the movement put more of its resources into immediate settlement work and that a special department of the Organization (to be located in Berlin), complete with permanent representation in Erez-Israel, be set up to put those (meagre) resources to best possible use. A forlorn attempt by Nachman Syrkin to reassert the primacy of political action was simply voted off the agenda without debate.[15]

This did not dispose of the irreducibly political question of the Turks. How *they* would respond to a concerted, let alone successful effort to build up the Jewish presence in Erez-Israel, in unspoken but clear defiance of their stated policy and published regulations, none could say. On this subject discretion remained the rule. Not even the most enthusiastic and single-minded 'practical' could offer more than the hope that somehow or other all would be well, as somehow or other all had been well, or almost so, in the past. When, to the surprise of the Zionists, as to most other foreign observers, internal changes finally came in Turkey with the seizure of power by the Young Turks in July of the following year, the response of all Zionists of all schools was electric. Hope piled on hope, enthusiasm hardly knew bounds.

iv

'We can diligently plead our cause before the Sultan and the Powers,' Nordau had once told the English Zionists, 'but we cannot force them to comply with our wishes and we must patiently wait for a juncture which will be favourable to our ends. [Meanwhile] we can prepare ourselves for the historical moment which is sure to come sooner or later.'[16] In the summer of 1908 the question in all minds was, was this the 'historical moment'? It was easy to believe

---

[15] *Protokoll VIII*, pp. 324–5. On Syrkin, see *Formative Years*, pp. 394–6.
[16] Report by the English Zionist Federation (EZF) to Central Zionist Office, Cologne. 17 December 1906. CZA. Z2/411.

so, especially in Russia where a certain parallel between the events
in Turkey and those in Russia three years earlier came quickly to
mind.[17] Even the two great critics of 'political' Zionism, Aḥad Ha-
'Am and Ussishkin, normally so sceptical and fearful of false dawns,
were not only sure that the Turkish revolution would have decisive
consequences for the entire Zionist enterprise in Ereẓ-Israel; they
rapidly agreed that it was now clear, as Aḥad Ha-'Am put it, that
'the *method* we had employed in our work thus far would have to go.'
Much would improve, but much would be demanded of the settlers
themselves and, above all, of those who backed them.

Now there would no longer be any room for petitioners in this or that
'court'. The door would be open for anyone with something to contribute to
the country wherever he might come from and we shall need new people, the
benefit from whose work will be evident to all. [On the other hand] Ereẓ-
Israel will no longer be a dark corner in which we can do as we wish once we
have paid the requisite *baksheesh*. For example, it will no longer be possible
to uproot trees planted by Arab labourers and demand highhandedly that
all the work be given to Jews only. Such behaviour would put us in a very
dangerous position. Generally, we must recognize our [true] place in the
country and try to entrench ourselves by *fruitful labour*. The competition
from various quarters will grow. . . . It is therefore time to drop the empty
phrases of 'diplomacy' on the one hand and 'socialism'[18] on the other. If we
have a future in the country it is not [diplomacy and socialism] that will
further it, but simple, useful work in the fields, in factories, and in schools
and other institutions and endeavours.[19]

[17] Sokolov to Wolffsohn, 30 July 1908. CZA, W62 II. For a typical analysis much
influenced by the proposition that 'conditions in Turkey and Russia have much in
common', see 'Turkiya ha-ḥadasha, ha-yehudim ve-ha-ẓionut', in the influential *Ha-
Shilo'aḥ*, xix, 1908–9, pp. 280–86. The journal's founding editor had been Aḥad Ha-
'Am. It still represented the finest literary and political writing of the intellectual-
national cultural revival trend in contemporary Zionism.

[18] A reference to the contemporary influx into Erez
AU-Israel of highly motivated young Jews from Russia much influenced by social-
democratic and socialist-revolutionary ideas who sought to build up a class of Jewish
'proletarians' who, eventually, would provide the basis for a revolutionary class
struggle. This brought them into conflict both with Jewish farmers who had no
objection to employing (cheaper) Arab labour and with the Arab labourers
themselves. See *Formative Years*, Chapter 11.

[19] Letter to Ussishkin, 17 August 1908. *Igrot AH*, iv, pp. 134–5.Emphasis and
quotation marks in the original. 'Zionism', Ussishkin pronounced early in 1909, 'has
ceased to be a question of generations and has become a question of years. . . . If we
work with courage and system the Land will be ours—at any rate part of it.' *Ha-
'Olam*, 24 February 1909. Zionists in Russia cannot have failed to be encouraged at
this time by the optimistic dispatches of the Constantinople correspondent of their
own journal, *Ha-'Olam*. For a typically enthusiastic report on the Zionists' new-found
freedom in the 'newly free country' and the opportunities for quiet and solid work
opening before them, see A. Ḥermoni, 'Ha-Ẓionut be-turkiya,' *Ha-'Olam*, 26 January
1909.

But there was more to it than the expectation that Ereẓ-Israel would be opened up and properly administered—presenting both advantages and fresh difficulties for the Zionists. There was the conviction that the change of regime meant the substitution of a liberal, parliamentary system for the old despotism. In such a system, not only would the rulers of Turkey be more approachable and vastly more attentive to plans for the economic and social improvement of their country, not excluding such outlying provinces as Palestine, but Ottoman society in general would at long last be an open one. There would be free political association. There would be a free press. Public opinion would inevitably count for much, where in the past it counted for nothing. And, since Ottoman Jewry would now reap the benefit of emancipation along with the other submerged and subject peoples of the Empire, the Zionists would be at liberty to seek to draw its members into the movement without fear of doing them harm, and in the legitimate interest of creating a substantial instrument of domestic influence in Turkey. What was needed, therefore, and needed urgently—the actual settlement work in Ereẓ-Israel apart—was a strong presence in Constantinople. There had to be a representative committee or mission there, and a newspaper, perhaps more than one in more than one language: French, Ladino, and possibly Hebrew, in Constantinople in the first place, perhaps in Salonika too.

In Russia, the Central Committee of the country organization, in its enthusiasm, promptly announced a special contribution of 50,000 francs (about £2,000) to the costs such new organs of the movement would entail.[20] In Cologne the mood was optimistic too, though moderated, as was thought proper, by statesmanlike caution, for indeed the auguries were not all favourable. Whatever might be hastily concluded in St. Petersburg, Moscow, and Vilna on the basis of general newspaper reporting, direct contact with representatives of the 'new, free Turkey' (as the EAC termed it in its regular confidential briefings to members of the Greater Actions Committee) could be sobering. Nordau, who had been asked by Wolffsohn to go to Constantinople to see on the spot how matters stood, refused outright, partly because he could not afford the journey, partly because, as he wrote Wolffsohn from Paris, he thought it would be fruitless.

[20] Resolutions adopted at Moscow, 16–19 October 1908. CZA, A24/104. Goldberg and others to Wolffsohn, 25 October and 18 November 1908. CZA, Z2/453. Also Ussishkin to Aḥad-Ha'Am, early January 1909. S. Schwartz, *Ussishkin be-igrotav* (Jerusalem, 1934), p. 146.

This morning I visited Ahmed Riz[a] Bey [a leading figure in the Young Turk movement]. I stayed from 11 to 12:30, an hour and a half, unfortunately without ever succeeding in being alone with him even for a moment. I found him surrounded by five persons, who remained sitting quietly when I entered, and while I was there three other persons came and went. Of the five, three were Turkish Jews: one a Mr Victor, an elderly gentleman, a former bank director, quiet, of good will; the other two, whose names I failed to catch, were of the worst type of boastful, French, Levantine assimilationists of the Alliance [Israélite Universelle] school. One was an Armenian who listened very attentively, but said nothing. The fifth, luckily, was Dr Nazim ... the man of greatest influence in the Committee of Union and Progress.[21]

I exchanged compliments with Ahmed Riza. He spoke a few meaningless phrases, then turned to his other visitors. In these circumstances I saw no point in asking him for a private meeting.[22] So I took Dr Nazim into a corner and talked to him for a whole hour. The substance of our talk is as follows:

'Prince Sabaheddin [leader of the more liberal, less Turkish-nationalist wing of the Committee of Union and Progress] is dead; he no longer exists; his programme of decentralization, of autonomous nationalities and provinces has been rejected. The [CUP] is intent upon centralization and Turkish supremacy [*Alleinherrschaft des Türkischen*]. It wants no nationalities in Turkey. It does not want to turn Turkey into another Austria. It wants a unitary, Turkish nation-state with Turkish schools, a Turkish administration, Turkish courts of law.'

He [Nazim] has nothing against Jewish migration [into Turkey]; he even positively favours it. The Ottomans apart, the Young Turks have more confidence in the Jews than in anyone else. But the immigrants must be distributed over the entire Empire; they must be dispersed and nowhere may they form a majority. His words were: 'We have 32 administrative departments (*kazas*). We shall take 100,000 Jews in each *kaza*; there will be room therefore for 3,200,000 Jews who must become good Turks. But we do not want one million Jews in a single place. For then they would become a new nationality—and to prevent that we are absolutely determined.'

Nordau asked about the prohibition on the entry of Jews into Erez-Israel. The matter was under discussion, he was told, and was on the way to solution. There had already been talks in Paris with

[21] Dr Nazim Bey was the secretary-general of the CUP and possessed of considerable influence on the Young Turk Government behind the scenes. Nordau hardly exaggerated his importance.

[22] Nordau may also have had in mind a disappointing meeting with Ahmed Riza five years earlier. See N. J. Mandel, *The Arabs and Zionism before World War I* (Berkeley, 1976), p. 59.

other Jewish organizations, the AIU and the Jewish Colonization Association (ICA). But this was not to Nordau's liking. These were non-, in fact (notably in the case of the AIU) anti-Zionist organizations; and he reckoned it would be a triumph for them if it was they, rather than the Zionists, who got the prohibition lifted. The fact was, he reminded Wolffsohn, that the AIU people had much in common with the Young Turks. The CUP's programme— no continuous Jewish settlement, no Jewish nationality, no auto- nomy, dispersal of the Jews, and (Turkish) assimilation—corres- ponded fully to their own. Still, in itself this should not be a cause for anxiety. It would be decades before there were three million Jews in Turkey, scattered or otherwise. And 'the Committee of Union and Progress would not endure as long as would the Jewish people'. It was his clear impression that

the leading Young Turks are well disposed towards the Jews, but hostile to Zionism. It seems that Zionism had been expounded to them by the ICA and Alliance people. That explains everything.

Our task, once the prohibition on entry has been lifted, is [therefore] to encourage immigration and to work tirelessly, if calmly, to alter the views of the leaders of the Young Turks on the matter of Zionism.

But he, in Paris, could do no more. The effort to influence opinion must be made in Constantinople.[23] On the method to be adopted Nordau offered no advice, and on the prospects for success he was silent.

v

David Wolffsohn, elected at the Seventh Congress of Zionists (1905) as Herzl's successor, had done nothing in the interim to alter his critics' view of him as a man of small ability and attainment who could not possibly do more than keep afloat the ship which his illustrious predecessor had launched eight years before. He had been a most loyal follower of Herzl—one of the few, indeed, who had become a family friend. He owed his election to the leadership partly because none of the other principal figures in the movement either would or could assume the post and the responsibility.[24] He had emerged as a candidate by the simplest of processes of elimination: he was independently wealthy (unlike most others) and therefore

---

[23] Nordau to Wolffsohn, 25 November 1908. CZA, W96 I.
[24] See *Formative Years*, pp. 422–4.

able to meet the heavy outlays the post would require; he was a resident and subject of Germany, therefore a member of a freer and more open society than that to which most of his fellow-Zionists belonged and fully at liberty to undertake political work; he was of stolid disposition (unlike the brilliant but temperamental and ever-questioning Nordau, for example) and so very well fitted to the job of bringing the rather ramshackle organization into administrative good order. But above all, he was, both in the eyes of the late Herzl's followers and his own, a firm disciple of the late leader. And this, so far as his place in the movement was concerned, was at once his greatest weakness and a source of real strength. It drew all the fire of the opposition on him. It gained him the support of the old Herzlian loyalists. It impelled him to take a view of things—he who was not in any important sense of a political cast of mind—that was, as best he understood it, political. It lent an aspect of system to what could easily have been dismissed as floundering. Therein lay his difficulty. For whereas the principles on which the political approach to the solution of the Jewish problem and the restoration of Jewish self-government among other self-governing nations was founded were clear enough, the strategy by which Herzl thought it could be effected had collapsed and none of the 'politicals' could offer a credible alternative. Least of all could Wolffsohn himself. He did his best to follow in the late leader's footsteps. He took up the contact with Arminius Vámbéry, the distinguished Hungarian-Jewish orientalist and traveller, sometime personal friend of 'Abd al-Hamid and secret agent (in the British interest), who had engineered Herzl's long-awaited, ultimately abortive meeting with the Sultan in May 1901.[25] He sought out one or two of Herzl's old contacts and informers in Turkey. In October 1907, the old regime still in place, he travelled to Constantinople, as had his master so many times before him. In the event he fared no better in the Sultan's Turkey than had Herzl himself.

Everything proceeded according to the old frustrating pattern: a preliminary meeting with Vámbéry in Budapest to be briefed; repeated meetings with contact-men in Constantinople, most of whom doubled as the Palace's informers on the Zionists themselves, some moderately well intentioned, others unmistakably mendacious and venal, all cautious, some downright fearful; a much sought-for meeting with the Sultan's powerful First Secretary Tahsin Bey,[26] at

[25] On Vámbéry, see *Formative Years*, pp. 110–13.
[26] On Tahsin's hostility to Zionism, see *Formative Years*, pp. 125–6.

which no business could be discussed but for which Wolffsohn had to wait half a day in an antechamber; a courtesy call on the Sultan's other Secretary, Izzet Bey, followed by an intermediary for Izzet offering good service in exchange for substantial remuneration; finally, a fresh invitation to the Zionists to arrange a large international loan to the Turkish Treasury as an earnest of their intentions passed to Wolffsohn through a semi-private, easily disavowable third party.[27]

The object Wolffsohn had set himself was modest enough. What he chiefly wanted of the Turks, he explained to his interlocutors, was explicit, if still limited permission for Jews to emigrate to Palestine and Syria.[28] He mentioned the moderate figure of two thousand families a year for twenty to twenty-five years. The immigrants would of course accept Ottoman nationality and obligations (military and other). And the entire project would be managed by a joint committee of Ottoman and Zionist functionaries.[29] It amounted to a very substantial diminution of the original Zionist aims and plans. It was less than what Herzl in his day had been so bold as to put to the Sultan and his minions as matters for negotiation, let alone what had been discussed privately within the Zionist family both in his lifetime and after his death.[30] Wolffsohn made no mention of self-government, nor of a 'charter', nor of international guarantees of any kind, nor of the precise terms under which the settlers would serve in the Ottoman forces, all matters on which the Zionists had once attempted to negotiate. In fact, there

[27] Wolffsohn kept a meticulous record of his conversations in Constantinople. CZA, W35/4.

[28] The practice of adding Syria to Palestine had developed over the years as part of the Zionists' continual effort to get the Turks to relax their restrictions. The idea was to meet the Turkish refusal to countenance immigration into Palestine by not insisting on it exclusively, while not going so far beyond the basic remit of the Congresses as to cause a scandal. 'Syria' was thought of as sufficiently close to Palestine geographically and historically to merge with it, as it were, and allow a compromise. But the Turks remained unmoved. So far as they were concerned, Anatolia and Mesopotamia were the only lands available for settlement by Jews—and then under rigorous conditions, the latest formulation of which Nordau had heard from Dr Nazim in Paris.

[29] CZA, W35/4.

[30] In July 1906 Nordau drew up a detailed 'sketch' of the 'demands' to be put to the Ottoman Government. It envisaged local self-government, complete with taxation and police powers, substantial payment for statelands to be purchased for the settlers, Jewish regiments in the Ottoman army, and *inter alia* recourse to the Hague Court of Arbitration in the event of differences. Nordau's memorandum does not seem to have been taken seriously. Certainly, it was never acted upon. 'Exposé-Entwurf Dr Max Nordau.' CZA, Z2/5.

was not so much as a hint of a political purpose or of a conception of things that went beyond the naked idea that the Zionist Organization was a body with which the Ottoman Government would do well to negotiate on a matter of public concern. In Wolffsohn's hands, in effect, 'political' Zionism had been whittled down to a method (negotiation at the highest possible level) of supporting and accelerating 'practical' Zionism, and 'practical' Zionism to hardly more than the old, excruciatingly slow build-up of the Jewish demographic and economic presence in Erez-Israel.

But even so modest a proposal and so limited a plan of campaign led nowhere. No one in Constantinople was seriously interested in what he had to say and Wolffsohn had no choice but to concede—at all events, implicitly—that for the time being all the Zionists could hope to achieve was something, and then not much, in the strictly 'practical' sphere. On that count at least he was able to come back from Constantinople with a small prize: Turkish agreement to the setting up of a branch of the movement's bank, the Jewish Colonial Trust, in the imperial capital itself. Strictly, it was to be a new bank, under a new name. But the JCT would have a controlling interest in it, and even if it was a very small affair financially it would be a toehold of sorts, so Wolffsohn and his friends hoped and believed, and therefore a step forward. For it was understood from the beginning, by both sides, that one of the two managers of the bank would be their own man and that he would double as the movement's representative. And thus, albeit in a rather shadowy way, the Zionists would have placed a permanent, if only indirectly recognized spokesman (and observer) at the centre of those things that mattered most to them, in Constantinople. Zionist diplomacy was to have its first diplomat. This was in itself a development that spoke of a gradual change of style in the movement's central institutions from one of somewhat haphazard voluntarism to something more akin to bureaucratic order.

Victor (Avigdor) Jacobson (1869–1934), the man chosen for the post, had been one of the group of Russian-Jewish students in Berlin, led by Leo Motzkin, who some twenty years earlier had formed the remarkable Russian-Jewish Scientific Society[31]—remarkable less for what it accomplished (essentially it was a debating society) than for the role many of its members would play in the

[31] See *Origins*, pp. 223–5.

movement later on. These included Motzkin himself and Chaim Weizmann, and lesser but still central figures such as Shmarya Levin and Jacobson himself. All four men had been among those who had joined Herzl in 1897. They had also fought Herzl; some covertly, some (like Motzkin) very openly. They had disliked Herzl's unbending supremacy in the movement, his lack of interest in the Jewish cultural revival which they, in the wake of Aḥad Ha-'Am, regarded as both the key means of achieving general national rejuvenation and the ultimate and most worthwhile end towards which that rejuvenation should be directed. They had been outraged by Herzl's willingness to take the East Africa project under consideration; and when the great quarrel between Herzl and his opponents was at its height, in April 1904, Jacobson (with Ussishkin) had emerged as one of the leading and most eloquent spokesman for the opposition.[32] But he differed from most of his associates in the anti-Herzlian, anti-political, 'practical' wing of the movement in at least two ways. In the first place he was of milder temperament. Jacobson was a man of cultivated tastes, at least as good a listener as he was a talker, more at home in the Russian than in the authentic Jewish culture, and probably as much at home in the French and German cultures as in the Russian. He had, indeed, a distinct fondness for, and an ability to adapt to, western Europe; he was something of a *bon vivant*; generally, he was what his Russian contemporaries tended to classify as a 'European'. Thus he was quite unlike the bearish Ussishkin, the ill-mannered Shimshon Rosenbaum, the arrogant Weizmann, the flamboyant Shmarya Levin—each one of whom was, in his way, of sharper and stronger character than Jacobson and more representative in their persons of the east European Jewry for whom they all spoke. But there was a more important respect in which he differed from most of his friends and allies. Although a member of the GAC for a number of years, Jacobson, in function and in disposition, evolved as a servant of the Zionist movement rather than one of its leaders. Like Sokolov[33] and Ruppin (of whom more below) he became one of the Zionist Organization's first salaried officials. Unlike Sokolov (Ruppin, as we shall see, was in a class by himself) he remained in all but name a salaried civil servant to the end.

[32] *Formative Years*, pp. 341–4.
[33] Ibid., p. 424.

Jacobson's appointment in Constantinople was not quite the first of its kind. In 1906 he had been named manager of the Beirut branch of the Anglo-Palestine Company, a subsidiary of the Jewish Colonial Trust (planned and created by Herzl from the first to serve as the financial arm of the movement). The APC had been intended to promote investment in Erez-Israel; at the very least to prove to the critics of Herzl and his school that something was being done on the ground. It evolved as a small commercial bank, hardly an engine of major investment and enterprise but effective enough in its limited way. By the end of the decade it had branches in Jaffa, Jerusalem, Hebron, Safed, Beirut, and Haifa. But if the APC in Jaffa and Jerusalem was an earnest of the intentions of the Zionist movement and a small increment to the total Jewish presence in the country, the *raison d'être* of the Beirut branch was unclear and there was little in the post to attract a man like Jacobson. Nor did his immediate superior in the bank's hierarchy (Z. D. Levontin), or Wolffsohn and his colleague on the EAC Jakobus Kann (himself a banker), think much of his work there either. The post in Constantinople, being more political in content, certainly in intention, was therefore better suited to the man. But it was not an appointment that Wolffsohn had found easy to make.

Wolffsohn had always been extremely reluctant to let any of the reins of administration fall from his hand. He rarely took advice (other than from exceptional figures like Nordau). He was apt to infuriate the country organizations by issuing what they took to be high-handed instructions. He treated the Organization's salaried officials in Cologne much as—so his critics supposed—he treated his clerks in his timber business. Even Sokolov was apt to be ground into the dust; and the obsequious tone which crept into Sokolov's written reports to Wolffson more often than not is (at least to a member of a later generation) painful to read.[34] In any event, the idea of a prominent figure like Jacobson in a semi-executive post, a man who had been one of Herzl's opponents (and was Ussishkin's brother-in-law into the bargain), could not possibly commend itself to Wolffsohn. He seems to have smelled rebellion and independent thinking from afar and was careful to lay down ahead of time strict terms of reference for the movement's new—and first—political representative. Primarily, Jacobson was to be an observer; he might

[34] One example among many: Sokolov to Wolffsohn, 9 October 1908. CZA, W62II.

seek to make and develop local contacts and connections, but he was not to negotiate without explicit authorization.[35]

Bound by these slender threads, after long delay, Jacobson arrived in Constantinople in August 1908 as the first dust of the Young Turk revolution had begun to settle and the clamour for action, especially in the Russian wing of the movement, was rising to a peak. The Ottoman Empire, it was asserted on all sides, was undergoing profound and rapid change. But what was the Zionist leadership in remote Cologne *doing*? Impatience with Wolffsohn and his associates grew, tempers flared, and much of the old caution that had characterized the 'practicals'' view of things, especially things political, was cast off in the general excitement. Far-reaching statements about the essential modesty of Zionist aims and pretensions coupled to demands that these be brought to the urgent attention of the Turks followed one another in quick succession. Roles were suddenly reversed. The Russian 'practicals'' proposal to mount a press campaign squared very easily with what had long been taken to be the characteristically Herzlian tradition of public action. And while Wolffsohn and most of the other 'politicals' could not and did not fail to approve it, at least in principle, in practice Wolffsohn kept his close, businesslike (and business man's) eye on the movement's resources, much in the manner the opposition had originally made their own, and tended to shoot down the more ambitious of the plans issuing from Vilna, St. Petersburg, Moscow, and now Constantinople (i.e. Jacobson) without mercy or regard for the authors' feelings.[36]

The view that the Ottoman ice-floe was now breaking up in earnest was, of course, well founded. It was the notion that the Zionists could find a place for themselves, even a very modest one, within a Turkish system of any kind that was really in question. In any event, the fact that much was in flux allowed two contradictory operative conclusions to be drawn. One, broadly that of Wolffsohn and his colleagues, was that they had all better be very cautious and wait and see how things turned out; and, indeed, the abortive counter-revolution in April 1909 and the subsequent tightening of CUP government and social control served to justify them. The other conclusion was that all haste had to be made, the truth about Zionism broadcast, friends gained, alliances formed (and the needs

[35] Mordechai Eliav, *David Wolffsohn, ha-ish u-zemano* (Jerusalem, 1977), p. 147.
[36] Ibid., pp. 151–3.

of the movement pared down to meet rock-bottom Turkish requirements), before things solidified again and a great opportunity was lost.

At the end of 1908, as a sop to Jacobson and his friends, a small subsidy was finally authorized for *El Tiempo*, a well-established Jewish journal published in Constantinople in Ladino. The sum involved would not be so large as to be a real burden (200 francs per month).[37] Its editor, David Fresco, seemed sympathetic to the Zionists (later he was to disappoint his sponsors).[38] The subsidy could be rated a first attempt to bring the Jews of the Empire into the movement. The larger project of breaking into the major arena of general public affairs and opinion had to wait until Wolffsohn returned to Constantinople at the end of June 1909 to see the new Turkey for himself.

In the event, Wolffsohn's talks with the new Ottoman personalities, official and unofficial, deviated hardly at all from the old pattern. He saw a great many people, but heard nothing new from anyone. Ahmed Riza impressed him not at all, and his talk with him he judged of no importance. He viewed his meeting with the Grand Vizier, Hilmi Pasha, as interesting, but the 'main thing', he noted, was that Hilmi told him very plainly that 'for the Jews, for the present, Palestine was closed—*fermé*—and [that] the Government was unwilling to cancel regulations that had been in force for 25 years.'[39] At one stage, a private plan to form a local company run by 'influential Turks' (one of them a Minister) in conjunction with the Zionists to purchase land in Erez-Israel in circumvention of the prohibition was brought before Wolffsohn. But he was doubtful of it from the start—rightly so, for in the end nothing materialized.[40] He saw some leading Jewish figures, including the Ḥakham Bashi

---

[37] Ibid., p. 153.

[38] In the following year Fresco turned his coat and published a small book, *Le Sionisme* (Constantinople, 1909), addressed to Ottoman Jewry, in which he praised the Turks for having granted emancipation ('Te rends-tu compte, Israélite ottoman, de l'immensité de la faveur qui vient de nous être accordée?') and went on to denounce Zionism for the extreme dangers for Turkish Jewry which it embodied: 'Israélite ottoman, peux-tu mesurer l'immensité du désastre qui s'abbattrait sur le Judaïsme du pays si nos compatriotes et particulièrement nos compatriotes musulmans qui constituent la majorité, se faisaient la conviction que l'Israélite ottoman n'est pas bien attaché à sa Patrie, qu'il court vers un autre idéal, qu'il rêve la création d'un État juif au détriment de l'unité nationale ottomane?' (pp. 71–2).

[39] Wolffsohn to Kann, 10 August 1909. CZA, W/16, p. 38.

[40] Wolffsohn to Kann, 13 July 1909. Ibid., pp. 26–8; 28–9.

(Chief Rabbi), who now treated the Zionists in friendlier fashion than had been their custom in 'Abd al-Hamid's time. But Wolffsohn found them much under the influence of the AIU and the ICA, if probably unaware that the Turks, as he had discovered to his amusement, did not much distinguish between the various competing Jewish organizations, tending to treat all—the Alliance, ICA, Zangwill's ITO, and the Zionists themselves—as so many cognate parties within a single 'Zionist' organization.[41] It could of course be argued that such confusion in the public and official mind had to be cleared up and an effort made to win it for the genuine Zionist cause. So the opposition to his leadership was now demanding of him. And in pressing this view they had Jacobson's vigorous support: his argument being that matters were still fairly fluid in Constantinople, that the new regime had not yet settled down, that it had no long-range policy, and that it was operating on a day-to-day basis dealing with issues as they arose. It followed that this was, truly, a time for action. Wolffsohn was finally won over.

Late in July he and Sokolov (who had accompanied him to Turkey) were joined by three representatives of the powerful Russian branch of the movement: Ussishkin, the most vociferous and unbending of Russian Zionists of the 'practical' persuasion,[42] Tchlenov,[43] his less incisive, more accommodating partner at the apex of the Russian wing of the movement, and Israel Rosov, a relative newcomer to its upper reaches. With the delegation from Russia was the brightest, most restless, and most favoured of Russian Zionism's younger men, Vladimir Jabotinsky.[44] The older men had come to see things for themselves and to hammer out with Wolffsohn the financial and organizational terms on which the press project was to go forward. Jabotinsky, a supremely adaptable and talented journalist, was their candidate for its actual management. For once agreement between headquarters and province was rapid. The Russians were to put up roughly half the money; Wolffsohn and the EAC were to find the rest. Jabotinsky would be a member of Jacobson's small staff. General political authority would be retained by the EAC in Cologne. The operational plans were unusually

[41] Wolffsohn to Kann, 5 [July] 1909. Ibid., p. 7.
[42] On Ussishkin's long campaign against Herzl, his exceedingly opinionated posture, and the rugged figure he cut then and later, see *Formative Years*, especially pp. 185–9, 313–20, 459–62.
[43] See ibid., especially pp. 285–7.
[44] See ibid., pp. 464–5.

ambitious: an independent weekly review to be published in French,
a participatory share in a Turkish journal, and subsidies for another
five named journals and one as yet unnamed, Jewish and non-
Jewish, in Constantinople and Salonika.[45] Finally, Sokolov was to
remain in Constantinople for some weeks to make sure things were
got going.

Taking stock, as the Orient Express took him back to central
Europe, Wolffsohn allowed himself a mite of optimism. It had
become his deepest conviction, he wrote to Kann, 'that we need a
press in Constantinople now if we want to achieve anything at all.'
And now the Zionists were going to have one—if, that is, they could
find the rest of the money and if the planned arrangements with the
local journals and journalists worked out as well as was hoped.[46] Of
course, there still remained the vastly more difficult question of the
precise content of the message or argument the 'press complex' he
and his colleagues hoped to build up would ultimately seek—or
dare—to put to Turkish opinion. That had not been seriously
discussed at Constantinople, nor was it later. But in any event, his
journey over, Wolffsohn's mind turned—possibly with relief—to the
more painful, but at least more easily manageable, issues that would
arise at the Ninth Congress of Zionists planned for the end of the
year and already in active preparation.

vi

Wolffsohn had good reason to be concerned about the Congress,
due to open in Hamburg on 26 December 1909.[47] He knew he would
be under attack. The Russian wing of the movement—to be
represented, once again, by about a third of all the delegates
attending the Congress—was now positively simmering with
impatience, irritation, and barely concealed contempt for him and
for most of his works which agreement on the single issue of the
'press complex' had done nothing to mitigate. The Russians were

---

[45] Memorandum by Jacobson, 2 August 1909. CZA, W84.

[46] Wolffsohn to Kann, 10 August 1909. CZA, W16, pp. 37–41.

[47] The Ninth Congress had been postponed until the end of the year (the
Congresses were normally held in the summer) in the hope that by then the state of
affairs in Constantinople would be clearer. Hamburg had been selected mainly
because it was in Germany, in which it was thought it might be useful to hold a
Congress for the sake of the impact it could have on local public opinion. It was also
the port through which a large proportion of eastern European Jews travelled on their
way to North America.

intent upon a show-down (although Aḥad Ha-'Am, as it happened, thought it premature and counselled against it[48], and they made no secret of their demand for radical and specific alterations to the structure and manning of the movement's institutions. Things had to move, was the nub of a public call from Vilna[49] drafted in mid-October in the immediate aftermath of another insufficiently successful attempt to get Wolffsohn to see things their way at a meeting of the GAC earlier that month. All Jews anxious for a freer national life, not Zionists alone, had great expectations of the coming Congress, it was asserted in a formal statement. 'The change of regime in Turkey had opened up broad perspectives for fruitful work,' it declared, 'and for the very first time had created, even for those who regarded our aspirations sceptically or negatively, the necessary material conditions for that work to be done. . . . But an entire year had gone by . . . hopes had not materialized, the hoped-for conditions had not been created.' Worse: a strong tendency to centralization was developing in Turkey itself, 'an attitude of suspicion of all nationalists and fear of anything that cast even a shadow of a shadow of autonomy and desire for self-determination.' The Ninth Congress must therefore make absolutely clear what Zionism really was and what it wanted and, above all, that our aspirations 'were not tied irrevocably to any possible, long-favoured external political condition.' The Ninth Congress must finally bring the long argument about the Charter to an end. And sooner or later it must 'shift the movement's centre of gravity, and before all else its policy, to Turkey, to Erez-Israel.'[50]

Appealing to other country organizations to support them, the Russians made no bones about what they wanted done in practice. The first step was to remove the EAC from Cologne, a city of small importance as much in the Jewish world as in the larger world of high politics and culture, to some great European centre, to Paris perhaps, or if that proved impossible, to Berlin. The prestige and influence of the Zionist leadership having visibly declined, a person of real international fame—Nordau was the man they said they had in mind—should be called to its head. The membership of the EAC must be enlarged to include major figures from the east (Ussishkin,

---

[48] Aḥad Ha-'Am to Ludizhinsky, 4 January 1910. *Igrot AH, vi, p. 215.*
[49] Vilna was the seat of the central office of the Russian Zionist Federation at this time. See *Formative Years*, pp. 460 ff.
[50] Circular letter number 11. *Ha-'Olam*, 10 November 1909.

Tchlenov, Sokolov, and Stand were specifically mentioned). And at
least three of its members must be actually resident in the city that
would serve as the new seat of the movement's headquarters. All this
because it was clearly owing to the present composition of the EAC
that 'the great tasks of the movement' had received such 'dilatory
attention and ... many favourable opportunities [had] been
allowed to pass unused'.[51] The mood was summed up by an
unidentified correspondent in the movement's main Hebrew-
language organ (published in Vilna under the auspices of the
Russian wing): 'What is clear is that we have *no political leadership at
all*.'[52] In brief, a massive campaign to remove Herzl's unfortunate
successor was in the offing.

In the event, to general surprise, Wolffsohn managed to beat off
the attack once again. He opened the Congress with the traditional
presidential review of the affairs of the movement. He asserted the
compatibility of Zionism with the laws, policies, and spirit of the
new, free Turkey. And, with what a canny correspondent for the
London *Daily Telegraph* called 'that sanguine spirit of optimism that
has done so much to keep the movement alive',[53] he declared that
the prospects for immigration and settlement had *improved*.[54] Nordau
followed him (as we shall see) with a much more powerful if
certainly less optimistic address. The campaign to unseat him was
then got under way, first in the 'standing committee' of the
Congress, over which Weizmann presided, then in the plenum;
whereupon it failed, hardly begun. The heart of the opposition's
proposal, to form a new, enlarged EAC of which Wolffsohn would
not even be a full member, proved to be unacceptable to too many
delegates, even to some of the candidates for the new EAC
themselves. It struck people as egregious, even offensive, and, as
Ahad Ha-'Am had warned Ussishkin, premature.[55] Wolffsohn's
stock actually rose somewhat in the course of debate when he replied
to his critics with a great deal more spirit and sense than they had
given him credit for. Worse, from the critics' point of view, in the
confusion and embarrassment that followed the collapse of their
effort to unseat him, there was no choice (and no time) but to

---

[51] Goldberg *et al.* to the English Zionist Federation, 7 November 1909. CZA, Z2/ 412.
[52] 'N. N.', 'Concerning the Ninth Congress', *Ha-'Olam*, 9 December 1909.
Emphasis in the original.
[53] *Daily Telegraph*, 1 January 1910.
[54] *Protokoll IX*, pp. 7–8.
[55] Ahad Ha-'Am to Ludizhinsky, loc. cit.

confirm the same, pale triumvirate of Wolffsohn, Kann, and Warburg in the official leadership for a further two years. And as a further consequence, the EAC was fated to remain for the time being in the obviously unsuitable city of Cologne, with a staff diminished, moreover, by the loss of Sokolov. For he, having joined the opposition, there where his heart had always been, had now no choice but to resign his post as Wolffsohn's chief salaried official. The discomfiture of the rebels was severe and evident. A chastened Weizmann, Wolffsohn's rage lapping at his feet as far as Manchester, felt obliged to write him a long letter, part pathetic exculpation, part fresh denunciation of the 'ruling party, . . . always imputing malice with wickedness' to those who opposed it.[56]

It may be, however, that the most powerful blow struck on Wolffsohn's behalf, albeit indirectly, had been Nordau's. He, after all, was Zionism's arch-Herzlian. More, he was the one truly major figure in an assembly of quarrelsome, unhappy and—with a handful of exceptions—rather mediocre men and women. He was certainly the only member of the declining band of 'politicals' who could deliver an authoritative review of the past two years' work and an authoritative statement of policy for the movement as a whole in terms which were difficult for any of those present to refute. None could match him for the sweep and clarity and sheer pungency of his review of the movement's—and indeed Jewry's—predicament. There was a sense in which Nordau's addresses to the Congress had always been and remained unanswerable.

The nub of the matter, Nordau told the Ninth Congress, was that there was *nothing* of true and lasting consequence the movement could now do except stick to its guns. True, with that 'regrettable instability' which was characteristic of the national temperament, the 'Zionist section of the Jewish people had been seized by a veritable fever' when they heard of the overthrow of Turkish absolutism, as if the revolution in Constantinople had been by far the most important event to have occurred in Jewish history and Zionism 'had been brought within arm's length of its goal.' Certainly, the Zionists must rejoice, not merely as Jews, but as men, at the prospect of progress, freedom, order, and peace, in Turkey as elsewhere.

But we must not forget that the revolution in Constantinople was not a

---

[56] Weizmann to Wolffsohn, 12 February 1910. *Weizmann Letters*, v, no. 173, p. 181.

Zionist event, after all, nor a Jewish event, but a Turkish one; and that we
are still not Turkish subjects, that we have no direct part in the internal
changes of the Turkish Empire . . . and that the Young Turks are merely
one party in the Ottoman Empire. . . . So let us curb our impatience.

So much for recent events. As for the future, the official Zionist
leadership needed no reminding (by the opposition) that Turkey
was central to its proper concerns, that the affairs of Turkey
deserved close study, and that the purpose and character of the
movement needed to be made known to its leading personalities. It
was (or should have been) plain to all that

the object of all our hopes, our desires and our labours, the Holy Land of our
fathers, is a part of the Turkish Empire. On its coasts and borders it is
Turkish soldiers who keep watch. The keys to the house which the Zionists
wish to make their home lie in the hands of the Turkish Government. It is
therefore only natural that all our aspirations point to Turkey as the needle
of a compass points to the magnetic pole. All our living enterprises, our
schools, our . . . bank, our information bureau, our experimental farm—all
lie in Palestine, which is to say Turkey. All the practical undertakings that
can be directly realized, those that we plan, those we prepare, all fall within
the framework of the Ottoman Empire. For years now we have done what
we could to study . . . the laws of the land. . . . We have colleagues in
Turkey whose very function is to inform us of everything affecting Zionism
and, whenever necessary, to work in our interest. What else, in present
circumstances, can be done? . . .

To transfer our headquarters to the Turkish Empire would be a serious
error. For we must never forget that our present task is a double one,
internal and external. Certainly, we must win the approval of Turkey and
the assistance of the Turkish Government. But it is just as necessary to win
the understanding and support of the Jewish people. . . .

Count your numbers! [he told the Congress] Measure your strength! Do
you really believe we are already strong enough to establish enterprises in
Palestine of such significance for Jewry and for the future of the Jewish
people that of themselves and in the natural course of events Palestine
would, today, be rendered the [effective] centre of our movement and seat of
its headquarters?

I do not believe it. I am much more strongly convinced that we are still,
unfortunately, very weak and that we must seek to gain a great deal more
ground within the Jewish people itself.

Besides, said Nordau, in the event of negotiations with the Turkish
Government, there were great tactical advantages in conducting
them from outside Turkey, in countries in which we enjoy greater
freedom than in Turkey itself.

There remained the question of the Zionist programme. It was still the Basel Programme, he told his listeners.[57] But there was this to say. The Zionist aim to create 'a home for the Jewish people in Palestine to be secured by public law'[58] did *not* mean, as some had thought at the First Congress, the re-entry of the Jews into Palestine under the auspices of the Powers. The movement's foundation Congress had only wished to stress that it rejected the idea of 'slinking' [*einzuschleichen*] into Palestine and wished to enter the country only on the basis of expressly granted rights.

Their opponents (meaning the anti-Zionist Alliance Israélite Universelle and the Jewish Colonization Association) were pursuing them with slanders[59] they would not dare repeat in Europe, but which less experienced Turkish listeners were taking seriously: that once in Palestine, supposedly, the Zionists intended to declare it an independent Jewish republic.

We therefore say to the Turkish statesmen: . . . None of us has ever thought of tearing Palestine out of the Ottoman Empire, setting up a kingdom or republic: thanking the Empire for its benevolent acceptance of the Zionists by striking a blow at its unity. What we do want is to form a nationality within the Ottoman state, a nationality like all other nationalities in the Empire . . . the most loyal, most reliable, and most useful of all the Turkish nationalities, and to contribute with all zeal to the culture, welfare, and power of the Empire—all that we wish to undertake, but as a nationality, a Jewish nationality.

On this point, Nordau emphasized, *no* concessions were possible. If the Zionists went to Turkey it was indeed to become Turkish subjects, but as Palestinian Jews—not as Turks in some outlying province of Asia Minor. If it were merely to assimilate, the Jews could do quite well where they were and save themselves the fare and the trouble of adaptation to new surroundings. If, on the other

[57] In the months leading up to the Congress there had been much talk of the need to revise the text of the Programme in the light of the changed circumstances. See, for example, Daniel Pasmanik's article "A[l] d[evar] shinuim ba-programma ha-bazilayit' ('Concerning changes in the Basel Programme'), in the official Hebrew-language weekly of the movement published in Vilna, *Ha-'Olam*, 17 August 1909; and with particular reference to the Zionist-socialist demand for revision, N. M. Gelber, *Toldot ha-tenu'a ha-zionit be-galizia 1875–1918*, ii (Jerusalem, 1958), p. 569.

[58] On the genesis and intended meaning of the Programme formulated at the First Congress in 1897, at Basel, see *Origins*, pp. 366–9.

[59] Later in the debates, Nordau gave chapter and verse for his charge that the AIU and ICA were systematically poisoning the minds of the Turkish authorities against the Zionists by inflating Zionist aims to unreal, untrue, and absurd proportions. *Protokoll IX*, p. 223.

hand, Turkey resolved that it was opposed to the realization of the Zionist ideal of a resettlement of the Jews in the land of their fathers, then the Zionists had no choice but to wait.

In sum, nothing could change the fact that the affairs of Zionism depended crucially on Turkey. If the new Turkey wanted the Zionists' devoted contribution to its welfare and prosperity, they offered themselves gladly. 'If what it requires of us is the renunciation of Jewish hopes, and assimilation, then Jewry says, "No!" '

The Congress, he concluded, could pass as many resolutions on the practical work in Palestine as time allowed, so long as it did not forget that the principle underlying all its work was 'national Judaism'. For this was Zionism's own, essential, and irreducible creation. Means were one thing, the end was another. 'In a movement which, because of a change in the Turkish constitution, altered not merely the means, but even the end, I would no longer see Zionism, but only assimilation, Turkish assimilation. Such Zionism would no longer be my Zionism.'[60]

Nordau was loudly cheered. The Herzlians cheered him for his restatement of the larger purposes of Zionism and for his reading of the political map. The opposition cheered him for his abandonment of Herzl's old idea of a 'Charter' or treaty under the terms of which the great Return would be organized and made secure, but also for his explicit statement that the Zionists would have to learn patience and concern themselves a great deal more with the strengthening of their position within Jewry.[61] This, in substance although not in tone, was only a step away from 'current tasks' and not impossibly distant from the Aḥad Ha-ʿAmian insistence on national consciousness and culture. The emphases were different. The terms grander. It was still far away from the other leg of the Aḥad Ha-ʿAmian recipe for rejuvenation still asserted by the master, namely that it was the concentration of resources in a *cultural* centre in Ereẓ-Israel that was vital.[62] For it was the contrasting territorial-political

---

[60] *Protokoll IX*, pp. 16–26.

[61] The Russian Zionist executive called its members' particular attention to these points in Nordau's speech. Circular to delegates, 30 December 1909. [OS] (12 January 1910, NS). CZA, A24/109.

[62] 'In the past, the "politicals" thought that Ereẓ-Israel could be obtained without working the country itself, but by means of intercession in the "court". Now that the "court" is no more, why even the blind will see that whoever conquers the country by means of cultural work, both material and spiritual, will in the end be its master.' Aḥad Ha-ʿAm to Mordechai Ben Hillel Ha-Kohen, 4 October 1908. *Igrot AH*, iv, p. 147.

approach to the problem of contemporary Jewry that had been indirectly restated, and it was the preferred strategy of orderly and large-scale access to Ereẓ-Israel and a firm and formal status for the Jewish settlement within it that had been declared Zionism's *sine qua non*. But equally, these great purposes had been judged—in all but so many words—to be out of reach for the present, and neither Nordau nor anyone else could suggest how progress towards them might be made. Nailing one's flag to the mast, muddling through, exploring every avenue, hoping for the best—this was the sum of his message. 'A long wait is an affliction,' was Nordau's characteristic comment on his own analysis; 'it is not a disgrace.' And it was a fair conclusion from all he had to say, although Nordau did not explicitly offer it, that in these circumstances a change of leadership would avail the movement nothing.

Back in Russia, the leaders of the opposition declared none the less that the moral victory had been theirs and that they were very far from giving up their fight. 'It must be stressed with all force', they stated in a message for the broadest distribution, 'that we will not move from the path we are on until we have succeeded in having at the head of our movement such leadership as will truly merit the name and correspond to the functions in question.'[63]

It was, indeed, a victory that would not be long delayed. But for what, precisely? One cannot tell how many of the more articulate members of the movement in any of its schools would have gone so far as did one of Aḥad Ha-'Am's own disciples who, reviewing the Ninth Congress with satisfaction, thought it marked 'yet another stage in the slow and painful process of evolution' whereby certain 'foreign' elements in Herzl's legacy were in process of being dropped; and that among such foreign elements as had been 'prominent in Herzl's mind', was an 'idea which had no necessary connection with the essence of Zionism—the idea of providing a "home of refuge" for persecuted Jews. This alien element was expelled from Zionism some years . . . ago,' this young Aḥad Ha-'Amian asserted, 'and is now embodied in the Territorial movement.'[64] Still, it was a fact that the gap between the schools had greatly narrowed; and that it was chiefly the refusal of the old Herzlian loyalists to cast the territorial-political approach to the major problems of contemporary Jewry totally out of mind that

---

[63] Circular to delegates, 30 December 1909 [OS]. CZA, A24/109.
[64] Leon Simon, 'Zionism after the Ninth Congress', *The Jewish Review*, April 1910, p. 74.

separated them from the forces now plainly dominant in the movement.[65] But whatever the approach, it was the poverty of the means available that undercut everything attempted and clouded and depressed all minds. No doubt, if all failed, Zionists could still take honourable refuge in sobriety, like most other Jews seeking to work in the Jewish public interest. 'What power-means [*Machtmittel*] do we have?' Sokolov had written to Wolffsohn soon after the Young Turks' seizure of power. 'We have our national spirit, our traditions, and so forth. . . . The first is of great value, but not for immediate negotiations, rather as a warrant for our future. The latter bears no relation to our grandiose aims. And even if we were already a major power . . . what do the great powers themselves do concerning the events in Turkey? They await developments.' This, thought Sokolov, was the honest and sensible thing to do.[66] And in essence it was not far from Nordau's position and that of many others. But it was a far cry from the note sounded by Herzl only a dozen years before. The iron of deep doubt had entered into more than one soul.

[65] Twice as many delegates had cast votes against Wolffsohn in the Ninth Congress as in the Eighth. The trend was unmistakable.

[66] Sokolov to Wolffsohn, 18 September 1909. CZA, W62 II .

2

Drift

i

The springs of Zionism had always been in eastern Europe. It was
there—mostly within the Russian Empire, partly within Romania
and the Polish region of Austria—that the greater part of Jewry was
located. It was there that the Jews formed a recognizable and
generally recognized national group with distinct linguistic and
cultural characteristics, buttressed, of course, by particular social
and religious institutions. In all respects but one, therefore, there
was a deal of sense in the Imperial Russian determination to see
them as a separate people, distinct from and on the whole un-
amenable to assimilation into the 'basic' or 'indigenous', i.e. Russian
and Russian Orthodox population of the Empire. By and large, a
distinct people was what they had always been; and by and large,
that was how the overwhelming majority of the Jews of Russia and
Poland most probably wished to remain.

West of the Russian Empire matters were generally otherwise,
both in fact and in theory. In Austria-Hungary a distinction was
commonly drawn between 'nations' and 'nationalities' (the former
supposedly 'great', certainly powerful; the latter supposedly 'minor',
but certainly powerless—subject nations, in fact). The Jews could,
with cause, have been grouped with the 'nationalities'. In fact this
was very rarely the case, [1] for while the distinction between 'nations'
and 'nationalities' had everything to do with power, and the Jews
were undoubtedly powerless, Jewry as an *ethnic* category was not
associated with power at all—least of all by those who composed it.

---

[1] In 1909, in the distant Austrian province of Bukovina, the Jews were recognized
as one of the constituent national groups and granted representation in the provincial
assembly. So far as I know, the case of Bukovina was unique in Europe in the period
leading up to the Great War.

Besides, both in the traditional lands of the House of Habsburg and in Hungary a measure of assimilation by Jews into the 'nations' of that Empire was now possible, by no means frowned upon by the authorities (even welcomed, to some extent, notably in Hungary), and not wholly unpopular among the Jews themselves. The result (as in much of *western* Europe) was a whole range of degrees of assimilation or half-way houses which stood between the poles of total, unquestioning loyalty to traditional modes of thought and behaviour on the one hand, and an effort finally to break free of the old bonds and into non-Jewish society by means of baptism, intermarriage, and in extreme cases, even open and declared hostility to Jewry itself, on the other hand. In Austria-Hungary, as in much of western Europe, a major, virtually irreversible disintegration of Jewry as a clearly defined and demarcated national group was thus in progress.

Not so in Russia. There only the extreme position of formal religious renunciation carried any real weight. Half-way houses and delicate distinctions were little understood and never much liked.[2] Baptism had always been necessary for intermarriage or for entry into the middle and higher bureaucracy, into secondary and university teaching (and indeed for free access to secondary and higher education itself), into the officer corps and the judiciary, and was virtually a requisite for acceptance into the higher ranks of the bar. It was therefore significant that, considering the vast Jewish population of the Empire (well over five million for the period under review), the number of conversions to the state church was extremely small: probably between 1,000 and 1,500 each year in the decade before the Great War. When, after 1905, a minor degree of religious toleration was instituted, there was even a moderate trend of converts back to Judaism.[3]

Difficult in itself on moral grounds (assuming none of a theological character) and redolent, inevitably, of opportunism, indignity, and betrayal, conversion was the rarer for Russian society, culture, and religious practice being on the whole less attractive in Jewish eyes, less 'superior', less 'advanced', and therefore ostensibly less promising culturally and intellectually than were the contemporary German or Hungarian or French or English

---

[2] An exceptional case was that of a deputy to the Second Duma, I. V. Hessen, who registered as a Russian Orthodox by religion and a Jew by nationality.

[3] Y. Ma-'or, 'Yehudei rusiya bimei ha-"dumot"', *He-'Avar*, vii, 1960, p. 83.

analogues in the eyes of the Jewish subjects of Germany, Hungary, France, England, or for that matter of Russia itself. There was the further circumstance that in the years after the 1905 revolution Russian nationalists tended to reject conversion to Christianity as a valid criterion for acceptance, and an ethnic or racial criterion—presenting an absolute obstacle to movement—began to replace it. But above all, the attitude of contemporary Jewry both within and outside the Russian Empire to Russia and to the Russian Autocracy and all its works was conditioned by the latter's own profound hostility to Jewry and to Judaism. For it was its consistent policy both to perpetuate a separate formal and legal status for the Jews *and* to build upon it a vast structure of social and economic restriction, administrative harassment, and systematic exposure to the mob.

Virtually alone among the established states of Europe (the one notable exception was Romania, which treated its Jewish minority with, if anything, greater harshness and less regard for the figure it cut in lands that lay to the west[4]), Russia chose openly to treat the very presence of Jews among its subjects not merely as regrettable or as a nuisance, or even as a misfortune, but as a matter of the first importance to the state, such that it was obliged to take draconian and, as it were, prophylactic measures against them. None of the measures actually adopted seemed to the regime ever to be adequate, ever to do more than scratch the surface of the 'problem' (apart from adding to the misery of the Jews themselves). Nor could the Autocracy resolve on how to attack the problem of a large Jewry in its midst 'finally'. There were always countervailing considerations of state. Not all Russians, not even all functionaries in the

---

[4] 'In no part of Europe is mediaeval prejudice against the Hebrew race more fiercely rampant than in Roumania,' remarked a well-informed, contemporary (non-Jewish) observer; 'for in no other part of Europe, save in Russia, are mediaeval conditions and modes of thought and conduct so rife.' (G. F. Abbott, *Israel in Europe* (London, 1907; new edition 1972), p. 379. A detailed discussion of conditions in Romania and the plight of its Jewry would be beyond the scope of this book. But it may be said that the characteristic circumstance was that, in defiance of their undertakings upon being granted full independence at the Congress of Berlin in 1878, the Romanian authorities continued to deny citizenship to the overwhelming majority of their Jewish subjects (numbering about a quarter of a million). They thus confirmed in formal terms and sought to excuse—if not to justify—their *de facto* and unashamed policy of exposing Romanian Jewry to continual physical, economic, and moral harassment. Even enlisted soldiers who fought in the ranks of the Romanian army in the 1913 Balkan war were refused citizenship after discharge. Inevitably, Romania was a steady source of emigrants to the United States and one of the minor strongholds of Zionism.

higher reaches of the administration, thought the persecution of the Jews either necessary or expedient, let alone morally justifiable. It was evident to all that the one sure result of the consistent persecution of the Jews was to earn the Autocracy the Jews' undying hatred and to drive them by their thousands into the ranks of the revolutionaries. But, perhaps inevitably, the failure to dispose of a large number of subjects disliked and held in contempt on arbitrary religious and ideological grounds and to compound the problem by steadily converting a normally passive population into a restless and rebellious one only increased the self-righteous fury and the brutality of mind and deed with which the state as a machine turned upon its Jewish subjects. After the crisis of the 1905 revolution and the huge increase in the intensity and regional distribution of licensed mob violence against Jews in its aftermath (of which the huge pogrom in Odessa—four days and nights of murder, rape, and arson leaving over 5,000 casualties, among them 300 dead—was the climax[5]), the physical battering of the Jews tended to diminish. But the *threat* of organized and officially sanctioned mob violence was permanent, and in every other way matters remained unchanged or worsened. The resulting combination of a certain improvement in terms of public order with a consistent rise in tension, to say nothing of despair, was not uncharacteristic of the mood and condition of Russia and the peoples of Russia as a whole. Yet there was a difference.

For most of the period between the first revolution and the outbreak of the World War the internal government and politics of Russia were dominated and, it might be said, typified by the somewhat enigmatic figure of Stolypin. Under his direction there occurred a substantial but incomplete reversion to pre-1905 norms of government. There was a real, if never thorough, attempt at social and economic reform, and a modest but certainly limited effort to work with the elected Parliament. A very restricted, successively less democratic, but still not entirely unrepresentative electoral system was retained. The years of Stolypin might be termed a period of ambivalence and twilight which it was not impossible at the time (or in retrospect) to consider, on balance, as preliminary to dawn rather than to further darkness. Progress, improvement, change, generosity, even freedom could not be ruled out for the future. Thus, at least, for Russia and the Russians. Not so for the Jews. So far as they

---

[5] See *Formative Years*, pp. 386–8.

were concerned, nothing fundamental had changed, and nothing indicated change in the future, except, probably, for the worse.

It was not only the constant tightening of restrictions and the steady elimination of whole categories (ex-servicemen, for example) from the very limited class of those who enjoyed some exemption from the anti-Jewish legislation, the periodic expulsion of great numbers of people, often groups of hundreds and more at a time, from cities outside the Pale and from the villages within it into the crowded towns of the Pale itself, the razzias conducted by the police in search of illegal residents, and numberless other harassments and obstacles put in the way of earning a decent living and pursuing a peaceful life that rendered all but the most stoic desperate for change. It was, too, the ever nastier atmosphere which the Jews of Russia were compelled to breathe: the endless, violent anti-Semitic abuse in Parliament, in the press, and in the street, and a state of affairs to which it was extraordinarily difficult for them to decide how best to respond. Should there be a considered reply to the constant public, officially approved condemnation of the Jews as an evil race given to evil practices? Should there be a formal refutation of the monstrous (and therefore perhaps inherently irrefutable) charges levelled against them? Or should Russian Jewry stand on its dignity and be silent? These came to be questions of the first order in Jewish public life, and it came at the same time to be reasonable to judge the issue hopeless: after all, to whose better judgement was one to appeal?

The degree to which the pariah status of the Jews had come to be accepted as part of the natural and therefore in some sense proper order of things is attested by the need even for such Russians of power or of eminence who did propose an amelioration of the Jews' condition to clear themselves of any possible charge of actual sympathy for the people in question. Stolypin's proposal for a change in the Jews' regime, put to the Tsar soon after taking office (and promptly rejected by his master), was couched entirely in terms of expediency. Even declared and committed liberals found the subject tricky, if not distasteful. When in 1911, the noisily reactionary anti-Semitic Third Duma was forced by a handful of courageous deputies, led by one of its two Jewish members,[6] to debate a proposal to abolish the Pale of Settlement in which the

---

[6] There were twelve Jewish deputies in the First Duma, four in the Second, two in the Third, and three in the Fourth and last.

greater part of Russian and Polish Jewry was confined, the liberal and generally decent Kadet party reluctantly resolved to support the motion. They had, indeed, no choice. But their spokesman, Vassily Maklakov, an eminent and respectable attorney, was careful to take the line that anti-Semitism in itself was *permissible*. Those who, for whatever reason, hated Jews were fully entitled to ostracize them socially and boycott them in their business dealings, to avoid looking at works of art they had produced or listening to music they had written. What was impermissible was for the *state* to engage in discrimination.[7] Later, in 1913, when the same Maklakov joined the team of defending attorneys at the notorious Beiliss blood libel case (in which an entirely innocent Jewish labourer was charged with the ritual murder of a Christian boy) he took an analogous line. The question whether certain Jewish sects did or did not practice ritual murder was an open one; all that was certain and all *he* wished to argue was that Mendel Beiliss was innocent of the specific charge levelled against him.[8]

[7] *Gosudarstvennaya Duma, tretii sozyv*, 4th session, part II, 54th meeting, 9 February 1911, cols. 1543–50.

[8] Ma'or, p. 70. It is right to add that, albeit on different grounds, Oskar Gruzenberg, the celebrated Jewish member of the team defending Beiliss, took a line that *in practice* was similar. Gruzenberg believed that to argue a negative proposition, namely that the Jews did *not* practice cannibalism, would be both impractical and undignified. It is well to recall that there was never any doubt, not even in the minds of the judicial authorities and the police in Kiev, that Beiliss was innocent. The evidence suggests that the procurator himself would have dropped the case, had the Minister of Justice in St. Petersburg, with political purposes in mind and with what Joseph Conrad called 'a Russian official's ineradicable, almost sublime contempt for truth' (*Under Western Eyes*, IV, i), not insisted on going through with it. The result was a desperate but massive effort to stage-manage the trial and procure a conviction by all available means. So with a jury of semi-literate peasants handpicked by the prosecution to confront, perjured (and paid) witnesses for the prosecution (one of them a Catholic priest) to serve it, a judge who was blatantly hostile to the defence, Gruzenberg had grounds for concentrating on the refutation of the specific charges and showing that Beiliss himself did not commit and could not have committed the crime. The public effect would be identical. In the event, the jury returned a tie vote and Beiliss (as the judicial authorities had privately anticipated) had to be acquitted.

The standard account (in English) of the affairs, complete with documents released after the revolution, is still A. B. Tager, *The Decay of Czarism* (Philadelphia, 1935). A more up-to-date, but untidy compilation (in Hebrew) is Meir Cotic, *Mishpat Beiliss* (Tel-Aviv, 1978). See also O. O. Gruzenberg, *Yesterday: Memoirs of a Russian Jewish Lawyer* (Berkeley, 1981), especially pp. 104–24. But the literature on the trial and its ramifications is large, extending to a cogently argued analysis of the way in which the affair may have set Franz Kafka on the path which led him to write 'In the Penal Colony' and *The Trial*: Arnold J. Band, 'Kafka and the Beiliss Affair', *Comparative Literature*, xxxii: 2, 1980, pp. 168–83.

Finally, it may be said of the whole gruesome affair that Gruzenberg's argument

But perhaps the most instructive—and in some ways the most poignant—aspect of the hopeless condition of Russian Jewry was that there was no way, no ground, no accepted method whereby its common needs and feelings might be put authoritatively to the Russian Government. No communal organization at a higher level than the local was permitted. No properly elected and representative body could be formed. Such supra-communal societies and parties as did exist (whether explicitly revolutionary, such as the Bund,[9] or only too anxious for legality, such as the Zionists) were held *ipso facto* to be subversive of the regime. The sole country-wide institution allowed Russian Jewry was a powerless body of religious and lay notables appointed by the Government itself to advise it on matters pertaining exclusively to the Jewish religion. It was rarely convened. It consisted mostly of wealthy laymen and eminent rabbis, not men inclined to take a forceful line. When in March 1910 some of the more distinguished members of the council were so bold as to ask to be received by Stolypin to express their concern about the general condition of Russian Jewry, the Prime Minister retorted that their business was with religion alone. It was not their function to discuss the general condition of their community at all. In any case it was the Jews themselves who, by joining the ranks of the revolutionaries

proved correct, but only up to a point. The authorities certainly judged the result a defeat, as it was, and responded by pressing charges against newspapermen and lawyers who had in one way or another offended them—chiefly by expressing support for the defence and criticism of the Government for the evil purpose behind the mounting of the trial. But the effect of centuries of anti-Semitic demonology was not easily dispersed. The author's father once recalled that when, as a young reporter, he covered the trial for his newspaper, he was flatteringly taken out to dinner by one of his senior (non-Jewish) colleagues. The great man assured him that all decent people knew Beiliss had been framed. But, he asked, 'Tell me, dear friend, what *do* the Jews consume at their Passover meal?'

[9] The 'General Jewish Workers' Party of Lithuania, Poland, and Russia' founded in 1897. The Bund was an explicitly proletarian, Marxist, revolutionary organization bound ideologically and (on and off) institutionally to the Russian Social-Democratic Workers' Party in an uncertain, unhappy, and ultimately tragic relationship. It sought to lead a sort of special, ethnic (and of course secular) Jewish wing of the Marxist revolutionary movement founded on the Jewish urban working class. Thus it hoped to effect a compromise between the Jews' desire to retain their identity and their almost equally strong desire to see the regime overthrown and replaced by RSDWP rule. That achieved, justice, they were sure, would finally be done them and equality between the nations reign throughout Russia. The Bundists were violently opposed to Zionism, which they reckoned bourgeois, excessively traditionalist, insufficiently interested in the here and now of Russian Jewry (the socialist Zionists being no better than their bourgeois brethren in this respect), and cravenly law-abiding into the bargain.

in great numbers, had brought their troubles down upon them. Russian Jewry, said Stolypin, had largely abandoned the Old Testament, without adopting the New. Educate your people in the spirit of religion and loyalty to the throne, he advised them; some gradual improvement in their condition might then follow. His visitors were then dismissed. The meeting had been short; the notables of Russian Jewry had been kept standing throughout.[10]

The cumulative effect of over thirty years of impoverishment, physical insecurity, administrative harassment, and continual verbal abuse from quarters high and low was to produce within Russian Jewry at almost all its levels the equivalent of a revolutionary situation: a tremendous disquiet, a nervous anticipation of, and desire for change, ever deeper alienation from the regime to which it was subject and from the broader society of which, in a limited but still real enough way, it formed a part. To this there was added a steadily growing rejection of traditional communal authority amounting to anything between outright repudiation and an amused shrugging-off of what was taken to be the irrelevant counsel of ill-informed old duffers. A thin stream of young, radical, and, it must be said, brave spirits did flow into the revolutionary underground—never in such numbers as the rulers of Russia claimed, but far from insubstantially. But the Jews *as a people* remained powerless in the face of the massed strength of the Russian regime and the deep hostility to them long bred into their neighbours. They could mount no national rebellion. They could retreat to no mountain redoubt. They were devoid of the sort of natural national leadership a hereditary aristocracy can occasionally provide. Their traditional communal leaders, the learned rabbis and the affluent men of business, rarely had influence extending beyond the local or the regional and were in any case unsuited socially, temperamentally, and perhaps, above all, morally for such a role. For the traditional leadership of Jewry was normally philanthropic and ameliorative in its purposes and profoundly cautious in its bent. Traditional public wisdom could be summed up as a general injunction to lie low and wait for the current storm to pass or, if it came to the worst, to strike tents quietly and depart. But in the present circumstances even the advice to depart was exceedingly uncommon (except among the radical spirits): the men of substance feared the charge of disloyalty to Russia that it could be made to

[10] Ma'or, pp. 67–8; *Jewish Review*, September 1910, pp. 193–6.

imply; the rabbis feared the further erosion of faith and religious observance that surely awaited their flock in distant America. And so, with none, neither the revolutionaries, nor the Zionists, nor, least of all, the traditional communal leaders, being able to offer the urgent relief they craved, eastern European Jews tended ever more strongly, ever more systematically, to shift for themselves. In practice, this meant migration: a great river of Jewish emigrants, passing out of Russia, Poland (and Romania too) *for good* to lands further west (chiefly, of course to the United States), fluctuating with the conditions of the lands of their birth, but always strong.[11] This, more than anything else, was the mark of the times. Yet it was the case that despite these circumstances Zionism—at the very heart of whose original programme lay the twin principles of migratory movement and social change—failed to convert itself into a mass movement.

ii

Russia and Russian Jewry were at the centre of the contemporary Problem (and problems) of the Jews, and the Russian Zionists formed far and away the largest contingent in the movement. They sent some 150 delegates to the Congress, roughly a third of the total. They formed between a third and a half of the formally enlisted membership. Theirs was the largest financial contribution to the Organization and to the Jewish National Fund set up in 1901 to collect donations for the purchase of land in Erez-Israel. Theirs, as we have seen, was increasingly the dominant—and soon to be the decisive—voice in the movement's internal debates. And as the years went by it was largely from within Russian Zionism that its chief and most original personalities tended to emerge. But within Russian Jewry itself Zionism was none the less a small affair. The figures are uncertain. Proper and comprehensive records do not seem to have been kept, partly for fear of the police, partly owing to slack administrative habits. Membership varied not only with the popularity of the movement (it was greatest in Herzl's lifetime and

[11] US Bureau of Immigration and Naturalization figures for immigrants of 'Hebrew' race: 61,000 (1900), 58,000 (1901), 58,000 (1902), 76,000 (1903), 106,000 (1904), 130,000 (1905), 154,000 (1906), 149,000 (1907), 103,000 (1908). The great majority came from Russia, Poland, and Romania. After 1908 the figures fell approximately to the level maintained before the revolution and the great wave of pogroms that accompanied it. Few returned, hardly more than 3 per cent (compared with 13–17 per cent of all immigrants to the United States at this time).

took years to recover from the shock of his death) but also with the degree of police repression. The number of full members of the Zionist movement, namely those who subscribed to its programme and paid the small membership fee—the *shekel* (40 copecks in Russia, more in western Europe and the United States)—seems generally to have fluctuated around the 70,000 mark, but may have reached 100,000 just before the outbreak of the Great War. But it could be affected by the fact that there was nothing so incriminating as possession of the *shekel* certificate unless it was the whole blocks of *shekels* held by the activists who distributed them. And while the *shekel* was distributed each year, there was a marked tendency for the numbers to rise in those years in which the Congress was held. Then, of course, the number of true activists was inevitably smaller than that of ordinary, largely passive members. The weekly printing of *Ha-ʿOlam*, edited in Vilna and very much the organ of Zionism's Russian wing (and therefore as good an indicator as any of the size of the ranks of the fully dedicated) was at most 6,000 (in 1911); postal subscriptions numbered 3–4,000. Subscriptions to the pro-Zionist Russian-language *Razsvet* may have reached 10,000. All told, throughout the Empire, there were at least one thousand local Zionist associations of various sizes, and in a country in which all such associations and activity were illegal and liable, as we shall see, to police repression, this was an achievement. But, again, measured against the five to six million Jewish subjects of the Tsar and the general restlessness among them so well indicated by the continual migration out of Russia to the west, it cannot be described as a truly powerful showing. [The fact was that the Zionist movement in eastern Europe was one in which the relatively well educated, modernist, and—again, *relatively*—comfortable classes were preponderant, rather than the impoverished, generally traditionalist, petty tradesmen, artisans, and *lumpenproletariat* of which classes most of Jewry in that part of the world consisted.][12] Figures for the Jewish press in Russia reflect this. A contemporary estimate put the maximum circulation of the principal dailies, weeklies, and monthlies in the three relevant languages (Yiddish, Hebrew, and Russian) at a little under 280,000. But it is the Yiddish publications that dominated (85 per cent) while Hebrew—the use of which for secular purposes was the very mark of Zionism in its national-cultural aspect—accounted for under 6 per cent.[13]

[12] For some observations on the social make-up of the movement at this time, see *Formative Years*, pp. 493–4.

⌐Such attraction as Zionism, in its early years, held for eastern
European Jewry, and for Russo-Polish Jewry in particular, had
much to do with the fact that it alone seemed to point a way out of
an ancient dilemma. ⌐It proposed a way whereby material and
psychological well-being could be improved without damage to the
national-cultural fabric, strengthening and renovating it. It accepted the proposition—indeed, it was originally founded upon it—
that there was no future for the Jews as private individuals in the
less-favoured, greater part of the Diaspora. It addressed itself to the
general condition of Jewry in the modern world in terms that
entailed a welding together of the Jewish people on what was hoped
to be an entirely sounder, safer basis. And so doing, it immediately
and inevitably set itself up in opposition, and indeed rivalry, to the
traditional leadership of Jewry, above all the rabbinate whose
members, as one of Russo-Polish Zionism's most articulate and
fearless spokesmen once put it, had not 'a fresh and live word' to say
to their flock, who wanted nothing better than the backing of the
Government to bolster their authority, who had nothing to say
about equal rights or even pogroms, and who behaved as if they
found the condition of the Jews within the Empire satisfactory.[14]
Thus, while Zionism could and did speak directly to the mass of
eastern European Jewry who wanted nothing so much as relief and
survival, it tended to have rather more to say to the Jewish
intelligentsia who, on balance, were concerned with general
categories at least as much as with immediate rescue. Thus even at
the beginning, but all the more as the original Herzlian *élan* and its
corresponding high purpose of a massive and rapid relief for eastern
European Jewry faded (much to the satisfaction of the intelligentsia,
who disappoved of what they held to be its 'messianic' and socially
irresponsible aspect). For then the relevance of Zionism to what
came to be known as the 'afflictions of the Jews', as opposed to the
more theoretical and cultural 'afflictions of Judaism',[15] began to fade

[13] These figures for membership, press, etc., were derived and collated chiefly from
the following sources: Jacobson and Hantke to Idelson, 12 August 1912. CZA, Z3/
880; indictment against A. G. Druyanov, 10 June, 1911, [OS]. CZA, Z2/457II; *Ha-
'Olam*, 26 February 1913; 'Circular No. 1' of the Russian Zionist Central Committee,
January 1910. CZA, Z2/457I; Report by Russian 'Secretariat' for May 1914. CZA,
Z3/892.

[14] Gruenbaum commenting on the deliberations of a rabbinical conference in
Poland. *Ha-'Olam*, 26 February 1909.

[15] A distinction much emphasized in the writings of Aḥad Ha-'Am. See for
example, 'Medinat ha-yehudim ve"zarat ha-yehudim"' (1898), *Kol kitvei Aḥad Ha-
'Am*, pp. 135–40.

too. And as the attention of the movement, led ever more effectively by its Russian wing, came to be riveted on the 'practical' work in Erez̧-Israel (the rest being relegated to an immensely distant future so far as any simple, straightforward mind in a dismal *shtetl* in the Pale could make out), so by an almost absurd paradox its attention came to be directed ever more closely to internal developments in Russia itself as well. Nor could things be otherwise if it was not to lose all popular support and all grounding in contemporary reality. This was the gist of the position adopted by the Helsingfors conference of Russian Zionists at the end of 1906 and which penetrated the thinking of Zionists throughout the movement, in time reaching even the crumbling Herzlian bastion in Cologne.

In practice, the changed position advanced matters little. The Zionists could never compete—nor did they propose to compete— in radical fervour with the true revolutionaries. Nor were they, nor could they be, interested in becoming a sort of ethnic Jewish segment of the constitutional democratic wing of the movement for general reform, so allowing their fundamental purposes to dissolve entirely. Their enemies on the left, notably the Bund, were therefore free to charge them, and not without reason, with weakening, by default, the general campaign for national rights in Russia.[16] In sum, so far as that part of the Helsingfors Programme which (loosely) prescribed participation in internal Russian political life was concerned, a degree of uncertainty and embarrassment seems to have clouded their vision throughout.[17] Their shift of emphasis may have been intended to be no more than tactical and temporary, part of the holding operation on which they believed the movement had no choice at this time but to embark. But if it made sense to its progenitors it added little to the movement by way either of clarity of public position, or prestige, or popular support. And what in some ways was worse, particularly to those devoted to keeping the whole delicate machinery of meetings, membership, propaganda, publications, funding, and contact with and influence upon the central institutions going, the new, less equivocal approach to the rulers and Government of Russia came to be matched by a less equivocal approach of the Autocracy itself towards the phenomenon of Zionism among its Jewish subjects.

[16] Koppel S. Pinson, 'Arkady Kremer, Vladimir Medem, and the Ideology of the Jewish "Bund"', *Jewish Social Studies*, vii, 1945, pp. 260–1.

[17] Thus Sokolov writing to Wolffsohn in evident discomfort, 31 January 1908, on the possibility of running for election to the Duma. CZA, W62II.

No doubt the severity of the Autocracy's post-revolutionary campaign against all forces judged to be hostile to it, and to the Jews of Russia in particular, rendered the Helsingfors policy futile at its very inception. But more specifically, for a movement which had managed to survive for a decade, even in some respects to flourish, in the twilight zone between tolerated illegality and deliberate repression, the impending clash between it and the Government was in danger of proving disastrous. 'So long as Zionism consisted of wanting to create an independent state in Palestine and promised to organize the emigration from Russia of a certain number of her subjects, the Russian Government could be entirely favourable to it', Herzl had been officially informed in his time. 'But once this principal aim of Zionism is dropped and replaced by simple propaganda in favour of Jewish national concentration in Russia, the Government naturally can under no circumstances tolerate this new Zionist course.' Thus the powerful, ruthless, but clear-minded Minister of Interior Plehve to Herzl in 1903.[18] Half a decade later, in a vastly more complex political situation and with the Zionists now ostensibly wedded to activity within Russia which the regime could not fail to note and was bound to resent, there could be no meeting of minds, let alone a (conditional) promise of help such as Plehve had given Herzl. On 1 June 1907 (OS), by decision of the highest judicial authority in Russia (the Senate), the Zionist Organization was explicitly declared illegal and police repression authorized and recommended.

Following closely the views of the Governor of the Minsk Province (where the formal question whether the purposes of the local Zionist association were or were not compatible with the law had first arisen), supported by the Minister of Interior in St Petersburg, the Senate agreed that the Zionist movement was a 'purely political movement'. It further concluded that 'the activities of the Zionist organizations reveal their aspirations to [effect the] national isolation of the Jewish mass[es] so as actively to fight the legal conditions established for Jewish life and thus necessarily exacerbate national hostility to the indigenous population' [literally: the 'basic local population', i.e. the Russians proper].[19] This, it was made plain, could not be permitted; and suitable instructions to that effect were handed down to the Provincial Governors by the Ministry of

[18] *Formative Years*, p. 251.
[19] State Senate, protocol number 5186, 1 June 1907 (O.S). CZA, Z2/453.

Interior from time to time from that point on.[20] There were cases where the relatively imprecise term 'Jewish masses' (*evreisky mass*) was replaced by the more precise (and significant) 'Jewish people' (*evreisky narod*).[21] But in any event, Zionism was now classed explicitly with tendencies held to be subversive of the regime; and seen from the point of view of a bureaucracy dedicated to the enforcement of uniformity and obedience to the best of its ability among all classes of subjects, it was perhaps a not wholly unreasonable position to have adopted. A typical Zionist circular of the time, headed 'Central Committee of the Zionist Organization in Russia', printed in Hebrew in Vilna, but with title, heading, printer's name and address, and date of publication all carefully indicated in Russian, avoids all explicit mention of the regime, but does speak clearly of almost everything else that was likely to vex the police: 'propaganda and agitation' among the Jews of Russia, 'the strengthening of Jewish national consciousness', the ways in which the former might bring about the latter (emphasis to be laid on national festivals, the annual day of mourning for Herzl, encouraging Zionist literature and periodicals, insistence on the right to keep the Sabbath, and the like). The right of the Jews to national organization, unity, dignity, and interests is assumed throughout.[22] None of this could the Autocracy have been expected to tolerate.

The effect of the resetting of Russian policy towards the Jews in general and the Zionists in particular under Stolypin was soon to be evident: there was to be no relaxation of the special, repressive regime under which 'Jewish life' was intended to be conducted. All attempts either to resist it head-on or to encourage independent national consciousness ('effect the national isolation of the Jewish masses') were to be put down. The Autocracy would not tolerate

[20] Thus for example, in connection with the 'increased agitation' among Jews in the Pale of Settlement in favour of the Jewish National Fund, which, it was pointed out, had the same purposes as the Zionist Organization and maintained directors in London and a central office in Cologne. This was impermissible, it was stated, on the grounds, already formulated by the Senate, that the Zionists had 'political purposes aspiring to the isolation of the Jewish mass[es]', etc. Secret instructions to Governors, no. 48, 21 December 1907 (OS). CZA, Z2/453.

[21] As in the formal charges levelled against A. G. Druyanov, editor of *Ha-'Olam* on the grounds that he and his journal had been instrumental in 'exciting the Jewish people to insubordination and to opposition to the law and provoking hatred between different classes of the population'. Prosecutor's office, Vilna, 10 June 1911 (OS). CZA, Z2/457II.

[22] *Mikhtav-hozer mispar 2*, Vilna, 1907. ('Circular letter number two', published simultaneously in Russian and Yiddish.) CZA, Z2/453.

insubordination neither in deed nor in sentiment, nor evidence of ill-feeling on the part of the Jews towards their Russian persecutors ('national hostilty to the indigenous population'). What was required of them was obedience and resignation. After all, the Jews, as Stolypin's predecessor, Goremykin, had occasion to tell the British Ambassador (Nicolson) with a freedom of expression that had appalled his visitor, 'were the vilest of people, anarchists, extortioners and usurers'.[23] Such was the view generally held in the Tsar's court and those who served it, and was well known—or soon to be made known—to outsiders. Ultimately it was a political datum none could ignore. And its effect over time, even on the most clear-minded of foreign observers, was rarely negligible. Even Sir Arthur Nicolson's original 'sympathy for the Jews', his son cautiously recalled, came to be 'somewhat damped by a closer study of the question.'[24] Other foreign representatives then and later, as we shall see, learned to express themselves on the subject of Russian Jewry in stronger terms, barely distinguishable in some cases from those of the ruling camarilla or its official servants. Attempts, even by the best intentioned and most discreet of foreigners, to intervene on the Jews' behalf were invariably met in St. Petersburg with great hostility and often with a covert threat that the interests of the foreign power in question, to say nothing of the wretched Jews themselves, were likely to suffer. Thus it could always be argued, and not wholly insincerely, by the British Foreign Office, committed by a Liberal Government though it was to a critical view of the Autocracy, that 'the effect produced [by intervention] could not fail to be the exact opposite of what is desired'.[25] And much the same thoughts and fears were current from time to time even in Jewish circles of impeccable loyalty to Jewish public causes. Even Zionists had doubts. When the EAC consulted their Russian colleagues about a plan to appeal formally to all European Parliaments to call upon the Russian Government to grant full civil rights to the Jews, Tchlenov was quick to turn it down. 'Such an act . . . could only make the situation of the Russian Jews worse; and as the initiative

[23] Harold Nicolson, *Lord Carnock* (London, 1937), p. 211.

[24] Ibid., p. 225.

[25] Thus the Foreign Office, on behalf of the Foreign Secretary, Grey, to D. L. Alexander and C. G. Montefiore who, as spokesmen for English Jewry, had asked for 'an unofficial intimation to be conveyed to the Russian Government that any large expulsion of Jews from Kiev would create a painful impression of this country.' Langley to Alexander and Montefiore, 31 May 1910. PRO, FO 371/979.

would proceed from Zionists, our Zionist position would be rendered impossible.'[26]

Of course, the matter of Zionism was never of central concern to the Russian authorities. And the initial response of the Russian Zionists to the new, precise formulation of the official view and operative intention was, not unreasonably, more optimistic than a literal reading of the decree seemed to entail. The Zionists did not, and knew that none took them to constitute, a positive danger to the regime; theirs was a movement whose purposes were only indirectly, almost unintentionally, inimical to it: an irritant, a factor disturbing the even, obedient, regimented mass of loyal subjects into which the Autocracy had always sought to convert the people under its rule. They were therefore fairly sure that things would work out in the end, the more so as the rigour and efficiency with which stated policy was generally pursued in Russia were never equal and consistent in all spheres.[27] But their prognosis proved wrong. Under the newly rigorous reaction instituted by Stolypin it was perhaps inevitable that they would begin to suffer after all. By the beginning of 1908 it had become clear in Vilna 'that we are caught in a totally negative attitude towards us'.[28] There were arrests. There was confiscation of documents and periodicals. Meetings were broken up. The collection of funds was hampered. Criminal charges were preferred against leading members of the movement. So once again, as in Herzl's time,[29] it seemed appropriate to seek a face-to-face meeting between the official and elected leader of the movement—Wolffsohn—and the ruler of Russia (under the Tsar). Several months passed before there was agreement on a meeting being held, but finally, late in June of that year, Wolffsohn was informed that Stolypin would receive him the following month.

It was Wolffsohn's hope finally to achieve the 'legalization' of the Zionist movement and its subsidiary institutions. His chief inform-ant on things Russian, and Herzl's before him, Nissan Katzenel-sohn, warned him that the chances of success were small and that it would be wise to stick to his central brief and purpose and refrain from entering into a discussion on 'general Jewish matters' in Russia. Stolypin, Wolffsohn was advised, was a former Governor of

---

[26] Tchlenov to Wolffsohn, 9 November 1910. CZA, Z2/4.
[27] Katzenelsohn to Wolffsohn, 11 September 1907. CZA, W90 II.
[28] Goldberg to Wolffsohn, 1 February 1908. CZA, Z2/453.
[29] *Formative Years*, pp. 245 ff.

Kovno, which had a large Jewish population. He was well versed in 'our business'. The right thing to do, he thought, was to ask for specific and positive steps and not be put off by general promises and delays.[30] None the less, Wolffsohn seems to have set out for Russia in a more optimistic and ambitious frame of mind than the advice given him, let alone the circumstances, warranted.[31]

The elected leader of the movement was received by Stolypin, but his chief encounter was with the Deputy Minister of Interior (Stolypin doubled as Minister of Interior himself), A. A. Makarov. It developed as a long and friendly talk, Wolffsohn reported to his colleagues. He himself was treated with the utmost courtesy; even the subtle interrogation 'as if by a public prosecutor' to which he was subjected during part of the conversation was conducted with the greatest politeness and consideration. He noted that the Minister was well informed about the movement, its personalities and institutions, the policies it had adopted, notably at Minsk in 1902[32] and at Helsingfors in 1906, and on the composition and affairs of Russian Zionism's headquarters at Vilna. He noted too that, 'as was common among non-Jews in their observations on Jewish affairs', many of the points made by Makarov were 'muddle-headed'. Wolffsohn sought to clear up as many of them as time would allow and, as there was no disagreement as to the actual plight of the Jews, to do his best to persuade the Russian Minister that the only radical solution to the problem lay in Zionism. To all this Makarov's response seems to have been to display attentive but firmly non-committal sympathy. In constrast, on the immediate question of the status of Zionism in Russia and the freedom it might be afforded, he spoke plainly. Legalization was out of the question: no foreign political movement could be tolerated. That it was politically and internationally neutral, as Wolffsohn stressed, that the politics concerned were *Jewish*, that Zionism was legal in Germany where foreign political movements were no less illegal than in Russia—all this was beside the point. This was Russia. Here things were otherwise. Besides, there were the Zionist socialists, Po'alei Zion; there were the Jews in the revolutionary movements; there was what had transpired at Helsingfors; and there were the

---

[30] Katzenelsohn to Wolffsohn, 1 July 1908. CZA, W90 II.

[31] Wolffsohn to Warburg, 25 June 1908. CZA, Z2/233.

[32] On the Minsk conference of Russian Zionists in 1902, see *Formative Years*, pp. 183 ff.

resolutions adopted by the Russian delegates at the Eighth Congress
at The Hague. In brief, there were reasons enough to disapprove of
Zionism. To Wolffsohn's protestations that the role of Jews in the
revolutionary movements was much exaggerated, that the Zionists
as such took no part, and that it was fair to ask how the Senate was
'capable' of condemning an isolationist tendency in Russian Jewry
when the Russian Government isolated them in its legislation,
Makarov replied in Russian officialdom's characteristic vein. 'The
Jews,' he told Wolffsohn, 'might have been created for revolution:
they were intelligent and they had nothing to lose.' It was necessary
to repress them: in this central respect there would be no change, he
was plainly trying to tell his visitor. Russian policy on the Jews and
Judaism was settled. The only sop Makarov was prepared to throw
Wolffsohn was a promise that he would be free from police
interference when meeting colleagues and supporters in the few days
left to him in Russia, and that Tchlenov would be received at the
Ministry for further discussion after his departure.[33]

Wolffsohn, unaccountably, thought his journey successful.[34] And
perhaps it was not a total failure. When Tchlenov was duly received
some days after Wolffsohn had left, the message transmitted to him
was much the same, the tone perhaps a shade sharper. Zionism as
an 'emigration movement' was acceptable, he was told; as a
movement which tolerated socialists in its ranks and concerned itself
with the internal politics of Russia it was not. If it wanted a change
of attitude it had first to dissociate itself from all elements opposed to
the Government both in principle and in fact. Then, perhaps, in a
year or so, there might be another meeting and it might be possible
to talk of legalization. First things first. Still, in the meantime, as for
the collection of funds and other low-key activities, Makarov seemed
to Tchlenov to have hinted that while no express permission to
conduct them would be granted, there would be less interference in
the future in practice.[35] And for a while, things were indeed easier
for the Zionists.

There was no change in fundamental attitudes on either side,
however. The Government of the Russian Empire remained
profoundly and actively hostile to its Jewish subjects and ever more

---

[33] Memorandum by Wolffsohn, undated but evidently written shortly after his
talks in St. Petersburg, very possibly even before leaving Russia.CZA, Z2/29.
[34] Wolffsohn to Katzenelson, 24 July 1908. CZA, W90 II.
[35] Tchlenov to Wolffsohn, 27 July 1908. CZA, Z2/29.

hostile to the Zionists for failing to limit themselves to the quality of an 'emigration movement'. The Russian Zionists continued to refuse to retract the Helsingfors Programme prescribing (admittedly restricted) participation in the internal political affairs of the Empire, let alone to forgo the encouragement and nourishment of 'national consciousness' (that which the Senate had termed 'national isolation'). At the caucus of Russian delegates to the Ninth Congress in Hamburg in 1909 they went so far as to reiterate their position publicly. By the following year the administrative and police repression duly gathered force once more. Arrests multiplied. At the end of 1910 twenty people were serving terms of imprisonment in Warsaw and Lodz alone.[36] In 1911, following additional arrests, the operations of the central office for the Russian wing of the movement in Vilna had virtually come to an end and the collection of membership fees was so badly hampered that it was feared for a while that no funds at all could be transmitted to Cologne.[37] In the summer of 1912 it proved impossible even to hold a proper meeting of the leading members of Russian Zionism to consider the situation.[38] Some 150 trials of members of the movement, chiefly on charges of illicit collection of funds, were held in the year 1913 alone.[39] At one point, in response to protests, the Central Office in Cologne was assured by the Russian authorities that no mass arrests of *Zionists* had taken place and that if people of such a 'category' had been arrested it was not on charges connected with the movement, but rather with such illegal practices as the collection of funds and membership in revolutionary organizations.[40] And the possibility that legalization be granted them at some future date and under certain conditions continued to be dangled before the Zionists from time to time.[41] But the seriousness of the Russian offer of toleration in exchange for what they judged to be good behaviour by the Zionists was never evident and it was inherently unlikely that the Autocracy could ever have reconciled

---

[36] Gruenbaum to the Central Office, Cologne, 11 November 1910, CZA, Z2/457.

[37] Goldberg to Wolffsohn, 21 June 1911. CZA, Z2/457.

[38] Recollections of A. Goldstein. CZA, Zenzipper collection, F30/28.

[39] Handwritten circular letter, n.d. (probably July 1912), marked 'secret' and copied to the EAC, Berlin. CZA, Z3/861.

[40] Department of Religious Affairs to [Wolffsohn], 29 May 1910 (OS). CZA, Z2/28.

[41] See for example: Katzenelson to Wolffsohn, (n.d.) March [1911] and 17 June 1911. CZA, W90 III.

itself at this late stage to the existence of a Jewish national movement in any form, even one really and truly limited to the encouragement of emigration alone. Zionism for its part, for all its weaknesses, was nothing if not a national movement. Nothing that it could do was likely to move the Autocracy from its set purpose of waging cold war against its Jewish subjects. Barring a fundamental change in Russian policy—at least as great as had been promised Herzl in 1903 (namely, positive political and diplomatic support for Zionism)—the Zionists had no choice but to place themselves among those who were hostile to the Autocracy even if they had been disposed to do otherwise, which none of them were. The hostility of the Russian Government to the Zionist movement was part and parcel of its profound and explicit hostility to Jewry as a whole and as such. In this sense, as in so many others, both the force and the fate of the movement were intimately bound up with those of the great community from which, largely, it had sprung.

iii

It is perhaps a sign of the inherent conservatism—not to say sluggishness—of Jewish public institutions, once established, that these events in Russia had no effect either on the balance of forces within the Zionist movement or on the policy it proposed to follow. The Tenth Congress (Basel, 9–15 August 1911) was held at the proper time and in the usual way; and its principal business was the orderly transfer of the leadership to new hands, from David Wolffsohn to Otto Warburg. What this meant in fact was that the shift of direction to which Herzl just before his death had had to agree to some extent, and was still resisted, weakly, by his successor, was now confirmed. And, further, that the solid bloc of Russian Zionists, who could not rule the movement either in name or in fact because conditions in Russian did not allow them to, but without whose support no other group could assume the movement's governance, had finally won.

The last campaign had been long in preparation—ever since the Congress in Hamburg. It had been deliberate and purposeful in every way. There had indeed been one last major, unintended row in the interim when Wolffsohn sought to assert his authority over the representatives in Constantinople on a matter in which the familiar elements of tension—poor administration, political distrust, and wounded self-esteem—were all miraculously combined. This was a tremendous fuss (not without traces of hysteria) precipitated by the impending publication in French of a book already published in German by the generally self-effacing third member (with Wolffsohn and Warburg) of the ruling triumvirate in the EAC, Jacobus Kann. In the eyes of the opposition of 'practicals' Kann had done the unforgivable thing. He had restated the aims of Zionism in unmistakably Herzlian terms. Protests were delivered and repeated. Umbrage was taken. Disavowals and resignations were demanded and rejected virtually all round (although in one case—Jabotinsky's—a resignation was both offered and gone through with). Wolffsohn himself stood firm throughout, but little credit accrued to him for refusing to disavow Kann. And his little victory probably did him more harm than good when the real breakthrough came just as the affair of Kann's book, as is the nature of such things, was beginning to evaporate.[42] This occurred at the 'annual conference'

---

[42] Kann had written up his impressions of a visit to Ereẓ-Israel in 1907. No one had paid much attention to the Dutch and German editions. It was the prospect of one in French (a language held to be one with which Ottoman officials were more familiar) that worried Jacobson and Jabotinsky who, in line with the opposition's view and the reluctant Wolffsohn's as well, considered that their function was to rid the Turks of the notion that the Zionists were after a special political position in Ereẓ-Israel. Kann had argued, explicitly, that what the Zionists must seek to do was to persuade the Turks to grant the 'Jewish people the right of settlement in Palestine with a Jewish autonomous government which recognized the suzerainty of H.M. the Sultan.' The constitution of the autonomous government would be such as to facilitate 'the free development of the Jewish people'. Relations with the Empire would be analogous to those of autonomous British colonies with the mother-country. The advantages that would accrue to the Empire were many, among them economic development and a stable, well-armed, and loyal population on one of its frontiers. Besides, world Jewry and 'la haute banque juive' would help relieve the Turks of their vast external debt. (*Erets-Israël: Le Pays juif* (Brussels, 1910), pp. 135–7, 142.) This, of course, was no less than a fresh presentation of the old Herzlian plan: something between the original blueprint for a Jewish state (1896) and its modification in the form of a Charter to which Herzl had resigned himself two years later. It was precisely that which the opposition was fighting. Jacobson did not go so far as Jabotinsky, who thought that if the book came out they might as well pack up and go home, but he was appalled. When the two men's protests to Cologne were unavailing, they turned to Vilna, upon which Wolffsohn's fury at what he took to be disloyalty and insubordination knew no bounds. The row only died down when, the book having appeared, nothing came to light to suggest that anyone in the Ottoman administration had taken notice of it. A representative sample of the numerous letters, resolutions, and dire predictions dealing with the case would include: Central Committee of the Zionist Organization in Russia. Minutes, 4–5 April 1910 (OS). CZA, A24/104; Russian Zionist leaders' conference, 22–24 May 1910 (OS). CZA, Z2/459; and Jacobson to B. A. Goldberg, 3 May 1910 (OS). CZA, A24/109. At the Congress the following year, on the central issue of the ends of Zionism, Wolffsohn repeated the agreed formula: it was not a state they wanted, but 'a home, on the ancient soil of our fathers, in which we, as Jews, without being persecuted or beset, could live a full national life.' *Protokoll X*, p. 11.

of leaders held in Berlin in June 1910: a regular event held in those years when no full Congress was convened. The long-planned resolutions laying down new rules for membership in an enlarged EAC and requiring the transfer of the Zionist Central Office to Berlin were now finally pushed through. The extremely cautious political line in fashion since 1908 was strongly reconfirmed. The direct attack on Wolffsohn's leadership was resumed; and for once even some of the Herzlian stalwarts failed to rally round him and Wolffsohn himself put up little resistance. He was now a tired, in some ways beaten, and—as was soon to be evident to all—a sick man. Perhaps the outcome was inevitable. In any case 'the struggle [*borba*] against the leadership begun after the Seventh Congress [1905] is over, we hope, for ever,' the triumphant Russian Central Committee informed its constituents upon the return of its representatives.[43] So it proved. Wolffsohn announced his retirement in his opening address to the Tenth Congress in the following year. It was received with calm in all quarters.

The Tenth was thus a quieter Congress than the movement had known for many years. There was no great debate on policy; policy appeared to be settled. Wolffsohn spoke about the affairs of the movement in optimistic terms, but his frame of reference was essentially administrative: he was leaving its institutions in good order was what he wanted to say. Nordau reviewed the general condition of Jewry in dark terms that contrasted strangely with Wolffsohn's, but which had no effect on the deliberations that followed—perhaps because Nordau's review of the condition of Jewry had become a regular fixture of the Congress and, perhaps, too, because while none could rival him for eloquence or sharp analysis, there was a sense in which he could tell the delegates nothing they did not already know. References to Turkey and the position of the Zionists there were few and cautious—with good reason, as we shall see.

There was some friction with the Mizraḥi, which represented an intellectually forlorn but politically important and ideologically sensitive effort to combine Zionism with religious orthodoxy. The anomalous presence of an orthodox element within the body of the movement had long constituted a problem. It was now made marginally more acute by the defeat of the 'politicals'. For they had

[43] Circular No. 3, Central Committee of the Zionist Organization in Russia, 30 June [?] 1910. CZA, Z2/457 I.

tended to be less interested in culture and education than the 'practicals', and so both less likely to tread on the toes of the religiously observant and more likely to co-operate with them at the expense of their rivals. The assembly was not overly put out when the Mizraḥi delegation, having failed to gain representation on the GAC, walked out in a huff. But a real show-down was avoided.[44]

There was a report (by Katzenelsohn) on the scale and direction of the great movement of migrants out of eastern Europe, and resolutions were passed calling for unified action on the part of all Jewish organizations to 'regulate' the flow. What the Congress had in mind was an effort to channel the migrants towards Ereẓ-Israel, so far as possible, and more generally to keep the Jews from dispersing in small and inevitably isolated groups in the new lands of settlement. But the spirit of the approach was not hopeful; and the reiteration of the principle, that 'Zionism adheres to its standpoint that the solution of the Jewish Question is contained only in the territorial concentration in Palestine'[45] was almost perfunctory.

On the whole the delegates looked inward. Their principal concern was with continuity and the shape of the new leadership. The new GAC (twenty-four members) reflected the change: easterners and their western allies formed the majority. More dramatically, Russian Zionists formed a majority on the EAC itself: three out of the five (Jacobson, Shmarya Levin, and Sokolov[46]). The fourth member of the EAC was Arthur Hantke, a Berliner, a rather proper German Jew, well educated (a lawyer), with a long record of service to the movement. In some respects he was, and certainly became, its prototypical organization man, rather than one with distinct political ideas of his own, although as one of the leading Zionists in Germany he had established his own channels of communication with his Russian colleagues and was acceptable to them. Appropriately, the EAC itself was now at last to be based in Berlin; and it would bear the mark of something like 'Prussian' administrative efficiency for some years to come. The fifth member and the EAC's elected chairman—and therefore Wolffsohn's

[44] On the origins of the Mizraḥi, and the issue of religious orthodoxy in, and versus, Zionism, see *Formative Years*, pp. 204–24.

[45] *Protokoll X*, p. 363.

[46] Sokolov might perhaps be more properly called 'Polish'; but as the Jews in Poland were rarely regarded as Poles either by themselves or the ethnic Poles, and Sokolov was a Russian subject, it is not inaccurate to class him with Jewish subjects of the Tsar from other parts of the Empire.

successor as leader of the entire movement in all but name—was Warburg, who could with reason be described at this stage of his career as the easterners' favourite westerner. All in all it was a clean sweep for the anti-political opposition.

Otto Warburg (1859–1938) was a member of a well-known family of bankers domiciled in Hamburg (and, later, in the United States). As a botanist of distinction with a professorial appointment at the University of Berlin he was one of the notables of Germany Jewry. Exceptionally, for one from a thoroughly assimilated, secularized, and established background, he had been drawn to Hibbat Zion in its German version (under the influence of his father-in-law, it was generally believed), and was an early recruit to the Zionist movement proper under Herzl. But he had never been much attracted to (or impressed by) 'diplomacy' and 'politics'. His intellectual and professional interests alike were in agricultural settlement: and it is not surprising that he played no role of consequence in the Zionist movement until the last year or so of Herzl's career, when even the inventor of Zionist diplomacy and politics had no choice but to make concessions to the 'practical' school. After Herzl's death Warburg's relative eminence as a man of means and established position made him a natural candidate for membership in the EAC. But even then the responsibilities and special perspective of office had no effect on his outlook. His concern, as before almost exclusively, was with 'practical' work in Erez-Israel; and while nominally a colleague of Wolffsohn's, he drifted steadily into the arms and hearts of the 'practical' opposition. For their part they had good reason to welcome him. The boost given to systematic and scientific agriculture in Erez-Israel under his leadership both in Wolffsohn's time (when he served as chairman of the 'Palestine Committee') and as Wolffsohn's successor was very great. Besides, as almost all agreed, he was very likeable, a man of the utmost integrity and of the greatest goodwill. 'A gentleman from head to toe'[47] was how those who knew him were apt to regard him, not without reason. But equally, again not without reason, few, if any, took him seriously as a leader of men. Not many seem to have gone so far as Nordau, who (privately) judged him 'an inferior project-maker, devoid of judgement, irresponsible, unrealistic, without a trace of foresight, [and]

---

[47] Richard Lichtheim, *She'ar yishuv* (Jerusalem, 1953), p. 214.

unpardonably reckless.'[48] But it was plain enough that Warburg, a man incapable of managing his own private fortune properly, was hardly one to blow fresh spirit into the Organization.

The new EAC's members (apart from Levin, who was a star performer in the lecture hall and a man of firm general principles and brilliant phrases, rather than one for the drudgery of politics and administrative action) were thus essentially organization-men, schooled in dedicated service to the movement and better equipped intellectually, socially, and linguistically for the institutional functions they were to perform than had been the majority of their predecessors. But they had no clear idea where they wished to go, let alone how they hoped to get there. All they were clear about was their intention to continue what had already been initiated, to preserve what had been achieved, and to wait upon events. They proposed to devote themselves 'to the further development of our work of information and enlightenment in Turkey.' Relying upon 'the progressive development of the Ottoman Empire', they 'cherish[ed] the firm conviction that our efforts will lead to the most favourable results.' On the 'activity in Palestine which we regard as the basis of all Zionist work' they proposed to ensure that it would be 'continued systematically'. For the rest, they would foster 'national culture', Jewish intellectual aspirations 'in all countries', and the national language. In this respect they pointed to the 'splendid service' already rendered by the Congress when it conducted one of its sessions entirely in Hebrew.[49]

In retrospect, the major outcome of the Tenth Congress—the new executive—seems to represent less a shining victory for the opposition than final defeat for the old school. At the time, nevertheless, it was certainly possible for the victors to put a brighter interpretation both on the changes made and on the changes avoided. Aḥad Ha-'Am, their mentor, seeking, as was his way, to look for the deeper causes and the longer trends, was greatly encouraged by the change.

One thing is clear to me beyond all doubt. 'Official' Zionism is dying and a new generation has arisen (especially in countries in the West) for which Zionism is *the very same national ideal in all its ramifications* for which we fought Herzlism all those years. True, the old phrases are still heard from the

---

[48] Nordau to Wolffsohn, 25 March 1911. CZA, W 96 I.
[49] Zionist Press Bureau, Bulletin, 25 August 1911. CZA, Z2/551.

platform, but only out of habit, as words emptied of their content. The 'generals' themselves, so it appears, recognize the fact that the camp is no longer drawn to the old flag.[50]

Following up his attendance at the Congress (the first at which he was present since Herzl's foundation Congress fourteen years earlier) with an extended visit to Erez-Israel, he summed up: both schools had implicitly recognized their failure. Once again, the 'politicals' 'had come with empty hands, speaking of a target they had no means of reaching, with nothing to rely upon except hope in an unlimited future when, perhaps, external conditions might favour "political work".' The 'practicals', for their part, still had no answer to the 'politicals" old question, 'Do you honestly believe that the purchase of a small parcel of land from time to time, the foundation of a small settlement with endless labour, some insecure "farm" or other for workmen, a school here, a high school there, and so forth— that *these* are the means to attain the "secure refuge"[51] as the "Zionist tradition" has it, a refuge that would put an end to all our afflictions by putting an end to our exile?' The truth of the matter, Aḥad Ha-'Am believed, was that so long as the 'politicals' had the stronger position, the 'practicals' dared not recognize that the purpose for which *they* laboured was not that which 'Zionist tradition', as he liked to call it, prescribed. The true aim of Zionism, namely the fostering of a new national life and a new national consciousness in all parts of scattered Jewry, was not the achievement of 'a secure refuge for the *people* of Israel', but of 'a fixed centre for the *spirit* of Israel'.[52]

This had long been his cause and he had some reason to be triumphant. No doubt, it was Zionism writ small. No doubt it marked—at least appeared to mark—the final disengagement of the movement from the greater, seemingly hopeless cause of direct rescue and relief for the mass of Jewry. But it was internally consistent, attractive to fine spirits, and, because modest in its purposes, rather more feasible and reasonable in the view of the sceptics both in and outside the movement. One way or another, in

[50] Letter to Ludizhinsky, 22 August 1911. *Igrot AH*, vi, p. 223. Emphasis in original.

[51] The accepted Hebrew translation at this time of *Heimstätte* (the key term in the Basel Programme of 1897 and best rendered in English as 'home') was *miklat batu'aḥ* —literally: 'secure refuge'.

[52] 'Sakh ha-kol', completed in March 1912 and published in *Ha-Shilo'aḥ*, xxvi: 3, 1912. *Reprinted in Kol kitvei Aḥad Ha-'Am*, pp. 421–8. Emphases in original.

fact if rarely in name, this was the direction in which the Zionist
Organization now strongly tended to move.

iv

If one did indeed subscribe to Aḥad Ha-ʿAm's astringent minimal-
ism, with its insistence on the peculiarly *moral* role of each element of
the Zionist enterprise in Ereẓ-Israel, then all depended on the
quality and staying-power of the new society arising in that country.
For the members of the larger, 'practical' school the brute criteria of
numbers, quantity, extent—in a word, sheer size—could not fail to
serve as the basic indicators of progress. Of course, in practice,
quality and quantity reinforced each other and could not be easily
disentangled. Upon them jointly depended that indeterminate,
Micawberish hope that had taken root, that somehow, in the end, in
circumstances that none could now foresee and about which, for the
present, it was both unnecessary and absurd to speculate, the
admission of the new *yishuv* into the class of political societies and its
acquisition of the privileges and instruments of self-government
would eventually occur. It was the hope, that, if all went well, the
time would come when the roots of the *yishuv* would have sunk so
deep and its solidity be so evident that the transformation from
community into polity would follow ineluctably. But it was, in the
nature of things, a hope which, if it was not to fail, had to be
nourished constantly by reports of what had been accomplished,
materially on the ground, in Ereẓ-Israel: there in Judea and Galilee,
not here in Prussia or Lithuania or Poland or the Ukraine. It was
there that the necessary—which is not to say the sufficient—
conditions of success for this Zionism writ small lay. To Ereẓ-Israel,
therefore, all eyes were now directed—more consistently and more
intently than ever before. It is therefore right to inquire what the
accomplishments of the Zionists there amounted to; and of what, in
the final analysis, could their hopes reasonably consist.

The short answer is that in the years just prior to the Great War
the new *yishuv* was a very small affair. Perhaps nothing illustrates its
slight proportions and its essential marginality to Jewry as a whole
so well as the rate of immigration into the Land (*ʿaliya*) both in
absolute terms and, especially, when set against the great migratory
torrent from east to west, at its height at that very time.

It is generally accepted that in the decade and a half between 1901
and 1914 some 1,600,000 Jewish migrants moved out of eastern

Europe. Of these, close to 90 per cent entered the United States and Canada, 2 per cent (about 35,000) Erez-Israel, 8 per cent all other countries; and whereas the average annual rate of migration to all countries for those years stood at about 115,000 (100,000 to the United States and Canada), the average annual *'aliya* to Erez-Israel was no more than 2,500.[53] We know a great deal about the social character of the immigrants to the United States, far less about those to Erez-Israel. But since the great majority of the latter (as of the former) were emigrants from Russia, and since most travellers from Russia to the Levant passed through Odessa, figures provided by the Hibbat Zion 'Odessa Committee', founded in the early 1880s,[54] still active, and still operating as the travellers' friend,[55] are of special interest. Of those who had recourse to their services, three-quarters were potential settlers in the full sense (for example: 1,692 out of 2,326 in 1911; 1,798 out of 2,430 in 1912); about 10 per cent were elderly people intent on spending their last days in the Land; the rest students and tourists. The distribution by sex was not markedly different from that in the greater flow of migrants to the United States (55–60 per cent men, 40–45 per cent women); nor was the proportion of youngsters under 15. But because of the relatively high proportion of migrants in late middle and old age wishing to die in the Holy Land, in contrast to those whose minds were set on living there, men and women in the most active and productive period of life formed a smaller fraction than was usual among Jewish migrants to other countries.[56] Indirectly, the disparity reflected the plain fact that, whereas religious and political ideology could never be significant motives for migration to the west, the pull of Erez-Israel, such as it was, was nothing if not mystical and ideological, closely bound up with the desire for collective and national—as opposed to merely private—salvation and well-being. Generally speaking, it was only where the balance of considerations tipped heavily towards the ideological that the decision to travel south, rather than west, was taken. The poverty of the country, the paucity

[53] Y. Lestschinsky, *Ha-demut ha-le'umit shel yahadut ha-gola* (Tel-Aviv, 1959), pp. 31–40; D. Gurevich and A. Graetz, *Ha-'aliya, ha-yishuv ve-ha-tenu'a ha-tiv'it shel ha-ukhlusiya be-Erez-Israel* (Jerusalem, 1944), pp. 10–21.

[54] See *Origins*, pp. 143 ff.

[55] The Committee published an admirable guide for emigrants packed with particulars of the climate, currency, handling of baggage, employment openings, and other useful information (*Svedeniya dlya emigrantov o Palestine* (Odessa, 1906, price 3 copecks); and maintained an information bureau to serve them on arrival at Jaffa.

[56] *Ha-'Olam*, 6 May 1913, pp. 9–10.

of its natural resources, and the hostility of the administration and of a large part of the local population all provided continual reinforcement to this rule—both by inhibiting immigration into Erez-Israel and by encouraging emigration from it. No complete and reliable records were kept locally either by the Ottoman authorities or by anyone else, nor could they be kept in the circumstances of lax administration and easily penetrable frontiers. But the occasional surviving hard datum tends to confirm the general impression of continual movement in both directions and, as had to follow, markedly slow overall growth. The Zionist Organization's Palestine Office reported scrupulously what it knew; and it knew, for example, of 3,400 arrivals and 1,450 departures through Jaffa in 1912. There were other ports of entry, but Jaffa was the country's main port at the time and the excess of arrivals over departures of about 2,000 through it in 1912—a relatively good year, so far as the reinforcement of the new *yishuv* was concerned—may be taken as representative.[57]

The other primary measure of size, growth, and above all potential for *future* growth was of course land. All but the most unbending of 'politicals' held the key to a change in the rate of growth, indeed the key to all forms of progress, qualitative no less than quantitative, to be land: the ownership of land, the settlement of land. This had much to do with an ancient Jewish thirst for those forms of stability, strength, and independence which seem to derive in all societies, uniquely, from the possession and cultivation of the soil. The Jews having been well-nigh universally deprived and handicapped in this respect for centuries, nothing fired the imagination of those calling for the reform of their condition so powerfully as the romantic, quasi-Tolstoyan vision of their people farming their land and tending their flocks in the country of their forefathers in true independence of mind and body and in starkest contrast to the dark, hopeless, squalid slum and ghetto life of the Diaspora that was the present lot of most of them. Accordingly, the road to national dignity and health ran through fields and forests. More mundanely, so did the road to economically efficacious resettlement—that, at least, was what the conventional wisdom of the age dictated. For almost all authorities were agreed that the natural and most effective method of transplanting people—of *colonization* in the essentially technical, apolitical sense in which the

---

[57] EAC confidential report to Zionist federations, 26 February 1913. CZA, Z3/427.

term was employed at the turn of the century—was settlement on
the land. It followed that the speed with which successful Jewish
farming communities could be established—they being the primary
target of 'practical' Zionist work—depended, immigration apart, on
the availability of land. But there being no benevolent Government
prepared to distribute it to would-be settlers, no matter how
promising, and regardless of what they might be expected to
contribute to the economy and general welfare, each piece of soil had
to be purchased from private owners at ever higher prices and by
repeated and ever more ingenious circumvention of the anti-Jewish
land regulations in force. Some land was acquired by the settlers
themselves; some through the instrumentalities set up by Baron
Edmond de Rothschild as early as the mid 1880s; some by the
Jewish Colonization Association[58] into which the Rothschild foundation was absorbed in 1900 and which was now the chief non-
Zionist institution engaged in the promotion of Jewish agricultural
settlement; and some consistently, over the years, parcel by parcel,
by the land-purchasing arm of the Zionist Organization itself, the
Jewish National Fund. But the funds available were absurdly
inadequate to any great national purpose. The JNF's total collections between 1902 and 1908 amounted to about £75,000, of which
only some £30,000 were successfully invested in land in Erez-Israel
and loans to various institutions. In later years the Fund's annual
income hovered around the £25,000 mark, at least a fifth of that sum
having been laboriously collected in the form of copper coins
deposited in little blue-and-white tin boxes kept in homes and
synagogues.[59] The results were inevitably meagre. In 1907 it was
estimated that land in possession of Jews of all categories (both new
immigrants and inhabitants of long standing) did not amount to
more than 1.4 per cent of the total (400 of the 29,000 square
kilometres that Turkish Palestine was reckoned to constitute),
whereas they formed at least 10 per cent of the country's total
population. In a good year, 25 square kilometres (25,000 dunams) of
land might be acquired. At the end of the Turkish period total
holdings by Jews did not exceed 650 square kilometres (2.25 per
cent).

---

[58] *Origins*, pp. 212 ff.; *Formative Years*, p. 374.
[59] JNF income from all sources: 424,000 marks (£21,200) in 1910, 542,000 marks
(£27,100) in 1911, 590,000 marks (£29,500) in 1912. *Ha-'Olam*, 4 February 1913. The
common price of land in these years seems to have been about 35 francs (or £1.4) per
dunam.

The growth in the number and population of the farming settlements, the surest measure of the success of the enterprise as understood by 'practical' Zionism, was correspondingly slow: some twenty settlements in 1907 (no growth to speak of since 1903) and a population of just over 5,000; twelve more communities and a total farm-based population of only 12,000 (about one-seventh of the entire *yishuv*) by 1914.[60] It is true that in some sort of final account, to the settlements proper there must be added the urban Jewish population. Jews formed a majority in Jerusalem, Tiberias, and Safed and substantial minorities in Jaffa and Hebron. And to the count of heads there must be added the new institutions which reflected, as they were intended, along with the farming communities, the particular social and cultural qualities with which the Zionists (of all schools) sought to endow the new Jewry in the old country: modern hospitals, elementary and secondary schools in which the language of instruction was Hebrew, an academy of arts and crafts, a teachers' training college, a Jewish national library, an institute of engineering and technology, a school of agriculture, and the celebrated experiments in egalitarian social and economic organization which came to be formalized as the *kevuza* (subsequently the *kibbuz*).

The achievement which was to crown the entire enterprise was to be the university: Jewish, but modern, Hebrew-speaking, of the highest academic worth and standards, a source of pride to all Jews everywhere,[61] a sort of engine of intellectual and cultural inspiration and revival. The university was to serve and reinforce the nation's intelligentsia, but equally it was to be an instrument whereby Jewish learning and the learning and science of Jews would finally be placed on an equal footing with those of other nations. And to these

---

[60] Firm numbers vary with the sources and with the categories employed: some 'settlements' were, strictly speaking, schools or experimental stations. For the Zionist Organization's own review, as presented to the Congress in 1913, see *Bericht des Actions-Comités der zionistischen Organisation an der XI. Zionisten-Kongress, Wien, 1913* (Berlin, 1914), pp. 110 ff. and *passim*.

[61] Except for the firmly orthodox, who had no use for universities or for secular learning generally. For the small, but articulate (or 'religious') wing of Zionism represented by the Mizrahi movement, matters were more complex and their attitude to the university project was ambivalent. They favoured it in principle, but wanted it restricted to the natural and social sciences. The humanities in general and studies in Jewish history, thought, literature and so forth in particular, let alone Scripture and rabbinics, had no place, they thought, in a Jewish university. See, for example, their contribution to the debate on the subject at the Eleventh Congress. *Protokoll XI*, pp. 327–328.

great purposes there was added the mundane consideration that such a national Jewish university would go a long way towards solving the problem of Jewish scholars and students who were denied access to, or their due status within, the universities of other nations. Talk of and actual planning for such a Hebrew university became an ever more prominent item on the agenda of the movement in the years leading up the Great War. At the Eleventh Congress of Zionists (Vienna, 2–9 September 1913) it was a major item of business; no other topic on the movement's agenda at the time epitomized the increasingly dominant Aḥad Ha-'Amian approach and programme so accurately or served so well to mark the absolute control of the movement by the 'practicals'.[62] The concentration of some of its best minds on the project (among them Weizmann's), virtually to the exclusion of other matters, showed how far the Zionists had travelled since the great crisis that had riven them a decade earlier and to what it was they now believed they might usefully apply themselves.

The university was not established until long after (in 1925); but in one cardinal respect the vision of a new and superior society—at all events, one element of it—was realized. This was the new man, the new Jew. Back straightened, brow sunburnt, his hands encrusted with grains of soil rather than the grime of cities, hard-working yet sensitive, a thoughtful peasant: remarkably, he corresponded with something approaching precision to the romantic ideal of which he was born. But what seems to have struck virtually all observers with special force was the fact that before their eyes were young men and women who were actually prepared to follow through with crushing labour and in circumstances of the utmost deprivation the ideas they advocated.

I travelled from Jerusalem to Galilee, and on a Sabbath eve, in the month of Av 5671 [July/August 1911], I reached Kinneret,[63] greatly moved by what lay before my eyes and by the deeds of my brethren. Coming towards me was the new man, the labouring man, the *kevuza* man, going down to his home from the field . . . tired, in ragged, patched, and repatched clothes, a

---

[62] Nordau, disgusted with the ways things were going and now convinced that the Herzlians had lost all vestige of influence, refused to attend the Eleventh Congress. 'It is painful, but inescapable' he wrote Wolffsohn; 'we shall have to let the "practicals" go their own way until they themselves have recognized their error.' 1 June 1913. CZA, W96I.

[63] Kinneret, on the southern shore of the Sea of Galilee, was the earliest of all collectives to be got going by the initiative of its members.

green patch on black cloth. At first I was shocked by the formlessness, surprised by the break with convention, by this ascetism and abstinence from all bourgeois practice: a sort of breaking of the vessels.[64] But with this he was wholly adorned with a new simplicity, a sincerity hitherto unknown to me, the lustre of the blessing of the soil and the divine presence of labour, as if he were one with the sheaf and the corn standing in the field.[65]

Even an observer of a different stamp, with an infinitely sharper eye for economic costs, problems, and probabilities and whose first impression of the *yishuv* was the sour one that it was in a bad way and 'prematurely aged',[66] found that the vision tugged at his heart-strings. And, what is more, that it was upon these people, the immigrants of the Second—'*Aliya*, predominantly socialist—some Marxist, some closer in outlook to the Socialist-Revolutionaries of Russia—virtually all, in fact, from Russia, that the social and economic future of the *yishuv* would very likely depend. 'In many ways,' Arthur Ruppin remarked, they were 'foreign to me (more emotional, disposed to endless argument, infirm of purpose, unpunctual, and inexact in their work); none the less I came to recognize that their honest enthusiasm for agriculture as the very foundation of the Jewish National Home was a priceless asset to be preserved at all cost.'[67]

Arthur Ruppin (1876–1943), like Herzl, Brandeis, and perhaps Zangwill, was one of the great outsiders in Zionism: western rather than eastern European, speaking neither Hebrew nor Yiddish, neither versed in nor especially attracted to the Tradition, entirely capable of pursuing a respectable profession (the law) in a comfortable society (Imperial Germany at the turn of the century), and infinitely removed in outlook, behaviour, and appearance from rebellion and non-conformity. He was a self-made man who had hoisted himself out of great poverty by his own efforts. He was of a severely practical cast of mind with a rare combination of instincts

[64] 'The breaking of the vessels' [*shevirat ha-keilim*] is a kabbalistic term connoting, roughly, the collapse of all structures.

[65] Zalman Shazar recalling his first meeting with Berl Katznelson, seen by many as the moral leader and ultimate social and political conscience of the Second 'Aliya. *Or ishim* (Tel-Aviv, 1955), pp. 311–12. Shazar himself (1889–1974) remained a city-dwelling, socialist intellectual, and his admiration for those who did what he and his colleagues all thought was the right thing, touched by shame for not doing so himself, was wholly characteristic of the group. In 1963 he was elected President of the State of Israel.

[66] Arthur Ruppin. *Protokoll XI*, p. 194.

[67] Ruppin, *Pirkei hayai*, ii (Tel-Aviv, 1968), p. 59.

and talents for law, administration, and business. He was tough, modest, and fundamentally apolitical. In many obvious respects he was the prototypical early twentieth-century bourgeois. He differed from the type in that the severity of his thinking was mitigated by great social curiosity and a powerful strain of imagination and sentiment. It is this, perhaps, which explains how and why he came to be the Zionist movement's great technocrat. Offered the post of director of the Organization's about-to-be-established first official, representative office in Jaffa, the 31-year-old lawyer from Magdeburg considered carefully. He had made an extended visit of inspection at Wolffsohn's and (particularly) Warburg's behest and had reported his dour findings with characteristic precision and astringency. But the idea of working in Erez-Israel in the Zionist interest, still very uncertain before that first journey,

> had upon my return, become firm. I had had an opportunity to judge the quality of the country and the quality of the inhabitants; and although I found many faults . . . I was sure none the less that extensive settlement was feasible. The subject won my heart. True, in Germany, my prospects in the world of business or law or in university teaching (when taking my doctorate my teacher at Halle, Professor Conrad, had advised me to take a post as *Privatdozent* in political economy) were considerable; but it seemed to me that even if I did achieve great things, I would always be regarded by those around me as foreign and contemptible. Not so in Erez-Israel where, so I hoped, I would be one of the community and would be able to work with it without inhibition.[68]

Others had been to the country on tours of inspection and inquiry before: Aḥad Ha-ʿAm, Motzkin, Ussishkin, Wolffsohn, Warburg, Weizmann, Lichtheim, Sokolov—it was a long list reaching back to Ḥibbat Zion and, in effect, never ending. All said their piece, some publicly, with precision and to considerable effect, others privately. Alone, in this twilight period of the *yishuv*, Ruppin returned and stayed on. He became the engineer, one might say the inventor, of systematic Jewish settlement. He brought system, facts, figures, prices, and clear purposes into the enterprise. He worked out how to make the most of exceedingly meagre resources: no more than £5,000 to draw upon at the outset. For the haphazard purchase of bits and pieces of land as they became available fortuitously on the market, he sought to substitute concentration in those areas (in

---

[68] Ibid., p. 38.

Judea and in Galilee) where there was most hope of building up a strong Jewish presence and a numerical majority. He formulated a policy of economic assistance and non-paternalistic guidance to the ill-trained, ill-equipped young settlers which encouraged independence and initiative without leaving them hopelessly to their own devices, his own function being to co-ordinate rather than dictate. He was horrified both by the spectacle of the 'old', i.e. non-Zionist *yishuv*, especially in Jerusalem, which struck him as constituting pauperized eastern European Jewry all over again, and by the sheer lack of economic prospect for the young of the modern new *yishuv*. Education was an excellent thing, but in a stagnant economy, he pointed out, it merely equipped the young for emigration. Simplistic Aḥad Ha-'Amianism such as the Master himself, in Ruppin's view, would hardly support, was therefore wholly counter-productive. In brief, everything had to be done to render the *yishuv*, indeed the country as a whole, economically viable and attractive not merely because its careful development was, supposedly, the only alternative to a political strategy, but because politics would avail the Zionists nothing in the absence of a sound, self-generating economic base to the society they wished to construct. Roads and railways had to be extended, medical services improved (he had had an unforgettable taste of what was on offer during his first visit when he himself was struck down by typhoid fever), mixed farming had to be encouraged (because it helped support the farming family in season and out) rather than cash crops. And step by step he began to get his way. He was young, scrupulous, dignified but unpompous, open to ideas, more than willing to explore (on horseback, if necessary, despite his never having ridden before). He was able to win and retain the confidence both of his nominal masters in Cologne and Berlin and of the new settlers by whom he set such store, to whom he listened carefully, and whose darling, in the end, he became.[69] It is wholly characteristic of the man that five years passed before he was ready to deliver a considered, public report to a Zionist Congress on the affairs and accomplishments of the 'Palestine Office' of which he was in charge. This was at the last (the Eleventh) Congress to be

[69] See, for example, Berl Ḱatznelson's immensely warm, utterly sincere obituary upon Ruppin's death in 1943. *'Al Ruppin* (Tel-Aviv, 1943), a pamphlet published for 'internal' distribution by the Histadrut (Labour Federation). 'An honest man in whom one can have confidence,' was Aḥad Ha-'Am's judgement quite early on. Letter to D. Schneersohn, 26 April 1913. *Igrot AH*, v, p. 115.

held before the outbreak of the War. The low key in which it was generally conducted and the unassuming and almost apologetic note sounded by the leadership were neatly encapsulated in a sentence from Warburg's concluding address: 'The Jewish people, in its two thousand years of suffering, learned patience and abstinence better than any other people on earth; and the necessary result of these two characteristics is satisfaction, even with small achievements.'[70] It may be said that it was Warburg's great good fortune that Ruppin was on the spot to do the little that could be done with the greatest possible efficiency. Certainly, given the direction the movement had taken, he was the man for this particular season.

What neither Ruppin nor anyone else could change was Ottoman policy, which set the outer limits within which he had to operate. Nor could he bring his particular talents to bear upon the slowly rising, unrelenting groundswell of Arab displeasure.

v

The Zionists were never blind (as some have claimed) to the presence of the Arabs as the settled, majoritarian inhabitants of Erez-Israel. Nor could they be. It was from Arabs that such land as was available for purchase had to be bought. It was Arabs whom the Jewish settlers had for neighbours, now friendly, now hostile, farm labourers in some cases, marauders in others. No one, least of all the members of the minute Arab intelligentsia who began to take up the national cause at the beginning of the century, seriously denied the economic benefit the Jews brought the country. But each case of an Arab watchman sacked for unreliability (or worse) and replaced by a Jew, or of a punch-up between youths of neighbouring villages, Arab and Jewish, or of Jewish farmers' fury at Arab goatherds for driving their flocks over their land in ways customary in Palestine but intolerable to Europeans, or of plain robbery, or rape, or murder in a hugely under-administered and badly policed land, or of the appearance of foreign, often arrogant new neighbours whose ways were incomprehensible and shameless to the Muslim peasant's eye, or even of decent (which is to say, relatively low) rates of interest offered by the Zionist's Anglo-Palestine Bank irritating established Arab money-lenders—all such cases and incidents tended to take on larger-than-life proportions and sinister, if still implicit, political implications.

[70] *Protokoll XI*, pp. 361–2.

Writing in 1891, after a visit to the country, Aḥad Ha-ʿAm, in a celebrated article, had warned his friends. The Arabs observed the settlers, but kept their own counsel, he told them. That was because they saw no danger to themselves in anything the Jews did, and meanwhile they profited: peasants were well rewarded for their labour, notables were well paid for the often marginal or even inferior land they sold. But if ever they thought their position was in danger, he warned, matters would change rapidly.[71] That was perceptive of Aḥad Ha-ʿAm, but too simple. In the event, the change from localized, low-level, and essentially spontaneous quarrelling, punctuated by bouts of violence and warnings of dire things to come, to the beginnings of organized thinking and pressure, and notably to the beginnings of an Arab *campaign* against the new *yishuv*, was precipitated by the collapse of the Hamidian regime in 1908. The institution of a constitutional, parliamentary, if still imperfectly democratic system of government rendered the Ottoman polity relatively fluid. The authority of the Empire's rulers was diminished and those in power were subject to competition. On the one hand, public order deteriorated; on the other hand, politically speaking, the Muslim peoples of the Asian parts of the Empire began to come alive, even in the Palestinian backwater. So while the Young Turk Revolution, as we have seen, struck many Zionists as opening up wholly new vistas and hopes, some of the best informed had forebodings. Jacobson, in Constantinople, for all his inveterate optimism, feared from the first that Arab opposition to Jewish immigration into Ereẓ-Israel would now be more effective.[72] Ruppin, more precise in his thinking and in his formulation of the new predicament, pointed out (privately) that while an autocratic sovereign could grant the Jews special privileges and maintain them with the full power of the state, in a constitutional regime there could be no special rights for particular communities, at least in principle, least of all for one that numerically was weakest.[73] In sum, from this point on, Arab-Jewish relations in Palestine/Ereẓ-Israel must be followed and understood largely in terms of the ensuing interplay between these three strikingly unequal forces: the Turkish, the Arab, and the Jewish. Broadly, it took three forms.

[71] See *Origins*, pp. 195–6.

[72] Wolffsohn to Warburg, 18 November 1908. CZA, Z2/233.

[73] Ruppin to Wolffsohn, 18 August 1908. CZA, L2/436. Cited in Y. Ro'i, 'The Zionist Attitude to the Arabs 1908–1914', in E. Kedourie and S. G. Haim, *Palestine and Israel in the 19th and 20th Centuries* (London, 1982), p. 38.

In the first place, a moderate loosening of the Turkish grip began to make a measure of public debate, protest, and agitation possible. In time there evolved a highly political, nationally minded Arabic press, much given to swift, harsh judgement and, when the spirit moved it, as was generally the case where Jewry in general and the Zionists in particular were concerned, to demagoguery in its editorial advice and tendentiousness in its reporting.[74] Ruppin and his staff in Jaffa, somewhat alarmed, began to monitor the new Arab press. The Zionist executive, in geographically and mentally remote Berlin, took note, and reports on Arab opinion and press began to appear in the regular confidential bulletins issued by the Zionist Central Office to members of the GAC and the leaders of the country organizations. It was not long before all informed members of the movement, certainly all with a claim to positions of leadership, had been made aware of what could not fail to appear as a campaign (part spontaneous, part concerted) against them. The response was cautious.[75] Ruppin, as the chief man on the spot, set the tone. The Zionists must see to it, he told the Eleventh Congress, that relations with the Arabs were peaceful and, if possible, friendly. Words were not enough; there must be deeds. Certainly, the new Jewish settlements had already brought the Arabs great benefits: many had found work with Jews; many had learned from Jews how to improve their methods of cultivation; the price of land has risen; Jewish medical services were available to them. But the Zionists, for their part, should only seek to purchase land for which the Arabs had no use. They must be better acquainted with the Arabs, learn their language and customs. They must seek to influence their press and fight the hostile influences, notably those emanating from Christian circles. It was not an impossible task.[76] Thus Ruppin, in public, on policy.

Efforts to talk what the Zionists regarded as reason to Arab

[74] On the Arab press in Palestine at this time, see N. J. Mandel, *The Arabs and Zionism before World War I* (Berkeley, 1976), pp. 85–92 and *passim*; and Y. Porath, *The Emergence of the Palestinian-Arab National Movement 1918–1929* (London, 1974), pp. 24–30.

[75] 'The article in *Ha-Herut* on the "danger" facing us in Erez-Israel as a consequence of the agitation against us among the Arabs has depressed me,' wrote Aḥad Ha-ʿAm. 'True, I had always thought that in the end this conflict would break out and I said so explicitly twenty years ago . . . but I never thought it would happen so soon, when our power in the country is still so limited and hardly to be felt.' Letter to Ha-Kohen, 27 November 1910. *Igrot AH*, iv, p. 317. The reference is to his article 'The truth from Erez-Israel' (1891). See above, p. 71.

[76] *Protokoll XI*, pp. 213–15.

editors, to move them to a more objective, if possible favourable view of the Zionist enterprise, and to open their columns to alternative views, even of the Zionist leaders themselves, were indeed continually made and not wholly without effect.[77] At one stage a plan to found an Arabic-language newspaper was discussed—to be rejected eventually as beyond the meagre resources of the movement. Some money was found to place advertisements in the Arabic press, buy copies of newspapers in bulk, and place small, discreet subsidies here and there, from time to time: all in the hope of nudging it in the desired direction. It does not seem to have been money well spent. In extreme cases of continual, essentially anti-Semitic slander, the courts were applied to with the help of the Ḥakham Bashi in Constantinople. However, when the editors of *Al-Karmil* (Haifa) and *Filastin* (Jaffa) were arraigned by the Ottoman authorities, they were acquitted by the courts, in one case on the grounds that the editor's intentions had been loyal (to Turkey), in the other on the grounds that relations between *Ottoman* peoples had in no way been harmed: the objects of the attack had been Zionists and foreigners.[78]

In a largely illiterate society in which the formulation of public issues and the formation of public opinion was to all intents and purposes the monopoly of a tiny class of land-owning, clan-leading notables and an exceedingly small semi-modern intelligentsia, it was hard for Ruppin and his colleagues in Jaffa, let alone the EAC in Cologne and Berlin, to determine what weight to attach to the Arabic press. But as a weather-vane showing in which direction the winds of opinion were blowing and to what tendencies weaker souls would do well to accommodate themselves, it was, and was so judged at the time, primordial. In its columns were displayed all the strands of the contemporary Arab *malaise*, in the exacerbation—or, at all events, expression—of which the tension between Arabs and Jews now began to play its ever increasing part. The attraction-repulsion felt for European-style modernism; the ambivalence

[77] On one occasion the editor of a Beirut newspaper went so far, in those relatively mild days, as to publish an article by Sokolov. (Thon to Sokolov, 6 April 1913. CZA, A18/12/12.) Minor coups of this kind were carefully reported. Thus the case of one Selim Salaḥi, described as 'a prominent Moslem citizen of Jaffa', who had written favourably of the Jewish settlements, asking 'What were all these places before the Jews came and brought them under cultivation?' in *Filastin* and *Al-Nafir*. (Zionist Press Bureau bulletin, 5 June 1911. CZA, Z2/551.)

[78] Y. Ro'i, 'Nisyonoteihem shel ha-mosadot ha-ẓioniim le-hashpiʿa ʿal ha-ʿitonut ha-ʿaravit be-ereẓ-israel ba-shanim 1908–1914', *Ẓion*, xxxii: 3–4, 1967.

towards the Turkish-held (and therefore, to many minds, illegitimate) caliphate; the confusion in minds faced with the conflicting claims of Islam and Christianity, of Ottoman loyalty and Arab national feeling; the ostensibly incompatible hard-minded, short-term political calculations which inclined towards Constantinople, as opposed to long-term, speculative aspirations which inclined towards Damascus, or Cairo, or (but still barely above the surface) Jerusalem; the still minor, but irritating problem of the Jews: were they potential allies or potential enemies, were they an example of thrift, intelligence, and efficiency to admire and follow, or an upstart and contemptible race to be squashed back into their proper place before they (with their mysterious, world-wide connections and evil, underhand ways) became too strong—all these were now increasingly in evidence. In combination they provided the soil on which the conflict with the Jews was to be further and continually nourished.

It is true that Zionism in these years was still far from being the maddening red rag to the Arab bull, the demon that *must* be exorcized if ever a proper social and moral order was to be imposed, that it later became. But some of the groundwork for its rise in the Arab public mind as a matter of first importance was being laid. It was in these years that the *terms* in which the matter came to be most commonly grasped began to be formulated and the arena in which what would be played out in a later generation may be said to have been in process of being cleared.

It is worth stressing that the Arab-Jewish conflict in this, its embryonic stage, was still chiefly a matter of spoken and printed words. The Ottoman authorities had no intention of relinquishing their overall control of the country, nor of letting local fire-eaters get out of hand. They, not the protagonists, determined the limits of conflict and argument; the more so because, as we shall see, their own hostility to the Zionist enterprise, maintained consistently as a matter of basic policy, was liable to minor mitigation in practice. This was partly because the Zionists in Europe and the members of the new *yishuv* in Ereẓ-Israel had access (if hardly more) to European centres of power and opinion; and partly because whatever danger to the integrity of the Empire might be discerned in the rise of Jewish national feeling and presence, Arab nationalism posed a greater problem and danger by far. In the interplay between Turks, Arabs, and Jews, what preserved the *yishuv* from truly major pressures from either Arabs or Turks or, worse, Arabs and Turks in combination, was thus, in the final analysis, its own weakness.

This interplay between the three almost comically unequal forces took a second form, more explicit in some ways, but ultimately of less consequence. This was the parliamentary form, a Parliament having been reinstituted upon *de facto* (1908), then final (1909) deposition of the Sultan and the accompanying promise of western-style democracy and political institutions. Ostensibly, the contenders for parliamentary representation in Constantinople were all loyal to the Ottoman regime and to the principles of ethnic pluralism. In fact, ethnic and religious identities (categories which tend strongly to merge in the Levant) were carefully monitored by all and formed the basis for political loyalty and political representation in all but isolated cases. And these latter cases, as often as not, were those of the least numerous and least powerful minorities, among them the Jews. None of the four Jewish members of the new Ottoman Parliament purported to be delegates of their Jewish constituents, although none of them could have been elected had their constituencies not included very large Jewish communities, and in one case, Salonika, been of preponderantly Jewish population. None were inclined to sympathy for Zionism; one was distinctly hostile. Their concern, as Jews, was for the safety and stability of the community, but they did not seek to function as a group. There was no question of their adopting a national, let alone nationalist line. In this sense, they were conservative—and wary of anything that might endanger the always fragile structure of Jewish-Muslim relations. Hopes that they would perform a function analogous to that of the Jewish members of the Russian Duma were soon dashed.

In Erez-Israel itself, matters were different, ostensibly. The Jews were in the minority in the country's two administrative provinces, but (notably in Jerusalem, where they formed the majority of the city's population) a substantial one in numbers, and of particular significance qualitatively. And, more immediately to the point, a radical political approach, uninhibited by centuries of firm (if generally mild) subjection to the ruling Muslims, was acceptable—in fact natural—to a very large proportion of local Jewry. It was therefore virtually inevitable that the leaders of the new *yishuv* should think of fighting the elections on an expressly national basis, if only to establish their presence in the political arena, and the *yishuv* as such, as a factor that others, Arabs and Turks, would do well to recognize and contend with. However, the obstacles to success were formidable. Only five deputies were to be elected to the Parliament in Constantinople, three from the *mutasrrıflık* of Jerusalem, two from the north of the country. The franchise was limited and the elections indirect: a restricted category of voters chose electors who in turn chose the deputies. Only Ottoman subjects were entitled to participate; as most Jewish inhabitants still held foreign nationality, the *yishuv* was thus heavily underrepresented even in the first round.[79] There were thoughts of promoting a mixed parliamentary delegation from Jerusalem, two Muslims and one Christian or Jew. It was soon evident that the most that could be done in practice was to try to form a Jewish voters' bloc and seek an alliance with the more accommodating wing of the Arab community. It might then be possible to get a relatively friendly Arab deputy elected. That too failed. Thus in 1908. In the subsequent elections in 1912 matters were complicated by the entry of the CUP into the electoral fray in force, but the results were much the same. Relations with the CUP were on the whole better than with their main opponents, the Liberals; and the CUP's face being set against the centrifugal tendencies which the Arabs were beginning to favour, it made sense to support it. But the Committee itself was reluctant to offend the Arabs by a public gesture to the Jews and it had its own reservations about the Jews as a political factor and about the Zionists in particular. The CUP's natural constituency, certainly the one to which it principally addressed itself, was Turkic in the first instance and Muslim in the second. The Jews were neither; and the Zionists in particular were suspected of having their own anti-Ottomanist purposes into the bargain. So far as the elections were concerned, all that remained for nationalist Jews of all strains in Erez-Israel to do was to choose between acquiescence and some small gesture of independence, if not defiance. They chose the latter and put up an independent candidate of their own. There was, of course, no question of his being elected. The results, therefore, were much as before: the Jerusalem district was represented in the new Parliament by one Arab deputy of relatively mild opinions and two others who were outstandingly hostile.[80]

---

[79] Of the some 50,000 Jewish inhabitants of Jerusalem only 6,300 had the right to vote, choosing 140 Muslim electors, 30 Christians, and 4 Jews. Of the 11,300 voters in the Jaffa-Ramleh district only 300 were Jews.

[80] P. A. Alsberg, 'Ha-she'ela ha-'aravit bi-mediniyut ha-hanhala ha-zionit lifnei

In the Parliament in Constantinople something like the full force of the Arab component of the Empire was clearly in evidence. A fifth of the some three hundred deputies were Arabs and it was not long before they had asserted themselves as a bloc with which the Ottoman Government had no choice but to contend, short of a reversal of constitutional policy and a return to repression. This ensured that the issue of the Jews in Palestine, Zionist purposes, and the tension between Jews and Arabs in the country would come before Parliament and on to the imperial political agenda, sooner or later, in a new form and under new, quite powerful, Arab auspices. The Turks, in consequence, would be faced more clearly than ever before with a choice: between holding the ring between Arab and Jew, or leaning in either one direction or the other. When the matter came up in Parliament on two occasions in 1911, chiefly as a stick with which to beat the Government, the ministerial response was indeed apologetic and left very little room for doubt about where it chose to stand. The charge was that Zionists and foreign bankers (Jewish and non-Jewish) were hand-in-glove with the Minister of Finance in ways (unspecified, but) clearly 'dangerous for the Ottoman Empire'. The Zionists, it was alleged, were intent on extending their influence out of Jerusalem and as far as Mesopotamia. True, the Government had rejected their demands, but they were persisting; and the attention of both Government and Parliament should be called to the 'manoeuvres of the Zionists in Turkey and to the fact that their agents pursued the realization of the secret aim of Zionism by a thousand means.' Two Jewish deputies rose to protest the blanket charges against Jewry, and the Grand Vezir himself dismissed the tale of collusion with the Zionists as 'pure fiction'. Some of the bankers with whom a loan for Turkey had been negotiated might be Jewish, he admitted, some were certainly not; in any case the question of their religion was irrelevant. They were all honourable men. So were the Turks, not least the Finance Minister himself. But he then went on to reaffirm the Ministry's own very firm opposition to Zionism—which he defined as 'the ideas of a few Jews in Europe', who sought, by massive immigration into Palestine, to establish 'a Jewish kingdom'. To which the deputy who had raised the question and presented the charges in the first place responded that evidently, on the matter of

milhemet ha-'olam ha-rishona', *Shivat Zion*, iv, 1956, pp. 164–6, 168–70. See also J.M. Landau, 'The "Young Turks" and Zionism: Some comments', in V. D. Sanua (ed.), *Fields of Offerings* (Rutherford, 1983), pp. 197–205.

Zionism, he and the Grand Vezir were in agreement after all.[81]

The subject came up again in May, this time in more specific terms and at the initiative of two deputies from Jerusalem. The Bible, Moses Mendelssohn, Herzl, and Nordau were cited; the *yishuv* was described as growing rapidly, as the scene of military preparations, as falling not far short of a state within a state; and the attention of Parliament was called, once again, to the 'peril' of Zionism and to Jewish national ambitions that extended into Syria and Mesopotamia. A Jewish deputy bridled at the Arabs' reference to the Bible, protested at the implication of Ottoman Jewry in the Zionist enterprise, and proposed a formal inquiry to establish the true facts. An Armenian deputy joined him to denounce the terms in which Zionism was discussed: their effect, he argued, was to incite an attack on all Jews, just as in the past there had been incitement against the Armenians. One Muslim deputy thought the whole issue was absurd: Zionism was not a danger at all; an Empire preparing for war against four separate neighbouring states had nothing to fear from 100,000 Jews in Palestine. The Minister of the Interior summed up with assurances that there was no intention to interfere in the religious and cultural affairs of the various nationalities or fuse them into a single nation; that Zionists were indeed a small minority in Ottoman Jewry; and that no sales of land in Palestine had been made without official approval.[82]

In Cologne the Zionist Central Office judged the second debate a distinct improvement on the first.[83] But Jacobson, in Constantinople itself, was gloomier for once. The relative improvement in the terms of political life in Turkey had not brought, nor could it bring, an improvement in the Turks' attitude to Zionism, he wrote (privately) to Ussishkin the day after the debate in May. The effect of the passing of the old, corrupt system and the new fear of public opinion would only make things more difficult. Regulations would be enforced more efficiently. The Zionists, if they did not reconsider their position and purposes, were fated to live, he thought, in continual trepidation, from thunderstorm to thunderstorm, the thunder being exceedingly unpleasant and a deal more serious than had been the recent debate in Parliament. Jacobson seems to have been as much alarmed by the (unstated) conclusions to which his

[81] *Le Moniteur oriental* (Constantinople), 2 March 1911.
[82] Ibid., 17 May 1911.
[83] Zionist Press Bureau bulletin, 26 May 1911. CZA, Z2/551.

own observations and analysis might be taken to be leading as he
was by the events themselves. 'Very confidential', he marked the
letter; 'for you *only*.'[84]

The third form of interplay between the three forces was more
distinctly and explicitly triangular. It followed from the major *Arab*
dilemma: were the Arabs to seek a place within a unitary,
centralized Ottoman state, or were they to press for a substantial
measure of autonomy within a *decentralized*, possibly federal system
of government and administration? Those who did not cleave to old-
style loyalty to Constantinople and the caliphate and sought a
degree of national self-determination (still short of outright
independence) were thus necessarily at odds with the ruling CUP
for which a unitary Ottoman state was explicitly (and Turkish
preponderance implicitly) a matter of first political principle. In
these circumstances, there was a move—at least in the major, more
sophisticated circles of Arab opinion, notably in Cairo and in
Damascus, rather than in Jerusalem—to look for allies and to
observe the Zionist enterprise with fresh, less jaundiced eyes. One
result was a series of meetings between representatives of the small
Ottoman Decentralization Party (Ḥizb al-la-Lamarkaziya
al-Idariya al-ʿUthmani) and a spokesman for the Zionists in which
the idea of political co-operation was very cautiously explored.[85]
The decentralists had the larger pan-Arab rather than local interests
in mind, and regarded Palestine as a southern province of Syria
rather than as a country with a discrete identity. Privately, few if any
were opposed to Jewish immigration; some declared themselves
warmly in favour. But none would go so far as to state their position
publicly (and to the Turks) for fear they would thereby be
discredited. The Zionist delegate noted that, on the whole, in this
particular case the Christian Arabs were for once better disposed
towards them than the Muslims. Some of the former positively
welcomed the prospect of a concentration of Jews in Palestine to
help counterbalance Muslim numbers and keep the vast Muslim
world divided by a substantially non-Muslim Palestinian land
bridge between Asia and Africa. In combination, Jewish and

[84] Jacobson to Ussishkin, 17 May 1911. CZA, A9/141.
[85] Discussed in detail in Alsberg, op. cit., especially pp. 172–4 and 185–206; and in
Mandel, op. cit., pp. 45–7, 148–64, 213–14. See also Roʾi, 'The Zionist Attitude', pp.
15–59.

Christian 'intellectual superiority', it was thought, would keep the great Muslim mass at bay.

By the same token, the Muslim Arab decentralists, while not wholly unfriendly, tended to be reserved. Their shift in opinion, so far as it went, owed nothing to approval, even on instrumental grounds, of the Zionist drive for Jewish national rights and everything to narrow and short-term calculations of expediency. Muḥammad Rashid Rida, a founding member of the party, who had long been outraged by what he judged to be the unwarranted pretensions of this 'the weakest of peoples', now began to think they should not only be emulated but made use of: the Syrians needed European technology and finance; it was therefore necessary to draw upon their resources. As for the dangers of Zionism—these, if and when the time came, could be controlled. Later Rida changed his mind again, as did others. Convinced that the Zionists were indeed in process of fulfilling their putative plan to dominate not only Palestine but Syria and Iraq as well, he turned his mind to the uses of organized violence against them: when the time came the Jews would be made to flee the country for fear of their lives.

It was an episode. On neither side were these talks handled by representatives of the front rank, least of all on that of the Zionists (except towards the end when some contacts were taken up by Sokolov). And if the Zionists were at any rate equipped with well-defined institutions and a reasonably clear chain of command, the Arab national tendency presented a different picture of which the decentralists were only one element. 'We are in contact here with several gentlemen who call themselves the chiefs and leaders of the different Arab groups,' Jacobson complained. 'Each one claims that it is he who is the real, the only real, the important one. . . . There is no way of knowing what truth there is in what they say, what is behind them. They do not have a *single* organization.'[86] Thus, in the event, precise demands, or the terms of a possible agreement, were put forward by neither party. Talks never went beyond an exploratory stage; it is doubtful whether they could have. There were no concessions the Zionists could make that would suffice to interest the Arabs and yet be compatible with the aims and ethos of the Zionist movement however moderately conceived. There could be no question of abandoning such central elements of the national revival (as Zionists of *all* schools conceived it) as free immigration

[86] Jacobson to Ruppin, 3 May 1914. Quoted in Ro'i, ibid., p. 36.

into the country, autonomous institutions, and a distinct national culture based upon the Hebrew language—to all of which, in one degree or another, Arab nationalists of the mainstream had always taken objection. Still, negotiations were never explicitly broken off and plans for a major meeting in the summer of 1914 at which progress towards a genuine *entente* was to be discussed were well advanced when the outbreak of war put paid to all inter-ethnic politics of this nature.

But in any case, it was the Turks who were the power in the land. It was from Constantinople that the concessions each side was after had to come. Indeed, when some were made to the Arabs at this time such small interest as there was in an alliance with the Jews was further diminished. For their part, the Zionists could not but approach the proposition that the Arabs were the allies they had long been seeking with the greatest doubt and caution. Did it mean that forces should be joined against the Turks, or more dangerously yet, in anticipation of the Turks' departure? Was it really safe to deal with the Arabs? Was it, ultimately, in the Zionist interest to do so?

Sokolov, in the course of an extended visit to the Near East in the spring of 1914, noted that the matter of relations with the Arabs was now one the Zionists had to try to come to terms with,[87] and recorded some bits and pieces of advice given him along with his own impressions. The Arabs had no organization, he had been told, and no leaders. They were unpatriotic and the only basis for co-operation with them was one of 'private deals, greed, profit, and bribery'. The Muslims were under the influence of the Christians, the Christians under that of the foreign Consuls. To treat with them was only to stimulate them to further political activity which would benefit the Zionists nothing. Besides, to co-operate, say on the basis of an Arab-Jewish newspaper, was necessarily to offend the Turks, and 'we are too much in their hands. [What] the Turks themselves desire is to weaken the Arabs.' And then the fact was, Sokolov concluded, that 'the Committee [of Union and Progress] was now

---

[87] Which is not to say there had not been repeated attempts to do so both on the spot in Erez-Israel and in Constantinople, and in formal debate at the Zionist headquarters as well; for example, at the GAC meeting of 4 November 1911 (Stenographic record, CZA, W142I) at which the issue was discussed at very considerable length. To the conundrum posed on that occasion by Motzkin, to take one instance, namely how an attempt to meet the probable opposition of the Arabs could be reconciled with (as he saw it) the need to 'identify' Zionist interests with Turkish none could offer a convincing solution.

favourable to Zionism;[88] [and that] we have an interest in the
Turkish national triumph because it would counter the Arabs.' As
for the Turks themselves, 'the chief condition' for acceptance of the
Zionists by the CUP was 'Ottomanization'.[89] In sum, the Jews
could not ally themselves with the Arabs, decentralists and others,
without destroying their by no means wholly intolerable relationship
with the Turks. They had every reason to avoid a quarrel with the
Arabs. They could seek to assist them technically, open their schools
to them, and generally help improve the condition of the Arab
peasant class.[90] But the immediate and visible prospects for political
co-operation were bleak.

What of the more distant future? At the beginning of the second
decade of the century the Sick Man of Europe was still in indifferent
health. As against the loss of Libya and virtually all of its Balkan
territories, the truncated Empire, it could be argued, was now more
compact and its rulers were more determined. The removal of a
large, restless, Christian population contiguous to independent
Christian states was perhaps all to the good, leaving only Christian
communities too well embedded in the Muslim heartland of the
Empire to constitute a present danger. On the other hand the
defeats in the Balkan Wars and by Italy had left their mark on other
subject peoples.

The Arabs are not yet organized and strong enough to be feared by us as a
danger [Ruppin's office in Jaffa reported to Zionist headquarters in Berlin],
but we must be aware that we are passing through a critical time and that
we shall have to reckon in the near future with an enemy who must be taken
seriously. Whatever results the peace negotiations [with the Balkan states]
will have, the Arabs will issue from the Turkish crisis strengthened. The
Arab movement for autonomy will now assume strength; and when the fear
of the Turkish officials vanishes the education and organization of the
populace by the intellectual class will proceed at a rapid pace. But if the
national consciousness among the Arabs becomes stronger we shall meet
with a resistance which can perhaps not be overcome any more by money. If
the Arabs should go so far as regarding it a national disgrace and treason to
sell their land to the Jews, the situation for us will become quite serious. It is

---

[88] In September of the previous year the Turks had abolished the 'red slip'
regulation that epitomized the restrictions on Jewish immigration. (See *Formative
Years*, p. 54.) The optimists took this as a sign of better times to come. In practice the
restrictions were maintained, though in a less offensive form.

[89] Diary jottings, April June 1914. CZA, A18.

[90] Ro'i, 'The Zionist Attitude', pp. 33–5.

therefore all the more a dictate of self-preservation to learn the importance of strengthening our present position and equipping ourselves for serious times. . . . It is exceedingly regrettable that the present moment is so little appreciated by our adherents. What we miss now we shall perhaps never be able to make good in the future.[91]

Here and there were voices suggesting that the Zionists should look beyond the present to a time when the Turks had departed. Greenberg, for instance, regarding the Italian occupation of Tripoli as proof that the Powers were 'not going to stand by the integrity of the Ottoman Empire', argued that this was the 'psychological moment for us to put to the Powers that there is a Jewish question, and that it can only be solved in Palestine; and that we ought to demand that, in any break up of the Turkish Empire (which is now proceeding) the claim of the Jews to Palestine must not be ignored.'[92] The views of a knowledgeable archaeologist, T. E. Lawrence, working near Aleppo, were reported privately and approvingly to Sokolov.

He [Lawrence] has a remarkable knowledge of Turkish conditions; he has been out in the country for 4 years and he is extraordinarily alive and awake. From what he says it seems that the Turkish power is in a state of utter collapse in Syria and indeed throughout Asia Minor, save in Anatolia, and that the seeds of dissolution cannot be removed. The Arabs are ready at any moment to break off and are very anxious to have English protection. They have at present no leader and no organisation. The Kurds in the interior are also ready to break away and are steady and able and may possibly supplant the Turks as the ruling power. The Armenians of course are turbulent and there is always the danger of Russian intervention.[93]

But such ideas and such a way of thinking had by no means taken root— not, at all events, as a basis for action. Far and away the most powerful tendency was to continue to seek an accommodation with the Turks, hoping against hope that the potential contribution of the Zionists to the Ottoman Empire would eventually be recognized and their own minimal requirements thereupon be met. The call for 'Ottomanization', namely the acceptance by the members of the

[91] EAC, Report to Members of the Executives of Zionist Federations (English edition), 26 February 1913.

[92] Greenberg to Wolffsohn, 25 September 1911. CZA, W79 II.

[93] Unmarked paper dated 18 August 1913 in Sokolov's files, CZA, A18/12/12. Internal evidence suggests Norman Bentwich as the author; the handwriting is possibly Albert Hyamson's, the latter having sent Sokolov an extract from a letter by the former.

yishuv of Ottoman citizenship with its obligations—subjection to Turkish law and service in the Turkish army—was constantly repeated and to some extent followed. And when the Italo-Turkish war broke out the Zionist leadership was instantly torn between that instinct that is deepest in the powerless—to play for safety and avoid involvement—and what seemed a golden opportunity to demonstrate loyalty to the Turks. A plan to form a 'legion' to fight with the Ottomans was discussed, but never got off the ground. A more serious proposal, to form a medical detachment to serve with their forces under the Red Crescent, had to be abandoned for failure to raise the some 100,000 marks it would have cost. In the end, the Zionists could do no more than express sympathy, thus, incidentally adding a small increment to the picture that had been building up in London and Paris over the years of Zionism as a movement that leaned on the whole towards the German side of the great European divide, its centre being in Berlin, its most visible activists and functionaries Middle European, the language in which it conducted its main business German, its closest interests in Turkey, and particularly suspected (by the British)[94] of close and malignant involvement in the affairs of the pro-German CUP—all, however, without any significant benefit to their cause in Constantinople itself.

It is not the least of the contradictions with which the Jewish *Risorgimento* is shot through that rarely was the primacy of politics in its affairs brought so clearly to the surface as by the workings of the essentially *non*-political approach the Zionists sought to pursue in the years before the Great War. The *yishuv*, the enterprise upon which most eyes in the movement were turned and upon which all its hopes and efforts were concentrated, looked very fragile. It was not moribund; but nor was it thriving. It endured, but it grew at a slower rate than the likely obstacles to its future welfare. It was not of a scale and structure to effect radically the condition of east European Jewry to which its origins and *raison d'être* must ultimately be traced. It lacked the strength in absolute numbers, as the Zionist movement as a whole lacked the quality of leadership, to cope with the multiplicity of rivals, opponents, and doubtful allies surrounding it and strike a path through the jungle of conflicting interests and

[94] Lowther to Hardinge, 29 May 1910. PRO, FO 800/193A. Also see below, pp.104, 195–6.

calculations in which it was embedded. None could suggest a tactic for breaking free of the structure of Near Eastern politics in which it was ensnared.

Thus the attractions of the 'practical' form of Zionism as a strategy for the movement were now beginning to be seen as illusory even by some of its adepts. As an alternative to political action it might serve the movement well so far as its internal cohesion and collective peace were concerned. But, as could now be seen, the more the *yishuv* as a 'practical' proposition prospered, the greater the local Arab opposition it was fated to arouse, the greater would be the misgivings of the Turks, and therefore the more surely the Zionists would be cast back into a *political* arena. The mood among the more perceptive and the better informed of the Zionists was therefore one of foreboding. There was a growing sense on all sides that faults of omission had been committed, even if none could specify their precise nature, and, dimly, that it was possible that time and circumstances had passed them by.

Only a little while ago [wrote a correspondent for the movement's Hebrew language weekly *Ha-'Olam*] it had been possible to do a great deal in Erez-Israel. At the time we dreamed of a Charter. The years passed. We did nothing at all: we were satisfied to dream our lovely dreams. The time when a Charter will be granted in Erez-Israel may now be near, but it will be given to those who inhabit the country and as we do not inhabit it, the Charter can do us great damage. The time has not yet come, but it is getting near. Will we at least understand now how urgently we must do our work so that we too will constitute a real force in the land of our hopes and make it impossible to remove us from our fatherland?[95]

No doubt there is a sense, however limited, in which something of the horrendous present may be discerned in this still relatively tranquil period before the eruption of the Great War. Two differences are crucial. It was a time when neither Jews nor Arabs possessed the advantages, responsibilities, and terrors of self-government (let alone independence), having only expectations or hopes or ill-defined stirrings of the political spirit. And it was a time when the decisive arena for either party was not in Palestine/Erez-Israel at all. In the first instance it was in Constantinople. Ultimately it was in Europe.

[95] 'Y.L.', 'Ha-tenu'a ha-'aravit', *Ha-'Olam*, 6 May 1913.

PART TWO

The War

3

The New Setting

The fortunes of Zionism were transformed by the Great War. It was not a predictable, let alone a necessary consequence of the upheaval. It was not the Zionists who wrought the change. Nor, as we shall see, did the movement's elected and established leadership intend the result or do much to advance it. The fundamental weaknesses of pre 1914 Zionism continued to pursue it throughout: its minority status in the Jewish world, its exceedingly limited political and material resources, the small scale of the new *yishuv* and its fragility, the dearth of effective leaders, and, above all, the inability of those who claimed to lead it to formulate an effective policy for the movement, let alone for Jewry as a whole, around which all would rally. The change in its fortunes was the consequence of two initially unconnected developments of vastly greater compass.

The first was that quite early in the war, minds in the Allied camp were set on an eventual large-scale amputation, if not dissolution, of the Ottoman Empire. Detailed and carefully considered plans for the future disposition of its territories were made and remade, approved at the highest level, and underwritten in practice by military operations. Turkey's adherence to the Central Powers by secret treaty in August and by full declaration of war in November 1914 set off a process of planning by its enemies for its post-war dismemberment. Palestine was among the Ottoman territories slated from the very beginning to be brought under new government. Accordingly, who would rule it, and in whose interest, became both open and real questions for the first time in centuries. To these questions a great variety of answers were advanced from time to time. What was never in doubt, so far as the Allies—Great Britain, France, Russia and, subsequently, Italy, and, in due course, the

United States too—were concerned was that the local regime would be an entirely new one. But to the circumstance that such plans, worked and reworked more than once, most notably by the British and the French, were the (secret) order of the day in respect of Palestine (along with other, greater territories), the Zionists themselves made no direct contribution. Nor, in the political and military nature of things, could they have. Nor were they aware of what was in preparation until a very late stage in the process, and then imperfectly. But that (if the Allies won the war) there would most definitely be a new order of things in the Near East was none the less a fundamental datum upon which—so far as the matter of Zionism was concerned—all else turned. Fundamental, but not unique.

The other crucial development was the change in the (terms and the light) in which the major political forces, notably the great European Powers, began to perceive the lesser forces in the international arena: the lesser states in the first instance, the lesser, or submerged peoples of Europe and the Levant in the second. What was new here was not the simple fact that the great military Powers and the leaders of the larger nations took cognizance of secondary and tertiary national forces, actual and potential, with a view to their recruitment or manipulation or overt or covert subjection. It was the intensity of the attention paid them, the relative lack of inhibition in the continual effort to exploit their ambitions, needs, and sensibilities, and the greatly enlarged class of those to whom truly systematic attention and court were now paid that was unprecedented. This had much to do with the *Zeitgeist*. It had more to do with the immense and unanticipated strains which the protracted, disastrous war put upon all the belligerent states. Much as unprecedented efforts were made to put all available domestic financial, industrial, and technological resources to maximum military use, so there were efforts on all sides to harness all available *political* resources (both domestic and foreign), and to block the hostile exploitation of all such resources as might be available to the enemy. The upshot was a fundamental change in the circumstances and prospects of a host of minor components of the contemporary political and economic arenas. Some were crushed, such as the Armenians. Some were wooed, such as the Irish. The Poles were wooed and crushed in rapid alternation by both sides as prospects changed and appetites and needs waxed and waned. Generally, it became the practice in all Foreign Ministries and intelligence establishments to monitor national sympathies and calculate national hostilities with care. And the longer the war lasted, the more whole theories and ideologies on the one hand and functioning political and military institutions on the other were constructed and harnessed to these matters—in practice to plans (or promises) for the imposition of a wholly new political and territorial order both in Europe and in the Near East.

For the longer the war lasted and the deeper and more painfully the costs and dangers of the fundamental strategic stalemate bit into the minds of the political and military rulers of the principal belligerent Powers, the more urgent became the search for additional increments of power and influence, however small, and for cracks in the opponents' armour, however narrow, that might, with advantage, be enlarged. And since four of the major belligerents were multinational empires and all the minor actual and potential belligerents and participants in the fighting in eastern Europe, the Balkans, and the Near East were either small states intent on expansion or subject nations bent on independence, the national drives of the lesser peoples of Europe and the Levant seemed to offer particularly fertile ground for political action to both coalitions. By lending an attentive ear to their claims, by playing on the sympathies of those who had their interests at heart, by painting attractive plans for the future, they might be drawn, it was thought, into one or other of the camps, if hitherto neutral, or induced to reverse their loyalty, if already committed—and the delicate balance of power thereby tipped, however slightly, in one direction or the other.

Among the peoples brought under fresh observation and to whose needs and aspirations, weaknesses and strengths, unprecedented attention was now paid were the Jews. That the Allies, as the conflict wore on, took greater note of them than ever before—in fact took *political* note of them at all—and that it began to be thought, especially in Paris and in London, that the Jews as a group, indeed as a people, might, under certain circumstances, be put to good account in the management of the war, was the second fundamental datum upon which the fortunes of Zionism can be seen to have turned. But it was the conjuction of the two developments—the placing of the future of Palestine on the international political agenda *and* the new light in which Jewry came, however briefly, to be held by the major Allied Powers—that was finally decisive.

ii

That, in the event⌊it would be Great Britain that would play the central role in these matters, rather than France, or, more remotely, Italy or the United States, was due primarily, as we shall see, to the role of its armies in the Middle East and the very high value the British put on a continuing and strengthened presence in the region.⌉ But it took time for all the relevant factors to evolve and to impinge upon the British official and political mind. It took time for a full understanding of the nature, dangers, and imperatives of the war to be reached and to take effect. And it took time for the notion that the question of Palestine and the question of Jewry might properly and usefully be linked to be taken up in Whitehall and Downing Street. Early attempts to move the machinery of British government in this direction—in practice, to interest those senior politicians and officials whose voices in such matters carried real weight—failed. Such was the fate even of the most interesting of such efforts, because it was the work of the most highly placed of all would-be promoters of a British Zionist orientation: Herbert Samuel, a leading member of the ruling Liberal Party, a member of Asquith's Government (President of the Local Government Board), the first Jew to serve as a British Cabinet Minister.

On 9 November 1914, within days of Turkey's entry into the war, Samuel went to see his colleague the Foreign Secretary. It was probable, he told Sir Edward Grey, that the Ottoman Empire would end by being broken up. The question of the 'future control of Palestine' was therefore likely to arise. Since 'the jealousies of the great European powers would make it difficult to allot the country to any of them[,] perhaps the opportunity might arise for the fulfilment of the ancient aspiration of the Jewish people and the restoration there of a Jewish State.' He himself, he explained, 'had never been a Zionist because the prospects of any practical outcome had seemed so remote that I had not been willing to take part in the movement. But now the conditions are profoundly altered.' Samuel went on to outline the benefits that the British (having regard to their strategic interests in the region) and the Russians (having regard to their large and increasing Jewish population) would derive from the establishment of such a Jewish state in Palestine. The other Powers did not count for much in this regard. In any case, it was important, 'that the new state should be founded under the auspices of the most progressive of the countries in which the Jews found themselves,' Great Britain.

Grey's response, Samuel recorded, was sympathetic ('The idea had always had a strong sentimental attraction for him.'), but very cautious. He would help 'if the opportunity arose'. He went so far as to tell Samuel, that 'If any proposals were put forward by France or any other Power with regard to Syria it would be important not to acquiesce in any plan which would be inconsistent with the creation of a Jewish state in Palestine.'[1] This latter undertaking was soon forgotten, at all events by Grey; but that was for the future. Meanwhile, Samuel, for his part, was sufficiently encouraged by the Foreign Secretary's response and by the response of at least one other member of the Cabinet, Lloyd George (who expressed himself as 'very keen' to see a Jewish state established in Palestine[2]), to bring the matter before the full Cabinet, formally. Two months later, he circulated a long paper in which his proposals were put forward in greater detail, but in a modified form. Once again, it was 'the prospect of a change, at the end of the war, in the status of Palestine' that was the starting point. It was joined now with what Samuel called 'a stirring among the twelve million Jews scattered throughout the countries of the world' and their feeling that 'now, at last, some advance may be made, in some way, towards the fulfilment of the hope and desire, held with unshakable tenacity for eighteen hundred years, for the restoration of the Jews to the land to which they are attached by ties almost as ancient as history itself.' True, 'the time is not ripe' for a fully-fledged Jewish state, if only because the present basis for it was too small and weak: 'The dream of a Jewish State, prosperous, progressive, and the home of a brilliant civilisation, might vanish in a series of squalid conflicts with the Arab population.' What could be done, however, what would be welcomed by the Zionists and 'the greater number of Jews who have not hitherto been interested in the Zionist movement', and what would meet *British* interests, would be the annexation of the country

---

[1] Handwritten memorandum, 9 November 1914. ISA, 100/1.
[2] Ibid.

by Great Britain. It would be best too for the country itself, 'blighted' for centuries 'under the Turk'. It would raise the prestige of Britain and 'add a lustre even to the British crown'. It would remove the danger of some other great European Power being established in the immediate proximity of Egypt. And it would 'win for England the lasting gratitude of the Jews throughout the world.'

The alternatives to British rule were then taken up in turn, analysed, and dismissed: annexation by France (its interests were strongest in northern Syria, and France would have enough on its hands if it recovered Alsace and Lorraine and obtained Beirut and Damascus); internationalization (inherently unstable and liable to lead, in time, to German control); annexation to Egypt (acceptable to some Muslims, but not by all, and much less desirable to the Jews); continued Turkish rule subject to certain guarantees (fated to revert to the miserable *status quo ante*).

But finally, Samuel concluded, there was the impact a wholly new British regime would have upon the Jews themselves. There would be a chance of large-scale relief for the hard-pressed people in Russia; and something else.

Far more important would be the effect upon the character of the larger part of the Jewish race who must still remain intermingled with other peoples, to be a strength or to be a weakness to the countries in which they live. Let a Jewish centre be established in Palestine; let it achieve, as I believe it would achieve, a spiritual and intellectual greatness; and insensibly, but inevitably, the character of the individual Jew, wherever he might be, would be ennobled. The sordid associations which have been attached to the Jewish name would be sloughed off, and the value of the Jews as an element in the civilisation of the European peoples would be enhanced.

The Jewish brain is a physiological product not to be despised. For fifteen centuries the race produced in Palestine a constant succession of great men—statesmen and prophets, judges and soldiers. If a body be again given in which its soul can lodge, it may again enrich the world. Till full scope is granted, as Macaulay said in the House of Commons, 'let us not presume to say that there is no genius among the countrymen of Isaiah, no heroism among the descendants of the Maccabees.'[3]

Now this was not at all the tone customary in Cabinet papers, nor was it what any of his colleagues would have expected from Samuel,

---

[3] 'The Future of Palestine', January 1915. PRO, CAB 37/123. Samuel was quoting from Macaulay's speech in the House of Commons (17 April 1833) in which he argued for the removal of all civil disabilities from the Jews.

respected for his clarity of mind and sound judgement rather than for breadth of imagination and generosity of feeling.[4] Asquith declared himself astonished by the 'vehemence' with which Samuel argued his case. 'It is a curious illustration of Dizzy's favourite maxim that "race is everything",' he wrote to Venetia Stanley (28 January 1915), 'to find this almost lyrical outburst proceeding from the well-ordered and methodical brain of H.S.' As for the plan itself, he did not like it. It was an 'addition to our responsibilities' to which he was not 'attracted', and he refused to take it up.[5] Samuel continued to press. He saw Grey once more on 5 February 1915, but got no further. This time the Foreign Secretary echoed Asquith's characteristically Liberal reluctance to add to British responsibilities.[6] When Samuel persisted and brought up his plan once more in a third, somewhat more astringent version,[7] Asquith liked it still less and (privately) was downright contemptuous of what he described as a scheme by which the British 'should take Palestine, into which the scattered Jews c[oul]d in time swarm back from all quarters of the globe, and in due course obtain Home Rule. (What an attractive community!)'[8] Besides, Samuel's strategic arguments cut little ice with the Secretary of State for War. Kitchener thought little of Palestine. He wanted Alexandretta.[9] In fact, few of the major figures in the limited circle to which the idea was exposed were friendly. One was Fisher, the First Sea Lord, briefly out of retirement, but shorn of much of his influence and soon to resign.[10] Haldane, the Lord Chancellor, had, at least at an an earlier stage, expressed 'interest and sympathy', but only privately and with a touch of scepticism.[11] The only firm partisan of the proposal, Asquith commented, was

Lloyd George, who, I need not say, does not care a damn for the Jews or

---

[4] 'Samuel is industrious, a good speaker, and clear thinker. His judgement is respected and his advice accepted, but everyone thinks him absolutely self-centred and his whole horizon bounded by his own career. He would never have time to pick any unfortunate fellow creature out of the mire.' Edward David (ed.), *Inside Asquith's Cabinet: From the Diaries of Charles Hobhouse* (London, 1977), p. 121.

[5] M. and E. Brock (eds.), *H. H. Asquith: Letters to Venetia Stanley* (Oxford, 1982), no. 281, p. 406.

[6] Handwritten memorandum, 8 February 1914. ISA, 100/1.

[7] 'Palestine', March 1915. ISA, 100/1.

[8] *Letters to Venetia Stanley*, no. 347, p. 477.

[9] Ibid., no. 347, pp. 477–8.

[10] Fisher to Samuel, 24 (?) April 1915. ISA, 100/1.

[11] Haldane to Samuel, 12 February 1915. Ibid.

their past or their future, but who thinks it would be an outrage to let the Christian Holy Places—Bethlehem, Mount of Olives, Jerusalem &c—pass into the possession of 'Agnostic Atheistic France'! Isn't it singular that the same conclusion sh[oul]d be capable of being come to by such different roads?[12]

And there was also, this time, violent opposition from the other major Jewish figure in the Liberal Party, Edwin Montagu, newly promoted to the Cabinet as Chancellor of the Duchy of Lancaster.

Montagu ('the Assyrian', as Asquith, his patron, called him behind his back with a balanced and consistent mixture of regard and contempt) was of a particularly complex character: sensitive, talented, profoundly unsure of himself, not without a touch of brutality—at least in language—and devoted to the not wholly tenable proposition that he was, or could be, a true Englishman. Like Samuel, he was rated highly by his colleagues for his ability. Unlike Samuel, he does not seem to have inspired respect. 'Montagu has a power of speech, clever, even brilliant,' his colleague Hobhouse noted; 'he will probably not desert his party, but always attach himself to its most conspicuous men, and is determined to achieve a career which he will probably do. He will probably swallow a good deal of boot blacking on the way. He has no courage, but some violence and bears malice and gossip.'[13] When, on 9 March 1915, in the course of a Cabinet discussion of military operations in the Near East and French aspirations in the area, Samuel put in another plea for a British protectorate over Palestine which would be 'consonant with the wishes of the Jews', Montagu kept silent. But a week later he sent the Prime Minister a fierce and in some ways malicious memorandum intended to demolish Samuel's case not so much piece by piece as by striking directly at the central idea of Jewish political, territorial autonomy. That Palestine held any strategic or material attraction for Great Britain he briskly denied. In practice, such interest as there was in the country was 'confined to the possibility of founding ultimately under British Protectorate a Jewish State'. But this would be disastrous. 'There is no Jewish race now as a homogeneous whole. It is quite obvious that the Jews in Great Britain are as remote from the Jews in Morocco or the black Jews in Cochin as the Christian Englishman is from the Moor or the Hindoo.'

---

[12] *Letters to Venetia Stanley*, no. 347, p. 477.
[13] *Inside Asquith's Cabinet*, p. 229.

How would the Jews occupy themselves in a Jewish state? Agriculture was never attractive to an ambitious people. 'I cannot see any Jews I know tending olive trees or herding sheep.' There were no great or remarkable Jewish literary men to-day. 'It is hardly worth while transplanting one-third of the Jewish peoples [*sic*] of the world for the sake of Zangwill.' If they prospered in commerce, the anti-Semites would press for a prohibitive tariff against Jewish exports. The community in the Jewish state would have no common tongue. 'Hebrew to the vast majority of the Jews is a language in which to pray but not a language in which to speak or write.' It would be forming a state out of 'a polyglot, many-coloured, heterogeneous collection of people of different civilisations and different ordinances and different traditions and the confusion could not be any very great improvement on that which followed the erection of the Tower of Babel.'

Samuel himself had admitted that the country could hold no more than a third of Jewry. What about those who would be left behind?

Much though it may possibly be regretted [Montagu continued], the Jew is not a popular figure in any civilisation. He is only tolerated in varying degrees in varying countries. . . . The sympathy which [Samuel] suggests is widespread and deep-rooted in the Protestant world, the idea of restoring the Hebrew people to the land which was to be their inheritance, is I fear very often a thinly cloaked desire to get rid of the Jewish ingredient in Protestant populations. I should not be surprised if the President of the Local Government Board [Samuel] has not often found at public meetings that he has been invited to get back to Houndsditch. What will happen when he is told to get back to Palestine? If Palestine became a Jewish State I am sure he would be asked to look after the Borough Council of Jerusalem rather than the West Riding of Yorkshire. . . .

[The Jews'] only claim to the hospitality of Russia, Bulgaria, France, Spain, is that they have no alternative home, no State of their own, and that they want to be and are patriotic citizens working for the good of the countries in which they live. When it is known that many of them have aspirations to go to Palestine if there is only room; when it is known that Palestine is the Jewish State which is really their home, then I can foresee a world movement to get them away at any cost, only comparable to the fervid expressions of opinion that a home may be found for the suffragettes in St Helena.

For all these reasons, he regarded Samuel's proposal

as a rather presumptuous and almost blasphemous attempt to forestall Divine agency in the collection of the Jews which would be punished, if not by a new captivity in Babylon, by a new and unrivalled persecution of the Jews left behind.[14]

Asquith, once again, was determined to be no more than amused as much by his protégé's 'very racy memorandum' as by some of the 'rather vicious digs at Cousin Herbert' (i.e. Samuel) it contained. There was no question in his mind of taking either the original proposal or the debate between the two Jews seriously. There were vastly more important issues to be dealt with. In any case, in May, when a new Cabinet was formed with Lloyd George at the new Ministry of Munitions and with the Unionists, Balfour among them, as members of the first coalition Government, no place was found either for Samuel or for Montagu.[15] The question—or possibility— of a *Jewish* Palestine was easily forgotten for a time in exalted circles. Not so Palestine itself.

iii

Early in April 1915 a committee of officials was set up on Asquith's instruction 'to consider the nature of British desiderata in Turkey in Asia in the event of the successful conclusion of the war.' This was the de Bunsen Committee. In many ways it was a typical Whitehall group composed of representatives of the Government departments immediately concerned (Foreign, India, and War Offices, Admiralty and Board of Trade), headed by a senior, unemployed Ambassador (who had once seen service in Constantinople), and serviced by the ever more efficient and powerful secretariat of the Committee of Imperial Defence. But it included one unusual figure, Sir Mark Sykes, neither a civil servant nor a military figure of much consequence (for all that he was a serving officer at the time). He was a Member of Parliament, but that was no qualification for such business either. His essential merit was that he had first-hand knowledge of the region in question. He had explored it widely, served briefly in the Embassy in Constantinople, added his mite of information from time to time to the War Office's store, and written enough to have established a public reputation both in Parliament and outside it as an expert on 'Asiatic Turkey'—although strictly, his expertise was of a private and somewhat eccentric nature rather

---

[14] Confidential memorandum, 16 March 1915. LlGP, C/25/14/1.

[15] However, Montagu was brought in again later in the year and Samuel early in the year after.

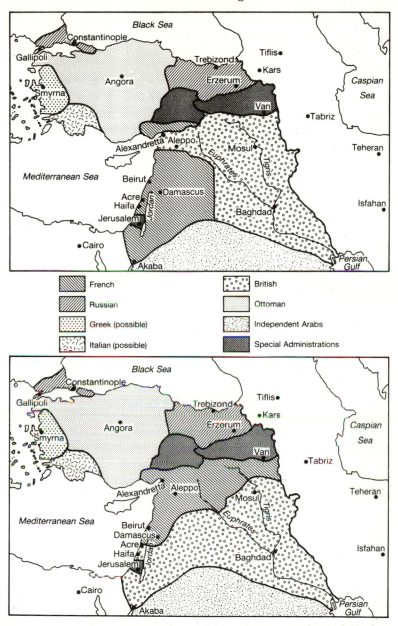

MAP 1. The de Bunsen Committee, June 1915: two schemes of annexation.

than of the kind which is normally characteristic of the professional scholar, diplomat, or intelligence agent. However, such were the flexible ways of British officialdom in wartime that his amateur status did not disqualify him, the more so as he had come to the attention of Kitchener and Kitchener had seen to it that he would be on the Committee. Nor did the fact that he had ideas of his own on the destinies appropriate to the peoples of the Near East rule him out—views which, as we shall see, he was to develop and promote at least as far as his brief (first Kitchener's, then chiefly the Foreign Office's) allowed him.

The Committee's starting point was a Russian claim to Constantinople as one of the spoils of war. It had followed upon the start of British operations at the Dardanelles which, in turn, had been prompted by a Russian request for a diversion in the face of Turkish operations through Armenia towards the Caucasus. In the event, the Turkish operations were unsuccessful, the British operations ended in the catastrophe of Gallipoli, and the Russian claim to Constantinople was fated to be renounced by the revolutionary Government. But the germ sown by Enver Pasha's ill-conceived northern campaign continued to live—in fact, flourish and mutate—with results that dogged all concerned long after its true origins had been forgotten. The Russian claim to Constantinople was accepted readily enough at the time both by the British and the French. In the customary way, it was then the latter's turn to consider what they would take for themselves. Contemplating the region, each of the three major parties, with well-remembered past and likely future conflicts in mind, looked as warily at each other as they did at their declared enemies. But with Russia's major interest already confirmed, France's central demand being for Syria, and Great Britain's 'special and supreme position in the Persian Gulf' being the cardinal principle upon which its policy was based, there was no immediately evident reason why insoluble conflict between the Allies need be envisaged. Great Britain, at all events, so the Committee believed (and as befitted one appointed by a Liberal Prime Minister), was not, and should not be, anxious to increase 'Imperial responsibility. Our Empire is wide enough already, and our task is to consolidate the concessions we already have, to make firm and lasting the position we already hold, and to pass on to those who come after an inheritance that stands four-square to the world.'

They added, not uncharacteristically, that '[i]t is then to straighten ragged edges that we have to take advantage of the present opportunity.'[16]

The Committee's chief strategic concerns, accordingly, were to maintain and strengthen Britain's existing military and naval presence in the eastern Mediterranean and secure land communications from the eastern Mediterranean to the Persian Gulf. Their chief political concern was to devise a system whereby the vast areas of Asiatic Turkey might be properly and effectively governed: with the Turks or, as was much more likely, without them. A great number of geographical divisions and administrative combinations were thought up, considered, and compared. Four threads ran through all: the Basra area at the head of the Gulf had to be British-controlled in any event; the conviction that the Ottoman Empire was indeed dying and efforts to resurrect it could not and should not succeed; the meagre military resources that would be available in Britain in the future—compared, for example, with the huge armies that Russia would always have at its disposal—dictated great caution; and, as the committee men put it at one point, one way or another it was 'with France that our difficulties will arise'.[17]

These were the major issues. The status and future of Palestine, in contrast, was a minor and dependent one. Geographically, it was loosely conceived. At times, 'Palestine' denoted the coastal area south of Beirut; at one point it was marked on a map as including all of modern Israel, all Jordan, and bits of southern Syria as far as Palmyra. De Bunsen and his colleagues noted that the French had laid claim to the country, but did not think it a claim that could be sustained, or should be. In any case, 'Palestine' as such, as a whole, and however defined, was of little interest to them. What was of interest was what it contained. There was Haifa: Great Britain would need it (rather than Alexandretta) as the Mediterranean terminal of its lines to Iraq; and there were 'the Holy Places of Christendom'. So far as Haifa was concerned, the Committee's members seem to have been sure that Britain would and could retain it, if not as an enclave then within a larger area under British control. The 'Palestine' of the Holy Places—clearly, in the collective

---

[16] 'Report of the committee on Asiatic Turkey', 30 June 1915, p. 4. PRO, CAB 27/ 1.

[17] Ibid., p. 11.

mind of the committee, the *Christian* Holy Places alone[18]—was a distinct and 'separate question'; and the Committee

felt free to deliberate on the assumption that the French claim [to it] will be rejected, since they [i.e. the Committee] are convinced that the forces opposed [among them, Russia] are too great for France ever to make the claim good. . . . For the same reason they consider that it will be idle for His Majesty's Government to claim the retention of Palestine in their sphere. Palestine must be the subject of special negotiations, in which both belligerents and neutrals are alike interested.[19]

This last was to be the point of departure for the actual and necessary negotiations with the French which were yet to come. At no point in the Committee's report, and so far as is known at no point in its proceedings, were Jewry in general or the Jewish interest in Palestine, sacred or secular, so much as discussed.

iv

The attitude of the British political and official classes to Jewry as a category and to Jews as individuals in the first twenty or so years of the century was substantially more complex than attitudes current among equivalent classes on the Continent. There was little visceral anti-Semitism. The passion and the hatred that infected much French upper-class opinion, the absolute social barriers that were virtually the rule in Germany, the unique combination of religious piety and brutality of mind that informed the Russian Autocracy and those who served it most loyally—these, in England, were virtually unknown. There was stereotypical thinking in plenty and it surfaced easily. 'Dirty coward,' Lloyd George once snarled after an argument with Montagu; adding: 'Men of that race always are.'[20] It seems to have stemmed, at least in part, from the ill-defined *objection* to Jews which coloured much thinking in all classes, but certainly in the upper social classes whence most officials and politicians still derived. Here and there it took the form of a little (forced?) shudder of revulsion at the very thought or prospect of Jews; but it was by no means simple, let alone absolute. As often as not it was mitigated by a not wholly unwilling respect for what were taken to be the Jews'

---

[18] There is no reference or hint of places in Palestine that might be holy to other religions. Moslem Holy Places in *Arabia* do receive attention, however, chiefly with a view to the likely repercussions in India of any change in their governance.

[19] Ibid., p. 28.

[20] W. J. Braithwaite, *Lloyd George's Ambulance Wagon* (London, 1957), p. 174.

salient qualities. Such complex feelings about the Jews—when notice was taken of them—are well exemplified in Virginia Woolf's recollection of her sentiments when she married one: 'How I hated marrying a Jew—how I hated their nasal voices, and their oriental jewellery, and their noses and their wattles—what a snob I was: for they have immense vitality, and I think I like that quality best of all. They can't die—they exist on a handful of rice and a thimble of water—their flesh dries on their bones but still they pullulate, copulate, and amass . . . millions of money.'[21]

'Sordid', 'squalid', 'oily', 'silken', 'vulgar', and like terms were adjectives applied very readily to Jews—as they were to some extent, and almost as easily, to Greeks, Armenians, and Italians; and they were readily and thoughtlessly accepted by middle- and upper-class English listeners or readers as fair and probably accurate comment. No doubt, there was in all this a large measure of national conceit, much as there was among the French and the Germans and, if in a much more troubled and unhappy way, among the Russians. There was very little doubt in the minds of the English upper classes, least of all in the minds of those who led or represented the nation, that they themselves belonged to a race that was superior in all those central respects (history, social practice, system of government, culture, even physical beauty, to say nothing of religion) in which the Jews were evidently deficient—not alone, perhaps, but markedly and notoriously so. But there were cardinal respects in which the English tended, by and large, to differ from the Continentals. They were not in the least afraid of the Jews. Inhabiting islands and having established a system of government in which national distinctions were formalized, accepted, and even in some ways encouraged, they tended not to be disturbed or irritated by Jewish social and cultural self-containment. They tended to limit the expression of anti-Semitic feeling to the domain of *private* conversation and correspondence. They tended too, in practice, to draw a distinction between such attitudes as they might have to Jewry as a whole or in the mass and *per contra* to the individual Jew into contact with whom circumstances might have thrown them. And generosity intermingled with dislike was not uncommon either: the less insular English observers of the foreign scene may be found tracing much of what they had found and detested in Jewry to roots

---

[21] Letter to Ethel Smyth, 2 August 1930. Nigel Nicolson (ed.), *The Letters of Virginia Woolf*, iv (London, 1978), pp. 195–6.

in their condition. Thus Mark Sykes: 'There dwell within this mass [of Russia] 6 million Jews, and such Jews as outside Russia are not to be seen in the world, repulsive, grasping, griping, fawning, insolent—of course all these faults are the faults of the environment, the [P]ale, the ghetto[;] it is a double tragedy of the Jewish mind oppressed by an undeveloped Russian mind. The Jews of Russia are what the Russians have made them.'[22] In a word, unlike the general run of Continentals, here, as in so many other respects, the English tended strongly to be flexible.

All this, it may be supposed, had much to do with the fact that the Jews were generally conceived of as a social, not a political category. The well-informed knew that elsewhere, notably in Russia, they were often regarded in a different light. Some imaginative but ill-informed British specialists in Ottoman affairs did think at one time that 'Jewry', along with the Masons, had played a particularly sinister role in the Young Turk Revolution.[23] One of the most influential and most distinguished of contemporary British journalists, Henry Wickham Steed, a star correspondent for *The Times* in central Europe for many years, devoted an immensely long chapter of his classic study of Austria-Hungary to them. He judged them 'first in importance' of the peoples of that Empire, and thought, writing on the very eve of the war, that 'no question deserves more earnest study [than the Jewish question]. It assumes a hundred forms, reaches into unsuspected regions of national and international life, and influences, for good or evil, the march of civilization.'[24] But in London few looked at the matter in these terms, if they looked at it at all. There was the nuisance of the east European immigration into Great Britain. Not all took kindly to the appearance of British Jews on the domestic political stage. But no one of consequence thought they constituted a *threat* to British society or institutions or civilization; and it would have been difficult

---

[22] Sykes to Simon, 6 January 1917. Hull, SP 4/136.

[23] See Sir Gerard Lowther's now notorious private letter to Sir Charles Hardinge (the former being Ambassador in Constantinople, the latter Permanent Under-Secretary at the Foreign Office), 29 May 1910 (PRO, FO 800/193A). For a careful analysis of this curious document, in which, among many other things, the Ambassador explained how 'the Jew' was entangling 'the Turk in his toils', much as he had already ensured that 'the Hungarian, who is of Turkish stock and is similarly devoid of real business instincts, has come under [his] almost exclusive economic and financial domination', see Elie Kedourie, 'Young Turks, Freemasons and Jews', *Middle Eastern Studies*, vii: 1; 1971, pp. 89–104.

[24] *The Hapsburg Monarchy* (3rd edition, London, 1914), pp. 145–6.

to find anyone in Whitehall or Westminster who thought that the Jews as a group were of any great political consequence so far as Britain and its Empire were concerned in the sense that they affected, or were capable of affecting, real British interests either at home or overseas seriously and directly.

Where the machinery of British government did take explicit note of them was in the context of the role they played (real or imagined) in other societies and polities and of the treatment meted out to them by other nations and governments. In the former case, they were simply subject to observation, the better to understand the foreign society in question and to deal with its Government. In the latter case they were the object of an exceedingly cautious but long-standing policy of doing what might be done to ameliorate the Jews' condition in those parts where, on the one hand, their condition was plainly intolerable and, on the other hand, London judged it both proper and possible for liberal, civilized Britain to act. In practice, it was not always judged politic to do so and there was never a great deal that could be achieved in any event. In the case of the persecution of Jews in Hamadan in the 1890s, London was prepared to instruct the British Minister in Teheran to tell the Shah plainly of 'the regret with which he had heard that the persecution had not yet ceased and . . . [of his fear] that a very bad impression would be created in England if it were allowed to continue.'[25] Romania's consistent ill-treatment of its Jewish subjects and equally consistent violation of its undertaking under the Treaty of Berlin was another subject to which, in certain periods, the British Minister in Bucharest had, a little less plainly, but 'repeatedly[,] called the attention of the Roumanian Government', the Foreign Office assuring representatives of British Jewry that the Minister would 'continue to do what he properly can to further the interests of the Jews.'[26] The Romanians were intransigent and slippery, however, and even concerted (if not very enthusiastic) representations by all the major European Powers brought no relief. So

While, therefore, it is greatly to be deplored that the intentions of the Powers in formulating the Treaty of Berlin have remained in a great measure unfulfilled [read a characteristically polite but faintly weary Foreign Office response to a fresh round of requests for intercession in 1907] it must nevertheless be borne in mind that the Roumanian Government have at

---

[25] Sanderson (Foreign Office) to Lord Rothschild, 26 May 1893. BD, C 11/2/1.
[26] Sanderson to Montefiore, 2 June 1902. BD, C 11/2/2.

least technically, put themselves in the right by passing the amendment of
article 7 of the Constitution to which I have alluded.

Having regard to the considerations enumerated above and to the still
critical state of affairs in Roumania, Sir E. Gray is of the opinion that the
present time would not be at all opportune for raising the question of the
disabilities under which the Jews of Roumania are still suffering in
practice.[27]

Certainly, there was much that was anomalous about the pressure
on the British to intercede, still more about such intercession when it
actually took place. The line drawn between foreign and domestic
affairs, between what was and what was not admissible as a matter
for diplomatic negotiation or even conversation between sovereign
states, was a familiar one and easily and, as a rule, sharply drawn.
Representations of this kind, on behalf of private groups of citizens
in one country related in one way or another to, or interested in the
welfare of, the inhabitants of another, entailed an incursion into
unfamiliar and awkward territory. The resentment caused in foreign
capitals by such representations was predictable, very notably so in
the case of the greatest target of Jewish pressure of all, Russia. The
benefit the miserable men, women, and children in the Russian Pale
of Settlement might actually derive from such representations—if
and when the Foreign Office and the British Ambassador in St.
Petersburg could bring themselves to make them—was likely to be
very slight. No chief of mission liked to take up such matters with his
hosts: British representations in the wake of the great pogrom in
Bialystok in 1906 were received by the Russian Foreign Minister, so
the Ambassador recorded, 'with exceeding stiffness'.[28] And a
request in 1910 for 'an unofficial intimation' to the Russian
Government that the anticipated expulsion of Jews from Kiev would
create 'a painful impression' in England was turned down flatly.
'Such an intimation', the representatives of British Jewry were told,
'would be calculated to cause irritation at any time as an
unwarranted act of interference on the part of a foreign Government
in the internal affairs of Russia and at the present moment, when
public opinion in that country is unusually sensitive as the result of
the intervention of various individuals and public bodies abroad in
the question of Finland, the effect produced could not fail to be the

[27] Campbell to Emanuel, 20 April 1907. BD, C 11/2/2.
[28] Harold Nicolson, *Sir Arthur Nicolson, Bart., First lord Cacnock* (London, 1937),
p. 221.

exact opposite of what is desired.'[29] When major diplomatic and strategic interests put a premium on amicable relations with Russia, as was notably the case upon the establishment of the Anglo-Russian *entente* in 1907, it became not only virtually impossible for the British Government to bring pressure, but particularly awkward for British Jews to seek to initiate it. When the Foreign Secretary himself, defensively but publicly, echoed the Russian argument that if there were pogroms on one side, there were 'the crimes of the other party of violence—the revolutionary party' on the other, it became still more difficult for English Jews identified with the establishment—and with the Liberal Party in particular—to continue to press their case.[30]

None the less they tended to do so, so far as they were able; and, it is well worth noting, without fear of ever being shown the door. For by these early years of the twentieth century it was not only well established that the Foreign Office was open and to some extent receptive to such pleas for help—certainly *in principle*—but a regular channel for such communication between it and the central representative institutions of English Jewry was in being, and a leading and guiding figure for these matters on the Jewish side had emerged.

v

The two main lay organizations in British Jewry at this time (and for some decades previously) were the Board of Deputies of British Jews, essentially a body composed of representatives of Jewish congregations; and the Anglo-Jewish Association, a philanthropic, voluntary body, composed preponderantly of notables, somewhat similar to the Alliance Israélite Universelle in Paris and, like it, concerned chiefly with welfare, security, and education in less fortunate communities, especially but not exclusively in the Muslim world. In 1878, the year of the Congress of Berlin, at which the independence of Romania was recognized and the status of its Jewish inhabitants made the subject of Romanian assurances and

---

[29] Langley (Foreign Office) to Alexander and Montefiore, 31 May 1910. PRO, FO 371/979. At the same time, privately the matter was gone into with some care: queries and reports were exchanged between London, St. Petersburg, and Kiev for almost three months following the Jewish representatives' initial application to the Foreign Office.

[30] See parliamentary debate on Foreign Office vote, 4 June 1908. Balfour, for the Unionist opposition, supported Grey. *Parliamentary Debates*, 4th series, cxc, col. 242.

(vague) international guarantees, the two bodies resolved to co-ordinate their 'foreign' affairs. They agreed that 'communication' with the British Government 'seeking the interference of the Government in reference to the affairs of Jews in foreign parts' would be made jointly and by agreement.[31] Each body would set up a special committee for this purpose and the two groups would join forces. In due course, the so-called Conjoint Foreign Committee was established to regularize and institutionalize this co-operation and was accepted by the Foreign Office as the principal channel through which all such business would be transacted. As was appropriate in Edwardian and early Georgian England, places on it were always found for some of the grandees of English Jewry, notably represent-atives of its two best-known families, the Rothschilds and the Montefiores. But in the years prior to the Great War, and more so during the war itself, the leading figure in the group was a man of much more modest origins, if, on the whole, greater attainments.

Lucien Wolf (1857−1930) was an English-born son of a Bohe-mian immigrant, a professional journalist of distinction (editor of the *Jewish World* at one point, assistant foreign editor of the *Daily Graphic* for almost twenty years, a regular contributor to the *Fortnightly Review*), and a serious non-academic historian. As with many of his generation, it was the onset of the great and overt persecution of Russian Jewry in the 1880s that had moved him to ever greater interest in, and activity on behalf of, east European Jewry. He mastered the subject in all its disagreeable detail, he initiated systematic, documented exposés of Russian policy and practice, and like Herzl before him, he did not hesitate to travel to Russia to meet the man thought to be chiefly responsible for the second great wave of persecution in the early 1900s, V. K. Plehve, the Minister of the Interior.[32] But Wolf was no nationalist, least of all a Zionist. He saw and described himself as an Englishman. He regarded both the English system of government and the status of the Jews in England as thoroughly satisfactory. It cannot be doubted that what he wished for more than anything was that that political system and that status or condition serve as universal models for governments and Jewries elsewhere. He thought it right to work for the dignity and freedom of Jews denied both the one and

---

[31] London Committee of Deputies of the British Jews, 'Heads of Arrangement with the Anglo-Jewish Association', May 1878. BD, C 11/1/2.
[32] *Formative Years*, pp. 256–7.

the other; and belonging to a community that had achieved emancipation, he believed it a moral duty to work for the emancipation of those communities which had not. In these sentiments he was not alone. But in the rather grey and mediocre human landscape of contemporary British Jewry Lucien Wolf was a remarkable feature: strong in character, clear of mind, efficient, hard-working, reliable, utterly dedicated. True, in his all-important relations with British officialdom some of this strength waned. The language in which he conducted his correspondence with the Foreign Office took on a pomposity and an artificiality that betrayed unease. The tone he adopted suggested—perhaps inevitably and necessarily—the supplicant. After all, what was his precise status? But if towards those securely placed within the magic circle of Government his approach was anxious, so far as those outside it were concerned, more especially those who, in his judgement, might upset the delicate balance of ideas and interests on which he relied, his approach was sharp and unforgiving, as we shall see. Historically, Wolf's importance lay in the fact that for some years, roughly until the end of 1916, a good many of the threads relevant to our subject were in his hands.

The outbreak of war did not materially change or weaken the Conjoint Committee's central, benevolent concern for east European Jewry. Its first response was that 'it would be improper at the present moment for the Jewish subjects of any of the Allied Powers to take any action, seeing that such action would inevitably be construed as an attempt to promote Jewish interests to the detriment of the united and single-minded prosecution of the war by the Governments and peoples of the three Allied Powers.'[33] But this extreme caution was rapidly modified. Increasingly, as the war continued and as it went badly for the Russians, the Jewish inhabitants of Poland, the Baltic lands, and western Russia began to suffer not only the direct impact of the fighting armies in their midst—fighting, as it happened, in those areas where the Jewish population was largest—but the added horrors of exceptionally brutal anti-Semitic action by the Russian Government and army— particularly the army. They were subjected to summary mass expulsions from their homes into the interior, to continuous public but baseless charges of treachery and espionage, to field courts-

[33] Emanuel to Hertz, 18 November 1914. ML, AJ/204/1.

martial and summary executions of alleged offenders, and the taking of hostages as guarantees of satisfactory behaviour. Sporadic pogroms by Cossacks were not uncommon.[34]

In private, the civilian Government (the Council of Ministers) had no doubt that the sweeping charges of espionage and disloyalty broadcast by the army against the Jews were unfounded, and that the supreme command under General N. N. Yanushkevich (which had assumed total control of the areas in question) was deliberately fomenting an anti-Semitic campaign within the army so as to represent the Jews 'as responsible for its own failure and defeat at the front'. They were also well aware of the impact of these developments on Russia's reputation and relations abroad. 'One does not like to say this,' the Minister of the Interior, Prince N. B. Shcherbatov told his colleagues in August 1915, 'but we are among ourselves here and I will not disguise my suspicion that, for Yanushkevich, the Jews are probably one of the alibis about which A. V. Krivoshein [Minister of Agriculture] spoke last time.' The situation, the Minister lamented, was as follows:

Hundreds of thousands of Jews of all sexes, ages and conditions have been moved, and continue to be moved, eastward from the war theatre. . . . The leaders of Russian Jewry are firmly demanding general measures and a legal basis for ameliorating the situation of their compatriots [i.e. allow them to reside outside the long-established Pale of Settlement for Jews]. In the heat of discussion I was told bluntly that a revolutionary mood was growing irrepressibly in the Jewish masses, that people are being driven to the last limit of despair, that every day it is becoming more and more difficult to struggle against the desire for active [i.e. self-] defence, that major unrest and disturbances are possible. . . . [And] it was pointed out to me that abroad too patience was wearing thin and that the day may come when Russia will not be able to borrow a penny.[35]

Ministerial reluctance to abolish the Pale of Settlement, or bring the question before the Duma, even as a temporary measure, was very great. It was, after all, the cornerstone of the whole edifice of legislation and restriction whereby the Jews had been kept down

---

[34] For a bitter, first-hand account by a Jewish serving soldier of brutalities committed by the Russian military against Russo-Polish Jews which he had been forced to witness, see Sh. Dubnov, 'Historiya shel ish zava yehudi: mi-ma'arakhot 1915', in *Ha-Tekufa*, i, 1918 (reprinted 1934), pp. 605–28.

[35] *Arkhiv Russkoi Revolutsii* (Berlin, 1926), xviii, pp. 43–4. (English translation: M. Cherniavsky (ed.), *Prologue to Revolution* (Englewood Cliffs, 1967), pp. 39–43, 56–72, 85–7, 121–3, 194–5.)

and, so far as possible, away from the Russian people, above all the peasantry. It would be, said S. V. Rukhlov, the Minister of Transport, 'a basic and irrevocable change in legislation which has evolved historically and which had, as its purpose, the guarding of Russian prosperity from Jewish grabbing and of the Russian people from the putrefying influence [*ot razlagayushchago vliyaniya*] of Jewish neighourhoods.'[36] But there were countervailing considerations.

We must be guided not by feelings [said the Minister of Finance, P. L. Bark], but by the demands of an extraordinarily critical moment. It is not we who created this moment, but those whom we have long and vainly begged to refrain from whipping up the Jewish question with Cossack whips. But it is we who have to pay for these whips, as the money for the war is being demanded from the Government. And we cannot obtain the money, for it is in the hands of that tribe which General Yanushkevich has visited with violence and injuries unthinkable in any civilized state. I must inform the Council of Ministers that of our last military loan of one billion, 480 million have actually not been placed—virtually half. . . . I must also state that the financial market abroad is closed to us now and we cannot obtain a penny there. . . . It is being openly hinted to me that we will not be able to extricate ourselves from our financial difficulties until some demonstrative steps are taken on the Jewish question.[37]

So if it was 'tragic' to have to think along such lines, nonetheless, 'Let us hurry,' the Minister of Agriculture joined in. 'One cannot conduct a war both with Germany and with the Jews.'[38] The Foreign Minister, S. D. Sazonov, heartily agreed. It would make 'discussions with the Allies much easier for me; they have been very embarrassed, lately, by the turn the Jewish question has taken in Russia.' Besides, the 'demonstrative steps' need not be far-reaching. Both he and the Minister of Finance had reason to believe that the Rothschilds were not asking for more than limited concessions. They did not ask for full equality for the Jews. They only needed a move sufficiently effective to keep 'the most agitated of the foreign Jewry' quiet.[39]

In the event, the concessions granted (some freedom of domicile and some easing of the bars to schooling) were no more than expressly temporary and very limited in scope. Resolved upon with great reluctance by the Russian Government and approved by the Tsar, they thus fell far short of their aims. Neither the notables of

[36] Ibid., p. 48.
[37] Ibid.
[38] Ibid., p. 49.
[39] Ibid., p. 50.

Russian Jewry itself nor the dignitaries of French and English Jewry, whom the Russian Minister of Finance met shortly after in Paris and London and sought to appease with references to a new dawn, were satisfied. They wanted an assurance that the concessions would be permanent; and they wanted—in fact argued that there was no other way of conciliating 'American and neutral sentiment'—true, real, and firm steps towards emancipation . And if, as a concession to war-time difficulties, emancipation itself might be left for the future, meanwhile, at the very least, as an earnest of good intentions, unrestricted right of domicile, the abolition of all restrictions on secondary and higher education, and an end to discrimination against foreign Jews travelling to Russia should all be instituted without delay. Their position, as put to the Russian Minister, was communicated to the Foreign Office[40] and subsequently backed to the hilt by the leaders of American Jewry as well.[41]

But to such demands there was—and in the nature of things political in Russia, there could be—no response. Worse, on the ground, within Russia, so far as the common people of Jewry were concerned, very little changed. The profound conviction that they were without legal protection, more than ever at the mercy of the whims of the meanest official and policeman, that they could be subject to court martial on the slightest suspicion and that nothing like serious proof of guilt need be adduced, all served only further to fuel older, still more deeply rooted fears and hostility to the authorities. And these grew steadily. A year later we find Motzkin writing of a general feeling in Russia that when the war ended things might well get even worse and that 'a catastrophe such as had never happened in history would occur. . . . [And] that it was not the possessions of the Jews anyone was now interested in, but their lives.'[42] As if to confirm Motzkin and his informants, we find the particularly well informed British Vice-Consul in Moscow reporting in much the same vein.

There seems no reason to doubt that the Jews are not only gravely discontented in consequence of the repressive measures of the last twelve months, but they are also in a state of considerable and not altogether unjustifiable fear of an outbreak of Jewish pogroms. There is also reason to believe that the Russian Government has been assiduously fostering anti-

[40] Memorandum by Wolf, 14 October 1915. BD, C 11/3/1/1.
[41] Louis Marshall to M. A. Guinzburg, 23 October 1915.
[42] Motzkin to Zionist Central Office, 12 May 1916. CZA, L6/88.

Semitic sentiments among the people, probably with a view to providing a safety valve for letting off some of the discontent which would otherwise fall on itself. . . .

That the Jews, as Jews, will be able to cause any serious trouble at the present moment is scarcely likely. The feeling of the country is against them, and a Jewish pogrom is far more probable than a revolutionary movement financed and fomented by Jews. The Jews can, however, and do act against the Russian Government in other ways. Needless repressive measures against the Jews at the present moment seem ill-timed, and the effect of a Jewish pogrom on public opinion in England and America might have far-reaching consequences.[43]

Finally, adding to the ever growing misery of the Jews of Russia and the ever more bitter relations between the Russian authorities and their Jewish subjects were two ostensibly extraneous factors. Polish nationalists, with a view to anticipated independence after the war and concerned about the large number of Jews who would certainly inhabit a free Poland however its borders were drawn, had already embarked on what was to prove their long and consistent campaign of anti-Semitic action, agitation, and incitement, some of the later fruits of which we shall see later. The Germans, for their part, now in occupation of large parts of Poland and western Russia, were beginning to make what they could of Jewish disaffection by encouraging it; and if, as the future would show, they had little or no intention of living up to the half-promises of emancipation and equal treatment which they were content to scatter, the effect, inevitably, was to deepen Russian suspicions and to cast the Jews virtually irrevocably in the twin roles of subversives and scapegoats. In sum, despite the great number (4–500,000) of Jews serving in the Russian armed forces, the entirely loyal conduct of the overwhelming majority of the Jewish civilians, and—as might be thought—the Russian Government's own direct interest in binding its subjects to it at least so long as the war lasted, the condition of Russo-Polish Jewry was now worse than before the war and steadily deteriorating. It was deteriorating, it was scandalous, it could not be hidden or—with any hope of success—denied, and it was on too large a scale and of too great an intensity not to have far-reaching political effects. Purely charitable action was continued: £200,000 were collected in Britain and the Empire for the relief of Russian Jewry at the end of

---

[43] Memorandum by R. H. Bruce Lockhart. Enclosure 2, Buchanan to Grey, 12 August 1915. Circulated to Cabinet. PRO, CAB 37/133.

1915, and appeals were repeated periodically. But the money was never either enough or directly relevant to the basic problems. If they were not to fail in their central, self-imposed task, the Jewish philanthropic organizations in the west could not refrain from applying as much political pressure as they dared, the more so as they were being continually pressed by representatives of Russian Jewry to ask for their Governments to intercede. And what was of greater and lasting significance, Allied Governments could not—in the interests of the effective prosecution of the war—entirely avoid taking direct notice themselves of what was taking place.

It was not only the internal unrest in Russia (about which they themselves could do nothing of substance) that worried them. It was the cumulative effect on public opinion in Great Britain and France in the first instance, and in the neutral countries, above all the United States, in the second, that was disturbing: an effect the Germans were at pains to strengthen and exploit.[44] There was the continuing embarrassment of claiming to be in conflict with militarist and despotic forces (the Central Powers) while being allied with what a representative figure of the moderate British left had once called 'a cruel despotism which is abhorrent to all thinking men'.[45] And if the exigencies of war and *raison d'état* served to damp down much of the resulting unease, even in the most liberal circles at home, abroad argument founded on the same wartime needs and *raison d'état* could lead equally in the opposite direction. This was especially the case, for particular and well-understood reasons, in the United States. For in the United States there were uniquely combined three crucial circumstances: vital sources of finance and military supply, a public substantially divided in its opinions on the merits of the belligerents and on the policy the United States should adopt, and a large, free, not uninfluential, and relatively uninhibited Jewish community.

Queried about the treatment of Russian Jewry, the Allied Ambassadors in Petrograd tended to play the matter down, or roundly deny mistreatment, or accept the Russian version of events as correct or at least reasonable: 'Since the beginning of the war

---

[44] In Ernst Müller-Meiningen, *Who are the Huns?*, a translation of a German propaganda vehicle *Der Weltkrieg und der Zusammenbruch des Völkerrechts* (Berlin, 1915) distributed in the United States, there is a chapter devoted to accounts of hangings, rape, expulsions, mutilation, arson and looting, and other Russian atrocities.

[45] F. W. Jowett (a Labour Member of Parliament), quoted in Max Beloff, *Lucien Wolf and the Anglo-Russian Entente 1907–1914* (London, 1951), p. 23.

Russian Jewry has suffered no collective violence whatsoever,' the French Ambassador firmly asserted. 'In the zone of operations a few hundred Jews have been hanged for espionage: that is all.'[46] His British colleague, took much the same line. But in Washington these matters took on different proportions and significance and at a very early stage of the war. True or false, these reports of mistreatment and the use the Germans were making of them were extremely damaging to the Allied cause, the French Ambassador (Jusserand) reported. Their repetition in many of the major newspapers was having its effect 'in a country where the Jews are powerful and numerous, forming *inter alia* 19% of the four or five million inhabitants of New York.'[47]

The British Ambassador (Spring Rice) was not as quick as his French colleague to see the connection between events in Russia and Jewish opinion in the United States, but he was never in doubt that Jewish opinion was very important, the Jews very powerful, and many of the Jewish notables pro-German. 'The German Jewish Bankers are toiling in a solid phalanx to compass our destruction,' he informed the Foreign Office in November 1914. 'Mr. Schiff, the head of the Jewish colony in New York, [is] an ardent admirer of Germany, which is the country of his origin,' he wrote Grey a fortnight later in connection with the movement for mediation between the belligerents and an end to the hostilities (which Schiff supported).[48] A few months later still he was a lot clearer in his mind about what really counted, so far as American Jewry was concerned.

It is very important indeed that the Jews who are a very strong element in the population here and even stronger than they are numerous, should not be hostile to us. The official chief of the Jewish party here, Mr. Schiff, is openly pro-German. I think the vast majority are pro-German or at any rate anti-Russian. Some of them however on political grounds and out of gratitude to England are very desirous that the Jewish Colony here should not compromise itself too much in favour of Germany. They very much wish that through the influence of the English and French Jews the Russian Government may be induced to make some concessions. This they regard as

---

[46] Paléologue to MFA, 4 February 1915. AE, Guerre 1914–1918, Sionisme, vol. 1197, p. 22.

[47] Jusserand to Delcassé, 26 January 1915. Ibid., pp. 16–17. See also Jusserand's dispatches, 20 November 1914, ibid., pp. 3–5; and 2 February 1915, p. 19.

[48] Spring Rice to Chirol, 13 November 1914. Stephen Gwynn (ed.), *The Letters and Friendships of Sir Cecil Spring Rice*, ii (London, 1929), p. 242; Spring Rice to Grey, 27 November 1914. PRO, CAB 37/122.

vital. Of course if we were to make this proposal to Russia we would not do the Jews much good and would do ourselves a great deal of harm. But they think that quietly and unoffically some steps might be taken at Petrograd. They are convinced that if the Russian Government would take action favourable to the Jews there would be a great revulsion of feeling here. It is significant that the principal Jewish journalists in New York, the editors of the 'Sun' and the 'Times', are strongly in favour of the Allies and they have done us a very great deal of good. But it is certainly true that the Jewish bankers are really acting for the Germans although they pretend to be neutral. The German Embassy lives almost entirely with the Jews and does most of its work through them. The most powerful German agent in Washington is Herr Warburg of the great Hamburg house, who is the most influential member of the Federal Reserve Board and has immense influence in the Treasury. The German Ambassador is constantly with him and through him is supposed to exert a great deal of influence over the head of the Treasury and over the financial part of the Administration. The Democratic party owing to its quarrel with the principal Christian bankers was thrown upon the Jewish rivals of Morgan and his friends for financial support and advice. This gives the Jewish community great influence in Washington and in addition to this they are certainly working all through the country, mainly in the German cause, and as they control the majority of the advertisements their influence is very great. It would be untrue to say that they are altogether on the German side but a very large number of them are and I am assured that one of the principal reasons for this is their dislike and fear of Russia. I think men like Montefiore and the Rothschilds could exercise a very salutary influence here by a timely message.[49]

Not everything Jusserand and Spring Rice reported and recommended was accepted without reservation, let alone acted upon. As the political and economic importance of the United States to the Allies became ever more evident, doubts as to their own personal suitability for so central a diplomatic role grew, as it happened, in both capitals. Nor was their assessment correct in every detail; and Spring Rice notably (Jusserand, a scholarly man and something of a historian, was both more precise and more sober) exaggerated Jewish influence and misconceived the degree and the ways in which such Jews as could throw political or financial or editorial weight into the balance in what they saw as the Jewish interest were

[49] Spring Rice to Primrose, 1 April 1915. PRO, FO 371/2559. Neil Primrose, Parliamentary Under-Secretary of State for Foreign Affairs, was of well-known lineage. His father was the Earl of Rosebery; his mother was a Rothschild. It is probable, but not certain, that Spring Rice had his maternal ancestry in mind when he addressed his recommendation that Jewish notables in England be impressed with the need to keep their American homologues in line specifically to him.

prepared to do so. Jacob Schiff could indeed be regarded as the most notable of the Jewish notables of the United States. As head of Kuhn, Loeb and Company, one of the two or three greatest investment banking houses in America at the time, he was very naturally the object of close attention by the Allies, hungry for loans. And Kuhn, Loeb was indeed put on the Allied black list as pro-German early in the war. But it was not on it for long, and the French, for their part (always more sensitive than the British to traces of pro-German feeling), soon came to regard the firm as being 'correctly neutral'. In 1916 it was regarded as positively favourable to the Allies. The real difficulty was to persuade Schiff to go beyond 'correct neutrality'. When in 1915 his firm was approached by Morgan with a view to collaborating in placing the great $500 million Anglo-French loan on the market, Schiff laid down conditions. He would agree to join the syndicate, as Jusserand later recalled, but only provided he could be assured that no part of the funds would go to the Russian Government 'whose attitude towards the Jews he judged contrary to the principles of humanity and justice. It being impossible to give an assurance on this matter, the House of Kuhn, Loeb refrained from joining the syndicate.' [50]

None the less, the essential validity of the ambassadorial theme— and it was one on which the two envoys were fundamentally in agreement— was questioned neither in London nor in Paris. It was very soon entered—with variations, as we shall see—into the accepted repertoire of political obstacles to an unimpeded pursuit of the war effort and as a matter to be dealt with, if possible by some form of counter-action. And reasonably so. In the upper reaches of American Jewish society as then constituted there was both some sympathy for the Germans and a great deal of resentment of the Russians, the latter sentiment tending strongly to reinforce and perpetuate the former. Jusserand's posthumous, quite respectful assessment of Schiff was correct: 'As a Jew he had ardently represented and supported in the United States the material and moral interests of his coreligionists. . . . German by origin and taste, he had retained very close ties with his first country, but he was before and above all else a Jew; his conduct at the time when the

[50] 'Note sur la maison Kuhn Loeb et Co. . . .', 17 June 1921. AE, Jusserand papers, box 33, Otto Kahn file, fos. 8–12. On just such grounds Schiff had been glad to render the Japanese financial services upon the outbreak of their war with Russia a decade earlier.

Anglo-French loan was floated showed this clearly.'[51] Indeed, it accorded entirely with the terms in which Schiff himself defined his position at the time.

My sympathies in this lamentable and terrible conflict are on the side of Germany, because I have not only been born and educated there, but because also my forbears have lived in Germany for many centuries. . . . Nevertheless, I have in reality no anti-English feeling, and am perfectly willing to concede that liberty—especially as far as the Jew is concerned—has in the past gained vastly more from England than from Germany, but whether this will be so in the future, with the venom and poison which the Russian Alliance appears to have already instilled into English feeling for the Jew, seems to be at least doubtful.[52]

Here, then, was the crack in the official wall through which the Jewish philanthropic organizations in Great Britain and France (but especially in the former)[53] could introduce their own arguments and expand them. The form the expansion took was, as we shall see, to press chiefly for thought, planning, and promises relating to the post-war period. This had advantages for all, even for the Russian authorities, if only, so it was argued, they could be persuaded to see the light. It seemed to offer a chance of exerting maximum pressure upon them while giving minimum offence and of compensating somewhat for the horrors of the war by holding out the promise of a new deal for the Jews when it was over. Plainly, if these matters were to be taken up at all, it would be at the eventual peace conference—subject, perhaps, to some quiet negotiation in the interim. Public representations and public action—to which there were objections all round—could be ruled out. But that said and that agreed, the argument that some immediate, limited improvement in the condition of the Jews, linked to a promise of eventual, radical improvement, would most certainly help the Allied cause remained a strong one. It was tenable in itself and it was consistent with the need, so powerfully felt by Wolf and his colleagues, to avoid 'the mistaken impression that we were pre-occupied by our denominational interests.'[54]

---

[51] Ibid. Schiff died in 1920.

[52] Schiff to Lucien Wolf, 14 June 1915. CZA, A77/3A.

[53] Broadly, French Jewry, as represented chiefly and notably by the AIU, was much more reluctant than its English analogue to press its Government in any direction but that in which it had already resolved to proceed.

[54] Wolf to Bigart (secretary of the AIU, Paris), 2 March 1915. ML, AJ/204/1.

That here too was the point at which, to the specific and inevitable post-war questions of the rights and status of the Jews in Russia and 'in the new and enlarged Poland' to come, there was added, as will be seen, 'the political future of Palestine'[55] at the hands of one of Zionism's firmest opponents is one of the many ironies that peppered the whole convoluted process whereby the question of a Jewish Palestine was restored to the agenda of the British Government.

[55] Ibid.

4

Disarray

It is important to recall that the Zionist movement was at a very low ebb in the period leading up to the Great War. Its institutional machinery was in working order: meetings great and small were held regularly, and in many countries, albeit often in difficult, sometimes semi-conspiratorial conditions; journals were published and distributed; problems were freely aired; plans were laid; work was done. But, as we have seen, its purposes and ambitions were now shrunken; its presence in Ereẓ-Israel—on which all thought and action had come to turn—was precarious; the mood of its members was increasingly sober, when not doubtful; and its accepted and elected leaders were, by and large, no better than mediocre, at all events dull. The livelier, not to say bolder (among them the more abrasive) spirits—Nordau, Zangwill, Greenberg, Ussishkin, Syrkin, Weizmann, Jabotinsky—had all either dropped out of the inner circle or, having failed to penetrate it, retreated to the periphery. The best of the new crop—Ruppin and Jacobson— were organization men, civil servants in a manner of speaking. In the shadows of his London exile, observing everything, commenting, advising those who would listen, but never venturing to take a public lead, there was Aḥad Ha-ʿAm. Only Sokolov remained at the centre to bridge the entire period from the pre-Herzlian beginnings: gifted, knowledgeable, dedicated, well-known, everything except of independent mind. And meanwhile, in Berlin itself, devotion to 'practical' affairs and to institutional and methodological consolid- ation was the order of the day. It suited the temperament and quality of the EAC over which Warburg presided (and which he typified), and was perhaps as much as could be expected.

The problems set the Zionist movement by the outbreak of war were thus extraordinarily severe. It put it to what might well be thought the ultimate test, namely that of its capacity, as a movement claiming primacy within the nation, to recover from shock, to reconsider its ways in the light of altered circumstances, and to restore order and direction when put initially to disarray. Flexibility, imagination, originality, and boldness of mind, rather than bureaucratic doggedness, solidity, and prudence, were now at a premium. Of course, that the established leaders were not prepared for the titanic conflict engulfing Europe, nor for the ensuing desolation, is not, in itself, surprising. They were neither less nor more perceptive than the general run of literate, publicly minded men and women of their generation within Jewry and outside it. And the failure of nerve and imagination they were to exhibit was compounded by a failure of structure. The effect of the war was to make it exceedingly difficult to initiate change, far more difficult than in the case of the government of a settled nation. The institutions by which the Zionist movement had governed itself since Herzl's time collapsed, as we shall see. Always slow-moving and awkward—except when dominated by Herzl himself—they were now revealed as hopelessly inelastic in form and spirit when faced with issues of extreme gravity and unquestioned urgency.

The hardest problem which the war set the EAC was whether or not to break free once and for all from the cardinal, very ancient rule of conduct in Jewish public affairs that Jews as a category and Jewry as a group should strive to avoid involvement in the conflicts of other nations—of *the nations* (*ha-goyim*), as the Jews traditionally termed them. As individuals they might have to take sides; they might even wish to do so. But the more violent the conflict, the greater its scale, and the more comprehensive the class of Jews liable to be sucked into it, the greater the corresponding dangers for all. For Jewry to side with one major protagonist against another was to play for perilously high stakes. In the end it was to risk betrayal whatever the result. The ancient rule was, therefore, to keep away and aloof so far as possible, to keep communal heads down until the storm had blown itself out, to assert neutrality in principle and to cleave to it in practice. If it was not a rule that could always be followed, it was always in mind, an unquestioned element of the conventional wisdom: Jewish public policy had necessarily to be prudential; deviations were always and everywhere deeply suspect.

No doubt, Zionism itself, in this regard, was in the nature of a venture into dangerous territory—and here lay not the least of the reasons for opposition to it. Herzl's argument that Zionism entailed no perils for the Jewish people because it could be shown to be in the interests of *all* parties operating in the central international political arena to render the Zionists assistance had never carried much conviction outside the circle of his closest adherents. The counter-argument—that as Zionism was political in nature and had political purposes it was bound sooner or later to make choices and enter into conflict—had always made much more sense to many more people. In the event, neither Herzl nor his successors had ever had to make a clear-cut international-political decision, least of all one that would have made them party to a major inter-state conflict; and it had been one of the hidden attractions of the 'practical' school that it seemed greatly to reduce the likelihood of Zionism being faced with really difficult political choices, energies being run in safer channels. It might even be said that the Zionists' success thus far in avoiding true political dilemmas was no more than the measure of their failure to make progress in the real political world—to which, on any interpretation of their purpose and ethos, they had never had any choice but to belong. One way or another, the war ended this age of innocence.

The deepest root of the change lay in the constant, fundamental circumstance that the Jews were a dispersed people: citizens (or subjects) of different states, members of different kinds of communities. The Zionists were Jewish nationalists and the Jewish people, as such, sought no quarrel with anyone. But for a great many purposes this availed them little or nothing. In the first place, the content of Jewish *national* feeling relative to other political, ethnic, and cultural sentiments varied from place to place in quality and intensity and even in clarity; and the degree to which it operated as a prime determinant of political outlook and identification varied enormously too. But, of course, regardless of outlook and sympathy, nationalist or otherwise, the Jews of Europe were drawn into the war willy-nilly along with most other Europeans and made to bear its impact no less (and in some cases more) grievously than others. Thus as soldiers (some 1.5 million serving in the various belligerent forces at roughly double their proportion in the population of the relevant countries as a whole);[1] and thus, as we have seen, as

---

[1] A. G. Duker, 'Jews in the World War'. *Contemporary Jewish Record*, ii: 5, September-October, 1939.

civilians harried (or worse) by the same great armies ploughing through, and fighting for, the lands of their settlement. But again, the response to conflict and the call to arms varied from country to country. Jews called to the Russian colours did their duty, by and large, but served their Tsar with little goodwill. In contrast, central and west European Jews tended strongly to be loyal not only in deed but in spirit.

Of none was this truer than of the German Jews; none were more anxious than they (except perhaps for the French) to prove their loyalty; none were more pained by (wholly false) charges voiced from time to time, even in exalted circles, that, as a class, they were shirking their duty to the Fatherland.[2] And in this respect, German Zionists, almost to a man, were at one with their compatriots within the German Jewish community as whole.[3] Perhaps this was to be expected. In any event, upon the soil of national *German* feeling to which virtually everything else—culture, habit, environment— predisposed them, concern both for the wretched Jews of eastern Europe and for the interests of the movement took a particular shape. One result was to convert the hitherto *incidental* German character of the main operational headquarters of Zionism into one of large and immediate significance.

The line distinguishing and separating the Zionist Central Office which served the movement world-wide from the Zionist country organization for Germany, the Zionistische Vereinigung für Deutschland (ZVfD), had long ceased to be a clear one. The seat of

---

[2] At one point in the war the German military authorities instituted a count of Jewish soldiers and casualties (the so-called *Judenzählung*).After the war, and as the atmosphere in Germany grew ever more poisoned, the association of German Jewish ex-servicemen published their own meticulous count of Jewish war dead complete with names and regimental affiliations. They found that of the some 555,000 Jewish inhabitants of Imperial Germany, 100,000 had served in the armed forces and 12,000 had died. The Jews being preponderantly urban, German Jewry's contribution should be compared, they thought, to that of the population of the city of Munich, numbering 645,000. They found that 13,700 citizens of Munich had fallen; and that the proportion of war dead to total population in the two groups, Münchner and Jews, was therefore precisely the same: 2.1 per cent. The compilation by the Reichsbund Jüdischer Frontsoldaten, *Die jüdischen Gefallenen des deutschen Heeres, der deutschen Marine und der deutschen Schutztruppen 1914–1918; ein Gedenkbuch* (Berlin, 1932), 423 pp., appeared with a brief preface by Hindenburg.

[3] A now well-known but at the time exceedingly rare exception was the young Gershom Scholem. It may be said, however, that his refusal to succumb to the general patriotic euphoria (and to the pressure of his immediate environment) owed more to his pacifist, semi-anarchist views than to his concurrent groping for a satisfactory Jewish identity.

the EAC had been in Germany since 1905 and in Berlin itself since 1911, as we have seen. The two institutions shared the same premises at Sächsischestrasse and, to some extent, the same personnel. Their working methods and language were the same. Leading figures of one could be found playing a prominent role in the other. It is not too much to say that they had developed a semi-symbiotic relationship. But that said, the identification of Zionism with things German, so far as it went, was not one with the German state. Since the failure of Herzl's attempt to enter into a political relationship with the German Reich no one had thought seriously of repeating it. Nor was there any sign of political interest in Zionism on the German side. Some of the more suspicious and ill-informed of the enemies of Germany thought there was more to the presence of the Zionist headquarters on German soil than met the eye. But there was not—at all events, not before the war transformed the situation in the eyes of many German Zionists and, marginally, in the eyes of the German authorities as well.

The impact of the outbreak of war upon the Zionists, as on so many other German Jews, was electric. In his first, comprehensive message to them, their president, Arthur Hantke (who doubled as a member of the EAC) predictably set the 'preservation of our Palestinian undertakings' as the Actions Committee's first concern, lamented the breakdown of communications with other branches of the movement, and spelled out some of the steps taken to keep things going. But he also asserted that he was especially proud to report that 'our friends in the movement have, without exception, fulfilled their duty by the German Fatherland. The members of the Zionist Federation of Germany have demonstrated practical patriotism [*Patriotismus der Tat*] in exemplary manner.' And while the Jewish Question would still be posed after the war, he believed relations between Jews and non-Jews would improve as a consequence of the 'heightened nationalism of all nations' which was evident all round.[4]

Equally powerful in the impression it made upon German Jews, Zionists and others, was the circumstance that Germany, with its allies, was fighting *Russia*, that it was pushing the Russian forces out of the western parts of the Tsar's empire, and that it bid fair to establish a new political and territorial order in eastern Europe. Whatever private reservations there may have been here and there about German conduct and German intentions, there was no doubt

[4] Circular to branches, 26 August 1914. CZA, A126/41/4.

in any Jewish mind (but least of all in the minds of German Jews) that German rule or influence was preferable to Russian. In any event, the naked fact was that German armies were moving into the parts of Europe that were most densely populated by the *Ostjuden*— the very people the western Zionists had from the beginning sought to succour; and Germany itself, perhaps, was cast for the role of liberator and emancipator of Russo-Polish Jewry. 'We feel pride in the thought,' wrote Hantke, 'that through the victory of German and Austrian arms . . . the Jews of the East will be set free from Tsarism.'[5] In the first flush of military success in the east, it seemed to many that it was the positive duty of German Jewry to work with and through the occupation authorities to ensure the eastern Jews humane and generous treatment, and that none were better placed to perform it than the Zionists. Not all German Zionists were convinced that they should project themselves directly into eastern Europe, but there were enough who were so convinced for a position to be established from which it would be difficult to make a complete retreat when, after more mature consideration, its political implications came to be judged undesirable.

Thirdly, there was the *yishuv*. It was evident from the beginning that it would be in difficulties. It soon became apparent that these would be very great. Turkish rule in Palestine, now a region of military operations, was changing in character and so far as its inhabitants were concerned, Arabs no less than Jews, for the worse. It was far from certain how long the Turkish administration under its new regional overlord, Djemal Pasha, Governor and Commander-in-Chief of Syria and Palestine ('an ambitious and unscrupulous megalomaniac', in one observer-historian's view[6]) would tolerate a large population of suspect enemy aliens, if at all. So, on the face of it, there were advantages in the director of the Zionist local office, Arthur Ruppin, being a national of the country that was Turkey's principal ally and the headquarters to which Ruppin reported being in Berlin. It might be possible—it would soon be necessary—for the Zionists to employ their German connections to help save the *yishuv* from the decimation that seemed to threaten. At the very least, they would have to press for intercession by the German Embassy in Constantinople to protect the *yishuv* from the high-handed and impatient Turkish military

---

[5] Ibid.
[6] A. P. [Lord] Wavell, *The Palestine Campaigns* (London, 1928). p. 28.

administration in its quest for supplies for man and beast, easy thoroughfare, and safety from real and imagined hostile elements in the rear.

But as the war progressed, even the enthusiasts in Berlin began to see that it was far from clear where the true balance of advantages lay. Neither the interests of Jewry—if these could be defined with precision—nor those of the Zionists specifically were, or could be, coincident with those of Germany. There might be much harm, moreover, in people, Jews and others, thinking that they were. The ability of Warburg and his associates in Berlin, of Lichtheim (who had replaced Jacobson) in Constantinople, and of Ruppin in Jaffa to protect and sustain the *yishuv* proved to be severely limited. The role of the American envoy in Constantinople, Henry Morgenthau, through whom much aid was channelled (not only from the United States, but from Great Britain as well[7]) was of equal weight, if not more, and depended crucially on the goodwill and the *neutrality* of the United States. Even the Russians played a part, for reasons of their own,[8] in the effort to keep the *yishuv* from withering under the combined burden of alien status, loss of markets for produce, military requisitioning, and a never-ending series of sanctions, punitive measures, and both explicit and implicit threats. The Bank was closed down, so were some of the schools; notables were arrested (some later freed, some deported); farm animals and carts were seized; and as reports of the fate of the Armenians began to filter through, fear that a similar disaster awaited the country's Jews began to take hold. Within a year some ten thousand members of the *yishuv* were obliged to leave. To add to their other trials, the country suffered a plague of locusts. Morale dropped catastrophically. 'We are intellectually humbled and economically done for,' one exile reported to the Zionist Central Office.[9] By the middle of 1916 it was estimated in Jerusalem (very roughly, no doubt), that of the some eighty thousand members of the total Jewish population of the

[7]   With the sanction of the British Government. Primrose (Foreign Office) to Gaster, 18 March 1915. CZA, A18/41/2/4.

[8]   'Considering that a weakening of Russian Jewry in Palestine is highly undesirable from the point of view of Russian state interests,' it was decided in Petrograd to take a forgiving view of Russian subjects who were obliged to acquire Ottoman citizenship and to seek the agreement of the British authorities for the temporary settlement in a neighbouring territory of those compelled to leave. Sazonov to Goremykin, 30 December 1914 (OS). CZA, L6/31II.

[9]   Lurie to Central Office, 21 November 1915. Confidential circular, 23 December 1915. CZA, L6/18/1.

country no less than three-quarters were in need of relief.[10] 'The situation in Palestine was frightful,' wrote Jabotinsky after his extended stay with the exiles in Alexandria. 'The mood was just as it was in Odessa in the week before the pogrom.'[11]

Similarly, it became evident after a while—and ever more clearly as the war continued—that the German Government and German military had limited interest in and no particular sympathy for the Jews of Poland and Russia. They were prepared to exploit the anti-Russian sentiment of the Jews. They sought to incite them to insurrection in Russian-controlled territory and to ensure as fair a welcome as possible for the invading German troops—which in fact was generally given spontaneously. 'In the early days of the German occupation,' one close observer noted, 'the Jewish populace of Warsaw was struck by a kind of madness, a joyful madness at having been released from Russian slavery.'[12] But once in occupation the Germans took a hard line—if still less brutal than that of the Russians—and they distinguished sharply from the first between those territories slated for annexation and those for some other, still undefined regime. In the former, the so-called *Land Oberost* (Das Land des Oberbefehlshabers Ost, i.e. Lithuania, Courland, and the areas immediately to the east of Prussia) the general call for a Jewish insurrection issued by the German General Staff in August 1914 (beginning: 'Der Tag der Freiheit ist endlich auch für die Juden Russlands angebrochen.'[13]) was not intended to apply.[14] What was instituted was a German military regime in which no ethnic, let alone independent, political sentiment was encouraged among any of the major national groups: Lithuanians, Poles, Jews, Latvians, or Byelorussians. In the other territories, the largest and politically most important component of which was the Polish heartland, it

---

[10] 'Palestine Report', 31 August 1916. CZA, L6/18II.

[11] Jabotinsky to Bernstein, 4 May 1915. CZA, Z3/88. On Jabotinsky's activities in Alexandria and upon his return to Europe, see below, pp. 143 ff. The reference is to the pogrom in Odessa in October 1905 which left over 300 dead and 5,000 wounded. See *Formative Years*, pp. 387–8.

[12] Yizhak Nissenboim, '*Alei ḥeldi* (Warsaw, 1929), p. 323. Nissenboim went on to remark that 'for once my heart was not with our people. I could not see the reason for joy. We had not been let out to freedom, but passed from one slavery to another; and who could tell if the later would not prove harder than the earlier?'

[13] 'An die Juden Russlands'. I. Friedman, 'The Austro-Hungarian Government and Zionism: 1897–1918', *Jewish Social Studies*, 27 (1965), App. I, p. 248.

[14] On this subject see especially Egmont Zechlin, *Die deutsche Politik und die Juden im Ersten Weltkrieg*, (Göttingen, 1969), chapter 6, 'Die Ostjuden in der deutschen Revolutionierungspolitik', pp. 116–25.

soon dawned on the more sober observers[15] that if any post-war concessions were to be made to the national sentiment of the subject peoples it was the Poles who stood to be the first beneficiaries. Moreover, the strongest tendency amongst the Poles themselves, even the Austrian Poles, by and large, was towards Russia, rather than to the Central Powers, on the grounds that most Poles were Russian subjects and that if there was to be national political union, it would probably have to be in some form of association with still undefeated Russia. What the fate of the Jews would be under such a regime could be imagined only very dimly, but it was likely, so all informed Jewish observers thought, to be exceedingly disagreeable. Here then, on reflection, were reasons to doubt whether Germany was the power to rely upon, and deeper reasons yet to refrain from public identification with either side. The results for eastern Jewry might be disastrous.

Finally, there were the stark facts that a large part of Jewry was caught up in a conflict that was not theirs and that great holes had been punched in the frail and uncertain network of communication by which the major communities and the leading figures of Jewry had maintained a form of consultation for half a century. Hantke might hope privately that, being compelled to fight one another, the Jews would end by finding their own virtually extinguished national sentiment rekindled by this 'last consequence of Exile being before their eyes'.[16] For few of his contemporaries could this have been more than a doubtful consolation. Most put this ultimate horror of the war out of their minds. As for the informal supra-communal system established for the co-ordination and dispensation of philanthropy, it was clear enough that the primary responsibility would now shift from war-divided Europe to neutral America. There, the steadily growing Jewish community was both affluent enough by virtue of the economic and financial achievements of its established members and close enough in sentiment to the Europeans, thanks to the newcomers within it, to be poised for the leading role. But for the Zionist movement—which, alone in Jewry, sought to define and promote *non*-charitable national interests— there could be no such shifting of major responsibility to other shoulders even as a temporary measure. It had to set a policy and

[15] Hantke among them. See his confidential circular, 12 November 1914. CZA, A126/41/4.

[16] Ibid.

lay down a course of action which would, at a minimum, do no violence to the essential needs of its constituents in all parts, maintain its existing structures, and prepare the movement for the political and social changes that would undoubtedly follow the war. If it did not, it would have abdicated its self-determined role. But was the minimum enough? Was it wise, was it even possible, to play for safety, to lie low, to wait for the storm to pass? Would not developments in the course of the war not go far to determine the political lay of the land when it was over? Did not strict non-identification and political self-abnegation sharply reduce the chance of a serious hearing at the great international conference that was likely to be convened at war's end and determine the settlement? Had the neutrality of the Zionists not been compromised already? In any event, if neutrality was the proper watchword, what did it entail in practice?

ii

When the shrunken Actions Committee[17] assembled for its first wartime meeting in the neutral capital, Copenhagen, early in December 1914, the effects of the war were fully apparent. Travel restrictions, fear of (or explicit prohibition on) 'intelligence with the enemy', and direct involvement by some in the war all played a part: of the six members of the Smaller Actions Committee (EAC), only four appeared; of the twenty-four members of the Greater Actions Committee (GAC) only five were willing and able to turn up.[18] This was awkward: the quorum had been set at eight members of the GAC over and above the EAC; the gathering was therefore formally without authority to take serious, binding decisions. But in the event, none of those present were unduly concerned by the irregularity, and the rump Actions Committee settled rapidly on non-involvement in the affairs of the belligerents as the sole principle

---

[17] The term 'Actions Committee' is used here, as was customary at the time, to denote the EAC and the GAC jointly when the two functioned as a single body.

[18] None of the three figures who were to play particularly important roles in the period to follow, Weizmann, Sokolov, and Jabotinsky, were present. Nor was Nordau. Sokolov was a member of the EAC, Weizmann of the GAC. Jabotinsky belonged to neither, but as a delegate to the last Congress held before the war he belonged to a larger, looser body, the 'Central Committee' which, in principle, could be called together as an interim Congress. Nordau, had he been invited and had he been willing and able to attend (there were recurrent efforts to draw him into the wartime affairs of the movement), would have been there in his own right, as the movement's grand old man.

of conduct on which all could agree. 'Neutrality' would be the key
term and concept; and early, ostensibly ill thought-out deviations
from it were denounced. The Russians had been particularly
incensed by the involvement of Bodenheimer, Hantke, and other
German Zionists in a group set up with other German-Jewish
notables at the outbreak of war to help make the best of the passing
of large parts of eastern Europe into German hands and act as a
recognized lobby on behalf of German Jewry: the Committee for the
Eastern Jews. The Committee had already gone through several
reconstructions and changes of name; but no reordering of its affairs
could alter what the Russians very reasonably judged its comprom-
ising nature. The German Zionists appeased their wrath by
announcing Bodenheimer's resignation from the chairmanship of
the Jewish National Fund; and the meeting approved a firm and
formal resolution condemning 'the participation of leading Zionists
in endeavours liable to endanger the security of Jews in any of the
countries at war'. However to the question what then should be
done in practice to alleviate the plight of east European Jewry
(discussed at length and reported on in particularly dark terms by
Tchlenov) there was no clear answer. Nor was there one to the
linked question, how and in what degree and on what terms should
the Zionists co-operate with other Jewish organizations that were
trying to help. Nor again was there a clear response to the old
dilemma which now, in an especially acute form, underlay the
general confusion of mind: where did the Zionists' priorities lie, in
Europe or in Erez-Israel? The wording of the delegates' formal
decision merely encapsulated the issue. Zionism, they resolved,
aimed 'at the fulfilment of the Jewish people's national demands on
the basis of concurrent work for our Palestine programme and for
the attainment of equal rights in those countries where these are not
yet possessed.'

Nor did any of this really dispose of the question what neutrality
for Zionism should actually entail. Least of all did it dispose of the
question that crucially epitomized the problem, had high symbolic
and no small practical significance, and, remarkably and exceptionally, was within the power of the delegates to resolve: the location of
the EAC for the duration of the war. It cannot be said that it was
shirked. The delegates were informed that Nordau had recommended that it be moved to the United States. They were aware that
at the end of August the American Zionists had formed a new body,

the 'Provisional Executive Committee for General Zionist Affairs', with the eminent lawyer Louis Brandeis as chairman, and had boldly proposed that they take over the management of the movement until such time as the Actions Committee was able to function properly. '[Shmarya] Levin and Provisional Committee insist absolutely necessary Central Bureau be temporarily in United States as neutral land and second largest Jewish center[.] Therefore imperative Tchlenov and either Sokolov or Jacobson come immediately,' was Brandeis's peremptory telegraphic message to them.[19] But there is no evidence that either proposal was seriously considered. A plan to remove the EAC to a neutral capital in Europe was discussed but turned down, chiefly, it seems, because Warburg objected. His grounds for staying put were that such a move was liable to be interpreted in Berlin as anti-German;[20] and he—which is to say, his residual authority—carried the day. Tchlenov, who three months earlier had been strongly of the view that the Zionist leadership needed to be 'reconstructed provisionally' in a neutral country,[21] did not now insist. Whether the delegates understood at the time that by letting Warburg have his way they were abandoning whatever chance they may ever have had of cleaving successfully, let alone profitably, to a policy—and posture—of strict neutrality is unclear. What is almost certain is that they did not realize at the time that by leaving the Zionist headquarters in Germany they had gone a long way towards compounding the disruption of the war: converting a reasonably well centralized organization into little more than a confederation of both well- and ill-defined groups that would grow steadily looser under the impact of the centrifugal forces set off by the war. They only sought to soften the immediate implications of their decision by approving a series of

[19] Brandeis to Tarschis, 8 November 1914. TP. Moritz Tarschis of Stockholm served briefly, until the Copenhagen Office got going, as the link man for correspondence between the various branches of the movement. Shmarya Levin, a member of the EAC, was in the United States when war broke out. Initially unable to return to Europe, he was induced to remain and work with the American Zionists.

[20] The other side of this particular coin was that in the course of time the Central Office in Berlin, in its contacts with the German bureaucracy, was able to refer to the Wilhelmstrasse's favourable view of the Organization as one working in the German interest. Warburg to Police Presidency, Berlin, 28 September 1915. CZA, Z3/501. For an example of the view in the German diplomatic service that Zionism did have its uses, see 'Exposé betreffend Dr Rosenblüth', Copenhagen to Berlin, 19 August 1915. Auswärtiges Amt, 130, D IV 4.

[21] Jabotinsky to Central Office, Berlin, 4 September 1914. CZA, Z3/86.

'fact-finding' missions by leading figures in the movement to the major belligerent capitals to which the EAC as such had just denied itself access, namely to London and Paris, and to the neutral United States as well. To service these missions a liaison office would be set up in a neutral country.[22] Denmark was judged more convenient than The Netherlands and it was not long before a Zionist liaison office was open and functioning in Copenhagen under Motzkin's direction. It was a cumbersome arrangement at best, but this at least can be said: it provided an essential link between the various branches of the movement for as long as the war lasted.

What was certainly not immediately apparent, although soon to be revealed, was that it was not only the institutional but the political structure of the organizations that had been changed. The established Zionist leadership had, at a stroke, departed from what passed for the commanding heights of the movement. Before the war, major issues had always been thrashed out in assemblies at all levels, in the movement's press, in private and official correspondence, and, above all, face-to-face. Now when the issues were of unprecedented gravity and when all business was urgent, when the barriers to private and public communication were severe, and when the fate of both the movement itself and the *yishuv* was likely, as all felt, to be in the balance, the elected leadership had entrenched itself in a position in which it could neither make policy freely nor freely promote such a policy as it had made. The results were disastrous not only for the prestige of the central institutions of the Zionist Organization, but for its internal discipline as well— grounded, as it had always been, on the habit of looking ultimately to the centre: if not always for guidance, then at least for coherence. In a voluntary movement in which all were free to come and go and no means of compelling obedience or conformity were available (or, indeed, had ever been sought or envisaged) the effect was the virtual dissolution of the delicate threads that had held the whole intricate, but loose, indeed rather delicate structure together. And as the authority of the EAC waned, so, inevitably, the energy with which the independent, dissident spirits within the movement struck out on their own in defiance and growing disregard of Warburg and his colleagues grew.

[22] GAC minutes, 3–6 December 1914. CZA, L6/371. See also the detailed, often acid comments of Jean Fischer, one of the delegates. Circular letter by Fischer, 14 December 1914. CZA, Z3/450.

Subsequent meetings of the Actions Committee illustrate these trends with some precision. The first attempt in 1915 to reconvene it failed totally: only two of the twenty-four members of the GAC were prepared to turn up at the appointed time and place.[23] When the Committee did meet finally on 10–11 June of that year in Copenhagen the attendance was no better than in the previous December. Neither the large Austrian nor the very small but increasingly important British branch of the movement were represented. But at least, along with Warburg and Hantke coming from Berlin, the notables of Russian Zionism were present in force: Ussishkin, Tchlenov, Jacobson, Goldberg, Motzkin, and Rosov. No policy changes were made: the principle of neutrality was reconfirmed, the fact-finding missions to the major capitals were to continue, the German Zionists were to lie low in the German-occupied territories of Russia. Once again, the Committee failed to make up its mind on the forms of co-operation with non-Zionists in matters of general Jewish concern. The mood was cautious, as before, the intention was preservative—the more so as the delegates now knew they were under attack.

The subject of liveliest discussion at this session of the Actions Committee was what already amounted to a public rebellion against their authority. For in the meantime, as we shall see, there had developed on the Organization's periphery—within the movement, but in open opposition to its constituted leadership—a move to form a Jewish Legion to join the Allied armies in the anticipated campaign to wrest Palestine from the Turks. To the Committee's collective mind, this was intolerable both on political and constitutional grounds. Such an undertaking, its members were agreed— and so asserted in uncharacteristically fierce language—stood in 'glaring contradiction to the whole character of the Zionist enterprise'. The Zionist Organization would have nothing to do with it, they stated, and they enjoined all Zionists from lending it support. Unquestionably, here was both a breaking of ranks and a violation of the principles of neutrality—with a vengeance. They could hardly fail to denounce it. On the other hand, it was far from clear to Warburg and his colleagues, even to the stronger-minded Russian Zionists in session with him, just what it was they could do about the rebellion. What they had anticipated when it had first broken out and what they still hoped for was that the movement for

[23] EAC circulars, 26 February and 10 March 1915. CZA, L6/371.

a Legion would fade of its own accord for lack of support. Their concluding decision at this their June 1915 meeting was therefore to keep their powerfully worded resolution to themselves for the time being, that is within the leadership circle itself. They hoped that, speaking softly about it or not at all, they might contribute indirectly to the project's ultimate collapse.

In the event, as we shall see, the soft line had no effect on the rebels and only a limited one on third parties. Motzkin, writing from Copenhagen to plead with the editor of the *Jewish Chronicle* to play the matter down,[24] could do some good, but not much and not for long: the campaign for all-Jewish units in the British army was public and newsworthy, certainly in London. The argument (one of those circulated) that because the movement had to be prepared for 'all eventualities' it must avoid any move that smacked of 'political adventurism' implied the elevation of inaction to a rule of conduct. And if the assertion that the important thing, when the time came, was to be in a position to state that the Zionist Organization really represented 'the masses of the Jewish people'[25] was one no Zionist would deny, as a response to rebellion it could only be taken as an infallible sign that the Actions Committee's loss of nerve, as well as of authority, was well advanced.

Meanwhile, the diversion of energies and confusion of mind precipitated by the upheaval of world war continued to eat away in other ways at the old simplicities and undermine the ever less effective efforts of those who might be termed the old guard of the 'practical school of Zionism' to keep everyone and everything in line. What was particularly worrying for the veterans of the long fight for the establishment of settlement work in Erez-Israel as Zionism's absolute priority was to see the enterprise in Erez-Israel receding from the vision of the Zionists of all ranks and degrees of involvement and commitment still living in Europe—much the larger proportion of the movement's membership. The causes were plain. On the one hand, the *yishuv* had lost something of its role of vanguard of Zionism (and the nation) and taken on much of the character of a community in straits: one more community on the list of those to which general Jewish philanthropy had to direct its attention and assistance. On the other hand, there was the huge rise and extension of distress in Europe and an inevitable diversion of

[24] 29 June 1915. CZA, A18/40/2.
[25] 24 and 26 October 1915. CZA, L6/18/1.

human and material resources by Zionists (as by others) anxious to mitigate it. This was notably the case in Austria, where successive waves of refugees pouring in from the war zones of Galicia and Bukovina cried out for relief. None could argue against bending all public energy in this new direction, but it was difficult for those who long had a set and very particular conception of Zionism not to see their view of it implicitly under threat all over again. Ussishkin, never one to mince words or soften the outlines of a dilemma, put his view of it bluntly: the plight of millions in the Diaspora should not lead Zionists to forget the one hundred thousand in Erez-Israel. True, there was a 'Jewish duty' to help the people in Europe; but there was a 'national duty' to stand by the *yishuv*/[26]

When the Actions Committee next met in March 1916, with a year and a half of the war behind them (and a rather different set of delegates in attendance[27]), the cumulative effect this continuing uncertainty and loss of direction, of known and recorded false moves, and of a mounting sense of frustration and loss of control all round was fully in evidence. The mood was tense, tempers were short. The twin issues of whether or not it had been a fatal error to leave the EAC in Germany and so entangle it with the policy and cause of the Central Powers and whether it was not too late to move it elsewhere were now very hotly debated, Jacobus Kann leading the attack. The ground for the original decision to stay put was gone over again: Germany's hegemonic position in central and eastern Europe, the interests of the *yishuv* and of east European Jewry, the likely response in Berlin if the EAC were removed. Not all were willing to accept that, on balance, it had been an error to remain in Germany. Almost all (Kann was the principal exception) felt that even if it had been, it was too late to correct it. But there was hardly a man present who did not express discomfort and irritation at the

[26] Copenhagen to Central Office, Berlin, 4 November 1915. CZA, L6/88; and circular letter from Copenhagen, 15 February 1916. CZA, L6/18/1.

[27] Meeting at The Hague, 23–24 March 1916, were Warburg, Hantke, and Jacobson for the EAC, seven of the twenty-four members of the GAC, and eight others (delegates to the last pre-war Congress). On this occasion, none of the leading Russian Zionists were present, nor were any of the English, nor was Nordau. Under the rules, the three categories formed the so-called Central Committee, a substitute or interim Congress (see above, n. 18). But 8 out of a possible 540 (the number of delegates at the Eleventh Congress held in 1913) was an absurdly small proportion and Berlin's decision to bend the rules and refuse to invite the principal proclaimed rebel against their authority, Jabotinsky (Berlin to Copenhagen. 27 December 1915. CZA, L6/37 II) did nothing to offset the 'rump' character of the gathering.

predicament they were now in: the Actions Committee had been too timid; it had allowed itself to be swept along by events; it had no policy; it was far from seeing the situation of the *yishuv* in its true, hard light. So far as the future was concerned, none ventured to suggest how the war was likely to end, although the tendency was to think the Central Powers had the upper hand; and none were hopeful. If Palestine came under Russian or French rule, things would assuredly go badly for the Zionists, one delegate volunteered; if under the British, things might be better, but the British, for their own special reasons, were bound to favour the Arabs; so too would the Turks if they remained in Palestine after all. Meanwhile the Turks still ruled the country and it was essential that the Zionists conduct themselves loyally and pick no quarrels with them. It was equally a fact that a very large part of Jewry was now under German control. The debate came full circle.

Once again the Actions Committee resolved to avoid change. The EAC would remain in Berlin, the Copenhagen office would be limited to liaison, the various country organizations would be asked once more to refrain from making policy on their own. No new ideas were raised, no reformulations of position proposed, no plan to reassert real as opposed to formal leadership outlined. The delegates took a brief look forward beyond war's end: preparations for the peace conference-to-be would be taken in hand, they decided, and thought would be given to the great migratory move of Jews out of eastern Europe that all expected to follow. That was all.[28] The Zionist movement, its elected leaders had resolved in all but so many words, had no choice but to sit out the war and hope for the best.

iii

Inert in essence, the position adopted by the official Zionist leadership was not entirely devoid of strength. Stripped of niceties, its force lay in the fact that it accorded well with the Jewish tradition of extreme circumspection in public affairs. To assail it was not only, in the nature of the case, to propose a venture into dangerous and unknown territory; it was to go against the very grain of custom. More, to oppose it publicly was to call down anger and obloquy from virtually all quarters—to be the object of a general fury that was all the greater for it being rooted ultimately in fear. In this

[28] GAC minutes, 23–24 March 1916. CZA, L6/37 II.

respect, covert opposition was safer. But secrecy and indirection in politics are wasting assets at best. They require for their effective exploitation, even in the short term, operational methods of a complexity, not to say deviousness, to which the Zionists had not thus far resorted and to which remarkably few among them were in any degree suited. So if it was soon evident to many that official Zionist policy bore a fatal stamp of poverty of thought and spirit—so much so that, as the war progressed, Warburg and his closest colleagues came almost to be forgotten by the movement at large—active opposition to it was initially the work of no more than a handful of notably bold and original, in other words rash and impertinent, souls. Four of the 'activists', as the most consistent and pugnacious of the rebels chose to call themselves, stood out: Yosef Trumpeldor (1880–1920), Pinḥas Rutenberg (1879–1942), Meir Grossman (1888–1964),[29] and the leading figure in the campaign, the very symbol of the movement for change, Ze'ev (Vladimir) Jabotinsky (1880–1940). What they had in common principally was the double conviction that the Zionists must declare openly for the Allies and that deeds must follow words in the shape of a Jewish fighting force as an integral component of the Allied armies. But not that alone.

It is of some interest that while, on the face of it, all four, like so many others of their fellows in the Zionist movement, were members of the Russian-Jewish intelligentsia, there is an important respect in which they were atypical of it. None had grown to manhood in a truly traditional Jewish environment, none had a command or even substantial knowledge of the Talmudic and rabbinical texts, familiarity with which is the hallmark of specifically Jewish learning. All had set their minds on secular education. For all four the fundamental language (and therefore culture) was Russian, not Yiddish or Hebrew. Jabotinsky, it is true, was in some ways an exception: he acquired modern Hebrew thoroughly, whereas the others never quite mastered it. But it remains, and it is fundamental, that none were in any sense *maskilim*. And finally they differed from the great majority of Russian Zionists—and, indeed, the general run of Russian Jews—in the further, striking respect that all four had operated socially and professionally in the non-Jewish environment in remarkable mental comfort and, it may be said, with still more remarkable if certainly only relative success.

[29] The author's father.

Trumpeldor was a wholly unique figure: the only Jew in his time to have served as a commissioned officer in the Russian army,[30] a distinction conferred on him for conspicuous gallantry in the Russo-Japanese war (and for which special authority had to be obtained from St. Petersburg). There had been nothing unusual in his doing military service as such: he had been a conscript and had no more reason than any other Russian Jew—or, indeed, a Russian of any race or religion—to look forward gratefully to several hard and socially disagreeable years in the ranks. It was his assimilation of the classic military virtues of daring and steadfastness and his whole-hearted identification with the purposes and duties of the unit to which he had been assigned that were unusual. The common feature of life in the Russian armed forces as Jewish conscripts experienced it was an alienation carried over from civil life exacerbated, as often as not, by the rigour and nastiness with which the officer corps tended to treat its Jewish subordinates. That Trumpeldor's father had been a long-service conscript as boy and man under the still harsher regime instituted by Nicholas I, and that Joseph himself had grown up in Rostov-on-Don, which is to say, outside the Pale of Jewish Settlement, in a part of Russia in which Jews were comparatively rare and somewhat freer in their private lives, may go part of the way to explain the relative goodwill and lack of inhibition with which he seems to have plunged into battle once involved in military operations. But there is no question that he was by any standard a natural soldier, and that in another country—certainly in his own, had he had one—he would have gone far. He was a strict, almost implacable disciplinarian. He proved exceedingly demanding of himself under fire (first under that of the Japanese, then that of the Turks). He took matters of duty, reputation, and honour absolutely seriously. It is plain that he returned from the Russo-Japanese war—one-armed, much decorated, spare, severe in appearance and, it seems, in behaviour—the very figure of a soldier-hero. But he returned with firm political ideas as well: socialist-

---

[30] There was one earlier case, that of a certain Herz Stamm, who served 6 years as a boy-conscript and a further 35 years as an adult soldier. Much respected by his immediate superiors, he managed both to sit the necessary examinations and to gain a commission. But his commanding officer's recommendation that he be promoted captain was too much for the War Ministry to swallow (Stamm had consistently refused baptism) and he was forced to retire—upon which he was awarded captain's rank as a parting gift after all. Y. Slutsky and M. Kaplan, *Ḥayalim yehudiim bi-ẓevaʿot eiropa* (Tel Aviv, 1967), pp. 112–13.

collectivist and Zionist. And these led him in 1912, as they had led other members of the Second *'Aliya*, to settle in Erez-Israel.

Here lay what seemed to those who knew him the paradox in Trumpeldor's mind. In explicit social and political ideology and in his general conduct and loyalties in Erez-Israel he was almost an archetypal member of the Second *'Aliya*.[31] But when the Great War broke out and Turkey joined the Central Powers, Trumpeldor refused to accept Ottoman citizenship as the price of permission to remain in the country, a price which many of his comrades among the wholly committed settlers and most of his friends in the Deganiya collective in particular thought a modest one to pay. True, it entailed total subjection to Turkish rule and its attendant risks. But it was what the Zionist Organization had long advocated (and offered the Turks, as we have seen), and it seemed at the time the only likely way to protect and preserve the foothold in Erez-Israel so laboriously carved out in recent years. Trumpeldor thought otherwise. He seems to have regarded it as impermissible for a former Russian officer (still in receipt of a modest pension) to join Russia's enemies and perhaps be forced to fight with them against her. It seems too that his international-political views led him to conclusions that differed from those of many of his associates. He was strongly anti-German; he loathed what he saw as Prussian militarism. He hoped and probably believed that the alliance with the Anglo-French *entente* would end by softening the Russian Autocracy. Whether in the end he was moved more by old-fashioned loyalty (to the uniform he had worn, as his contempories put it) or by much more general political views and sympathies it is impossible to say. One way or another, early in 1915, he allowed himself to be shipped off with other exiles to Egypt. (There, curiously, it turned out that he was somewhat better placed than his fellows, thanks to the military pension now paid to him through the Russian Consulate in Alexandria.)[32]

Rutenberg, far from bearing a measure of loyalty to the Russian Autocracy, was a proclaimed and active rebel against it. He was a native of Romny, a small town in the south-eastern Ukraine. On the eve of the First World War Jews formed about a third of the population. Their principal occupation was trade. They had suffered severely (eight killed, thirty wounded) in the major wave of

[31] On the Second *'Aliya*, see *Formative Years*, pp. 385, 390–4, 397–411.
[32] Shulamit Laskov, *Trumpeldor: Sippur ḥayyav* (Haifa, 1972), pp. 89–92.

pogroms that hit Russian Jewry in October 1905. In no way, then, did it differ significantly from the many other such towns of its kind in the Jewish Pale of Settlement. Rutenberg himself, however, was, if not unique, certainly unusual. He was a qualified engineer (employed for a while at the great Putilov works in St. Petersburg) and, from an early age, had been an active—indeed, 'professional'—revolutionary, a member of the Socialist-Revolutionary Party and associated with its 'fighting organization'. He suffered imprisonment on several occasions and played a role of some importance in the revolution of 1905. It is notorious that when his party concluded that Father Gapon of 'Bloody Sunday' fame was a police agent, it was Rutenberg who, as instructed, organized his assassination. When the first revolution failed, he was obliged to flee Russia. When the second, February Revolution broke out he returned, a strong supporter of the Provisional Government against the Bolsheviks. Accounts are unanimous that he was an impressive man with a daunting manner, 'perhaps the most remarkable Roman of them all,' wrote a not notably friendly English observer, reviewing major figures in the Zionist movement whom he had come to know in the immediate post-war period. 'Thick-set, powerful, dressed always in black; a head as strong as granite and an utterance low and menacing through clenched teeth. He is no politician, he explains . . . no politician? He was with Kerensky in the last pre-Soviet days; and had his advice, which was to shoot Soviet leaders quick, been taken, something better than Bolshevism might have reigned in Russia now.'[33]

As all this suggests, Rutenberg was very far from being a Zionist in the familiar mould. It is an open question whether, in terms of inner belief, he was ever a Zionist, or Jewish nationalist, at all. His conception of a Jewish Legion had no necessary connection with Erez-Israel and was elaborated and even promoted in advance of Turkey's entry into the war. But he was very well aware not only of the afflictions of Russian Jewry (it could hardly have been otherwise) but of the significance of the Russian-Jewish problem for the wartime configuration of international politics. Like some others (not all) in the Socialist-Revolutionary camp, he saw the war in its essence as a conflict between Prussian militarism and western European democracy—the ultimate effect of which would be to propel Russia further and faster along the democratic path. Jewish

---

[33] Ronald Storrs, *Orientations* (London, 1943), p. 417.

hostility to Russia, legitimate in itself, was an obstacle to this process. It was therefore in the interests of all concerned, not least those of the democratic Powers, to seek to meet Jewish needs and aspirations. One way in which this could be done was to provide units within their armed forces in which Russian Jews *outside* Russia—all men who had very good reasons for refusing to return to Russian for military service—could play their part, under their own flag, in the general struggle against the forces of reaction. Shortly after the outbreak of war, Rutenberg, probably under instruction from his party comrades, sought support for the idea of a Jewish Legion, first from the Italians, hovering at (but not yet over) the brink of war, then the French, then the British. There was some official and some private sympathy in Rome, but it was too early for a decision on a hypothetical case. He got nowhere with either the French or the British.[34] Towards the middle of 1915 Rutenberg moved to the United States. Well before his return to Russia in 1917 he had dropped out of the campaign for a Jewish fighting force. But he was generally known to have been associated with it, and Zionists of the main (conformist) stream were free to draw appropriate conclusions.

Grossman's origins, in one respect, were much like those of the general run of Russian-Jewish *intelligenty*: his father was a man of rabbinical training and some, possibly limited, rabbinical functions, who doubled in a small way as a businessman and manufacturer. But there was much in his life initially to set him apart. He was born and had grown up in the Kuban region, north of the Caucasus, an area that had been largely set apart for Cossack governance. It was well beyond the Pale of Jewish settlement and exceptions to the rule prohibiting Jews from settling in the Kuban were rare. The Jewish population of the province was minute: 0.1 per cent for the region, 1 per cent in the town, Temryuk, in which the family lived.[35] Like Trumpeldor, Grossman had only had a scratch Jewish education, and like him again had had great trouble acquiring a formal secular education in Russia because of the obstacles set Jews by the rule of *numerus clausus* in state schools and universities. Nevertheless, he made his way successfully into the world of Russian (non-Jewish) journalism, studied for a while in German universities, and on the

---

[34] Matityahu Mintz, 'Yozmat Pinḥas Rutenberg le-hakamat gedudim 'ivriim 'im peroz milḥemet ha-'olam ha-rishona', *Ha-Ẓionut*, viii, 1983, pp. 181–94.

[35] 1897 census figures.

outbreak of war moved to Copenhagen where he represented the
well-established political and financial newspaper, the St. Petersburg *Birzheviya Vedomosti*. He was by no means a stranger to Zionism.
For a while in Russia he had been a member of the socialist wing of
the movement; in Germany he had been a leading member of the
Zionist students' society He-Ḥaver. But there was a strain in his
approach to, and his feelings about the problems of Jewry—Russian
Jewry above all—which he shared with Trumpeldor, Rutenberg,
and Jabotinsky. It was a double vision of the Jews: within Russia
and outside it, both as part of the mosaic of nationalities in which
they had a right to a place and as necessary candidates for
evacuation from the 'prison of the peoples' to their own country in
Erez-Israel. Jabotinsky, one of the authors and promoters of the
Helsingfors Programme, had once stood for election to the Duma.
Rutenberg, as has been suggested, was for long more Socialist-
Revolutionary than Zionist and the balance was not tipped the other
way until well after the October Revolution, if then. Trumpeldor
returned to Russia in 1917, if only briefly. So did Grossman, who
remained long enough to sit as a deputy for the Jewish national
minority in the Parliament of the ill-fated Ukrainian republic. What
may be said too of all four men was that they were powerfully
disposed to action and hugely impatient of sloth, passivity, and fear.
Writing of the criticism which the project for a Legion encountered
from the beginning, Jabotinsky denounced it as 'conscienceless'.

People seated peacefully in their soft armchairs, people who cannot be
persuaded to travel to Paris or to Alexandria for the affairs of Zionism
because there are mines and submarines in the sea—such people should
stand to attention, it seems to me, and shut their mouths when it comes to
young men doing their duty under a hail of shrapnel [at Gallipoli].[36]

This was a spirit—a romantic spirit in some ways—that appealed to
the young journalist and colleague in Copenhagen. In him
Jabotinsky found his first true—and for some time his only—
political ally.

   Vladimir Jabotinsky himself was the only one of the four to have
gained a reputation and a place for himself in the Zionist movement
in earlier years and in different circumstances. But on the eve of the
war he was no longer its *Wunderkind*.[37] The Helsingfors Programme

[36] *Di Tribune*, 2, 1 November 1915.
[37] See *Formative Years*, pp. 464–5, and above, pp. 25, 55.

had proved unworkable, if not irrelevant, as political reaction reasserted itself in Russia. In what seems, in retrospect, a thrashing about for a new position to take and a feasible policy to follow, he had moved in the direction of 'cultural Zionism'. He had taken up the cause of modern Hebrew (Hebrew as a spoken language and Hebrew as a vehicle for contemporary literature) with great earnestness and he had joined actively in the campaign for the establishment of a Jewish university in Jerusalem. Whether his heart was fully in such matters is hard to say. What we do know is that his response to the outbreak of war was immediate. He promptly applied to, and successfully persuaded, the important Moscow daily newspaper *Russkiya Vedomosti* to send him to western Europe and to the neutral countries as a roving correspondent. The still greater alacrity with which he responded to Turkey's entry into the war— his instant conviction that Turkey would be defeated and his proposal to his editors that he travel to North Africa to observe Muslim reaction to the *jihad* proclaimed in Constantinople—equally suggests a man grown weary of the small beer of contemporary Zionism, a man drawn magnetically to greater affairs and ostensibly nobler causes.

In December 1914, after duly visiting French North Africa, Jabotinsky reached Egypt. He found the bulk of the refugees from Erez-Israel assembling in Alexandria. And there, already burning with the conviction that the war had become the Jews' war, no less than that of any other nation, he conceived the idea of a Jewish Legion and thought he saw the makings of one before his eyes. He made his first great recruit, Trumpeldor, in February. By the beginning of March they had together collected the signatures of the first hundred volunteers. The British military commander in Egypt to whom they applied had no plans or instructions for operations in Palestine, however, and was not entitled to enlist foreign nationals into the regular ranks of the army anyway. On the other hand, the Dardanelles campaign had just commenced. What he would agree to readily enough was the formation of a humble regiment of muleteers. Trumpeldor, the soldier, reluctantly accepted the offer. It promised action and perhaps a foot in the door. Jabotinsky, not for the first time, demonstrated his obstinacy and singlemindedness by parting from Trumpeldor almost immediately and returning to Europe to pursue the project of a Legion as *he* understood it— namely, as a political act before all else and as a first step towards what in later years would be thought of as the 'revision' of Zionism.

It was at this point that Jabotinsky became—and was to remain all his life—a supremely controversial figure: loved by some, loathed by others, fated to be surrounded (in later years) by a circle of personal loyalists for which there had been no precedent in Zionism (except perhaps in Herzl's case), an object of derision to the ostensibly hard-headed, a hero to many more. It is unlikely that in these early years Jabotinsky saw himself, or sought to project himself, as a hero. But it is central to the deciphering of this unusual man that there was nothing he wanted so much as for the Jews as a people and as individuals to re-enter history heroically: to play a great role, to pick themselves up, to take their destiny in their hands, to earn the general admiration of the nations, to merit self-respect. It followed that for him service, self-sacrifice, and total absorption in the national cause—a cause defined in necessarily large and simple terms—were of the essence of decent behaviour; and that clarity of position, the nailing of one's flag to the mast, fair dealing with the allies, and even enemies—these were the requirements not only of honour but of good sense. There was thus much in Jabotinsky's outlook and public conduct that recalled Herzl. Indeed, he and Grossman made the need, as they saw it, to restore the Herzlian mode of Zionism one of their major themes. But Jabotinsky was not a diplomat. He was never a man for slow and considered *démarches*, for moving sideways, for speaking softly and exclusively, or even chiefly, in private. It may be that he was not sufficiently self-important to play such a role with success. It is certain that he had very little patience with intricacy and complexity, that he favoured a large brush and a broad sweep, that he did not understand nor was he able to cope with complex institutions except in so far as he was able to ascribe to them some general character. In his political logic he tended to be either devastatingly correct or catastrophically wrong. It may perhaps be said of him that he was not really a man of *politics* at all, certainly he was no politician. Rather, if anything, he was a tribune.

iv

The activists' fundamental charge against the established leadership was that the latter misconceived the general trend of international events and failed to see that in a world of rapid and violent change it was essential to establish yourself as a *participant* if you were not to be ignored. To be ignored was to be emasculated; to emasculate yourself was to ensure that you were ignored. It was wholly mistaken to shy away from the arena of high politics; it was essential, although far from easy, for the Jews to enter it, fatal to their interests if they failed to do so. As for neutrality, there could be none where the vital interests of the nation were at stake: to proclaim it in such a case was to discount, indeed to demean those interests.

The underlying mood of those who thought (and *a fortiori* wrote and talked) along such lines was similar in some respects to that which swept through the movement upon the seizure of power by the Young Turks in 1908. There was the feeling that the political ice in which Zionism had been entrapped for almost two generations was breaking up, that fresh opportunities were available and had to be seized, that it was easy enough to preach caution and play for safety, but that passivity could be the movement's death. But whereas the changes in Turkey in 1908 and after—the changes hoped for, no less than the changes which materialized—suggested a policy that, while a variation on, was none the less continuous and consistent with positions struck earlier, the world at war implied not much less than a revolution both in thought and in method. For now at last the Ottoman Empire, by virtue of its having joined one group of major European Powers warring against another, risked not merely a further wasting away of its resources and territory at the periphery, but general collapse and dismemberment. No doubt this could be disputed, in the sense that the Central Powers might emerge victorious. What could not be disputed, so the 'activists' held—or disputed no longer—was that the Ottomans had set their face against the Zionist enterprise finally and implacably. The war, far from encouraging them to meet the Zionists part of the way, was beginning to figure in the eyes of some Turks as an opportunity to deal with the *yishuv*—an irritant and an obstacle (among many other irritants and obstacles) to the full political control to which they aspired—once and for all. The *yishuv* was certainly in great danger. But its safety, the 'activists' argued, did not lie in the appeasement of the Turks. It lay rather in the prospect of Erez-Israel being in other hands. In short, the Jews must plunge into the fray *as such and in their own name*, the Zionists leading them, fighting under twin flags: their own and that of the Power in whose army their armed force would be incorporated.

The concept of a distinct national group fighting in the ranks of another nation's army was a familiar one in contemporary Europe. In the present war there were, or would be, among others, Poles fighting Russia under Austrian command, a Czech Legion fighting the Central Powers under Russian command, Russians and Americans fighting under French command. The Zionists themselves, as we have seen, had toyed with the idea of forming a Legion to fight with the Turks against the Italians in 1911.[38] Now a Jewish Legion, it would be argued, offered unique advantages: high symbolic value, an enhanced prospect of participation in the making of the eventual political and territorial settlement, a military role, however limited, in the fight for, and the occupation of Ereẓ-Israel that was bound to come. It was politic and it was honourable: precisely the mixture of realism and sentiment that lay at the heart of both the appeal and the programme of Zionism under the original Herzlian dispensation. Moreover, the men who would form the nucleus of such a force were already to hand, in Alexandria. The British military authorities had not refused the gift outright, only just firmly enough to discourage all but truly determined promoters of the scheme. And meanwhile a proto-Legion, as it might be called, had rapidly been formed and put into action at the Dardanelles.

In the event, the 'Zion Mule Corps' proved to be something of a disappointment. Its members were not enlisted formally in the British army. Only the sprinkling of British officers and non-commissioned officers brought in to provide a skeleton command structure carried proper rank and received normal pay and allowances. Volunteers promoted to positions of command, even the most notable of all, Trumpeldor, who served as second-in-command to the British colonel of the corps, were accorded honorary rank only and none of the men's families received the allowances customary in the British forces at the time. The men were ill trained. There were frequent grave misunderstandings between them and their superiors. For long periods morale was poor. Insubordination, bordering on at least one occasion on mutiny, was for some time endemic. The men were unquestionably on active service and subject to its inevitable concomitants: dirt, discomfort, fear, injury, and death. But they were deprived of those marginal, but necessary rewards which the British army has always valued and known how to employ to brilliant effect: regimental pride, status, badges, a little bit of glory. True, in the end, by the time it was disbanded in 1916 a

[38] See above, p. 84.

little over a year after its formation, matters had improved. In the course of their service at the Gallipoli front, where their time had been as arduous as that of any unit participating in that miserable venture, they had finally pulled themselves together. They had been mentioned in dispatches. The commanding general had explicitly commended them. There were one or two awards for bravery. But as regards the larger purposes and larger dangers of the enterprise, it could not be said that either the case for or the case against a Legion had been made out. No *armed* Jewish component of the British army had been formed. No operations in Palestine in which a Jewish unit might have participated had been launched. On the one hand, a small, local, non-combatant battalion of muleteers, however useful on the spot to the military formation of which it was a part, could not be of the stuff of politics as the advocates of a true Jewish Legion conceived it. On the other hand, there was no evidence that the Turks had noted and responded directly to its existence and that the *yishuv* was faring worse on its account.

Thus those who had always opposed the idea of a Legion had some grounds for thinking that the wisest course was to ignore the Zion Mule Corps and wait for it to be forgotten, and those who favoured the idea had still to decide whether to persist. But since to persist was necessarily to carry the campaign out of Egypt and into the vital centres of Zionist (and, generally, Jewish) opinion, to pursue the matter was to meet the Zionist establishment head on— and, by the same token, to compel it to make some response. This, as we shall see, was precisely what happened. The campaign for a proper Legion was not allowed to die; and it became, inexorably, part of a campaign against established and recognized authority within the movement. By the same token, it became a cause in support of which new men appeared and, above all, an alternative approach to the issues facing Zionism was publicly articulated. But while the fight for the Legion and the larger rebellion against institutional authority within the Zionist movement were inter-calated and mutually reinforcing, they were not identical.

v

Jabotinsky's first stop in Europe after Alexandria was in Brindisi where, at the end of March 1915, he met Rutenberg at the latter's invitation. They agreed on a rough plan of campaign. Rutenberg's steps in Europe would be retraced: in Italy jointly with Jabotinsky,

in France and Great Britain by Jabotinsky alone. Rutenberg would
then move on to the United States (with an appeal to its large Jewish
immigrant population, not the Government, in mind). In Rome the
two men saw members of the pro-war party and a junior Minister,
but it was still too early for the Italians to take up a project of this
kind and, it may be surmised, too remote from their central interests
and ambitions for it to be considered seriously. Then they parted.

Jabotinsky began with high hopes for success in Paris: he did not
doubt, and with good reason, France's interest in the Near East and
in Palestine specifically. But the Foreign Minister, Delcassé, to
whom Jabotinsky had been introduced by Gustave Hervé, returned
a disappointingly dusty answer, and Jabotinsky's characteristically
swift conclusion was that the French 'knew' that they would not be
allowed to annex Palestine and that in any case Zionism did not
interest them.[39] He turned to Britain, but in London, in May, did no
better. It was the British who would play the capital role in the
region, in his view; so he had thought from the beginning.[40] It was to
England that he, like so many other Russian Zionists, was drawn by
the image it projected of a state that, uniquely, was both a liberal
democracy and a great imperial power. It was from the English that
he expected both understanding and help: after all, it had been with
them that a beginning had been made at Gallipoli. But he got
nowhere. At the War Office he was told that Kitchener wanted no
'fancy regiments'. A promise by Weizmann to introduce him to
Herbert Samuel fell through—Tchlenov and Sokolov, then in
London, having refused to sanction it.[41] The 'diplomatic' possibilities open to him at this stage were thus exhausted and what was as
serious was that now, back among his colleagues in Europe,
Jabotinsky could not but take note of the heat with which, by and
large, his views and purposes were resisted within the Zionist
movement itself. It was not long before he was called to Copenhagen
for a firm (still private) show-down with the EAC. This was just
prior to the Actions Committee meeting in June 1915 at which, as
we have seen, the Legion project was high on the agenda.

The hostility he had aroused within the inner circle of the
established and elected leadership was enormous. Warburg, Ussishkin, and Klee (a member of the GAC) insisted on 'the Legion

---

[39] Ze'ev [Vladimir] Jabotinsky, *Avtobiografiya* (Jerusalem, 1958), pp. 138–41.
[40] Letter to Rosov, 5 November 1914. CZA, L6/86.
[41] *Avtobiografiya*, p. 143. And see below, pp. 160–1, 165.

question being settled' before all else.[42] With Ussishkin in particular breathing down their necks,[43] Tchlenov and Jacobson had Jabotinsky join them for a private meeting to listen to what they had to tell him. His own views were known: he had just set them out for Jacobson at length.[44] It does not seem that much attention was paid them, but in any event there was no mincing of words on either side. For three hours, as Jabotinsky related it, his two senior colleagues,

aided by the brave Dr Hantke from Berlin, argued that [not only the Legion project but] the Mule Corps too was a criminal offence, [and] that if I continued to conduct this propaganda—why I would be burying the Zionist enterprise for all eternity. Jacobson and Hantke particularly distinguished themselves. . . . Dr Hantke proved to me, on the basis of political economy, history, and statistics, that Turkey would never give up its rights to Erez-Israel. The man demonstrated to me, with the clarity of the multiplication tables in the noon sunlight, that the victory of Germany was assured on all the fronts. And both together revealed to me the awful secret that rebellions would soon be breaking out in Egypt, Algeria, and Morocco.

Jabotinsky's reply, by his own account, was that they were thoroughly mistaken. They had come to neutral Denmark from a blind Germany and a sick Russia. He himself had come from England, France, Egypt, and French North Africa. He had no doubt at all that Germany was incapable of winning the war and that Turkey would end by being smashed to pieces. But why argue? he asked them. Why not compromise? Why should they not proclaim the absolute neutrality of the Zionist Organization while he, for his part, left it, formally and actually, and continued on his way as a wholly private person? The offer was refused.[45] The Actions Committee would neither make its peace with Jabotinsky nor would it ignore him. It resolved, as we have seen, to fight him, initially by denouncing him in confidential instructions to all the principal figures in Zionism; and Jabotinsky, as he himself recorded, 'suddenly found [himself] alone, locked in battle with the entire Zionist movement. [Yet] in fact, not wholly alone.'[46] For it was at

[42] Memorandum by Tchlenov, 'Ueber die Beteiligung des Herrn W. Jabotinsky an der Sitzung des GAC vom 10–11 Juni 1915.' CZA, L6.37 I.

[43] Jacobson to Tchlenov and Sokolov, 17 May 1915. WA.

[44] Jabotinsky to Jacobson, 25 May 1915. CZA, Z3/2.

[45] Ibid., pp. 144–5. For Tchlenov's account of the confrontation see his letter to Weizmann, 15 June 1915. WA. 'It is painful that a man who has so many good aspects should be so childish, so unyieldingly stubborn, and so boundlessly ambitious,' he remarked of Jabotinsky *inter alia*.

[46] Ibid.

this point that he teamed up with Grossman and the two together began what became a systematic public campaign as much for a Legion explicitly as for a new, 'activist' brand of Zionism by means of public meetings, private argument, and—especially galling to the Actions Committee and to the liaison office in Copenhagen—a press campaign with a fortnightly journal of their own published in Copenhagen itself and distributed world-wide.

vi

There was no precedent for a public fight of this nature within the movement. The great quarrel, a little more than a decade earlier, over the British offer of a Jewish autonomous region in East Africa had been very severe. It had led to a split in the movement (when Zangwill and his colleagues had left it to form a separate organization). It had determined the general direction of Zionism from that time on. But the common will to unity and to the preservation of the institutions and their authority had largely prevailed. What Zionism had lost in *élan*, and to its rivals, by moving away from the very largest issues in Jewry cannot be estimated. But the movement as *organization* remained intact and at no time was it truly under threat. No doubt, this had much to do with the fact that the fundamental issues at stake were never fully articulated and that the years 1903–5, frightful though they were for Russian Jewry, were, when all is said and done, of a familiar pattern.[47]

The present quarrel was very different. There was no great founder-leader to draw the fire of the opposition and crystallize the respective camps. The specific and immediate questions before the movement were vastly clearer, but at the same time pregnant with great and evident dangers. The attack upon the established leadership could not fail to be an attack not only upon their policy but upon their competence. And that such an attack had been mounted in the first place was regarded by the defenders not only as evidence of reckless disloyalty, but as betokening possible disaster in itself. Hence the heat of the argument, the tone of the protagonists, and the trimming, not to say deviousness, exhibited by those who could not bring themselves to make up their minds and declare themselves one way or the other.

The gravamen of the 'activists'' charge against the official

---

[47] For a discussion of the issues at stake in 1903–5, see *Formative Years*, chapter 10, 'Looking Back and Thinking Forward', pp. 348–64.

leadership was their passivity and lack of moral courage. The theme was articulated over and over again in their Yiddish-language journal *Di Tribune*, which Grossman edited and published regularly from mid-October 1915 to the end of August 1916.

The saddest thing [wrote Jabotinsky in the lead article of the first issue] is not that nothing is done, but rather that there is no plan and no purpose. Our leaders are satisfied with such degree of activity as they themselves [choose to] develop and turn angry when others are dissatisfied. . . . It is not only a question of lack of talent, but of a pathological fear of action, of a kind of aversion to the very smallest creative step. One would have to be blind not to recognize this as a disease. Not, I think, an organic disease, but the result of the deeply rooted influence of upbringing. At this moment in history, one that may never return, it is a disaster. . . .

As for the argument that the *yishuv* must be protected and the Turks appeased, the matter should be seen from our point of view. None should be allowed to think that if we [the Jews] are struck only lightly, only with the tip of the stick, that we shall take no offence, that we are used to [such treatment]. . . . Not that this is written to arouse hatred for the Turks. It makes no difference whether we love or hate them. What is important is that we open our own eyes and understand the true meaning of the events in Palestine. The lesson they have to teach is simple and clear: the Turks do not want Jewish settlement in Palestine. And really I do not understand why it is so difficult for this truth to penetrate our consciousness. . . .

All this leads to two conclusions: the first is that it is not in our interest for Palestine to remain under Turkish rule. The second is that if Turkey is against us we should seek other connections and other friends. Today, in 1915, when affairs are governed solely by clear and open calculation, and all can see who is who's friend and who is who's enemy, it is for us too to establish new bonds—openly and in the public eye.[48]

Alas, Jabotinsky and Grossman argued, it was plain to anyone surveying the scene that clear thinking and a clear step in one or other direction were simply not forthcoming, not now—nor, indeed, later at the peace conference that would follow the war. The mood in Jewry, and in the movement in particular, was deeply pessimistic. There was a loss of faith and hope all round. There was a feeling that whatever happened the Jewish people would be the losers.[49] Little or nothing was left of Herzlian Zionism. 'Of a Jewish State one heard nothing.' As for the angry debate itself, at least it had revealed those

[48] 'Aktivizm', *Di Tribune*, 1, 15 October 1915.
[49] Meir Grossman, 'Der Anhoib', *Di Tribune*, 2, 1 November 1915; and 'Pesimizm', ibid., 7, 20 January 1916.

who *should* have been concerned 'to revolutionize Jewish life' in their true colours. It had caused an outcry; but that was no reason to shirk it.

There are indeed profound differences between them and us [wrote Grossman]. . . . It may be that our leaders have grown old; it may be that Zionism itself has been struck with a sickness of age. Whichever is the case, an operation is called for, even if it should be a difficult one, even if the times appear unsuitable. . . . Why, we speak almost different languages. You [the leaders] argue: what will the gentiles say? We for our part want the truth itself, no matter how bitter. . . . You speak to us of harmony within the family. We reply: Zionism itself and the freedom of our people matter a great deal more than the Organization. . . . You speak to us of discipline, obedience, and silence. Are we to hide? . . . We want to illuminate both Zionism and the Organization, to see that the Idea matches the gravity of the hour. . . . So what you must know, is that we will sell neither our right to criticize nor our striving after great achievements for the mess of pottage known as *shelom bayit* [domestic harmony].[50]

There was initially a tendency to forgive Jabotinsky, 'a charming and kind person, not only sincere . . . but chivalrous and noble', only to wonder, as Jacobson put it, at his lack of 'responsibility' and his 'unforgivable recklessness'.[51] He had, after all, won a certain reputation for himself and was much admired by the less stolid of the Russian Zionists. Grossman, eight years younger, had made no such mark. Reports upon him from Copenhagen to Berlin tended to be bilious. Promises to put a stop to his activities and of an early opportunity being taken 'to rub the young man's nose thoroughly'[52] were made with some regularity. The appearance of *Di Tribune* brought a particularly angry, at times ferocious, response in the loyalist press—coupled, for the most part, with a (countervailing) dismissive advice to the public to pay the rebels no attention. Grossman was a 'revolver journalist',[53] Jabotinsky an adventurer whose 'tragical-comical', 'heroic-romantic' project for a Legion was an affair of 'political tricks' for which 'we have neither the spirit . . . nor the time.'[54] They had aroused 'the antipathy of all democratic Jewish society'.[55]

[50] 'Shelom bayit', *Di Tribune*, 8, 5 February 1916.
[51] Jacobson (in Berlin) to Bernstein (in Copenhagen), 21 July 1915. CZA, L6/88.
[52] Bernstein to Rosenblüth, 22 July 1915. CZA, L6/88.
[53] *Yudishe Folkshtimme* (Copenhagen), 26 November 1915.
[54] *Di Warheit* (New York), 30 November 1915.
[55] *Di Welt* (London), 10 January 1916.

It was not only natural for two gifted journalists to have founded a review, there was little else they could have done if they were to persist. The public meetings held in Scandinavia had been successful so far as they went, but no real follow-up or support was forthcoming, and Scandinavia even in wartime was a backwater. Jabotinsky subsequently paid a brief visit to Russia to propagate his views on his own home ground, but he had very limited success; and it was the bitter resistance there to what he was trying to do that was plainest to his eye. Ussishkin in his rage, so it transpired, had gone so far as to stop Jabotinsky's aged mother in the street in Odessa to tell her (in so many words) that her son deserved to be hanged.[56] So after the founding of *Di Tribune*, leaving Grossman to run it, he moved back to London. In the end it was there that the campaign for a Legion would finally be decided. But the 'activist' campaign in its wider sense, namely for a thorough change in the composition and direction of the official leadership of the movement, was kept up too and intensified. Its gist now was the argument that the Zionists were deeply divided, that there was now a new 'political' opposition to the old 'practical' leadership, that this opposition needed to be recognized, and that only its incorporation in a new composite leadership and the formation of a 'coalition government' would save Zionism and enable the Organization to function properly.[57]

Progress was slow. Jabotinsky found himself relatively isolated: a man on the margin of Jewish political life, although not quite the pariah the more passionate loyalists made him out to be. The fact was that the note of restraint and quiet reason struck by the EAC in its confidential circulars to loyalists ('It would be difficult for anyone—Mr Jabotinsky and his friends apart—to take the idea that the Jewish Legion might influence the conquest of Palestine, and contribute to the establishment of an autonomous Jewish state seriously;' other factors would influence a Power adopting such a course, 'not the fact that the Jews had put several thousand men at its disposal.'[58]) had not been wholly successful. Nor was the routine adopted for dealing with what were taken to be the more outrageous of the 'activists'' charges: refraining from a direct response, and channelling the EAC's views through Copenhagen for confidential distribution to the Zionist country organizations.[59] Nor again had

[56] *Avtobiografiya*, p. 149.
[57] *Jewish Chronicle*, 17 December 1915.
[58] Copenhagen Office, confidential circular, 26 October 1915. CZA, L6/18/1.
[59] For example: Copenhagen to Berlin, 16 June 1916. CZA, L6/88.

the equivocal (but ostensibly authoritative) presentation of the state of affairs in Ereẓ-Israel been without a possibly confusing but certainly soothing effect on the recipients of the confidential circulars in which such reports were embodied. Detailed accounts of the trials of the *yishuv*, many of them first hand, would be regularly offset by such hopeful quotations from reports of men on the spot as could be gleaned. ('There is no place for despair and discouragement . . . there is none who has the slightest intention to give up the fight.'[60]) And where there could be no question of the gravity of the situation (as after Ruppin's expulsion from the country by Djemal Pasha in the autumn of 1916 which had led the EAC to lay down that 'we have to be prepared that this measure might represent the beginning of new persecutions, the possibility of which we, indeed, have always been afraid of.'), there the reports were distributed as 'absolutely confidential' with a warning of the dire consequences of a leak of their contents to the press.[61] No change was made in this practice right to the end of Turkish rule.[62] The upshot was that while the 'activists' made only slow progress towards their stated goals and the oppositional camp they claimed to lead remained very small, the effect of their offensive was substantially to accelerate the erosion of the established leadership's prestige and authority.

In politically and socially invertebrate Jewry the instinct for consensus and joint action and the reluctance to break ranks had always been powerful. Thus for whole communities, thus for particular groups, societies, and institutions within them, thus especially in the case of the necessarily fragile supra-communal institutions and movements. At the same time, a persistent feature of Jewish public life in the modern era has been the multiplication of views and divisions of opinion on matters of general concern. Thus, inevitably, between strong convictions which pull centrifugally and a conventional wisdom (which lays down that there is little to be gained and probably much to lose by displays of disunity) that pulls centripetally, a great tension arises. The Jews' profound but ancient sense of membership in a 'community of fate' vies continually with a modern freedom of mind which leads at least some of them to regard the world around them in unconventional terms and to consider

[60] Copenhagen Office, confidential circular, 23 November 1916. ML, Gaster Papers, vol. 54.

[61] Ibid., 27 October 1916. CZA, L6/18 II.

[62] See for example, ibid., 17 August 1917. CZA, L6/18 III.

afresh what it might be best in the general interest to do. Strong leadership can dissolve this tension for a time; weak leadership tends eventually to be resented because it serves to perpetuate it. Strong leadership may draw support regardless of the specifics of its stated policy; weak leadership must rely substantially on the specifics of whatever policy it seeks to promote. Ultimately, indecision, obscurity of purpose, and failure to face—and outface—opposition have much the same eroding effects on leaders in Jewry as in other societies and polities. Only the *process* of wasting tends to be more protracted, and the moral agonies which such a fight entails are often greater.

So while the campaign against the 'activists' was not without its successes, the fundamental problem of the existence of an impenitent public opposition was not disposed of. If anything, it was exacerbated. What the activists had done was not only to denounce what they took to be the weakness of the leadership; they had, unwittingly, led the established leaders of the Zionist Organization to demonstrate that weakness for all with sensitive eyes to see. And evidence that this was the case was ever more easily come by. The Jewish press did not ignore the rebels, and reports and comment on them moved out of the relative obscurity of the Yiddish press into the relative light of the English-language periodicals. From time to time there were hints of support from notables: from Joseph Cowen, the president of the English Zionist Federation, from Leopold Greenberg, editor of the *Jewish Chronicle,* and, distantly and indirectly, from Israel Zangwill as well—all old Herzlian 'politicals'. The matter of the Legion, not identical with, but indissolubly linked to the political management of Zionism, was made once more to penetrate the official bureaucracy in London, both at the War and Foreign Offices, and more effectively than on the first occasion. There was no decision as yet. But the voices calling for a favourable response within the British establishment (C. P. Scott and L. S. Amery among them) were multiplying. There had even been a sympathetic leading article in *The Times*.[63]

The dilemma of the official Zionist leadership was certainly acute. To have taken up the mavericks' challenge openly and directly would no doubt have converted what it was determined to treat as a public nuisance into something like a legitimate and respectable

---

[63] C. P. Scott to Lord Robert Cecil, 11 December 1915; and L. S. Amery to Cecil, 11 January 1916. PRO, FO 371/2835. *The Times*, 15 July 1916.

rival for the moral and constitutional government of the movement. But that was not only to concede a measure of defeat; it was to endanger the whole rickety policy of neutrality as they understood it. And there was a technical and constitutional problem: at a time when the institutions of the movement had virtually fallen into abeyance, it was not at all clear how such a conflict could be resolved properly and formally—had anyone been of a serious mind to do so.

You know my position on the whole Jabotinsky question [Shmarya Levin wrote to Victor Jacobson]. . . . Let Jabotinsky now say what he likes, let him keep coming with demands—his name will be eternally associated with the miserable idea of a Legion and no one can deal him a greater injury than he has dealt himself. . . . The call for a coalition ministry cannot fail to be dismissed out of hand by anyone with any understanding whatsoever in politics. . . . A clear-minded man will certainly ask himself: who precisely would elect the new men to the executive; and if indeed they were elected to the executive—who precisely does he think would grant them the right to take decisions in matters on which they and the legal executive are divided? Jabotinsky's demand, which is identical, by the way, with Cowen's, can only be understood as a call for the dismissal of the [Greater] Actions Committee and not the EAC alone. But it seems he himself is afraid to express his demand in clear language, and so doing condemns himself.[64]

In the end, if there was to be a radical change in the government of the Zionist movement while the war lasted and in a direction contrary to that which the official leadership had sanctioned, it would have to be engineered by more subtle and circumspect means.

vii

Chaim Weizmann was a rebel of a different order. In some ways he was hardly a rebel at all. In character and in achievement he was in another class. In reputation he stands to this day with and between Theodor Herzl, the man who precipitated the re-entry of Jewry into the world of politics, and David Ben-Gurion, the man who presided over its definitive reincorporation therein. What his specific role and precise achievements were is less clear; and as he and his times recede from memory, and their attendant myths, convictions, and controversies dissolve, it is ever more difficult to pin them down. Again, few would question (there was a time when none doubted)

---

[64] Shmarya Levin to Victor Jacobson, 16 February 1916. [n.a.] *Igrot Shmaryahu Levin* (Tel-Aviv, 1966), p. 345.

that his attainments (whatever they might be) were of a very high order, that he does indeed bear comparison with the two indisputably pre-eminent figures in the history of Zionism—and so with major figures in the modern history of Jewry as a whole. But if so, how and why? Weizmann, as we shall see, was the man who, at the end of the Great War, emerged as Zionism's virtually undisputed leader—Herzl's first true successor, it may be said, having regard to his supremacy within the movement. But the roots of that supremacy, the ways and means by which a wholly secondary figure in 1914, one moreover who had largely shut himself away in northern England, many hundreds of miles from the centres of Jewry—thousands from Erez-Israel—had propelled himself within a very few years into Herzl's vacant seat, are not without their obscurities. All that is not obscure is that Weizmann's rise within the body of the movement was in all cardinal respects a function of what he accomplished and of what he was reputed to have accomplished in the course of the war. It follows that for an understanding of the progress of the movement in this its crucial phase, no less than for a proper charting of the progress of the man who became its leader, it is necessary that some of the strands of fact, fiction, and merest supposition which had come to be fed into his *ex post facto* public reputation be disentangled.

Chaim Weizmann (1874–1952) was a man of revealing contradictions. He was an early and notably fierce critic of Herzl, whose methods and very conception of Zionism he despised and whose authority he resented.[65] But in the end it was his thorough-going adoption of Herzl's central purpose (a special status for the Jews in Erez-Israel under the benevolent auspices of a major Power) and his brilliantly effective personal 'diplomacy'—the face-to-face contact, the direct confrontation, with the great men at the very apex of state power that Herzl had always sought and greatly believed in—that won him the succession. Weizmann was always profoundly conscious of his origins, of his having emerged from what he saw as the living heart of the Jewish nation pulsating within the larger, unhappy, shapeless body of world Jewry as a whole, but animating and nourishing it all the while: the Russian-Polish concentration. He frequently insisted on his membership in that community, on his being flesh of its flesh, on its special quality: 'We who come from

---

[65] *Formative Years*, pp. 193–8.

Russia are born and bred in an aspiration towards a new and better Jewish life.'[66] In the rather simple, unsystematic, virtually non-ideological way he made his own when dealing with such questions, he was nothing if not an eastern European Jewish nationalist, a man who was sure he knew his people and understood them, and one who never hesitated to speak for them, nor in the event, to decide for them—if necessary without consulting them.[67] It was in such terms that he presented himself, on the whole with success, to some of the semi-assimilated notables of Anglo-Jewry. It was how he presented himself to the great men of Whitehall and Westminster. It was in that role, to the end of his days, that he was most impressive and most effective too at touching chords of sentiment and decent fellow-feeling where a lifetime in politics and society in London had not caused them wholly to wither away. On the other hand, not one of his colleagues and proximate contemporaries in the chief, east European wing of the movement had gone as far as had Weizmann in removing himself physically from its geographical and demographic centres and from the political centre of Zionism in Berlin. On the eve of the war, of the thirteen Russian members of the Actions Committee, eight still lived in Russia. Four more lived in Germany or Turkey in direct, full-time service of the movement. None had attempted, none seems ever to have envisaged, anything comparable to Weizmann's heroic effort to create a fresh, as it were parallel life for himself as an academic scientist in England, largely adapting to English ways in his private life in the process.

Weizmann became a British subject in 1910. At no point thereafter, not even during the last painful years of his life, did he want to sever his ties with his adopted country. Few things pleased him so much as his acceptance for wartime work in the laboratories of the Ministry of Munitions and his later appointment as Chemist to the Admiralty. After the war it was proposed that he be knighted

[66] Letter to the Marchioness of Crewe, 19 June 1915, *Weizmann Letters*, vii, no. 176, p. 213.

[67] Thus long before he was in a position to influence events. 'The Jewish masses in London are in the throes of an Africa fever,' he wrote to Ussishkin at the height of the great quarrel occasioned by the British offer of an autonomous Jewish region in East Africa in 1903; 'but they are so unenlightened that tomorrow they might just as easily be fired with enthusiasm for America and the day after for Palestine. If this is the so-called voice of the people that our Africans speak so vociferously about, one can ignore it with a clear conscience.' (20 October 1903, *Weizmann Letters* iii, no. 60, p. 64.) The 'Jewish masses in London' were preponderantly recent immigrants from eastern Europe. The 'Africans' were the supporters of the scheme, Herzl at their head.

and it was duly 'ascertained' at Downing Street that he would 'welcome' the honour.[68] How disappointed he may have been when, in the end, the knighthood was not forthcoming, one cannot tell: perhaps less than by his failure to attain a professorship in chemistry at Manchester and the possibly more galling failure to be elected Fellow of the Royal Society. But again, deepest of all, was his devotion to Zionism as a cause—the only social and political cause in which he was really interested.

Can these diverse, seemingly less than compatible sentiments and loyalties be squared? At heart, Weizmann's was an Aḥad Ha-'Amian view of the matter of Jewry: an essentially stern, in some ways pitying, in other ways pitiless, but above all paternalistic outlook on Jewry in which anxiety for the fate of the Jews as a group historically was combined with a resigned, even fatalistic writing-off of their chances as individuals existentially. It owed a great deal to first-hand knowledge of the depth of the social, political, and economic mire in which east European Jewry was entrapped, and of the enormous social, political, and economic forces militating against their being extracted from it. It was shot through with disbelief in the possibility of any such large-scale rescue and rehabilitation of the Jews as Herzl, Zangwill, Nordau, and their school had envisaged. It placed its chief hopes on an effort— necessarily long term—to draw something finer, newer, improved, altogether more promising, but substantially reduced in scale, from the hopeless shambles of contemporary Jewry. Its values were therefore ultimately moral and cultural; and despite the scepticism and caution, the dislike of the grandiose and the obviously ambitious, the preference for what was modest and carefully contrived with which all plans and projects were examined—among them the project for a Jewish university in Jerusalem, to which Weizmann was much attached and to which he was devoting a great deal of his time on the eve of the war—there was much in this approach to, and interpretation of, Zionism that was Utopian. It was selective and perfectionist, a matter of pilot projects and institutions. It was not well attuned to considerations of power and

[68] 'Honours: Dr Charles Weizmann', memorandum [by Phillip Kerr, private secretary to the Prime Minister], 13 December 1920. SRO, GD 40/17/1169. Upon naturalization in 1910 Weizmann had changed his first name to 'Charles', but used it only on what might be termed bureaucratic occasions. See also Kerr's letter to Herbert Samuel, 4 January 1921. ISA, 100/8.

high politics. In the final analysis, it was preparatory. For direct
participation in it few would be called, fewer still chosen. The *yishuv*
as 'spiritual' or cultural centre would inspire and stimulate change
in the great, only very slowly changing bulk of Jewry. Accordingly,
while the task of the leading Zionist militants was to promote the
centre in Ereẓ-Israel, its exigencies would keep most of them back in
the Diaspora with most of the Jews. Those who were not members of
the movement's inner hierarchy and bureaucracy and did not wish
to be because they were too proud, or too independent, or too
dissatisfied with the pace or direction set by the central office in
Berlin had necessarily to find a parallel occupation and a source of
independent income. The logic of their situation was compelling.

So it had been with Aḥad Ha-ʿAm himself—to whom alone of all
the notables and worthies of the movement Weizmann was
attached, and for whom he seems never to have wavered in respect.
But whereas Aḥad Ha-ʿAm was content to perform the role of sage,
to give advice when it was sought and to hand down analyses and
judgement *ex cathedra* whenever he could bring himself to break one
of his long, dark silences, Weizmann was a man driven to action by
consuming personal ambition and driven to seek the top in all his
endeavours. And driven too, it should be said, by an unusual, almost
artless confidence in the value and validity of his own judgement
and the ultimate propriety of anything he might do in practice to
execute it. It was a measure of a self-confidence that revealed itself,
most notably perhaps, in a consummate ability to rationalize private
choices and inclinations in terms of the general interest. It is this, it
seems, that accounts best for the absence of any trace of modesty or
self-criticism in the man.

His extraordinary, at times blind self-assurance may also partly
explain the instances of deviousness and lack of scruple—mostly
minor, many trivial—that pepper his career. What else could have
moved him, for example, to write explicitly on one occasion to a
correspondent whom he was anxious to impress with his views that
he had personally witnessed the great pogrom in Kishinev in 1903,
and then to go on to recount his exploits there as a defender of the
Jewish quarter when he had been nowhere near Kishinev at the time
and the evidence is that he was in Geneva all the while?[69] Why
should he have allowed Rutenberg and Jabotinsky, especially the

⎯⎯⎯⎯⎯⎯⎯

[69] Letter to Dorothy de Rothschild, 22 November 1914. *Weizmann Letters*, vii, no.
45, pp. 52–3 and n. 6.

latter, to believe they had at least his tacit support for the Legion project, while making it clear to others, among them Aḥad Ha-ʿAm, that the contrary was the case?[70] What manner of man was capable of striking so richly chameleonic a variety of tones in his correspondence: now respectful, now comradely, now severe, now humble ('You were kind enough to allow me to write to you,' he once began a letter to the Marchioness of Crewe; 'I hope you will forgive me if I avail myself of this permission so soon after our interview. I have to thank you for the patience with which you have listened to my sad and sordid story.');[71] and, over and over again, patronizing or dismissive (as when writing to Sir Mark Sykes about Jabotinsky, with whom he had been on close enough terms to share an apartment in London: 'An excellent fellow, highly intelligent, honest and very energetic, but it is a pity that the idea of a Jewish Legion has almost become his *idée fixe* and he has subordinated important Zionist interests to this idea. I am sure your letter will put him right.')?[72] How was it that he did not think it improper and damaging both to his cause and to his personal reputation that he should have promoted both the interests of the movement and the matter of private financial reward for his services as a scientist through the same channels and at the same time?[73]

Whatever interpretation is put on the energy with which he pursued general and private interests in tandem and the ever growing determination and skill with which he learned to project himself as the man of the hour, it is probable that he himself gave no thought to the question how he might ultimately be judged by others. At bottom, Weizmann was neither a moralist nor an intellectual. He was not a man of letters nor a connoisseur of any of the arts. In taste, in deportment, in aspirations, and in pleasures he was profoundly bourgeois. There is much to suggest that he was happiest and most relaxed in the laboratory. His handwriting—in

[70] Compare Weizmann to Aḥad Ha-ʿAm, 18 December 1914, ibid., no. 79, p. 93, with his letter to Rutenberg of 5 February 1915, ibid., no. 109, p. 135, and Jabotinsky's evidently well founded conviction that Weizmann favoured the project, although reluctant to support it publicly, as recounted in Jabotinsky's autobiography, op. cit., p. 154; and see Aḥad Ha-ʿAm's indignant letter to Weizmann (4 September 1917, *Igrot AH*, vi, p. 84) when Weizmann came out in public support of the Legion, once it was a *fait accompli*, reversing what Aḥad Ha-ʿAm had long understood to be his true position.

[71] 19 June 1915. *Weizmann Letters*, vii, no. 176, p. 212.

[72] To Mark Sykes, 15 February, 1917. Ibid., no. 307, p. 329.

[73] C. P. Scott's diaries, entries for 22–26 May 1916, 26–30 January, 27 February, and 9 August 1917. BL, Add. MSS. 50903, fos. 9, 144–5, 165; and 50904, fo. 93.

half a dozen languages, available to inspection in many hundreds of letters written over an immensely long period—reveals much of the inner man: exceedingly regular, undeviatingly legible. Taken together, these may be clues to the hard, pragmatic streak in Weizmann of which he was not in the least ashamed, but on the contrary rather proud: realism raised to the level of a principle. Weizmann's vision of the future to which the Jews should strive and the path they should tread meanwhile were both grounded on a deliberately sharp perception of the world around him, heightened and intensified by a profound, indeed excessive sense of the weakness of Jewry, and by a kind of paternal and generally forgiving scorn for the pretensions of the Children of Israel to operate unguided in the larger world which they were now re-entering. It was an approach that in its origins owed a good deal to Aḥad Ha-'Am. But Weizmann was never the compleat Aḥad Ha-'Amian. If his respect for the Master never wavered, his devotion to him was subordinate none the less to his own independent reading of the current state of affairs. He trusted no one's judgement as he trusted his own. It was not the least of the sources of his strength and of his success.

It is in this sense that his reaction to the events of the summer and autumn of 1914 and the surge of energy which charged his thinking and behaviour from that time on were characteristic. For a while he thrashed about seeking 'action', hardly calmed by Aḥad Ha-'Am who, no less characteristically, thought it much too early to chart any kind of course and that anything done in the spirit Jabotinsky had begun to exemplify was a positive 'sin against the Jewish people, no one having been authorized to act in its name.'[74] But it was not long before Weizmann began to strike out on his own in directions of his own devising—not so much to rebel against the Zionist hierarchy and to fight its policy as to circumvent it. His grounds and his purposes as he himself outlined them were almost identical with those of other rebels, notably Jabotinsky. He envisaged the dismemberment of the Ottoman Empire. He wished to align Zionism, indeed Jewry, with the *entente* whose victory he desired and believed in. He judged the existing structure for the management of the movement to be incompatible with its interests: in effect, he wanted the Actions Committee in Berlin to vacate its authority. And he passionately wanted Zionist policy and interests restructured on

---

[74] Weizmann to Aḥad Ha-'Am, 14 September 1914. *Weizmann Letters*, vii, no. 7, p. 7; Aḥad Ha-'Am to Weizmann, 15 September 1914. *Igrot AH*, v, p. 306.

the basis of close association with England—that country, as he saw it, 'which champions the cause of small nationalities [and which] will—I believe—guarantee the maximum amount of justice to a world tired out by this terrible war'.[75]

The last point was cardinal. There is no mistaking the fervour with which he held to the view that it was in the English that the Jews would at last find their champions, and that it was in the Jews that the English for their part would find remarkably solid and loyal partners such as even a Great Power had need of. When the time came for a 'general reckoning' after the war, the Jews would put in their claim for 'an organized autonomous Jewish community in Palestine'; Palestine, he had no doubt, would 'fall within the influence of England'; England would support the Jewish claim, out of self-interest if for no other reason. For, developed by the Jews, Palestine would serve British regional strategic interests admirably; they alone could turn it into the 'Asiatic Belgium'[76] of which the British Empire stood in need. Thus all would prosper, all would benefit, justice would be done.

Weizmann, like so many other members of the Russian-Jewish intelligentsia, held Britain in exceedingly high esteem: a free, liberal society that stood in strongest contrast to virtually all other societies and regimes in early twentieth-century Europe; and he believed, by what might be termed a variation on a basic Aḥad Ha-'Amian theme (one which the Master could never quite bring himself to accept) that nothing would suit the needs of Jewry better on its first steps towards renewed independence than to be under British influence and tutelage. Necessarily, it would be an unequal relationship. But his belief in it probably derived—at all events fitted—the somewhat deferential esteem in which he held the English, and his consistent lack of confidence in his own people's capacity to manage their collective affairs. Yet it cannot be said that he loved the English. It is doubtful whether he ever understood English ways as thoroughly as he believed he did. It is certain that in his rather wry, paternalistic way he did love the Jews and that he understood their ways very well indeed. The important thing is that he thought the latter needed the former for purposes that went far beyond what pertained strictly to the world of politics. He thought himself remarkably well placed to engineer the conjunction, as

[75] Letter to Zangwill, 19 October 1914. *Weizmann Letters* vii, no. 22, p. 26.
[76] Ibid., pp. 27–8.

indeed he was; the more so as, so defined, it was a task which not only resolved all contradictions in his private position, but necessarily built upon them. In practice, what had to be done upon the outbreak of war, initially, was to prepare the ground for the coming 'general reckoning', namely to put forward the proper arguments to the proper people and to avoid any act or work that might spoil steady progress towards the desired end. The task, in a word, was a diplomatic one. It was a task which Weizmann embarked upon almost immediately when the war broke out.

In logic, and to some extent in spirit, this was Herzl's quest for an ally all over again: founded on much the same belief in the power of rational argument, in the ultimate harmony of interests among nations, on the goodwill and high purposes which motivate at any rate the best of the world's leaders and on the conviction that to stimulate them to action it would be necessary, in the last resort, to confront them personally.[77] Of course, the international circumstances were vastly different from those of 1896–1904. On the whole they were more favourable. In Weizmann's case the search for an ally was simplified by it being confined to Great Britain alone. In practice, the soundings and gentle propaganda he had in mind at this stage were entirely directed to preparations for the great international conference that would assuredly follow the war; and as they were intended to be conducted privately, failure entailed no serious risk, let alone danger. His purpose and activities necessarily ran counter to the Zionist movement's officially proclaimed neutrality and would have repelled that great part of the membership that still relied upon the EAC's authority and wisdom had it but known what he was up to. But as yet nothing impelled Weizmann to declare against authority publicly. He was flexible and cautious. Privately, he encouraged the Americans in their effort to take temporary charge of the movement, then retreated when the EAC resisted and failed to yield to Brandeis's pressure. Essentially, it was a negative position that he struck: consistently keeping his distance from the men in Berlin. 'I shall not go to the conference,' he wrote Shmarya Levin when the first important wartime meetings of the Actions Committee was planned. 'I cannot do this either as a Jew or as a British subject.'[78] His grounds for refusing the invitation and his criticism of Warburg and Hantke for holding the meeting and

[77] See *Formative Years*, Chapters 3, 4.
[78] Weizmann to Shmarya Levin, 18 October 1914. *Weizmann Letters*, vii, no. 21, p. 23.

keeping the EAC active and in Berlin were ostensibly much the same as those of Kann and Jabotinsky. But he was not prepared either to argue the issue with the German Zionists face-to-face as did Kann, or to strike out in open rebellion in the manner of Jabotinsky and other 'activists'. In their sense of the term, Weizmann was not an activist at all. He, for his part, marvelled at their readiness to submit to the odium their public dissidence brought down upon them. In sum, his own rebellion was subtler. Far from quarrelling with Sokolov and Tchlenov when they arrived in London as legates of the EAC or explicitly rejecting their authority, he sought their co-operation.

In the case of Sokolov, who spent most of the war years in London, he initially went out of his way to humour his senior, to seek to work with him in tandem, and finally to enlist him with great manipulatory skill in a programme of action of his own devising. With Tchlenov he was less successful. But Tchlenov returned to Russia and remained there with only a few interruptions for the greater part of the war.

All this helps to explain how it came about that in the end it was Weizmann and those who gathered round him, leaders of a covert opposition, not Jabotinsky and his 'activists' seeking to mount an open opposition, who were best placed to assume effective leadership of the movement at war's end. It was by indirection and disconnection, not public polemics and confrontation, that the EAC was ultimately reduced to a cipher. And, perhaps, in the institutional hiatus forced on the movement by world war there could be no other way, as Levin had pointed out.[79] That it should have been Weizmann, the loyal, life-long Aḥad Ha-'Amian, the leader (with Motzkin) of the first organized opposition to 'political' and 'diplomatic' Zionism in general and to Herzl the leader in particular, who did more than anyone to re-establish Zionist policy on a political and diplomatic basis is of course ironic. But it speaks volumes for his ability to set out to seize the opportunities which, in his judgement, were now presented both to the movement and to himself with hardly a backward glance or thought for old positions now abandoned: proof positive of his high, native, political talent.

Talent, cunning, and determination are far from being the whole of the story, however. Some time would pass before Weizmann

---

[79] See above, p. 156.

found a way to put his ability and energy to use in a specific direction; and when the opportunity came it was not—nor, in the nature of things, as we shall see, could it have been—of his own making. Nor was it entirely clear to him at the time (and, possibly, later) what his true and precise role would turn out to be. But in any event, when it came, he seized the opportunity with the speed, directness, and confidence that betoken a master.

PART THREE

Decisions

5

A Plan Aborted

i

The matter of the Jews and their interests, obviously peripheral to the major concerns of the belligerents, impinged upon the management of the war through a particular (but by no means unique) mix of categories among the myriad competing forces in the arena: both regular offices and officers of state and some of the informal groups, private institutions, and remarkable individuals operating, some before, some behind the scenes of government proper. The wartime state of affairs was of course one in which individuals and collectivities of all kinds tended as never before, and with unprecedented ease, to propagate new, often wholly unexpected and irregular (and, in retrospect, often astonishing) currents and crosscurrents of policy and opinion. These were liable to appear, disappear, reappear, and shift course, to push a subject to the top of the official agenda one day, its sponsors dismissing it without a tremor of regret the next. It was out of what may be described as this political market of unprecedented freedom and flow of information and opinion, or as some might think unprecedented chaos, that British policy on the Jews, like on so many other matters, emerged. In consequence, only a drastic cutting away of the clutter of detail encumbering it and a consistent effort to distinguish action actually taken from mere fancy and intention are likely to yield an account that will render the improbable dénouement with which we are concerned intelligible. Even then it remains an episode (as much in the diplomatic history of Great Britain as in the political revival of the Jews) that will bear more than one interpretation.[1]

Three of its aspects, all interconnected, contributed particularly to its inherently convoluted and therefore problematical nature.

[1] See Select Bibliography, pp. 382–4 below.

Taken together they go some way to explain the ease with which varying, indeed contradictory *ex post facto* accounts of it have always been both possible and common. In the first place, it was throughout an affair of leaders and their entourages: Ministers and senior diplomats, functionaries of central national institutions, national and communal spokesmen (some authorized, some self-appointed); and was a component of high politics: marginal to, but still intercalated in Great Power rivalry. In a word, it was a matter of élites. The public, the parliaments, the 'street', even, in large measure, the press were not involved, at all events never integral to the process. They might be referred to and invoked; they were not consulted.

Secondly, owing partly to its essential (i.e. political) nature, partly to the terms in which it tended to be conceived by those most closely involved, and partly to the *modus operandi* to which most of those concerned had long been habituated, and, partly too and not least, to the exigencies of wartime diplomacy, the intricate, somewhat crab-like moves by which the players progressed (or retreated) from time to time were largely secret. Secrecy covered not only moves, but considerations; and not only at the time, which is to say during the war, but, in many cases, in the long aftermath.

Thirdly, by one of those paradoxes that serve both to reveal something of the peculiarities of political behaviour and to enliven its study, the central concern of the various secret negotiators—none of whom were ever fully in command of all the relevant facts of the matter, or fully informed of the identity and purposes of all others engaged *de facto* in the affair—was with *public* opinion after all. But it was the opinion of a public very imperfectly known to most of those concerned, a public whose views and likely responses to political events therefore formed the subject of continuous, often ill-founded speculation and argument, and a public which itself was almost wholly unaware of what was afoot. In the final analysis, the political decision in favour of the Zionists, fought for by some, opposed by others, emerged as the end-product of a series of arguments conducted within an inner arena on the subject of the interests, behaviour, views, and desires of people who were immensely distant from it in space, condition, concerns, and mental set.

ii

'I must confess to being considerably alarmed to notice that, to judge by the Foreign Office telegrams, there is a recrudescence of

attempts to satisfy the Zionist movement,' Edwin Montagu complained privately in mid-March 1916.[2] A year had passed, almost to
the day, since his first, ferocious response to the ideas Samuel had
presented to the Cabinet upon Turkey's entry in the war.[3] Neither
his horror at the prospect of an explicitly pro-Zionist British policy
nor the force with which he stated his conviction that such a move
would do neither Great Britain nor the Jews any good had
diminished. As a member of the Cabinet again since November of
the previous year, he seems particularly to have resented the fact
that this 'new and unauthorised policy of the Foreign Office' had
been launched without sanction at the highest level. But there was
nothing he could do to obstruct it. The Foreign Office was
unquestionably the relevant and competent department in this
matter. The Foreign Secretary, Grey, was now failing in health and
had to be replaced regularly by the Marquess of Crewe; but
together—and indeed separately—Grey and Crewe carried a great
deal more weight than Montagu. Nor could there be doubt in
anyone's mind, not even in Montagu's, that they and their officials
had been 'animated [to employ Montagu's own language] by the
desire to help Great Britain' rather than the Jews or any of *their*
causes. And there was the crowning oddity (of which Montagu was
not immediately aware), that a principal role in this fresh stage in
the process whereby the question of a Jewish Palestine had been
restored to the British Government's agenda had been peformed by
a personage on the Jewish side who was almost as wary of the idea as
were Montagu and Montagu's special confidant in these matters,
Rufus Isaacs, Lord Reading.[4]

For the established leaders and institutions of English Jewry, the
plight of the less fortunate communities, Russo-Polish Jewry before
all others, was still a matter of central concern and their particular
mission in their relations with the Government. It had been neither
deflected nor diminished by the war. The condition of east European
Jewry having further and very sharply deteriorated, as we have seen,
their concern and desire to render help were greater than ever. But
so were the obstacles to doing so. Short-term charitable work in

---

[2] Montagu to Reading, 17 March 1916. IOLR, MSS. Eur. F118/95.

[3] See above, pp. 96–8.

[4] To Montagu's complaint of 17 March 1916, Reading had replied at length,
managing to express both support for the Foreign Office's new position and
sympathetic agreement with most of Montagu's strictures.Reading to Montagu, 19
March 1916. IOLR, MSS. Eur. F118/95.

regions now largely in the war zone and under enemy occupation was virtually out of the question. Pressure on the British Government to intercede with Britain's (and France's) principal militiary ally and induce a change of heart in Russia and the eventual emancipation of its Jewish subjects met with greater resistance than ever and was easily repulsed with arguments that Jewish communal spokesmen tended to find unanswerable. When a Russian-Jewish notable from Petrograd was brought to the Foreign Office by Lucien Wolf to give a first-hand survey of the condition of Russian Jewry, especially in the eastern war zone, he was listened to 'most attentively and sympathetically' by Lancelot Oliphant, the official responsible at the time for affairs relating to Jews. But there could be no question of any action being taken. It was extremely difficult for the British Government to do anything at the present moment, Oliphant explained. And Wolf, loyal as ever, accounted himself not entirely displeased. 'It was especially noteworthy,' he reported to his Committee, 'that Mr. Oliphant used the words "extremely difficult" in regard to action on behalf of the Russian and Polish Jews, whereas on previous occasions he has invariably emphasized the "impossibility" of interfering in the domestic concerns of the Russian Empire.'[5]

The Jewish establishment as represented by the Conjoint Foreign Committee (CFC) had found itself torn as never before between what seemed to be conflicting duties and responsibilities: as Jews on the one hand and as British subjects on the other. Of all conflicts of interest and principle this was the one they had always dreaded and which, led by their authoritative and articulate secretary Wolf, they were most anxious to resolve. At the technical level they made it their practice to report in detail to the Foreign Office on their contacts with non-British bodies and personalities and to ask for the Office's sanction for much of the content of their correspondence before despatching it. At the policy level there occurred a certain paralysis of will, if not loss of direction. 'While realising to the full the gravity of the Russo-Jewish question,' ran an early formulation of their position a few months after the outbreak of the war, 'it would be improper at the present moment for the Jewish subjects of any of the Allied Powers to take any action, seeing that such action would inevitably be construed as an attempt to promote Jewish interests to

[5] Wolf to Alexander, 4 July 1915, enclosing memorandum of 2 July 1915. BD, C11/2/6.

the detriment of the united and single-minded prosecution of the war by the Governments and peoples of the three Allied Powers.'[6] It was incumbent upon them, they thought, 'to avoid the discussion of questions which might lead to controversy between the Allies.'[7] Their conclusion, at this stage, was that the best they could do was 'to watch very carefully the progress of events so as to be prepared to make due representations in the proper quarters when the time for discussing terms of peace might arrive.'[8]

Ostensibly, this left them with very little to do but consider the future and make interim 'representations'. They did both the one and the other, but with increasing foreboding. The notion that the war would end as briskly as it had begun, to be followed in good order by a peace conference on the old model (it was the Congress of Berlin of 1878 that Wolf and his colleagues had in mind), evaporated as the huge conflict dragged on. The sense that they must be ready to argue Jewish causes and cases with unprecedented energy when the lines along which the new political order to be established were in process of being laid down grew. The fear that, so far as Russia was concerned, there was 'no prospect of direct alleviation from the Peace Conference' was ever stronger.[9] Given the deep, active,[10] generally mindless anti-Semitism with which Polish nationalism was shot through, the further prospect of several million Jewish subjects of Russia and Austria falling under Polish rule, should the Poles achieve autonomy or even independence, was wholly appalling. The future of Romanian Jewry—possibly much enlarged if Romanian territorial ambitions were satisfied at war's end—was likely to be as bleak. Generally, if the map of Europe was going to be redrawn and whole communities were to be transferred from one sovereignty to another, it was evident there would be dangers (along with opportunities) all round. The principle the CFC was determined to cleave to—the principle it would press the Powers to adopt—would be, as in 1878, equal rights for all

[6] Emanuel to the Chief Rabbi, J. H. Hertz, for transmission to the Grand Rabbi in Paris, 18 November 1914. ML, AJ/204/1.

[7] Wolf to Bigart, 2 March 1915. BD, C11/3/2/1.

[8] Ibid.

[9] Ibid.

[10] Even in London—where Paderewski, as an unimpeachable British source informed Lucien Wolf early in 1915, 'had been very active . . . in explaining the Polish grievances against the Jews and . . . had even seen [Asquith] on the subject.' Wolf to Leopold de Rothschild, 28 April 1915. BD, E3/204/2.

inhabitants of the territories in question. Its members do not seem to have been very hopeful, but at least on this the CFC was clear in its collective mind.

It was less clear in its mind on what its members and its secretary took to be the decidedly secondary matter of Erez-Israel/Palestine to which, however, its thinking ahead to the post-war period naturally led it once the break-up of the Ottoman Empire began to emerge as a major war aim of the Allies. All that Wolf and his colleagues were certain of was that they did not agree with the Zionists: they did not, as they put it, 'contemplate any special political privileges [there] for the Jews'. True, they did not think it was enough to approach the safeguarding of Jewish interests there along the lines thought appropriate to eastern Europe. It was not enough, that is, to ask for equality of rights and status. 'It may be desirable,' they conceded, 'to ask for special facilities for Jewish immigration and colonization and for the free development of Jewish institutions and Jewish cultural life.[11] What 'special facilities' might mean precisely and how these might be obtained without the underpinning of special political rights were questions which they did not attempt to work out, however, and for all that they recognized the special historical, religious, and 'sentimental' attachment of the Jews to the country, there was no doubt in their minds that the truly great 'practical questions' were those that confronted Jewry in Russia, Poland, and Romania. It was there, as before, that they believed their own and everyone else's attention should be directed. So it should be throughout the war. So it should be in the aftermath. Meanwhile, they wished to play as effective a part as possible in the general effort to push the war to a successful conclusion.

At the same time, the members of the CFC and the circles and institutions they represented regarded themselves as bearing a particular responsibility for the conduct and, not least, the repute of the Jews as a component of British wartime society. And what lent special weight and quality to their role in Jewry was the custom and strong instinct of the relevant British Ministers and officials to accept them as the primary and authorized (if somewhat tiresome) spokesmen for English Jewry. It was a role which they themselves, naturally enough, were intent upon retaining. It was common wisdom that such a well-established channel of communication with the Government—and with that most prestigious of departments,

[11] Wolf to Bigart, 2 March 1915. Loc. cit.

the Foreign Office, in particular—was one that it was in the interests of all members of the community, indeed of all Jewish communities, to preserve; and, besides, it placed the CFC in a position of moral superiority, as it were, and of power *vis-à-vis* other Jewish bodies. Any serious attempt to challenge their primacy was open to charges of disloyalty, irresponsibility, and intrigue. At the same time, the effort to maintain that primacy obliged them to treat with—and, to some extent, co-operate with, and even represent— groups and tendencies within Jewry for which they had little liking or regard. Arguments with rebels, would-be competitors, and plain independent spirits could be fierce, however, in a community founded on voluntary public service and voluntary obedience in which none could *impose* a view, let alone discipline. The members of the Conjoint Foreign Committee of the Board of Deputies of British Jews and the Anglo-Jewish Association were liable in such cases to be driven back for their own guidance to a restatement, if not reformulation, of their fundamental views on the nature and needs of Jewry in the contemporary world, a procedure which did not always advance matters. The more clearly they found it necessary to define and articulate their views, the more difficult cooperation with groups holding other views could become. Worse, by one of the paradoxes with which the modern history of the Jews is shot through, their set notion on the role it was their duty to play could lead them to take up ideas that were deeply foreign to their way of thinking and incompatible with the underlying principles upon which that role was founded. It was thus that we find Wolf and his colleagues reluctantly but bravely believing that they must take up the question of the Jewish interest in Palestine as a matter of high priority after all.

iii

The Conjoint Foreign Committee was moved to rethink its approach to a Jewish Palestine in two (overlapping) stages and as a consequence of two distinct sets of considerations. These corresponded to the CFC's conception of its role within Jewry and on behalf of Jewry respectively. The one moved it to enter, reluctantly, into talks with a group of Zionists; the other to seek a way of contributing to the general effort to win the war.

In mid-November 1914 Harry Sacher, a close friend and political associate of Weizmann, called on Lucien Wolf to (in Wolf's words) 'find a means of co-operation between the Zionists and the leaders of the Community, as represented by the Conjoint Committee'.[12] Wolf was sceptical, but this was not an offer that could be refused out-of-hand; and, on the face of things, some form of co-ordination and co-operation was not out of the question. Like Wolf, Sacher was English-born and an established journalist who had worked for the *Manchester Guardian* and the *Daily News*, and he was devoted to Jewish causes. He was not even a 'political' Zionist, he explained to Wolf, rather an Aḥad Ha-ʿAmian. Indeed, the chief influence over him was Weizmann, to whom he had been drawn virtually since Weizmann's arrival in England and on whose behalf, in effect, he was now acting. When Wolf asked him whether the Zionists would be able to 'modify their political aspirations' in return for the CFC's agreeing to work with them—in itself a substantial concession on the Committee's part as most of its members and constituents 'did not regard Palestine as a practical solution to any of the problems with which they have to deal'—Sacher replied that for the Zionists 'such a concession would be very easy, more especially as the last Zionist Congress had practically eliminated political Zionism from its immediate programme and had resolved to rely on Cultural Zionism and Peaceful Penetration.' The political problems might therefore be left to solve themselves.[13] Sacher evidently hoped that Wolf and his colleagues could be relieved of their fear of 'the bogey of political Zionism, of a Jewish State which will pose them with awkward questions of allegiance'. He seems also to have hoped that he could manage to instruct them in 'Zionism in the sense in which we understand it [and of which] they all, including Lucien Wolf, have no knowledge or glimmering of knowledge.'[14]

A certain antagonism was inherent in the relations between the two parties, and hints of difficulties and tensions and points of mutual incomprehension to come emerged early. Sacher and Weizmann refused from the first to take the CFC people at their own high estimate. Referring to them in his private correspondence, Sacher habitually put 'leaders' within quotation marks. Weizmann, fiercer in his feelings and not yet wholly in control of his style, spoke of Wolf as Rothschild's 'porter' and laid down that 'gentlemen of the type of L.W. [Wolf] have to be told the candid truth at present and

[12] Memorandum by Wolf, 17 November 1914. BD, E3/204/1.
[13] Wolf, ibid.
[14] Sacher to Weizmann, 17 November 1914. WA.

made to realize that *we* and not *they* are the masters of the situation, that if we come to them it is only and solely because we desire to show to the world a *united Jewry* and we don't want to expose them as "self-appointed leaders"'.[15] Wolf, for his part not without reason, had doubts whether Weizmann and his friends had authority to speak for the movement. 'I find at the outset,' he wrote Sacher, 'that I am confronted by the enquiry: who are the persons and organisations representing your views and in what measure do they represent the great body of Zionists? I must answer this question specifically and I hope you will enable me to do so.'[16] Sacher replied that he and his friends were 'convinced' that their cause was the cause of the Jewish people, that 'We know that we are the spokesman of 200,000 organized Zionists', and that Weizmann was the representative in England both of the EAC and the Provisional Zionist Committee in America 'which during the war has taken over the direction of Zionist affairs'.[17] It was not a truthful answer, as Wolf was aware, and the prospects for an understanding were not improved when reports of Weizmann's other activities (interviews with Balfour and Samuel, for example) began to filter through to the established leadership.

I took the opportunity of pointing out [Wolf reported to his principals] that in my opinion Dr. Weitzmann [*sic*] would be very ill-advised to pursue his negotiations with politicians if he were really anxious to cooperate with Members of the Conjoint Committee. The Conjoint Committee was the appointed body elected for that purpose by the Anglo-Jewish Community, and it would only make for trouble if the Zionists were to trespass on their functions. In that case, indeed, the proposed cooperation would be useless, and impossible.[18]

But finally, after further talks and some acrimonious correspondence, the CFC being impelled, it seems, as much by fear of the trouble the Zionists would cause if no attempt was made to meet them part of the way[19] as by hope that the Zionists would ultimately modify their position, a formal meeting between the two sides was

---

[15] Weizmann to Sacher and Leon Simon, 28 November 1914. *Weizmann Letters*, vii, no. 48, pp. 57–8. Emphases in original.

[16] Wolf to Sacher, 26 November 1914. BD, E3/204/1.

[17] Sacher to Wolf, 1 December 1914. Ibid.

[18] Wolf to Alexander, 16 December 1914. Ibid.

[19] 'The Zionists are exceedingly active,' wrote Claude Montefiore to Samuel; 'and those who like myself, regard their policy and aims as most dangerous and false, can no longer afford to go to sleep.' 3 March 1915. CZA, A77/3/8.

convened on 14 April 1915. In the event, neither Weizmann nor Sacher attended. The Zionists were represented by Sokolov and Tchlenov—the unquestionably accredited legates of the Actions Committee who had arrived meanwhile in London[20]—and three prominent veterans of the English movement: Cowen, Gaster, and Herbert Bentwich, all senior to Weizmann in terms of past or present office. The two leaders of the CFC, D. L. Alexander for the Board of Deputies and Claude Montefiore for the Anglo-Jewish Association, along with Wolf and one other member, H. S. Q. Henriques, confronted them. The Zionists seem to have done most of the talking (much of it in German).

Tchlenov led the discussion. He reviewed conditions in eastern Europe. He conceded readily that all should aim at an improvement of the Jews' legal and political status there. But, he argued, it would be a very extended process and would not and could not lead to a 'complete' solution of the Jewish problem. That could only be obtained by Zionism; and the Zionists, as might be supposed, were intent upon it, the more so as there was now a 'unique' chance of restoring Erez-Israel to the Jews. If the Allies won the war the Ottoman Empire would be broken up. It was likely that the country would fall to England, and it was entirely conceivable that England would give the Jews a chance to establish a Jewish commonwealth within it. In such circumstances it would be a 'crime against the Jews of the world' if the great Jewish organizations did not come together to press the Jewish people's claim at the coming Peace Conference. Other nations would be pressing their claims. Those that did not thus stand up for themselves would be ignored. But the Jewish case must be represented by a *single* set of delegates; and since the Zionists were determined to make the most of the unique opportunity that had been presented them, unity depended on *all* Jewish organizations adopting a common stand on both central issues: that of Erez-Israel as well as that of the Jews' legal disabilities in Europe. The Zionists were convinced there was no contradiction between the two. The question now was whether the CFC agreed and whether they were prepared to co-operate on the lines indicated. Finally, the Zionists emphasized (probably in response to a query), they—that is, Tchlenov and Sokolov—were indeed the competent spokesmen for the Organization, and the

---

[20] See above, p. 132.

Organization was still governed, as before the war, by the regularly elected EAC.[21]

Wolf and his colleagues were cautious. They wanted to know more of the terms in which the Zionists envisaged a Jewish 'commonwealth' (*Gemeinwesen*): its probable size, its status in Jewry relative to other communities, the special rights that would be asked for the Jews within it as a collectivity and as individuals. At pains to be reasonable and moderate in their response, the Conjoint Foreign Committee took some time and went to some length to examine the Zionists' views and proposals—in the light, inevitably, of their own view of the current conditions and desired future of European Jewry. But the result, when it came, was a firm restatement of the anti-Zionist position, Lucien Wolf's hand apparent in virtually every line. The nub of the argument was a refutation of what the CFC correctly took to be the core of the Zionists' position: the thesis that the long campaign to secure the welfare and the full rights of citizenship of east European Jewry was doomed to failure. 'If there were any reason to believe that this [our] programme had become impracticable, we should necessarily have to turn to some other, and we could not refuse to study the Zionist proposals in that light.' They were far from such a belief. They did not deny that the struggle for Jewish emancipation was beset with difficulties, nor that the contemporary outlook was 'profoundly discouraging'. But they were convinced that there was 'no solid ground to despair of eventual success'. Social and political conditions in eastern Europe were changing,

the whole tendency of the national life [there] is necessarily towards a more enlightened and liberal policy. . . . The very magnitude and growing embarrassments of the Jewish question, and the certainty that it cannot be solved in any other way, afford a guarantee that sooner or later the statesmanship of the countries concerned will, for their own protection, deal with it in the way in which it has been successfully dealt with in Western Europe and America. . . . Antisemitism is [not] ineradicable, [nor are] the Jews . . . inherently unassimilable. . . . It is, of course quite possible that we are over sanguine in this view, but this does not make the plan of the Zionists any the more acceptable to us.

In any case, Zionism was inherently mistaken and dangerous.

[21] 'Report on a conference of the honorary officers [of the CFC] with the delegates of the Zionist Organizations,' 27 April 1915. BD, E3/204/2.

In no sense can it be regarded as a likely solution to the Jewish problem. It will not diminish the number of Jews in the Russian Captivity; it can do nothing to abate the rigours of that captivity. . . . [And] it would seriously compromise all prospect of solution by the alternative way of emancipation.

This latter danger derived from what lay at the very heart of their objection to Zionism:

The idea of a Jewish nationality, the talk of a Jew 'going home' to Palestine if he is not content with his lot in the land of his birth, strikes at the root of all claim to Jewish citizenship in lands where Jewish disabilities still exist. It is the assertion, not merely of a double nationality—a doctrine which is just now in extremely bad odour—but of perpetual alienage of Jews everywhere outside Palestine. This would not only create a new and perhaps insurmountable bar to Jewish emancipation in lands like Russia and Roumania, but it would have the most deplorable consequences for the Jews in other countries where legal disabilities no longer exist, but where some sense of the strangeness of the Jew, or some ungenerous antipathy to him as such, still lingers.[22]

There were other objections, among them that an eventual Jewish state as the Zionists conceived it would be founded on a special status for its Jewish inhabitants, therefore on 'civil and religious disabilities of the most mediaeval kind'. Such a state could not endure and 'would bring lasting reproach on Jews and Judaism.'[23] But central in their thinking was the fear that the Zionist programme and the Zionist idea—perhaps the Zionist idea above all, if ever it gained wider ground—struck not only at the foundations and prospects of their own programme, but at the bases of their own social existence and security as well. In brief, they recognized in Zionism not only a rival school of thought drawn to different purposes and values, but a threat to their constituency and to themselves. It followed that there could be no meeting of minds and no joining of forces, unless, of course, one or other party modified its position. *They* would not, they informed the Zionists.[24] Privately they had considered going so far as to agree with the Zionists 'that efforts should be made to bring Palestine under British . . . Protection, as being favourable to Jewish development in that country.'[25] But the passage was struck out, almost certainly on the

---

[22] Ibid.
[23] Ibid.
[24] 'Resolutions of the Conjoint Committee, April 27 1915, presented to the adjourned conference [with the Zionist delegation] on April 29 1915.' ML, AJ/204/1.
[25] Ibid., BD, E3/204/2.

advice of the Foreign Office, to which it seems to have been submitted for approval.[26] No other common ground could be identified.

The Zionists' reply, conciliatory in tone, amounted to a restatement of their own position on Jewish rights, on the Jewish problem in general, and on the alleged interconnection (which they denied) between assertions of Jewish nationhood and anti-Semitism. Nothing the Jews did affected anti-Semites one way or another. 'The only way for Jews to satisfy anti-Semitism,' they argued, 'is to cease to exist, and that is a solution no Jewish body can contemplate.' They denied that any responsible member of the movement had ever suggested, 'that under the guise of Jewish nationalism, there should be any restrictions or prohibitive measure against Arabs or other dwellers in the land.' Finally, they pointed out, to follow the CFC and limit the future Jewish claims in Erez-Israel to what Jews might require

'as a matter of conscience or communal convenience', is to mistake the whole object of the demand. What is wanted is that ... such measures should be taken as would avoid any hindrances to the new progressive elements while they remain a minority in the land, and that special facilities for colonisation and development would be granted to the Jewish bodies or organisations which will undertake the work. The basis must be established for a great and rapid development of the country through the labour and energy of the Jewish settlers, and such 'concessions' must be secured as will enlist the support and interest of Jews all over the world.[27]

This was not Ahad Ha-'Amian Zionism, but nor was it political Zionism strictly constructed. Anything less than 'special facilities' for settlement and development would have reduced the Zionist purposes in the country to such minimalist formulations as had been presented from time to time, in desperation, to the Turks. But the statement was still too strong for the CFC; and was judged, at any rate by Wolf, (perhaps because the Zionists had tried too hard to meet him at least part of the way) 'a feeble document, and where it is not feeble, extremely disingenuous'.[28] In any event, the exchange was at an end[29] and the disjunction confirmed, never effectively to

---

[26] Memorandum by Wolf on conversation with Oliphant, 28 April 1915. ML, AJ/204/4; and CFC confidential minutes, 9 June 1915, ibid.

[27] 'Reply of Zionist representatives on the memorandum of the Conjoint Committee', 11 May 1915. BD, E3/204/2.

[28] Wolf to Leopold de Rothschild, 25 May 1915. BD, E3/204/2.

[29] Wolf to Sokolov, 11 June 1915. CZA, A18/22. On the abortive attempt to restart the talks, see below, p. 225f.

be bridged. On the Zionist side the lead would be assumed ever more powerfully by Weizmann directly, as we shall see. The CFC, for its part, having submitted all the relevant papers to the Foreign Office (without the Zionists' knowledge or consent) and been confirmed in their rejection of an altered order of Jewish priorities,[30] resumed their efforts in the direction in which they believed and to which they had long been accustomed. Their essential dilemma— how concern for the welfare of Jewry might be squared with their desire to prove themselves loyal subjects of their country—had still to be resolved. Late in 1915, help, conceived in what seemed to them to be precisely the right spirit, came to them unexpectedly from Paris.

iv

Official French and British observers of the American scene continued to register and report on Jewry's preoccupation with the condition of its Russian branch as an obstacle to Allied purposes. Allied Ambassadors in Petrograd might seek to play down the continual hammering of the Jews[31] and, on occasion, to excuse it. But if in France and Great Britain Jewish protests and moral discomfort could be kept quite easily within manageable limits, and in any case could have no effect on the conduct of the war, matters in the United States itself were otherwise. Russian disclaimers and denials of ill-treatment, even when delivered formally by Government spokesmen of the highest rank, had no effect on opinion in the face of the continually accumulating reports of ill-treatment from Russia itself. Liberal France and England—engaged, as they wished all the world to know, in a struggle against anti-democratic forces— could not easily escape the embarrassment of association with despotic Russia. And while the Jews were not the only victims of that despotism, their case was a particularly blatant one (if only because it was grounded solidly and openly in Russian law and administrative practice) and they had great numbers of energetic and devoted spokesmen in the west. Since it had long been agreed by

[30] 'An interesting sidelight on Zionism, showing how hopelessly impracticable Zionists are,' was a Foreign Office reponse on reading Wolf's account of statements by Tchlenov and his colleagues at the 14 April meeting. Minute by Oliphant [29 April 1915]. PRO, FO 371/2488.

[31] For example, Paléologue to Delcassé, 15 September 1915. AE, Guerre 1914– 1918, vol. 1197, fos. 99–101.

all the belligerents that public opinion in rich, neutral America had to be fought for, since American Jewry, as represented notably in the press and in Wall Street, was believed (as we have seen) to carry great weight, and since, as the war continued, the Allies looked to the United States ever more intently for political and financial support—the concern of their representatives with Jewish opinion became ever more enxious, not least because none regarded the prospect of a change of heart in Russia as anything but improbable. This was true especially of the French.[32]

In December 1915 it was decided in Paris to deal with the problem directly. A 'Committee for French Propaganda among Jews in Neutral Countries' was formed under the joint auspices of Parliament and Government. The chairman of the Foreign Affairs Committee of the Chamber of Deputies assumed the leadership. Jewish and non-Jewish notables—deputies, members of the Academy, university professors, and men of letters, some of them of great distinction—were co-opted. Lines of possible argument and apologia were laid down. One of the initiators of the project, Victor Basch, a professor at the Sorbonne, was despatched by the Foreign Ministry to speak directly to leading figures in American Jewry. And finally, the Conjoint Committee in London was informed of the plan and invited to co-operate. Wolf thereupon informed the Foreign Office, proposed that a parallel committee be established in London (if the Foreign Office agreed), and submitted his own views on the problems posed by the state of Jewish opinion in the United States and on the lines that might most usefully be adopted.[33]

There is no mistaking the enthusiasm with which Lucien Wolf rose to the French initiative and sought to improve upon it in the hope that 'the formation of such committees, in close collaboration with the British and French Governments, would probably provide a new leverage for the purpose of obtaining concessions from the Russian Government.'[34] He thought an English-speaking committee

---

[32] See for example, Jusserand to Delcassé, 12 February 1915; and, especially, Homberg, French financial delegate to the United States, to Briand, 21 February 1916. AE, Guerre 1914–1918; Sionisme, vol. 1197.

[33] Bigart to Wolf, 10 December 1915; 'Note' by Victor Basch, n.d.; Wolf to Lord R. Cecil, 16 December 1915; Comité de propagande française auprès des Juifs neutres, minutes for 16 December 1915; and Meyerson to Wolf, 24 December 1915. BD, C11/3/1/1.

[34] CFC Reports [15 December 1915], p. 62. ML, AJ/204/1.

likely to be far more effective in the United States than one from France. He argued that it ought not to be of an 'official character' on the French model (although it had to be 'in the closest confidential relations with His Majesty's Government') because 'Americans did not like the intervention of foreign governments in their domestic affairs'.[35] He offered the Foreign Office his own close analysis of the problem American Jewish opinion presented the Allies, and suggestions for dealing with it which were at once more detailed, more incisive than anything the French had had in mind and, in one respect, quite novel.

It was not enough to counter old arguments against Russia and adduce new ones for supporting the democracies, which *grosso modo* was what the French had in mind. The Jews were all 'more or less hostile to Reaction'. There had to be a positive appeal to their sentiments and loyalties.

I am not a Zionist [Wolf wrote], and I deplore the Jewish National Movement. To my mind the Jews are not a nationality. I doubt whether they ever have been one in the true sense of the term. . . . Still, the facts cannot be ignored, . . . in any bid for Jewish sympathies to-day, very serious account must be taken of the Zionist movement. In America the Zionist organisations have lately captured Jewish opinion, and very shortly a great American Jewish Congress will be held virtually under Zionist auspices. This is the moment for the Allies to declare their policy in regard to Palestine. . . . [They] cannot promise to make a Jewish State of a land in which only a comparatively small minority of the inhabitants are Jews, but there is a great deal they can say which would conciliate Zionist opinion. If, for example they would say that they thoroughly understand and sympathise with Jewish aspirations in regard to Palestine, and that when the destiny of the country came to be considered, those aspirations will be taken into account, and that in addition they would be guaranteed reasonable facilities for immigration and colonisation, for a liberal scheme of local self-government for the existing colonists, for the establishment of a Jewish University, and for the recognition of the Hebrew language as one of the vernaculars of the land, I am confidant they would sweep the whole of American Jewry into enthusiastic allegiance to their cause.

What the Zionists would especially like to know is that Great Britain will become mistress of Palestine. This may be difficult to say in view of French claims and of the assurances which have already been given to France in regard to the whole of Syria, which is held in Paris to include Palestine. But,

---

[35] Wolf to Cecil, loc. cit.

if, without dealing with this question, the guarantees I have indicated could be given, I am sure they would suffice. What the Zionists fear above all is an increase of Russian influence, or an Italian annexation which would fill the country with Sicilian peasants, or an International Commission which would be soulless if it were not a hot-bed of demoralising intrigue.[36]

The initial reception accorded Wolf's proposals in the Foreign Office was a hesitant one. His argument was not dismissed out of hand. But nor could anyone suggest what might really be the 'best method of tackling [the] extremely delicate problem'[37] he had raised. Inevitably, the papers were sent to Sir Cecil Spring Rice, the Ambassador in Washington, for his opinion.

The Ambassador's reply amounted to a restatement of the now accepted view of the matter, namely that 'the influence of the Jews here is very great' and 'a strong hatred of Russia . . . really is the governing motive' in their approach to the belligerent powers. But his operative conclusions were different from anything Wolf or his friends in Paris had in mind. Spring Rice did not oppose propaganda. But he thought there was no prospect whatever of removing Jewish disabilities in Russia which were 'likely to last as long as the ordinary Russian [was unable] to compete with the ordinary Jew'. 'Our weak point', the Jews' hatred of Russia, was therefore insurmountable. That said, however, there was no reason, in his view, for the Jews to help the Germans against France and England, the more so as, if the French and the English ever took careful note of the conduct of the Jews, the 'reaction . . . will not be advantageous to them'.

My personal suggestion would be (given in all diffidence) that the heads of the Jewish communities in France and England should be warned of the general impression which exists here of the anti-ally sympathies of the great mass of the Jews in the United States, although many of the most prominent members have the strongest sympathies for France and England and the cause for which they are fighting. There is a danger threatening the Jew in England and France of which they should be warned and of which I believe the Jews here are fully conscious.

In sum, it was not so much for the British Government as for the community leaders in France and England 'to explain to their

---

[36] 'Suggestions for a pro-Allies propaganda among the Jews of the United States', 16 December 1915. PRO, FO 371/2579.
[37] Minute by B., 20 December 1915. Ibid.

Jewish brethren here [in the United States] what would be the effects of taking sides with us.'[38]

The Ambassador's proposal was acted upon only indirectly and with nothing like the energy he had had in mind. Lord Robert Cecil, in the course of his correspondence with Wolf, did venture on one occasion to refer to circumstances in which Jews unnamed might 'lose a great part of the sympathy which at present exists for them in France and England', but went no further, perhaps because of Wolf's shocked reply.[39] The original proposal to form a committee on the lines of the one in Paris was approved, but, in the event, the project never got off the ground either. Lord Reading, Lord Chief Justice at the time, proposed as a key member, pronounced in favour of the operation, but declined to participate. The Foreign Office at all the relevant levels was none too enthusiastic about Wolf playing the central role that he evidently planned for himself. And, perhaps decisively, within the Foreign Office itself, the question of what was to be said, and offered, to the Jews came to be debated with greater attention and urgency—and, on the part of some officials, greater excitement—than that of the vehicle by means of which they were to be approached.

Wolf himself had put forward three specific recommendations: that the British and the French promote an understanding between Russia and the United States on the old issue of discrimination against Jewish citizens of the United States travelling to Russia; that Great Britain and France 'urge' upon the Russians the abolition of certain restrictions on Jews 'pending the complete revision of the laws relating to the Jews already promised by the Imperial Government' after the war; and that there be made 'a public

---

[38] Spring Rice to Cecil, 29 January 1916. PRO, FO 371/2835. Spring Rice's full letter to Cecil, as quoted here, was in fact mislaid and not seen until early in April. But the gist of it had been telegraphed in February, read by all concerned, and sufficed in practice.

[39] Wolf had promptly and solemnly written to Cecil, that 'while we shall always do our best to induce our coreligionists in other countries to support the policy of His Majesty's Government, we cannot be held responsible for anything they may judge proper to do in the very different circumstances in which they are placed. The Jewish communities are religious communities, like any other. They have even less of international organisation than many Christian denominations, and it is always difficult—in the present circumstances, indeed, impossible—to obtain any unity of action from them.' He was then assured by Lord Robert that his views were 'appreciated' and would be borne in mind. Cecil to Wolf, 24 February; Wolf to Cecil, 29 February; and Cecil to Wolf, 1 March 1916. ML, AJ/204/2.

statement on the Palestine Question'.[40] The first two proposals were now swiftly rejected. 'Any attempt at the present moment,' Wolf was told, 'to induce the British and French Governments to intervene directly or indirectly in Russia's internal questions, would be a great mistake.'[41] That left only the 'Palestine Question', advanced as a 'definite concession [that] must be made to Jewish opinion. . . owing to the great organised strength of the Zionists in the United States'.[42] It was on this that the Foreign Office, at all relevant ranks up to and including the Foreign Secretary (Grey) and the Minister deputizing for him in his absence (Crewe), fastened as the basis for a policy it would make good political sense for Britain and France to pursue. (It was at this stage, as telegrams on the subject were exchanged between London, Paris, and Petrograd, and people outside the immediate Foreign Office circle but on the regular distribution list of Foreign Office telegrams became aware of the direction taken, that Edwin Montagu, now Chancellor of the Duchy of Lancaster, protested.)[43]

'The one ruling consideration,' it was argued in the internal memorandum which most clearly set out the terms in which the British diplomatic machine saw the issue in the spring of 1916, is what

would appeal powerfully to a large and influential section of Jews throughout the world. . . . It is clear that the Palestine scheme has in it the most far-reaching political possibilities and we should, if I may be allowed to say so, be losing a great opportunity if we did not do our utmost to overcome any difficulties that may be raised by France and Russia.[44]

It was recognized in London that French objections might be serious, although how formidable they would prove to be no one at this stage had estimated. The Foreign Office was also aware in a general way that Jewry itself was divided on the question of Palestine. The Russians, it was estimated correctly, were unlikely to be difficult.

So far as the French were concerned, it was decided to approach the Government in Paris directly (the Ambassador in London had

[40] 'Memorandum' [18 February 1916]. PRO, FO 371/2835.
[41] Cecil to Wolf, 24 February 1915. Ibid.
[42] 'Memorandum', loc. cit.
[43] See above, p. 170–1.
[44] Minute by O'Beirne, 8 March 1916. PRO, FO 371/2817.

been sounded and had been dismissive of the plan) in the hope that if it was explained 'fully to them the political object which we hoped to attain by turning in our favour the Jewish force in America, the Near East and elsewhere,' the 'result might be completely different'.[45] As for the Jews, the feeling was that 'Mr. L. Wolf cannot be taken as the spokesman of the whole of Jewry'; that 'if and when we are allowed by our allies to say anything worth saying to the Jews it should not be left to Mr. Lucien Wolf to say it'; and that the subject ought to be pursued in spite of the divisions of opinion in Jewry 'since the advantage of securing Jewish goodwill in the Levant and in America can hardly be overestimated, both at present and at the conclusion of the war.'[46] The upshot was that the French and Russian Governments were formally invited to consider the offer of 'an arrangement in regard to Palestine completely satisfactory to Jewish aspirations'. The advantages hoped for were duly explained. The opposition of part of Jewry to Zionism was conceded. And the carefully formulated 'definition of Jewish aspirations in regard to Palestine' which Lucien Wolf had submitted to the Foreign Office[47] was transmitted verbatim:

In the event of Palestine coming within the sphere of influence of Great Britain or France at the close of the war, the Governments of those Powers will not fail to take account of the historic interest that country possesses for the Jewish community. The Jewish population will be secured in the enjoyment of civil and religious liberty, equal political rights with the rest of the population, reasonable facilities for immigration and colonization, and such municipal privileges in the towns and colonies inhabited by them as may be shown to be necessary.

This, as we have seen, was more or less what the CFC had been prepared to agree upon with the Zionists late in 1914 and what Sacher (and presumably Weizmann) had originally called for at the very earliest stage before the central issue of principle—the nationality or otherwise of the Jews—arose and aborted the talks. The Foreign Office saw nothing to object to in Wolf's formula, but they did wish the French and Russians to know that they, for their part, were in favour of going a good deal further.

We consider . . . that the scheme might be made far more attractive to the

[45] Ibid.
[46] Minutes by Crewe, 8 March 1916, and Cecil, 14 March 1916. PRO, FO 371/2817.
[47] On 3 March 1916.

majority of Jews if it held out to them the prospect that when in the course of time the Jewish colonists in Palestine grow strong enough to cope with the Arab population they be may be allowed to take the management of the internal affairs of Palestine (with the exception of Jerusalem and the Holy Places) into their own hands.[48]

Only a year before, the Zionists and Zionism had been dismissed as 'hopelessly impracticable'. The change is striking; and one, it must be admitted, that cannot be neatly accounted for. There is no evidence of ministerial, let alone prime ministerial intervention. Grey and Crewe (Grey's regular replacement) had simply agreed with what had been put up to them by the officials: the view set forth was now, broadly and at least for the moment, a collective one within the Office. The Zionists themselves had had no direct contact with anyone in the Office, virtually since the start of the war, except for a single interview granted Weizmann by Lord Robert Cecil in August 1915. Cecil seems to have disliked Weizmann at sight, but had been impressed none the less by what he had been told of Jewish national feeling and by the intensity with which the argument had been put to him.[49] No doubt, something of what Weizmann had said to him had registered. But it was a single incident and relatively long ago. Sokolov had sought to be received, but had failed. It is possible that Crewe had heard something of Zionism from his wife,[50] to whom Weizmann had been introduced and whose ear he had. It is certain that Samuel's memoranda of the year before had not been wholly forgotten, at any rate at the ministerial level. And there was the coincidence that just at the time Wolf's memorandum was under consideration a report of a conversation with the head of the Jewish community in Alexandria was received from Cairo and read with attention by all the men who had a hand in the decision to gain French and Russian approval for the new departure. Its substance was that which in milder form Wolf had argued for, namely that a declaration of support for Zionism would swing Jewish opinion sharply in Great Britain's favour. The response in London was mixed; it was observed that approval would lead to difficulties with other Powers (France, chiefly), and that there were divisions within Jewry to be taken into account. But no one contested the basic

---

[48] Telegram to Bertie, Paris, and Buchanan, Petrograd, 11 March 1916. PRO, FO 371/2817.

[49] Cecil to Russell, 18 August 1915. PRO, FO 800/95.

[50] The Marchioness of Crewe was the daughter of the fifth Earl of Rosebery and Hannah Rothschild.

argument outright; and it is evident that it was turned over in the minds of men who, even if they were not all enthusiastic, were ever more strongly of the view that Jewish opinion did count and ought to be catered for in one way or another. It was a view epitomized in Lord Robert Cecil's oblique comment on the despatch from Cairo when placed before him: 'I do not think it is easy to exaggerate the international power of the Jews.'[51]

'The international power of the Jews.' It was an odd notion, not one—it seems—that was ever thought through by any of those who were ready enough to employ and act upon it. The Jews, as the professionals of British diplomacy could have known, had no 'international power'. That is to say, they had no means—and what mattered more, by and large (the Zionists apart) they had little desire—to come together to wield power in their own collective interest. They had no means either of ascertaining in just what their collective interest might consist, the more so as it was always a fair question whether there was, and whether there could be, a 'collective' Jewish interest at all, except perhaps *in extremis*. No doubt the steady peppering of Paris, London, and Petrograd with reports on Jacob Schiff and other Jewish notables, their views and their loyalties, real and alleged, had had their cumulative effect on all three Governments. But the evidence which we know to have been placed before these generally sensible men does not suffice to account for the dramatic conclusions they seem to have drawn from it. It is their predisposition to read a lot more into it than it could bear that must have been decisive. It certainly derived from the common and very ancient propensity among non-Jews of all classes and all levels of social and political sophistication to ascribe organic unity to what was at best an aggregate of groups, parties, communities, institutions, societies, and particular individuals, all of widely differing types and purposes, bound—if that is the word—only by exceedingly tenuous and uncertain ties which boiled down to things of the mind and the heart, never to defined, recognized, and compelling *interests*. It was precisely for lack of a strong, evident, common interest and for lack of a strong, generally accepted leadership to articulate and pursue it that the Jews were devoid, and mostly chose to be devoid, of 'international power'. The Jews themselves and those who claimed to speak for them in their different ways—the Schiffs, the Wolfs, the Montagus, the Readings,

[51] McMahon to Grey, 11 February 1916. PRO, FO 371/2671.

the Rothschilds, the Montefiores, the Samuels, the Ah'ad Ha-'Ams, the Weizmanns, the Tchlenovs, the Jabotinskys, the men of the Alliance Israélite Universelle, the Jacobsons, the Warburgs, the Hantkes, and the many, many others—all knew this. It was only among those observers of Jewry who were themselves placed outside it that the myth of an organic Jewry and of consequent Jewish international power held a fascination, was believed or half-believed in, and tended actually to influence not only the interpretation of data but to serve as a basis for action. It may be too that in the third year of the war the urge to grasp at any straw was irresistible: anything was worth trying if its mite could be added to the enormous total effort. With the balance between the real powers on earth so even and precarious, the fear or hope that the smallest increment might tip it one way or the other had solid origins. It is also the case, as we shall see, that there were always strong minds and sharp eyes that saw through the clouds of prejudgement and lore in which the matter of the Jews had always been enveloped. Within less than a generation, the notion of the Jews' 'international power' would of course be revealed throughout Europe and in the United States as well as empty of real content, for all to see. But that was later; and meanwhile it had passed from a notion present chiefly in the back of the minds concerned, a matter hardly relevant to the political business of the day, to the forefront of those same minds and directly relevant, in their view, to their major concerns.

That said, the uses of a position favourable to a Jewish Palestine lay in the logic of the concern with Jewish opinion *per se*: not so much concern with such power as the Jews could wield, rather with their hostility to the Allied cause and the need to deflect or neutralize it. It was clear to the British, to the French, and to the Russians themselves that Jewish hostility was almost wholly a function of Russian oppression. It was clear to all that a change of Russian policy would quickly precipitate a radical shift of attitude and sympathy (or, as one Foreign Office man minuted quaintly, 'restore Jewish confidence in Russia').[52] But it was equally clear that no such change was forthcoming. And lastly, there was intense opposition in London and Paris to any attempt to press the Russians in a direction it was evident they would refuse to move. The Allies could decide to resolve to remove the issue from the agenda. But once they had, by stages, come to accept it as one of importance which required

[52] PRO, FO 372/2817, fo. 24.

treatment, the inclination to look for a solution to the dilemma was strong. By the same token, constant reminders by the established Jewish organizations in London and Paris that the central problem of Russian Jewry was unsolved were intensely irritating; and, once it was broached, the 'Palestine idea' looked exceedingly attractive, a release from the peculiar frustration of recognizing a problem while being unable to deal with it.[53] Thus, at any rate, in London.

The response in Petrograd was encouraging. Sazonov, the Foreign Minister, told Buchanan that there was no objection, in fact his Government 'would welcome [the] migration of Jews to Palestine'. Their only reservations concerned the Holy Places—clearly conceived as being preponderantly Christian—which must be placed under an international regime.[54] The British themselves did not think otherwise at this point.

In Paris the question was examined much more closely and in a different light. Unlike Petrograd, where Buchanan had gone to see Sazonov, there was no interview between the Ambassador and the Foreign Minister (Briand) or any of the senior officials at the Quai d'Orsay. Besides, Lord Bertie himself was unenthusiastic. When he had first heard something of Zionism from a Zionist—Weizmann, as it happened, in Paris, early in 1915—he had noted in his diary that Edmond de Rothschild had

sent a Russian coreligionist established in Manchester to 'talk' about what I think an absurd scheme, though they say it has the approval of Grey, Lloyd George, Samuel, and Crewe: they did not mention Lord Reading. It contemplates the formation of Palestine into an Israelite State, under the protectorate of England, France, or Russia, preferably England. ... What would the Pope, and Italy, and Catholic France with her hatred of Jews, say to this scheme?[55]

Now he wrote to Grey to warn him that the 'idea' would meet with no encouragement in Paris. He himself did not think German and German-American Jews would be moved from their hostility to Russia by promises in regard to Palestine. He thought that such promises, if made, would become known to the Arabs and that

---

[53] 'What is discouraging,' O'Beirne minuted after reading yet another report on the weight American Jewish opinion ascribed to matters in Russia, 'is that so much more stress is laid on the emancipation of the Russian Jews than on the Palestine idea.' 14 March 1916. Ibid.

[54] Buchanan to Foreign Office, 14 and 15 March 1916. PRO, FO 371/2817, fos. 34–6.

[55] *The Diary of Lord Bertie of Thame* (London, 1924), i, pp. 105–6.

1. David Wolffsohn

2. Otto Warburg

4. Nahum Sokolov

3. Yehiel Tchlenov

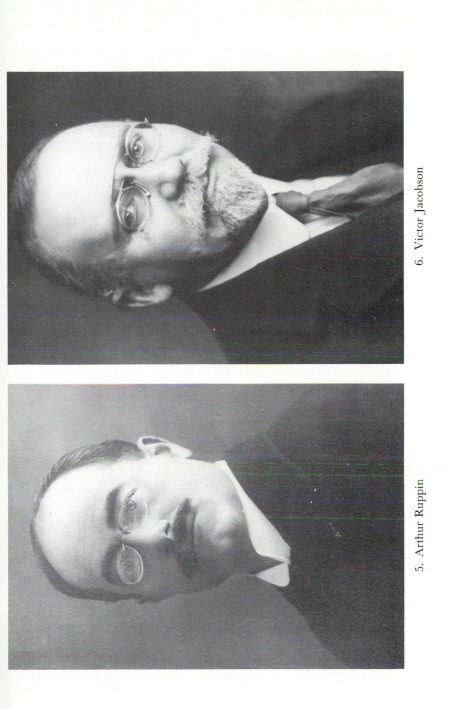

6. Victor Jacobson

5. Arthur Ruppin

8. Ze'ev Jabotinsky

7. Yosef Trumpeldor

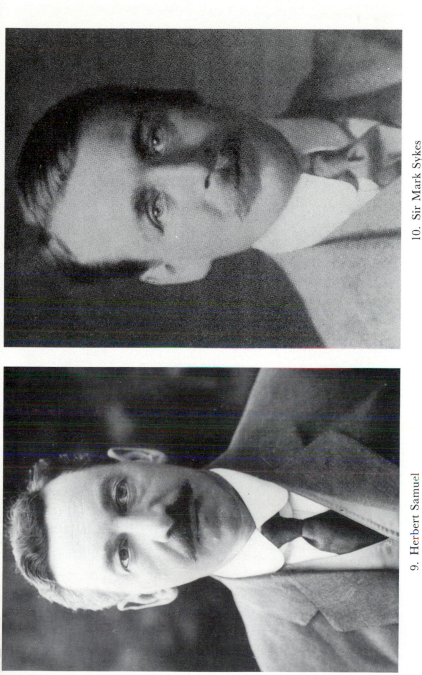

9. Herbert Samuel

10. Sir Mark Sykes

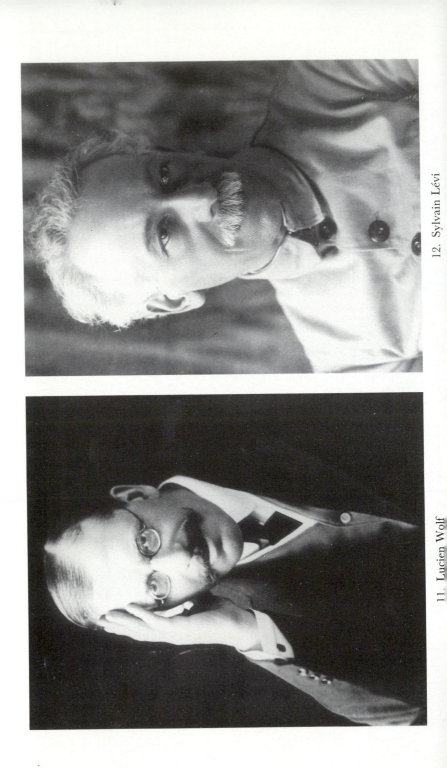

11. Lucien Wolf

12. Sylvain Lévi

13. Arthur James Balfour

14. Chaim Weizmann

the results would be 'disastrous . . . so far as Arab aid to the cause of the Entente Allies is concerned'. Besides, he warned his minster, 'The Jews are not a combative race. How would they fare against the warlike Arabs unless physically supported by England and France?'[56] But he followed his instructions and presented the proposal with care. He rearranged the original Foreign Office text to give somewhat more emphasis to Grey's *caveat* that, so far as London was concerned, there was no firm view about the nature of the regime under which Palestine ought ultimately to be governed. He toned down the Foreign Office's firm 'Our sole object is to find an arrangement which would be so attractive to the majority of Jews as to enable us to strike a bargain for Jewish support.' 'Attractive' became 'appealing'; 'us' became 'the Allies'; 'bargain' became 'arrangement'.[57]

The French response, as Bertie had anticipated, was polite, firm, and negative. It stopped short (as relations between wartime allies necessarily dictated) of outright rejection of Great Britain's 'Palestine idea'. The French doubted whether the project was likely to have the hoped-for effect. Jewish hostility to the Allies was inspired, they believed, by matters that had nothing whatever to do with Zionist aspirations and the realization of those aspirations therefore would do nothing to cause that hostility to disappear. Secondly, there was an Arab factor, namely the danger that such a project would arouse Arab susceptibilities 'which it would be proper to treat with caution' (*ménager*). It was their view, accordingly, that the greater question of 'the creation of an Arab empire' must be settled before the one now set before them could be studied to any good purpose.[58] In sum, the French view of Zionism and of its place in contemporary Jewry differed from that of the British; and, the crucial point, they would only consider it—if at all—within the governing context of their interests and purposes in the Near East in general and Palestine in particular.

v

In fact the terms in which the overwhelming majority of French diplomats, soldiers, and politicians approached these matters cannot be

---

[56] Bertie to Grey, 13 March 1916. PRO, FO 800/176.

[57] Grey to Bertie, 11 March 1916; Bertie to MFA, 12 March 1916. Ibid., fos. 23, 41.

[58] Briand to Bertie, 21 March 1916. Ibid., fos. 43–5.

disentangled from the terms in which French higher society as a whole—and the nationalist, Catholic, and conservative parts of it in particular—tended to conceive them. To say that this approach— shot through, as it surely was, with bias, misinformation, sharp likes and dislikes, and a large measure of narcissism and self-satisfaction—was anti-Dreyfusard in essence would be to overstate the case. But something of that pugnacious, explicitly Christian, suspicious nationalism—intermixed with the popular conviction that the Jews were not only mean and disloyal but major participants in the fight for the very soul of France ('la lutte . . . entre la France catholique et la France juive, protestante et libre-penseuse'[59])—was forever seeping into ostensibly serious political-strategic discussions of affairs in the Near East. It can be detected, as we shall see, as a kind of permanent background hum of set, right-of-centre attitudes to what were generally intended as rational considerations of where the interests of France lay and how they might be furthered. One result was to lend a dogmatic quality to positions advanced both in the course of internal debate and in the course of debate with allies: the terms thought appropriate being, as often as not, those of rights and duties and supposedly self-evident facts rather than needs and observed circumstances. A paper submitted to the Foreign Ministry by a prominent (if aged) member of the establishment as the outlines of the proposed post-war settlement in the Near East began to be known laid down, as matters that were beyond question, that Palestine was part of an indivisible Syria; that Syria so conceived must be governed by a single Power, one capable moreover of imposing order on the various competing races, sects, clans, tribes, and other groups that divided the country; and that

That Power cannot be other than France, designated by its traditions, its centuries-old role, its lavish generosity, the education it has provided, the language it has propagated, the culture it has spread, [and] the noble example the missionaries of its civilization and charity have given.[60]

---

[59] *La Croix*, one of the standard-bearers of Catholic anti-republicanism, reporting the opening of the trial of Émile Zola, 8 February 1898. A week later, on 15 February, the journal carried a long piece on 'Le Secret de la puissance juive' written up in the spirit which became familiar after the war in the form of 'The Protocols of the Elders of Zion.'

[60] Memorandum by the Marquis de Vogüé, 23 May 1916. AE, Série A. Paix, vol. 174, fos. 103–9. Vogüé, a member of the Academy and sometime director of archeological excavations in Palestine, had served as Ambassador in Constantinople and Vienna in the early years of the Third Republic.

In similar vein, 'The question, "*should* Palestine be French?" was badly posed,' Senator Flandin wrote to the Prime Minister.[61] 'For Palestine, like the rest of Syria, *is* already French.'

What is interesting is that such views and such ways of 'posing the question' were not only typical of what might be termed the political classes, but that they were not views that anyone chose to question even in the inner reaches of officialdom. Nor did they—or the form in which they were cast—seem in any way out of the ordinary. At the start of the negotiations with the British on the division of the spoils at the end of the war (of which more below), the instructions to the French representatives were drafted in very much the same spirit and even language. It was the French Government's fundamental concern to obtain British recognition of France's established *rights* on 'the eastern shores of the Mediterranean' that was particularly and characteristically emphasized.[62]

Of Zionism itself, however, little was known in Paris, and little interest in it had ever been displayed. France was the one European Power to which Herzl had never applied for understanding or political support, possibly because official Paris was indelibly associated in his mind with what he had learned of it during his years there as a newspaper correspondent. Long after, Nordau had made an attempt to establish contact, but nothing came of it and Nordau himself had had to leave Paris when war broke out because he was, technically, an enemy alien. So far as Zionism and Zionists did come to the notice of the Quai d'Orsay and the Intelligence branch of the General Staff, it was chiefly in the context of Near Eastern politics and especially as rivals of the Alliance Israélite Internationale, official France's chosen instrument for activity among the Jews of the Levant and the Balkans. In their eyes it was a movement deeply suspect for its German connections and supposed German loyalties.

Zionism and the Alliance are two opposing interests [a French representative in Belgrade reported in 1913] ... two mentalities, two cultures. Zionism in this part of Europe represents a national Judaism that is essentially German, the Alliance an international Judaism of French inspiration [*d'idée française*]. Zionism paves the way for German penetration; the Alliance fortifies Mediterranean resistance.[63]

[61] 18 April 1916. AE, Guerre 1914–1918, Turquie (Syrie Palestine VI), 144. Emphases in original.

[62] Briand to Picot, 2 November 1915. AE, Guerre 1914–1918, vol. 871, fo. 32.

[63] Cited in Catherine Levigne, 'La Politique française à l'égard du Sionisme de 1896 à 1917,' (1974, unpublished).

When interest in Zionism quickened somewhat in 1916, it was at first this notion that it was to all intents and purposes a German-oriented movement that coloured the view taken of it. The seat of the EAC in Berlin, the connections in Constantinople—notably Jacobson's quasi-diplomatic function there—and the role the German authorities were being pressed to play in the effort to protect the *yishuv* from Turkish depredation all contributed to its reinforcement.[64] If some experts knew better and saw deeper, that is not to say that they took the Zionists at their own estimate of themselves. A French declaration in favour of a Jewish state 'would be laughable', Jean Gout, Director of Asian Affairs at the Quai d'Orsay, observed in August 1916.[65] And in the following year, when Allied policy on the subject was finally about to be determined, he summed up what had plainly been his long-standing view of the entire matter of Zionism, Jewry, and the political attention France might usefully pay to one and the other, all in two pungent paragraphs in which remarkable ignorance and equally remarkable insight are peculiarly mixed.

The millennary aspirations of the Jews, especially of the proletarians of Poland and Russia, are neither socialist, as their social situation would lead to believe, nor nationalist, as the declarations of their intellectuals claim. Essentially, they are Talmudic, which is to say religious. The legends which have served to soothe the misery of these poor devils have made them see Jerusalem [restored?] as the end of all their ills, Paradise on earth where the God of Israel would reign in triumph. . . .

One should not exaggerate the import of these dreams, but nor should they be thoughtlessly disparaged. Even after attaining positions of distinction in countries of civil equality, intelligent and educated Jews retain the dream of the ancient ghettos in a corner of their hearts for several generations. Thanks to their wealth, the ties they maintain among themselves, and the influence they bring to bear on ignorant governments, they do carry a certain international weight. But they are not and cannot be a *factor*. A wise policy would [therefore] allow the Jews to envisage the possibility of [Jewish] association [*groupement*] in Palestine, but within the limits of existing nationalities, and not as an independent one.[66]

---

[64] For a representative, rubbishy intelligence report, duly transmitted to the Quai d'Orsay by the War Ministry, 31 August 1916, see AE, Guerre 1914–1918, Sionisme, vol. 1198, fo. 50.

[65] AE, Guerre 1914–1918, Sionisme II, vol. 1198, fo. 45.

[66] Gout to de Margerie, 7 May 1917. AE, Guerre 1914–1918, Sionisme III and IV, vol. 1199, fo. 7.

The difference between the French approach and that of the British to the political dilemma posed by the Jews was thus fundamental. Both believed benefits would accrue to them in the United States if the Jews' hostility to Russia were appeased. Neither were willing to press the Russians to mitigate the regime under which the Jews were held—the British in some discomfort, the French with little or no embarrassment at all. (On one occasion, asked to respond to fresh reports from the United States on the depth of Jewish feeling there, Paléologue, the Ambassador in Petrograd, replied with a blunt warning: 'The least sign of foreign meddling would be fatal to the Jewish cause; for it would immediately provoke a revolt of religious and national conscience in the whole of Russia.')[67] Pressure on Russia to mend its ways being ruled out, both sought a solution. Here lay the difference. The British, somewhat less hostile to Jewry *per se* and with a better grasp of the nature of Zionism and of currents of opinion within Jewry as a whole, were inclined none the less, as we have seen, to ascribe considerable weight to what they took to be Jewry's 'international power'—which is to say, its capacity to act and interact purposefully and on a world-wide scale. In their eyes, it made sense therefore to establish a connection between Jewish opinion on one continent (America) and Jewish interests and aspirations in another (Asia) if it would bring the desired result. Besides, for the British—at this stage—the Levant in general and Palestine in particular figured largely in instrumental terms, as we have seen: their essential interests lay much further to the east, in India, upon which everything else, including actual and hypothetical footholds in the Mediterranean, turned.

The French, in contrast, more hostile to and less understanding of the Jews, were inclined to ascribe much less weight to their supposed 'international power'. And they were not only sceptical of the attempt to establish the kind of link between Jewish opinion in the United States and Allied plans and purposes in the Near East that the British had in mind, they strongly resisted it. But above all, they wanted Syria (conceived, it must be said, in generous terms) for itself and for themselves. Thus, even had they been disposed to go as far in meeting Jewish needs and desires as were the British, even if they had had to deal with as forceful a set of Jewish institutions and

[67] Petrograd to MFA, 18 July 1915; and MFA to Washington, 23 July 1915. AE, Guerre 1914–1918, Sionisme, vol. 1197.

personalities as there were in London, rather than with the comparatively spineless Alliance Israélite Universelle—an institution only too glad to serve as an instrument of French foreign policy, and to which the Quai d'Orsay had long been accustomed to give political guidance—they would have been faced with a conflict of interests. In fact, at this stage of the war, and of the allies' effort to determine the future of the region, there was no question in the minds of French officialdom where France's decisive interests lay. But nor was it a matter of calculation alone. Not the least of their contributions to the long debate with the British that now ensued was a singular element of passion, as one characteristic episode will illustrate.

Sykes and Picot, the appointed negotiators for the disposal of Turkey's Near Eastern territories, were in Petrograd to obtain Russian agreement to their proposals when Grey's telegram of 11 March reached Buchanan. Sykes reported his colleague's reaction: 'M. Picot, on hearing the sense of the telegram, made loud exclamations and spoke of pogroms in Paris. He grew calmer, but maintained [that] France would grow excited.' The Englishman sought to mollify Picot. 'I urged on M. Picot [the] inestimable advantages to [the] allied cause of [the] active friendship of the Jews[,] of the world force of which he reluctantly admitted.' Sykes went on to suggest that the Zionists, for their part, should give some practical 'demonstration of their power'—bring about an 'accentuation of German financial straits', for example; and then took up the question of the regime under which Palestine would be governed. The Zionists, he knew,[68] and seems to have explained to Picot, wanted the British; and the British, for their part, thought an international regime undesirable. The implication was clear. Picot exploded and Sykes duly reported his fury. France

would never consent to England having temporary or provisional charge of Palestine [Sykes reported]; not even if we offered Cyprus as a gift and appointed [a] French governor for Jerusalem, Bethlehem, Nazareth, and

[68] Sykes had Samuel's Cabinet memorandum of March 1915 in mind, Samuel having given him a copy before his departure for Russia. (Sykes to Samuel, 26 February 1916. ISA, 100/2.) Grey was furious at this indiscretion and Sykes was instructed to 'obliterate from his memory that Mr. Samuel's Cabinet memo. made any mention of a British Protectorate.' He was informed that Grey had told Samuel at the time that a British Protectorate was 'quite out of the question' and that Buchanan was asked to impress upon him 'that he should never mention the subject without making this point clear.' Nicolson to Buchanan, 16 March 1916. PRO, FO 371/2767.

Jaffa. They seem hardly normal on this subject and any reference seems to excite memories of all grievances from Joan of Arc to Fashoda.[69]

vi

The famous Anglo-French Agreement on the post-war partition and control of the Near East concluded (with Russian sanction) in May 1916 had been the fruit of long, laborious, and often irritable negotiations almost throughout. This was at least partly because it was founded on the *hypothesis* of Allied victory at a time when in none of the territories concerned did the Allies have so much as a foothold.[70] The negotiations therefore took the form of an effort, more or less genuine, to reconcile such interests and desiderata as each side was prepared to assert explicitly, and of somewhat embarrassed manoeuvring to attain and protect positions which for one reason or another could not be proclaimed (because they ran counter to the needs or wishes of the other side or were even founded on the other's presumed hostility.) The French, led by François Georges-Picot (with the Ambassador in London, Paul Cambon, watching over him), and the British, led at first by Sir Arthur Nicolson and then by Sir Mark Sykes, oscillated continually between the pole of co-operation, amity, and consideration set by the fundamental fact of a wartime alliance and the pole of long-standing suspicion and rivalry in all that concerned the Near East. Apart from Russian concern lest its interest (in practice: the interest of the Russian Orthodox Church) in having a hand in arrangements made for the supervision of the Holy Places in Palestine be neglected, and the exclusion, by agreement, of the somewhat vaguely defined territories that would accrue to the new and independent Arab state that would rise in the Arabian peninsula, there were few solid political or military facts to limit the scope and quality of the envisaged settlement, and to determine at what point between the opposite poles the negotiators would be obliged to come to rest. Virtually everything that was external to the parties was speculative: the defeat of the Turks, an Arab decision to join the Allies, the value of such aid as the Arabs would render, the post-war needs of France and Britain, the methods of government likely to prove most efficacious in the areas to come under their respective

---

[69] Buchanan to FO, 14 March 1916. PRO, FO 371/2767.
[70] The disastrous Mesopotamian campaign had ended with the surrender of the British forces on 29 April 1916.

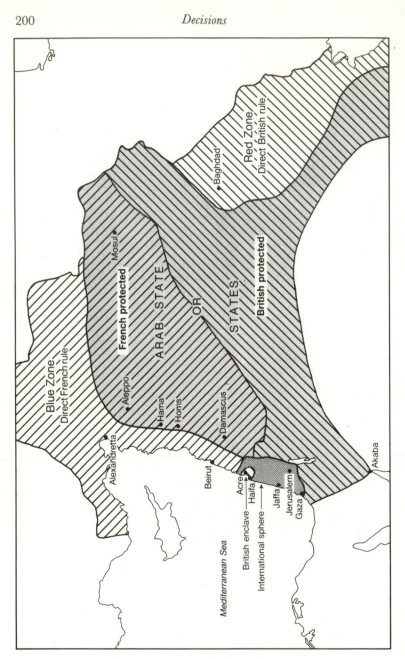

MAP 2. The Sykes-Picot Agreement, May 1916.

control, the response of the populations in question to that control, the turn Anglo-French imperial rivalry would take in later years. And because all was speculative, purposes rather than circumstances dominated their thinking. Given the concomitant conviction —never stated, but always in force—that France and Great Britain between them would be free to impose their will, once they had defined it, the only major impediment in the negotiators' minds to its free exercise was the need to take account of each other. Matters extraneous to specifically Near Eastern questions—apart from the overriding need to accommodate an ally and seek a compromise when it became clear beyond all question that he could not be persuaded to let one have one's own way—were excluded from consideration. Taken as a whole, it was a diplomatic-strategic exercise shot through with hubris and tunnel vision.

Palestine did not figure as a major item on the negotiators' original agenda, but it did soon become a central issue of controversy. The French position was that it was, and had long been, an integral part of Syria. Picot was instructed to insist that the territory to be placed under French control 'end only at the Egyptian frontier'. So far as the Christian Holy Places were concerned, France, as the 'traditional protectress of the Christians of the Orient', was at least as well qualified as any other power for the task. Suitable arrangements and international guarantees such as would satisfy the various Christian sects, the Jews, 'and even the Muslims' could be devised. As a last resort, if the British made difficulties, a neutral enclave, strictly limited to Jerusalem and Bethlehem, might be agreed to.[71] The British, as we have seen,[72] were interested chiefly in Mesopotamia and the Persian Gulf territories. For the rest, they wished to keep France as far away from Egypt as possible (as the French well knew) and they wanted a port on the East Mediterranean littoral with good rail connections to the interior. For the latter purpose, Haifa had finally been picked as the most promising, although interest in Alexandretta had not entirely faded. In these circumstances, an arrangement between the Allies was possible, but could only be arrived at by stages. At one point the French thought of dividing Palestine into three: the northern part of

---

[71] Briand to Picot, 2 November 1915. AE, Guerre 1914–1918, vol. 871, fos. 32–6. 'It seems,' wrote Gout, 'that the British, no doubt under the joint influence of clergymen and partisans of a greater Egypt, have tried to establish the idea that Palestine has ever had an independence existence.' 2 January 1916. Ibid.

[72] See above, p. 100.

the country under their control, the greater part of the *mutasarrıflık* of Jerusalem internationalized, and the south under the British.[73] The difficulty was obliquely reflected by Sykes and Picot in their preliminary joint memorandum in which they laid down as axiomatic that the 'principal parties must observe a spirit of compromise'.[74] The compromise eventually worked out provided for Palestine (as loosely, but generally conceived) to be divided into *four* parts, each under a different regime. Upper Galilee would be French, part of the area to be assigned to them for direct rule. The southern part of the country (the Negev) would be part of an Arab-state-to-be under British protection. The Haifa and Acre bay area would form a small enclave under direct British rule. The rest, the major part of the country, the 'brown area' in the terminology adopted, would be placed under 'an international administration, the form of which is to be decided upon after consultation with Russia, and subsequently with the other allies, and the representatives of the Shereef of Mecca'.[75]

It does not seem that the matter of the Zionists and their aspirations in Palestine was discussed at any stage of the negotiations leading up to the conclusion of the Sykes-Picot Agreement. The 'conscientious desires' of Judaism, along with those of Christianity and Islam 'in regard to the status of Jerusalem and the neighbouring shrines',[76] were briefly mentioned, as a matter of course, but no more. The Director of Naval Intelligence, Captain W. R. Hall, did point out *inter alia* in a long critical comment on the first joint draft agreement by Sykes and Picot that 'the Jews have a strong *material*, and a very strong *political*, interest in the future of the country. He went on to argue that 'In the *Brown Area* the question of Zionism . . . [has] to be considered.'[77] But these considerations were not pursued—at all events, not in the immediate context of the Anglo-French agreement-in-the-making. (It may be that Captain Hall's views contributed something to the proposal of 11 March to think in terms of the Jews obtaining 'the management of the internal affairs of Palestine (with the exception of Jerusalem and the Holy Places) into their own hands'; but that proposal came later when the

[73] Briand to Cambon, 5 January 1916. AE, Guerre 1914–1918, vol. 871.
[74] 'Arab Question', 5 January 1916. PRO, FO 371/2767.
[75] Grey to Cambon, 16 May 1916. War Cabinet Paper GT 368. IOLR, MSS. Eur. F112/265.
[76] 'Arab Question', 5 January 1916. Loc. cit.
[77] Hall to Nicolson, 12 January 1916. Ibid. Emphases in original.

terms of the Sykes-Picot Agreement had already been settled in all but name and the two negotiators were in Petrograd to seek Russian assent.) Sykes himself got his first serious introduction to the topic in February 1916, on the eve of his departure for Russia, when Samuel gave him a copy of his Cabinet memorandum 'Palestine' of March 1915. At that stage, his understanding—possibly reflecting initial caution as much as what he took to be the general official view—was that the Zionists were interested in the 'realization of the ideal of an existing centre of nationality' rather than in something expressly political.[78] But it is clear that these new ideas germinated rapidly, and in Petrograd, upon receiving word of what the Foreign Office had in mind, he was on his way to becoming the greatest enthusiast of all for 'the Palestine idea'. For the time being, his fertile mind was busy devising an exceedingly complex plan whereby all—French, British, Arabs, Jews, and Russians—would have a hand and a stake and recognized status in the internationalized part of the country and all be more or less satisfied.[79] It led nowhere. Sykes thought he had persuaded Picot that an arrangement that would satisfy everyone could be devised,[80] but if he had, and if Picot followed it up, it is certain that there was no interest in such a plan in Paris. The French had accepted the internationalization of the major part of Palestine with great and undisguised reluctance. They were not prepared to make further concessions. Least of all were they prepared to consider a special status for the Jews. They did not want them. They did not take them at the British estimate: the Jews were not, in their view and in Gout's terminology, a true *factor* in international politics. And, it seems, they had already begun to suspect the Zionists of serving, or of being likely to serve, as some sort of Trojan horse for the British.

It was now London's turn to grasp that Bertie's scepticism had been well founded: the 'Palestine idea', whether in its milder form as proposed by Wolf or in its stronger form as proposed by the Foreign Office itself—let alone in the still ill-defined terms adumbrated by Sykes—was unacceptable to the French. The discussions with their ally which the British officials, proponents of the 'idea', had wanted as soon as Briand's immediate, icy response had been digested, were

[78] Sykes to Samuel, 26 February 1916. ISA, 100/2.
[79] Buchanan/Sykes to Nicolson, 14 March 1916. PRO, FO 800/96; andBuchanan/Sykes to Nicolson, 18 March 1916. PRO, FO 371/2767.
[80] Ibid.

not insisted upon and did not take place. Nicolson's advice, given as far back as the beginning of March, to 'leave it alone'[81] was followed, additional reasons for following it being adduced. Wolf was waiting impatiently for a reply, but the feeling that he and his colleagues were not the right interlocutors for a dialogue on Zionism, if there was to be one, had grown. In June 1916 the Arab revolt had started and if there was not much faith in it in London ('Are these Arabs of any military value', Asquith had asked, and Sykes, called to give evidence, had replied, 'They have a negative value—they are bad if they are against us . . . but I do not count them as a positive force. They are armed, but they do not fight to win.'[82]) it was beginning to be sensed that the Arabs, plans for whom were, after all, at the heart of the matter of Sykes-Picot, might not like the parallel, if even vaguer, plans for the Jews, and that it might be necessary to tread warily in this respect as well.[83] Finally,

---

[81] Minute by Nicolson, 3 March 1916, reporting a conversation on the subject with the French Ambassador. Cambon had told him that 'he was sure that his Gov[ernmen]t. would not be disposed to entertain the proposal.' PRO, FO 371/2671.

[82] War Committee minutes, 16 December 1915. IOLR, MSS. Eur. F112/128. Crewe, acting for Grey, and O'Beirne, the Foreign Office official most closely concerned at this stage with the topics with which the present study deals, were both in attendance.

[83] Concerning the notoriously controversial question of what the Sherif of Mecca was and was not promised by McMahon, the British High Commissioner in Egypt, in the course of the famous exchange known as the 'McMahon Letters' and the degree to which these promises were compatible, if at all, with undertakings to the French and, later, to the Jews, it may suffice to say (although some would not agree), that while the Sherif did assert his claim to Jerusalem, McMahon did not confirm it and, indeed, made no mention of Palestine at all. His specific reservations related to the famous 'portions of Syria lying to the west of the districts of Damascus, Hama, Homs and Aleppo' and to Britain's freedom being limited to these territories where it could act 'without detriment to the interests of her ally France'. But taken in context, namely the repeated assertions by Great Britain, France, and Russia that the question of Palestine was a question apart and that the only issue (at this stage) could be whether it would fall under an international or a French administration, it is clear enough that the British, at any rate, did not think they had made any undertaking concerning Palestine to the Arabs.

This was confirmed explicitly by G. F. Clayton, at the time Director of Intelligence in Cairo, several years after the event. 'I was in daily touch with Sir Henry McMahon throughout the negotiations with King Hussein, and made the preliminary drafts of all the letters. I can bear out the statement that it was never the intention that Palestine should be included in the general pledge given to the Sherif; the introductory words of Sir Henry's letter were thought at the time—perhaps erroneously—clearly to cover that point. It was, I think, obvious that the peculiar interests involved in Palestine precluded any definite pledges in regard to its future at so early a stage.' Clayton to Samuel, embodied in a letter from Samuel to Grey, 12 April 1923. ISA, 100/10.

Hardinge, who had replaced Nicolson in the meantime as Permanent Under-Secretary, was opposed 'on principle ... to the
publication of all formulae as they invariably create embarrassment'. In brief, the wind had shifted and the decision was taken to
tell Wolf (in writing) that the moment was not 'opportune' for a
statement of policy on Jewish settlement in Palestine and to brief
him (verbally) on some of the reasons for the retreat.[84]

'The real reason,' Wolf was informed by Oliphant, was that the
French had objected to his formula, and that the French grounds
were that 'a very large body of Jewish opinion' would remain
unsatisfied by it. Nothing was said to him of French plans for the
country, let alone of the (still secret) agreement concluded with
them. Nor did Oliphant explain that the original French argument
against the 'Palestine idea' was that it would not affect Jewish
opinion, because it was *Russia* that was of central concern. Wolf, for
his part, thereupon jumped to the wholly mistaken conclusion that it
was the *Zionists* the French had in mind when speaking of Jewish
opinion, and that it was they who had interfered because they
thought his formula inadequate. (He knew nothing of the stronger
formula proposed by the Foreign Office.) 'That is to say,' he
reported bitterly to his Committee, 'that they [i.e. the Zionists]
would rather have no privileges at all in Palestine than have the
equal rights and the colonising and immigration privileges we ask
for.'[85] Several days later, in Paris, he was astonished and further
confused to hear from Briand himself that 'no formula on the
Palestine question had ever come before him.' Had the officials at
the Quai d'Orsay acted in their Minister's name without consulting
him? It was not impossible, he was told. Or was it perhaps the
British who had misunderstood and misreported the French?[86] The
shrewdest comment he heard was Edmond de Rothschild's: one
reason for French opposition might be fear lest the effect of a public
declaration of Palestine would be to admit 'that the destiny of
Palestine was not exclusively a French concern.'[87]

By the summer of 1916, then, as a matter of immediate diplomatic
business, the 'Palestine idea' had run into the sand; and the notables

---

[84] Minutes by Grey, Cecil, Hardinge, Oliphant *et al.*, 27 June 4 July 1916. PRO,
FO 371/2817.
[85] Memorandum by Wolf, 5 July 1916. BD, C11/3/2/1.
[86] Extracts from Wolf's diary submitted to Foreign Office. Wolf to Oliphant, 18
July 1916. PRO, FO 371/2817.
[87] Ibid.

of French and English Jewry, especially in their established
institutions, turned their attention and energies once more to
preparations for a peace conference-to-be. And yet, in the official
mind, something had been embedded, at any rate in London. There
the 'international power' of the Jews had come to be accepted as a
factor to be dealt with and catered for, and not at all in the terms
that Spring Rice, from Washington, continued to advocate.[88] The
Jewish interest in Palestine had been recognized, as indeed had the
differences in Jewry on that very topic. The Zionists had ceased to
be viewed almost automatically as members of an absurd or
negligible movement. In one of Sykes's characteristically exuberant
but generally influential papers one finds them listed as a matter of
course, along with the papacy and the Orthodox Church, as a given
factor in the Near Eastern ethno-politico-religious complex which it
would be well to bear in mind.[89] In short, the climate of general
ideas—as opposed to views on immediate political tactics—had
changed. Set views on a large variety of subjects including the
subject of the Jews, their interests, and their uses, had undergone a
mutation. It is true that in the meantime, under the Sykes-Picot
Agreement, there had been established a framework of reference for
the Near East which seemed to set the seal on the terms on which the
Levant was due to be rearranged territorially and politically. Given
the primacy of the alliance with France as Britain's fighting partner
against Germany—the cornerstone of British foreign policy so long
as Asquith and Grey had charge of it—there could be no serious
question of moving towards their revision, no matter where British
interests in the Near East were thought to lie. But it would not be
long before both the state of affairs in the region itself and the light in
which it was viewed in London for immediate practical purposes
would change radically. Once that occurred, the 'Palestine idea'
was free to float once more to the surface of British political
consciousness.

[88] 'I think it would be a very good thing to warn English Jews of the very great
danger the Jews will incur in the allied countries if in this neutral country [the United
States] the Jews as a whole use their organisations and political power against the
Allies.' Spring Rice to Hardinge, 14 July 1916. PRO, FO 800/242.
[89] 'The Problem of the Near East', 20 June 1916. PRO, CAB 17/175.

6

The Terms of the Final Equation

i

It is characteristic of the spirit in which the belligerent Governments managed their affairs throughout the Great War that the effort to define the 'terms of peace'—i.e. the outlines of the post-war political and territorial settlement—was pursued with a degree of energy that seems (in retrospect) hardly compatible with the immediate military perils to which they were subject. It is true that on the Allied side the protracted internal discussions and the incessant external diplomatic manoeuvres relating to the ultimate fate and governance of large parts of Central Europe, the Balkans, and the Near East had much to do with the enlargement and continued cohesion of the alliance and the mustering of all possible sources of material and political aid while the war was in progress. It is striking, none the less, that the exceedingly elaborate plans for the Near East were laid by Great Britain and France (both separately and jointly) while the the battle for Verdun, to name only one ghastly and extended episode, was raging, and long before there was a serious prospect of military victory, or even of major military operations, in the Near East itself. The composure and confidence with which the Cabinet's special, and specifically entitled, Committee on the Terms of Peace conducted its deliberations is remarkable. Its members (Curzon, Cecil, Austen Chamberlain, and Smuts among them) considered the questions put before them—even the smallest: how the French, say, might be persuaded to part with the tiny islands of St Pierre and Miquelon, and how Chile might be talked into leasing Easter Island to Great Britain in the interests of improved imperial wireless telegraphy—at a time (April 1917) when German submarine warfare was at its peak and the series of battles being waged under General Nivelle's command (the British at Arras, the French on the

Aisne) was in progress and its disastrous outcome already beginning to be comprehended.

It may be that the urge to look past the war to the peace that would follow was consequent upon the fact that the *civilian* government of Great Britain, from the Prime Minister down through the ranks of lesser ministers and civil servants, had (by the standards of our own times) little to do with the higher direction of the war and was left with time to think about other matters. Lloyd George's famous forcing of the convoy system on a deeply conservative Admiralty was a rare exception. His successive failures to achieve control of affairs on the Western front accorded with the rule. His predecessor Asquith never even attempted anything so bold. What was true of the two Prime Ministers was doubly true of their ministerial colleagues, even of the Service Ministers (with Churchill when in the Admiralty as a borderline case). It was true *a fortiori* of the successive Foreign Secretaries, their deputies, and the Foreign Office and Diplomatic Service as a whole. The latter's prime function, it was tacitly agreed on all sides, was to provide the political equivalent of munitions: to recruit allies, to counter or pre-empt attempts by the Central Powers to do the same in their own interest, to help keep the existing alliances and understandings with France, Russia, and the lesser Powers—later with the United States—sweet, and to watch those bonds for signs of weakness and decay. It was not to ensure that strategy encompassed political calculations. In such circumstances, it is perhaps not surprising that some of these talented and, in certain cases, imaginative men should have turned their minds to the likely structure of the world at war's end. Intellectually it was the more satisfying enterprise. Morally it was more rewarding. Politically it was necessary in any case if promises to potential allies were to be both made and kept. And perhaps most profoundly, the carnage in France and Flanders (of which they may not have known enough, but which was none the less the ultimate determinant of the climate in which they lived and operated) did not fail to move the great majority of them to believe it was their positive duty to establish a new and improved world order. Of course, it would have to be one in which Great Britain (and its allies) could expect to be safe and, so far as possible, preponderant. It would have to be one that was organized with due attention to political, geographic, and demographic realities. It was accepted that a balance would therefore have to be struck between whatever general principles were thought to apply and the uncomfortable, irreducible difficulties that would inevitably arise. But one way or another, a new order of things was necessary.

The principal object of the War is the attainment of a durable peace, and I submit that the best way of securing this is by the double method of diminishing the area from which the Central Powers can draw the men and money required for a policy of aggression, while at the same time rendering a policy of aggression less attractive by rearranging the map of Europe in closer agreement with what we rather vaguely call 'the principle of nationality.'[1]

Thus Balfour to his colleagues, in his inimitably succint style, as Asquith's leadership was drawing to its end.

But finally, and more immediately, the fall of Asquith in December 1916 and his replacement by Lloyd George brought a new administrative system and new ideas to the fore—and a new urgency even to old ideas. The new, small, and exceedingly potent War Cabinet became the political powerhouse of the country. Its staff—in effect the Prime Minister's personal staff—became an instrument whereby great political matters could, by prime ministerial choice, be drained away from the established departments of state (the Foreign Office among them) virtually at will. One such matter to be appropriated (for a time) by the Prime Minister and his Cabinet Office was the Near East.

In their essentials British desiderata, policy, and expectations in the Near East underwent no change under Lloyd George. The thread of ideas and concern leading from the de Bunsen Committee set up two years earlier[2] remained unbroken. But Lloyd George set about reaffirming the 'disruption of the Turkish Empire' as a major British war aim (along with the rolling back of Germany from the lands of its conquests and the 'democratisation of Europe') with a purpose and a fervour (some thought obsession) that stood in contrast to Asquith's reluctance to sanction further expansion of Britain's overseas interests and responsibilities if such could possibly be avoided. Hostility to Turkey, while not new in England, had much intensified in consequence of the war and the brutalities inflicted by the Ottomans on the Armenians and on British prisoners of war. Under Asquith the British, with the French and

---

[1] 'The Peace Settlement in Europe', 4 October 1916. PRO, CAB 37/157/7.
[2] See above, pp. 98–102.

the Russians, had gone so far as to warn the Turks publicly in 1915 that their persecution of the Armenians was regarded as a crime 'against humanity and civilization' for which 'all members' of the Ottoman Government would be held responsible.[3] The warning was delivered as a manifest matter of duty—but not with discernible vigour. It was vigour particularly that Lloyd George now brought to the question of Turkey conceived in moral, political, and strategic terms combined. He had long been an 'easterner' in the established sense that he favoured a greater military effort on the flanks of the Central Powers and on the weakest links of the chains binding them (as did his newly powerful and influential Cabinet Secretary, Maurice Hankey). But his strategic views were compounded with a detestation of the Turks for what he judged their long 'misrule' and for having, as he put it, left lands that were 'the richest in the world' a 'blighted desert'—a detestation that was nothing if not Glad-stonian in depth and sincerity. At the same time his feelings about the military campaign just beginning in Sinai and about the higher significance of the expeditionary force now set 'on the road to Jerusalem' were shot through and through with a romanticism and a historicism that were too simple (in so complex a man) to have been anything but sincere. In some ways, Lloyd George's views had more in common with the undercurrents in Paris than with the usual thinking in London. So had his language: 'There have been many expeditions from Christendom into that part of the world to wrest [Syria, Palestine, and Armenia] from the grip of the Turk,' he told the Imperial War Cabinet early in 1917. 'I believe that this is the last. . . . We have entered the land of the Philistines. . . . I hope we shall conquer [them].'[4]

It was, of course, the fact that British troops were indeed poised for the invasion and conquest of the country that had raised the question of the future of Palestine to the rank of an immediate issue of interest and policy both in London and in Paris. On 30 March the British Cabinet, more optimistic than the commander of the Egyptian Expeditionary Force (EEF) himself, ordered him to make

---

[3]   Ulrich Trumpener, *Germany and the Ottoman Empire* (Princeton, 1968), pp. 209–10.

[4]   20 March 1917. IOLR, MSS. Eur. F112/134. The convening of the Imperial War Cabinet, composed of representatives of the United Kingdom, the Dominions, and India, some three months after the change of Government in London, was an occasion for a general review of the progress of the war and the purposes arising out of it.

for Jerusalem. The French were unable either to participate in the campaign (apart from despatching token forces) or to object to a genuine and, at first sight, promising military effort to clear Palestine and even Syria of Turkish forces. But the prospect of British forces entering lands in which they themselves had a declared interest dismayed them. 'We must wish our allies success in their enterprise with all sincerity,' the French representative in Cairo telegraphed Paris as soon as he learned what was afoot, 'but shall we allow them to operate alone when they will have crossed the Egyptian frontier?'[5] 'Jerusalem cannot be left to the mercy of looters nor can the British flag be allowed to fly over it alone,' the Ambassador in London insisted, and urged Paris to authorize political co-ordination with the British without delay in the hope of avoiding a French political defeat.[6] This was promptly conceded and it was thereupon agreed that Sykes and Picot, who had fathered the 1916 Agreement and were known to be able to work amicably in tandem, would go out to Cairo together to uphold it. For the French this was a great deal better than nothing and for the moment it looked as if their interests were safe. 'Anxious to fulfil their engagements in our regard,' it was laid down authoritatively in Paris at the end of the year, 'under the terms of which they have recognized our preponderant influence in Syria and agreed to Palestine south of Haifa being subject to an international regime, His Majesty's Government have proposed to the Embassy of the Republic in London that an understanding be promptly entered into in the interests of a joint, provisional administration.'[7] On the British side, however, matters were seen otherwise. The May 1916 Agreement was not, and could not be, repudiated, but the will to implement it in *all* its particulars was rapidly dissolving.

What had happened was that under Lloyd George, with much of the handling of Near Eastern political affairs transferred at least for a time (with Sykes himself) from the Foreign Office to the Cabinet Secretariat, old British reservations about a French presence in Palestine had finally mutated into an explicit (but still secret) determination to establish fully-fledged British control over the

---

[5]   Defrance to MFA, 7 December 1916. AE, Guerre 1914–18, Turquie, vol. 20.
[6]   Paul Cambon to MFA, 9 December 1916. Ibid.
[7]   Briand to Minister of War, 26 December 1916. Ministère de la Guerre, État-Major de l'Armée, Service historique, *Les Armées françaises dans la grande guerre*, tome ix, vol. 1., annexes, no. 163, p. 236.

country. 'To ensure this,' Curzon's Committee on the Terms of
Peace recommended in the spring of 1917,

it is desirable that His Majesty's Government should secure such a
modification of the [Sykes-Picot] agreement with France of May 1916 as
would give Britain definite and exclusive control over Palestine and would
take the frontier of the British sphere of control to the River Leontes [i.e. the
Litani] and north of the Hauran. Turkish rule should never be restored in
Palestine or Mesopotamia.[8]

No one of consequence in London now explicitly supported the
internationalization of Palestine. 'Palestine' for present purposes
was conceived in larger terms than those implied in the 1916
Agreement: i.e. roughly both the *mutasarrıflık* of Jerusalem and the
two southern *sanjaks* of the *vilayet* of Beirut. And while, ostensibly, it
was from German influence in the Balkans and 'what was left of the
Turkish Empire' that British interests in the Levant had to be
protected, it was agreed on all sides in London that the immediate
obstacle to control of the country was France. This was the view
early in 1917, if not before; and having as its implicit object the
repudiation of an agreement with Britain's closest ally, it was an
exceedingly awkward one to have been adopted. It may therefore
have been in an effort to soothe some troubled consciences that the
Committee's secretary, Leopold Amery, took it upon himself to
inform its members that the French too had been secretly
considering the establishment of their own undivided rule in
Palestine 'in contravention of the provisions . . . contained in the
agreement of May 1916.'[9] But however awkward, no one was
prepared to argue that what were seen as French pretensions should
be allowed to override what were judged to be solid British interests.
Curzon affirmed the asymmetry with characteristic bluntness when
he too stated that the French were 'very jealously attempting to peg
out claims' to the country. The only 'safe settlement', in his opinion,
was that Palestine would become a British protectorate. He found it
convenient to point out, moreover, that there were others who

---

[8] Imperial War Cabinet, Report of Committee on Terms of Peace, 28 April 1917.
PRO, CAB 21/77.
[9] Ibid., minutes, 23 April 1917. There is a note suggestive of psychological
projection in Lloyd George's comment, on learning of a French plan to send a
disproportionately senior officer to command the handful of inferior infantry
battalions they had earmarked for the Palestine campaign, that it was clear to him
that they 'had ulterior political designs.' War Cabinet minutes, 10 April 1917. PRO,
CAB 23/2.

wanted the British in place. 'The Zionists in particular,' so he understood, he told the Committee, 'would be very much opposed to Palestine being under any other flag or under a condominium.'[10] In their instructions to Sykes, about to take up the post of Chief Political Officer to the Commander of the EEF at the beginning of April, Lloyd George and Curzon were explicit.

They impressed on Sir Mark Sykes [it was recorded], the difficulty of our relations with the French in this region and the importance of not prejudicing the Zionist movement and the possibility of its development under British auspices. . . . The Prime Minister suggested the Jews might be able to render us more assistance than the Arabs. . . . The Prime Minister laid stress on the importance, if possible, of securing the addition of Palestine to the British area. . . . The Prime Minister suggested that Sir Mark Sykes ought not to enter any political pledges to the Arabs, and particularly none in regard to Palestine.[11]

The ascription of great strategic importance to Palestine ('German control of Palestine, combined with a German reacquisition of East Africa is, indeed, the greatest of all dangers which can confront the British Empire in the future,' wrote Amery in a paper submitted to Curzon's Committee.[12]) in combination with the view that one way or the other the Zionists might be useful allies in the effort to overturn the Anglo-French Agreement was certainly the chief cause of the reappearance of the 'Palestine idea' on the Government's active agenda. It had been in the air for some time, as we have seen. It is possible that the objections the French had expressed the previous year to the idea of a special status for the Jews in Palestine had even done something to revalue it. For the problem, as Sykes saw it, and as others came increasingly to accept, was how to break down—or at least counter—the French 'pretensions' and 'sentimental' claims to Palestine, and so disconnect it from Syria (the 'pretensions' and claims to which the British had no intention of questioning at all). The first great step had been taken when Picot and his colleagues had been talked into agreeing to the internationalization of the southern half of the country, but under Lloyd George this was no longer judged sufficient. The difficulty lay not only in the fact that a formal, written agreement to which the Russians too were party had been concluded, but of course in the

[10] Committee on Terms of Peace, minutes, 19 April 1917. PRO, CAB 21/77.
[11] 3 April 1917. PRO, CAB 24/9, fos. 306–8.
[12] 'Notes on Possible Terms of Peace', 11 April 1917. PRO, CAB 24/10.

fact that it was a matter that impinged directly on relations and trust between wartime allies. Besides, it had been Sykes himself, a passionate supporter of the *entente*, who had negotiated the agreement. What was needed, therefore, so this ingenious man had grasped, was the introduction of an additional 'pretension' and 'sentimental' claim into the equation: to complicate the issue, to provide room for fresh manoeuvre, to make it possible to take the issue up once more at a later date, to muddy the waters. It could not be a British pretension or claim. It had to be that of others. It had to be along the lines of the internationalization already agreed upon, but taking it a step further. British control of the country did not require formal sovereignty. It could be achieved by indirection. In a general way, Sykes explained to Scott, so far as Palestine was concerned,

he was rather inclined to compromise . . . France was very insistent on pressing her claims to something like a condominium. . . . That would not do as we must have military control except as regards the Holy Places and perhaps the railway from Jaffa to Jerusalem which might be internationalized and policed by the French, but he thought we might secure all we wanted if we acted as the 'mandatories' of the powers—e.g. exercised a delegated authority. But he said it would make a great difference, when we came to the Peace Conference, if we were already in military possession of the country the invasion of which we had already begun.[13]

This was what the Zionists, representing and promoting 'Jewish national aspirations', could provide. To employ the Zionists to this end made good sense to people (among them Curzon, for example, at least initially) who had no particular sympathy for their cause or for Jews in general. For those who did sympathize with the Zionists, it became a powerful argument in their favour.

A second cause of the restoration of the 'Palestine idea' to the Government's agenda was the revival, in stronger terms and at a higher level of authority than had been usual in British diplomacy in the past, of the view that the problem of the Jews of eastern Europe not only deserved, but positively required treatment. Such was Balfour's view. And for all the differences between two men whose social origins, temperament, habits, and appearance stood in striking contrast, there is a sense in which something of the conviction (it is impossible to speak of fervour in Balfour's case) that

[13] Entry in C. P. Scott's diary, 1 March 1917. BL, Add. MSS. 50903, fos. 182–3.

Lloyd George brought to his treatment of Near Eastern affairs and to the issue of Palestine in particular may be detected in Balfour's dealing with the issue of Jewry: Jewry, it must be said, in its larger, *European* context. For Europe, not the Near East, was Balfour's abiding interest and, of course, with a great European war raging, his central responsibility. When it was his turn, as the new Foreign Secretary, to review foreign policy before the assembled dignitaries who formed the Imperial War Cabinet in March 1917, he duly concentrated on its problems and prospects, among them the likely fate of Russia after the February Revolution, while none the less following Lloyd George in affirming that 'the practical destruction of the Turkish Empire is undoubtedly one of the objects which we desire to obtain.' After his presentation, after questions, answers, and interpositions by other Ministers, he himself interjected that 'I should like to take this opportunity of expressing satisfaction at the idea of the Jewish lot being improved in Russia.' It was a reference to the emancipation decreed in revolutionary Petrograd ten days earlier. After further brief exchanges Balfour went on to state, this time plainly for the record and without explicit connection with anything said earlier by any of those present, 'I am a Zionist, but I do not know whether anyone else is.' He did not elaborate. Nor did any of those present take up the subject—perhaps because of Milner's remark, the only recorded response, that 'It is impossible to go into that now.'[14] It was of course a tiny episode, soon forgotten, no doubt, by most of the participants. Its interest lies only in the fact that the note Balfour had struck—with deliberation—was one of peculiarly personal conviction and commitment and hardly typical of this most sophisticated and experienced of British statesmen.

Balfour had long been anything but indifferent to the problems of Jewry or ignorant of its outlines. In an age when hostility to and ignorance of Jews not only permeated the class to which he belonged but was very freely expressed, he seems to have had a deep and consistent—it may be said, *gentlemanly*[15]—dislike of anti-Semitism,

[14] 22 March 1917. IOLR, MSS. Eur. 112/134.
[15] Winston Churchill's celebrated characterization of Balfour rings as true as ever: the man who 'passed from one Cabinet to the other . . . like a powerful graceful cat walking delicately and unsoiled across a muddy street. . . . [Who accepted] invitations from all sort of people, never broke an engagement for something more tempting, and left behind him a trail of satisfaction and even happiness. . . . The best-mannered man I ever met—easy, courteous, patient, considerate, in every society and with great and small alike.' *Great Contemporaries* (London, 1962), pp. 194–5, 204. 'Of

the more so perhaps as he may have had a troubled conscience so far as the matter of the Jews in England specifically was concerned. It was under his premiership that unprecedented restrictions on the free immigration of aliens (in practice, Jews for the most part) were enacted by Parliament. It was on that occasion that he thought it necessary to state his view, that the 'medieval treatment of the Jews was a permanent stain on European annals; and [that] he agreed that if [the Government] could do anything to wipe it out, if they could do anything to diminish its effects in the present time, it would be their bounden duty to do it.'[16] It was under his premiership that the not unconnected negotiations with the Zionists, first on settlement in El Arish, then on settlement in East Africa, had taken place.[17] Balfour had played no direct part in them, but he could not have failed to have been aware of what was going on and to have approved. That said, his interest in the Jews, a certain sympathy for them, and an evident distaste for the language and activities of their enemies were controlled by his dispassionate and sceptical outlook on the world of politics as a whole. When, on the eve of the war, he was asked by Lord Rothschild to join Theodore Roosevelt, Clemenceau, and some other world-class notables to support an international committee for the defence of religious liberty and the protection of minorities in eastern Europe, Jews among them, Balfour's reply was friendly, but exceedingly cautious and worldly-wise.

In the course of our long experience we have seen minorities monstrously ill-used in more than one country—Bulgarians, Armenians, Christians, Jews, to say nothing of aborigines in various parts of the world. Their wrongs have deeply moved public opinion in many countries, and not least in America and Britain. Societies have been formed for their protection; speeches denouncing their oppressors have been made without number; pressure has been put upon various Governments to intervene on their behalf; but I am doubtful whether any of these proceedings have done good to those they were intended to benefit, while they have undoubtedly produced much international bitterness.[18]

course, as you know only too well,' another contemporary wrote, complaining of the way Balfour had been running the Admiralty under Asquith's premiership, 'A.J.B. is very misleading because he is such a charming gentleman and many people have imagined that they have made an impression upon him when they haven't.' L. J. Maxse to Sandars, 16 June 1916. Bodl. MS. Eng. hist., c. 769/146–7.

[16] 10 July 1905. Parliamentary Debates, 4th series, vol. 149, col. 154.
[17] *Formative Years*, pp. 132 ff.
[18] Rothschild to Balfour, 16 December 1913; Balfour to Rothschild, 30 January 1914. BL, Add. MSS. 49745, fos. 163, 170–1.

Now, some four years later, to champion a Jewish cause in such forthright terms as he had chosen was thus to go very far and in an unusual direction.

The change in Balfour's attitude had much to do, no doubt, with the changed circumstances of the war, the first results of the February Revolution in the Russia, the adoption by all, not least by himself, of the 'principle of nationality' as a general guiding rule for the peace settlement, and by much the same ostensibly canny assessment of ways in which the Jews might be mobilized in the British interest as informed Lloyd George's and, of course, Sykes's approach to present operations and future arrangements in the Near East. But there was in Balfour's approach an additional ingredient in default of which there is much in his treatment of the matter of Jewry that remains inexplicable. Balfour seems to have come to believe not only in the uses (for Great Britain) of the modern Jewish national tendency, but in its intrinsic value and propriety. He not only agreed with the Zionists; he tended to accept their arguments in the terms they themselves customarily employed and on the grounds they themselves adduced to support them. In this sense he had indeed become, as he had said, a Zionist. It is true that Balfour's role in the higher direction of the war and of wartime diplomacy has never been easy to assess, and the weight carried by the Foreign Office in the central processes of political decision-making in Great Britain continued to diminish under his rule. Still, his personal prestige, his long experience of affairs (no other British politician had then, or has since, served so many years as a Cabinet Minister), his extraordinary political and diplomatic skills, his disinterested loyalty to Lloyd George as the man best qualified in his view to run the country in wartime—all these made him a formidable champion of any cause he chose to adopt.

Balfour was not alone in his sympathy for the Jewish national cause in its specifically Zionist form. Approval of Zionism *in principle* was becoming fairly common in the higher reaches of the British political and administrative establishment. But whereas Balfour's approval was at heart of a philosophical character and essentially detached from considerations of direct policy and interest, in most other cases it is virtually impossible to say where political calculation ended and moral sympathy began. As in the year before, both the underlying reasons and the stated arguments for taking up Zionism and 'the Palestine idea' had a great deal to do with a third active current of contemporary diplomatic and strategic thinking.

The Jews continued to figure in British (and, of course, French) official minds as capable of playing an ill-defined, possibly harmful role in the world arena, constituting a power of some sort to be circumvented or, if necessary, appeased. Changed conditions in the United States and Russia had modified this concern in London and Paris without removing it.

As regards the United States, Wilson's and Congress's decision to join the war against Germany (but not Turkey) had done less than anticipated to reassure the British (and the French) about the state of public opinion there or about the aid in money, men, and matériel they might expect to receive. Far from promising an increase, America's mobilization for war seemed likely to divert resources away from the *entente* Powers and into the vast effort to arm the United States itself, whereas the need to hasten and expand American participation in the war in Europe in all forms—financial and industrial as well as military—was all the greater and more urgent for the catastrophic wasting of men, matériel, and money to which Britain and France had been subject in the course of almost three full years of warfare. The official American position on many of the political issues engendered by the war, notably those touching on the post-war territorial settlement, were plainly different from those of its European allies and seemed likely to be pursued by the Americans with embarrassing vigour.

It is sometimes forgotten [Britain's chief intelligence officer in the United States reminded his Government several months after America's entry into the war], that the Americans are not among our Allies. Technically, the United States made war against Germany to protect the rights of America and is not bound by any inter-Ally treaties. She has reserved for herself the right to make peace with Germany at any time she chooses. . . . They regard themselves not as Allies but as a species of super-Ally. They place themselves in the position rather of arbitrators than as Allies. This is a strong feeling throughout the United States and cannot be neglected.[19]

American hostility to participation in the war on general pacifist and neutralist grounds was still alive. Hostility to Britain on the oldest grounds of all—as the former colonial power—was not dead. In sum, an effort to win American opinion to the Allied cause—and certainly to mitigate hostility—was as necessary as ever and against this background of concerns American Jewry continued to figure as

[19] Cabinet memorandum by Sir William Wiseman, August 1917. PRO, FO 800/209.

an element of some consequence. 'The Jews seem to have changed their attitude to a considerable extent since the Russian revolution,' the British Ambassador in Washington reported in July, 'but the richer Jews have got their funds invested in Germany and I do not think their sympathies can be altered now whatever happens.'[20] Spring Rice remained somewhat out of touch with views in London,[21] but his anxieties—in a general way—were shared by his colleagues at home. If the need to appease American Jewry had diminished, it had not dissolved. In the course of Balfour's visit to the United States from late April to late May—a journey born directly of a drastic weakening of Britain's financial resources and the need to do whatever possible to moderate the unpopularity, both ancient and new, of the British in the United States—it was inevitable that meetings with Brandeis, the leader of the American Zionists, but equally well known for his access to Wilson, should figure on the Foreign Secretary's agenda. Brandeis, as expected, and urged on by the Zionists in London,[22] pressed for a 'national home for the Jews in Palestine' under a British protectorate. Balfour was friendly. He said nothing about Sykes-Picot or the direct British interest in the country. He only spoke of French and Italian 'sensibilities'. But he did promise his 'personal support.'[23] The Foreign Office could therefore feel they had one more friend in Woodrow Wilson's court as well as having done something to drive a wedge between those Jews thought likely to support Britain in any way possible and those who still tended to hold back.

In Russia too, matters relating to the Jews had eased in one respect, while deteriorating (it was thought in London) in another. The overthrow of the Autocracy had yielded a democratic regime which had in turn removed an ancient source of friction with Russia

---

[20] Spring Rice to Balfour, 20 July 1917. BL, Add. MSS. 49740, fo. 143.

[21] The urge to replace him strengthened in the summer of 1917. See for example Drummond to Balfour, 5 July 1917. PRO, FO 800/197.

[22] The relevant telegram to Brandeis from James de Rothschild and Weizmann (21 April 1917, Yale, Wiseman Papers, 91/130) was transmitted to the United States through British intelligence channels. It may be assumed in consequence that Balfour knew precisely what to expect when Brandeis called on him.

[23] Brandeis to de Haas, 8 May 1917. *Herzl Year Book* (New York, 1963), p. 340; and minute by Drummond, 18 June 1917. PRO, FO 371/3053, fo. 298. Balfour was almost as worried about the degree to which the Americans would and could be dedicated to the prosecution of the war at the end of his journey as at its outset. 'Please remember,' he telegraphed home on 28 May, 'that there is a considerable party in America who dare not openly attack [the] war but endeavour by every expedient to prevent its vigorous prosecution.' BL, Add. MSS. 49699, fos. 25–6.

and with it, as everyone knew, the root cause of Jewish disappro-
bation of the Allies and such preference for the Central Powers as
there was. But meanwhile Russia was in turmoil, and in what
direction the 'rapidly moving cinematograph of Russian politics,'[24]
as Balfour called it, was likely to move, none could say. The danger
that the Russian state would suffer total administrative and military
collapse was real and recognized. That the call in Russia to leave the
war was growing rapidly in volume and popularity, particularly on
the political left, was evident. That newly emancipated Russian
Jews were now prominent in public life, notably on the left, had been
recorded, and had been combined in the minds of some British
observers with older, set notions about Russian Jewry and its
allegedly iniquitous role in Russian society. In Russia itself, the
Embassy under Buchanan, along with some of the consular
representatives, held to the view that the Jews remained hostile to
the British and that pro-German sentiment was still alive among
them.[25] In London the plea for a policy that would win them wholly
and finally to the Allied cause began to be heard once again and to
carry fresh conviction. 'We are advised that one of the best methods
of counteracting Jewish pacifist and socialist propaganda in Russia
would be to offer definite encouragement to Jewish nationalist
aspirations in Palestine,' the Ambassador was informed a little
under two months after the fall of the Autocracy and asked whether
he agreed. He did not. Buchanan did not believe there was much
enthusiasm for Zionism among Russian Jews anyway and he
continued to think that the 'Jewish question here is always a delicate
one and . . . that the less said about the Jews the better.' But his
advice was not taken, and the change in the climate of ideas in which
the matter of the Jews now tended to be discussed is well illustrated
in the heated response to Buchanan's strictures from Sykes,
telegraphing from Cairo. The British Embassy in Petrograd did not
and could not know the facts of the matter, whereas he did, he
argued. He knew, as Buchanan did not, how such a question as
London had raised should be put, and to whom. He knew who were
Zionists and who were not. For he knew, as Buchanan evidently did
not, that inquiries about Jewish opinion had always to be made with

---

[24] Imperial War Cabinet, minutes, 22 March 1917. IOLR, MSS. Eur. 112/134.
[25] See for example, consular reports forwarded (and evidently approved) by
Buchanan and judged of 'sufficient interest' to circulate to the Cabinet. Buchanan to
Cecil, with enclosures, 6 May 1917. PRO, FO 371/2966.

the greatest delicacy and care if correct answers were to be obtained. 'Allowance must be made in this for 1900 years of oppression, secretiveness, indirect habit of thought and action, and distrust of Christians.'[26] Sykes had his way. No one in London seems to have presumed to argue with him.

For all these reasons—because in the Near East France appeared as almost as serious an obstacle to British purposes as Germany or Turkey, because in the United States the battle for the favour of the American public was far from over, because in Russia internal decomposition and the rise of hostile political forces threatened to amputate the triple *entente* before serious military aid from America ever materialized—the Jews emerged once again as a 'factor' of which it would be well to take account. Thus in British eyes, at any rate, and in the very sense which the Quai d'Orsay's resident expert on the subject had dismissed as erroneous.[27] But how far the Jews were to be seen as allies, how far as tools, few now stopped to consider. Nor, for that matter, with rare exceptions did those Jews who were specifically in question. On neither side did any seek (perhaps none now needed) to define and determine the precise nature of the unprecedented political relationship into which the British Government on the one hand and a small, self-appointed, and in many ways unrepresentative body of Jewish notables on the other were now about to enter.

The indeterminate nature of the relationship had much to do with the fact that by and large to what each party thought of as its interest there was added a measure of belief not only in the political but the moral value of the relationship. In the event these feelings were to prove ephemeral and, so far as both Jews and Englishmen were concerned, a wasting asset. Nor were these bonds of sympathy and mutual regard the only ones of their kind that were now in the making. They were never to be as famous, as long-lasting, and half so pregnant with far-reaching political consequences as their contemporary analogue, the ties established with the Arabs of the Hedjaz. But if they lasted for a moment in history it was a crucial moment, at any rate for the weaker partner: for they hinged on the central circumstance that the Jewish national tendency in its Zionist

[26] [Cecil] to Buchanan, 24 April; Buchanan to Foreign Office, 27 April; and Sykes to Graham, 28 April 1917. PRO, FO 371/3053.
[27] See above, p. 196.

form had, under the 'principle of nationality', finally fallen into place in the British scheme of things. It was a principle that was ever more strongly believed to be one of universal validity. In the eyes of those concerned in Whitehall it followed ever more smoothly that Zionism was no longer an absurdity or aberration. Thus for almost all, but particularly for those whose romantic and generally imperfect notions about the Jews of antiquity were troubled by what they saw (or thought they knew) of *contemporary* Jewry. For them Zionism, with its promise of a Jewish *Risorgimento*, made much the same sort of sense and carried much of the same appeal as the revival and liberation of Greece and Italy had carried in the previous century. Sykes, Amery, and Ormsby-Gore (all three Members of Parliament, as it happened, and of an independent cast of mind) in the Cabinet Office, Cecil and Graham in the Foreign Office, Lloyd George himself too in his somewhat devious way, and perhaps above all Balfour—all in some degree were under the sway of such notions. So were many others in journalism, in parliamentary politics, even in the armed services. Zionism, in short, had come to be regarded in London in 1917 as not only useful but *worthy*: always a potent combination of attributes in this particular seat of government. But again, just how Zionism *as a tool* was to be employed in practice and how closely it would be possible and desirable to work with the Zionists *as allies* had still to be determined.

Not the least of the causes of the uncertainty—one which was to appear and reappear in a great variety of forms over many years—was the fact that in the early stages of the process, even as late as April 1917, the question how strongly France was to be fought, if at all, for control of Palestine had still to be settled. The Prime Minister's men, led by Sykes, were clear enough in their minds. At the Foreign Office, however, there was unease, if not confusion.

His Majesty's Government are now committed to support Zionist aspirations [ran an internal Foreign Office memorandum which wholly misconstrued what Sykes was trying to do]. Sir Mark Sykes has received instructions from the Prime Minister (and Mr. Balfour) and has been taking action both in Paris and Rome. . . .

However admirable the Zionist idea may be and however rightly anxious His Majesty's Government are to encourage it, there is one aspect of the situation to which attention should be drawn. Every Zionist with whom I have discussed the question . . . [is] of the opinion that their project would break down were Palestine to be internationalised [as laid down in the Sykes-Picot Agreement]. . . . We cannot, of course, inform the Zionists of this Agreement, but are we justified in encouraging them in so great a measure when the prospect of Palestine being internationalised is distinctly stronger than the prospect of the country coming under our protection? I know that the Prime Minister insists that we obtain Palestine and that Sir Mark Sykes proceeded on his mission with these instructions. But those who are best qualified to gauge French opinion, including Lord Bertie, are convinced that the French will never abandon their sentimental claims to Palestine.[28]

But whether tools or allies, there was the question of *who*, for present and practical purposes, were 'the Zionists': a question that had to be answered if the topic was to be moved from the plane of discussion to that of action. Sykes thought he knew: Sokolov, Weizmann, and Jabotinsky were the men—at any rate the type of men—he had chiefly in mind. He thought he knew what they were aiming at; he was sure of the benefit that would accrue to Britain if their aims were achieved.[29] They were men with whom a working relationship could be established. It was in the logic of things to proceed to do so. The groundwork had already been laid. It was indeed at this point and for these reasons that the paths and purposes of the British Government and that branch of the Zionist movement which was best known to it (not least because it had made it its business to make itself known) began to intersect.

ii

This crucial phase in the history of the Zionist movement can barely be separated from what was now to be the steady rise of Weizmann to a position of leadership—initially of that branch of Zionism which wanted the co-operation and protection of the British, ultimately of the movement as a whole. It may be that in a final reckoning Weizmann was more the epitome of the momentary alliance that was now in the making than its engineer. But his drive to the top was nothing if not a function of his ambition, his political

[28] Graham to Hardinge, 21 April 1917. PRO, FO 371/3052. Hardinge, who had never much liked the policy of supporting the Zionists, thought that 'a British Palestine . . . seems at present unrealisable' and that the relevant conclusion should be drawn. Cecil, Acting Foreign Secretary in Balfour's absence, and much more closely identified with that policy, thought the most useful thing to do would be to get the French 'to join us in an expression of sympathy for Jewish nationalist aspirations.' This was the line that was followed.

[29] Sykes to Graham, 28 April 1917. PRO, FO 371/3053.

talent, and his sheer determination to lead. Even if he was hugely favoured by circumstances which were more often than not either fortuitous or incidental to the purposes of Zionism, or the work of others, or unknown to him, or if known then misunderstood, it was his ability to make the most of what was to hand that was decisive for his acceptance both by his colleagues as their leader and by the British political and administrative establishment as a man worth working with. Sykes, whose interest in Zionism had been intense at least since early in 1916, as we have seen, who continued to believe that the Zionists were 'the key to the situation' and that 'with "Great Jewry" against us there is no possible chance of getting the thing thro"', had wanted badly to get the Zionists 'fired up' in the interests of settling 'the Franco-Arab difficulty'.[30] For a while, after his return from Russia, his principal contact and informant on Zionism was Moses Gaster, the *Ḥakham* (Sephardi Chief Rabbi) to whom he had been introduced by Samuel. Gaster had been an early adherent of Ḥibbat Zion and an immediate recruit to Herzl's movement. With Zangwill lost he was by any account the senior veteran Zionist in Britain. He had been prominent in some of the Congresses. He had been president of the English Zionist Federation. He was still anxious to continue to play a role in public affairs. In the narrow world of communal politics in England he could scarcely be circumvented; and it is a measure both of his position and of Weizmann's almost unerring eye for useful connections that in the latter's early years in the country he did what he could to cultivate and humour the *Ḥakham*. But Gaster was a difficult, quarrelsome, and somewhat unpopular man, and in no sense an effective leader of others. The chemist, like many before him, eventually fell out with the rabbi. And Sykes, for his part, within a very few weeks of his first meeting with Weizmann at the end of January 1917, transferred both his attention and his essential business to the new man—and to Sokolov too, it must be said—with no recognizable hesitation.

By this time, in February 1917, the grounds for seeing Weizmann as a public figure of the second rank with disproportionately large political pretensions had virtually dissolved. Thanks to his technical and scientific inventiveness he was well on his way to becoming

---

[30] And with a characteristic flourish he drove home his point slightly misquoting Shakespeare: (*Troilus and Cressida*, I,iii) '"Untune that string and mark [*sic*] what discord follows"—Assume Zionists satisfied the contrary is the case.' Sykes to Sir Arthur Nicolson, Permanent Under-Secretary at the Foreign Office, 18 March 1916. PRO, FO 800/381.

persona grata in Whitehall and so to neutralizing the residual effects of his unhappy last year or two at Manchester University.[31] He had made such progress in his long-standing effort to cultivate the magnates of western European Jewry that it was to him specifically that the one most favourably disposed of all, to whom the Zionists owed the greatest of their debts, turned in the summer of 1916, calling Zionists and non-Zionists to co-operate: Baron Edmond de Rothschild, the 'father of the *yishuv*', who in its early years had saved it from economic collapse and had followed its fortunes and those of the Zionists generally with a critical but decidely warm and avuncular regard.[32]

Edmond de Rothschild had learned of the Foreign Office's decision to drop Wolf's plan and formula for a British pro-Zionist statement and when Wolf saw him in the course of his visit to Paris in July 1916[33] he pressed the CFC's secretary to join forces with the Zionists, notably with Weizmann. 'The Baron has a very exaggerated opinion of Weizmann's position and influence,' Wolf reported to his Committee. 'He thinks, for example, that he (Weizmann) is President of the Zionist Organisation in London.'[34] But he did not demur, and in London in August the two men met under the roof of the Baron's son, James, this time as equals. In the event, the Baron's good intentions led nowhere. The fundamental difference on the 'nationality' or otherwise of the Jews formed the subject of one sterile argument. The questions whether the British Government had or had not agreed to the Zionists being granted a Charter in Palestine (as Wolf thought Weizmann had told him, but Weizmann denied) and whether a Charter (in practice: special settlement rights for Jews) was proper and acceptable in principle formed the subject of another argument and of a long and acrimonious correspondence into which, in one way or another, half a dozen other Jewish notables were drawn. Weizmann stuck to his guns and allowed Wolf to rage against ideas of which he profoundly disapproved. He had no

[31] On Weizmann's failure to attain a professorship, the cloud which gathered over his head at Manchester towards the end of his time there as a result of his involvement in an industrial patent dispute, and his much happier career as a chemist in wartime government service, see two articles by Jehuda Reinharz: 'Chaim Weizmann and the Elusive Manchester Professorship', *AJS Review*, ix: 2, 1984, pp. 215–46; and 'Science in the Service of Politics: The Case of Chaim Weizmann during the First World War', *English Historical Review*, c: 396, 1985, pp. 572–603.

[32] See *Origins*, pp. 212–18.

[33] See above, p. 205.

[34] Diary, 10 July 1916. ML, AJ/204/2.

intention, he said, of allowing 'the bitterest opponents of the Jewish National Movement [to] have anything to do with the Palestine question', and professed 'failure to understand why they should at all desire to deal with such a question and not prefer to leave it *strictly alone.*'[35] A long, fatherly letter from Baron Edmond ('Be moderate, my dear Mr. Weizmann, and above all conciliatory.') advising compromise with Wolf and speaking of the wisdom of the old, non-political approach to the settlement of Erez-Israel[36] had no effect and does not seem ever to have been answered. But that it should have been written speaks volumes for the solidity of Weizmann's growing reputation as the central Zionist figure in wartime England in everything but title. Before long he had the title too. In February he was elected president of the English Zionist Federation, wholly on his own terms, having successfully insisted on a team of like-minded people being placed on the Federation's committee with him, and having been accorded general recognition —enthusiastic in some quarters, resigned in others—that within English Zionism he had no competitors for force, authority, and increasingly important political connections. The days when his precise status might be questioned [37] were virtually, but not entirely, over. He could speak for the (tiny) English Zionist Federation. He could be accepted as one who knew a great deal about the affairs and mood of the vastly more important Russian branch. But he could not speak for it; still less could he speak for Zionism's central institutions, against which, in practice, he was in rebellion, or claim a residual authority in consequence of their collapse.[38] Nahum Sokolov, a member of the EAC and its appointed legate (with Tchlenov) for the countries of the *entente*, could do both.

Among the notables of Zionism in wartime London, Sokolov's seniority and prominence in the movement were unrivalled (greater

[35] The principal items are: memorandum by Wolf, 17 August 1916. CZA, A77/3A; Wolf to James de Rothschild, 31 August 1916. Ibid.; James de Rothschild to Wolf, 31 August 1916. WA; Weizmann to Wolf, 3 September 1916. *Weizmann Letters*, vii, no. 271, pp. 291–2; Weizmann to James de Rothschild, 5 November 1916. Ibid., no. 287, pp. 310–12. Further exchanges in the form of memoranda by Zionists and Wolf: 11 October, 20 November 1916. ML, AJ/204/3. Wolf submitted the major items to the Foreign Office for their information. PRO, FO 371/2817 fos. 166 ff.

[36] Edmond de Rothschild to Weizmann, 10 November 1916. WA.

[37] See above, p. 177.

[38] His credentials questioned, Weizmann tended to be on the defensive in the early stages of the war. See for example his letter to Magnes, who had inquired more than once whether he had Tchlenov's and Sokolov's sanction for what he was doing: 9 January 1915. *Weizmann Letters*, vii, no. 100, pp. 124 ff.

by far than Gaster's, let alone Weizmann's). So were his knowledge of its affairs and his single-minded devotion to its causes. Of the six-man EAC elected in 1913 and still nominally in office, only he was both willing and able to co-operate with the British by lending his authority to the alignment to which Sykes and Weizmann—in their different ways and for their distinctive purposes—were driving. Neither Sykes nor Weizmann could do without him. And it is therefore Sokolov, older by thirteen years, the acknowledged veteran, the more erudite and cultivated of the two, of milder and more humane disposition, who by his growing acceptance of the younger, tougher Weizmann as the dominant member of the partnership provides the sharpest indicator of Weizmann's growing strength, political achievement, and striking ability to project his own self-confidence.

If Weizmann was favoured by the contingent presence in London of the loyal and relatively pliant Sokolov, by the fact that the movement as a whole, seen world-wide, was in disarray and its central institutions in virtual collapse, and by the circumstance that there was no one among the committed Zionists in Great Britain itself of comparable talent, independence of mind, and sheer energy, his greatest good fortune lay in the tactic upon which the British Government was now resolved. This was, as we have seen, that with the military occupation of Palestine impending, the attempt would be made to employ the Zionists in the effort to evade those terms of the 1916 agreement with France which applied to that country. It was a tactic to which he was not party and of which neither he nor any of his colleagues were informed. It is not clear when—*if at all*—he and they became aware of it and grasped what their intended role was to be. As we have seen, the role Sykes (under Lloyd George) had allotted the Zionists was not immediately clear to all concerned at the Foreign Office either. There it was the thesis propounded originally by Lucien Wolf, that Zionism alone would provide an effective key to the hearts of Jewry (the anti-Zionist minority notwithstanding), that was held to be of central validity. There was the second thesis that the lesser nations deserved a place of some sort in the sun and that the Jews, so it seemed, were one of their number. And finally, as the war continued and spread to the Near East, the Jews—some Jews, at any rate—were known (by some) to be capable both of playing a role behind the Turkish lines on behalf of British intelligence and within the Egyptian Expeditionary Force proper as uniformed troops. There were thus several distinct grounds for arguing the case of Zionism in high places in London.Each was of some weight. Each was more or less popular with one or other of the political figures and diplomatic and military institutions involved. But in each case, as we have seen, there was a counter-argument or countervailing factor strong enough to meet it, or at any rate greatly to reduce the value of a pro-Zionist policy in the eyes of those considering it. It was the tactic associated with Sykes that tipped the balance decisively. On the one hand it was urged as promoting a central British strategic interest. On the other hand, being directed—in effect—against France, it dissolved the major objection to the original proposal put to the Foreign Office by Wolf and provisionally accepted by it, namely its incompatibility with the military and political logic of the Anglo-French *entente*. Once Sykes's tactic had been approved and employed, the British Government was *ipso facto* 'committed' to sponsoring Zionism, as most British diplomats immediately concerned recognized. For it followed that if the Zionists were to be made use of and edged towards the target Sykes had set them, their involvement and integration in British affairs had positively to be encouraged. That this was the crucial circumstance upon which all else hinged, and from which to a great extent, all subsequent developments flowed, is attested by the dramatic change, once it had been instituted, in the fortunes of other Zionists who, in defiance of the set policy of the central institutions of their movement, had been intent upon a pro-British orientation all along.

The 'activists' had been labouring throughout 1916 to impress both upon the British Government and upon the Jewish community in London, especially in London's East End, the uses and virtues of a Jewish Legion in the British army. Jabotinsky had made a few more friends in high places, but he could do nothing to overcome the War Office's dislike of 'fancy regiments', disbelief in Jews as fighting men, and a general sense that this was a political and therefore inherently doubtful scheme. The Foreign Office thought no better of it. Only the Home Office, now headed by Samuel (reincorporated into the Cabinet at the beginning of the year) was mildly attracted to a scheme which seemed to promise an end to the scandal of some 30,000 young men, mostly Russian subjects, who would neither volunteer for military service nor could they, under the new conscription laws introduced at the beginning of the year, be forced to do so. Jabotinsky argued that if they were offered the carrot of service in their own national cause no stick would be necessary; and with Samuel's unofficial blessing, and with Grossman, whom he had called from Copenhagen to join him, he set about campaigning for his Legion in Whitechapel. He failed. The established Jewish community (with rare exceptions) was appalled by the very notion of separate units for Jews, even foreign Jews. Most other Zionists in England, as elsewhere, opposed the scheme on the ostensibly not unreasonable grounds that Jewish/Zionist units in the British army fighting in Palestine would seal the fate of the *yishuv* at the hands of the Turks. As relatively few volunteers for service in the Legion came forward in any case—no more than two hundred, not the thousands hoped for—it was clear that the scandal of the thirty-odd thousand young Jewish men in London's East End would not go away. And finally, Jabotinsky and Grossman had a hard time of it personally. They encountered huge opposition to what they stood for in the very crowds they went out to harangue, and were pelted with vegetables and severely jostled for their pains. All this was noted by the authorities, and the scheme thereupon dismissed once again (with somewhat amused appreciation of Jabotinsky's noble intentions) as trebly unhelpful: politically controversial, administratively eccentric, and militarily—having regard to the numbers likely to be involved—insignificant. When at the end of the year some 120 veterans of the Zion Mule Corps who had volunteered for the British army proper arrived in England and were incorporated into a battalion of the Royal Fusiliers, Jabotinsky, in evident desperation, joined them as a private soldier.

Jabotinsky was then 37 years of age. He had long been exempted from conscription into the Russian army; nothing required him to serve in the British. But he thought it not only the useful but the honourable thing to do. It accorded with his deep romantic streak. It might be seen, too, as an act resolved upon in the moral-political style of thinking common among Russian radicals of the day (by whose example he seems in some ways to have been deeply influenced), for whom it was all but axiomatic that political conviction entailed moral commitment and moral commitment required action. But in the larger political sense it was an error for Jabotinsky to have enlisted, as he himself came to realize. For so doing, he removed himself by degrees, in the end almost totally, from what had become and would long remain the central political arena: London.[39] (Weizmann, it may be said parenthetically, was not given to making that kind of mistake.[40] A man of exceedingly high ambition, he knew better than to demand of himself what he demanded of others. But then still less did he demand of others what he demanded of himself.)

However, so far as the Legion was concerned, Jabotinsky was fortunate in the end. He had made a last attempt at the end of January 1917, just before enlistment, to bring the matter before the Government, writing to the newly installed Prime Minister. This time his ideas were accorded a much friendlier reception: Leopold Amery (now serving with Sykes in the Cabinet Office) had advised him to emphasize the role and conduct of the Zion Mule Corps at Gallipoli and its having been mentioned in dispatches; to play down the political uses of the scheme; and to address the memorandum directly to the Prime Minister with a request that the project be considered by the War Cabinet.[41] Amery himself, all enthusiasm, then pushed it further along the line on expressly political grounds. Its 'effect . . . upon the Jews in America and elsewhere, who have been largely anti-entente because of Russia, might be very good,' he argued, asking Balfour to bring it up before the War Cabinet. 'Even in Austria-Hungary, where the Jews are such a big factor, the formation of such a unit and its military successes in Palestine, coming on top of the Russian revolution, might cause a revulsion of feeling.' He addressed the Foreign Secretary specifically on the strength of Balfour's having 'expressed himself so freely in favour of Zionism at the War Cabinet the other day'. The War Office's objections, 'may have been applicable', Amery argued, 'when it was only a question of raising a battalion or so, but it would hardly apply when there is the possibility of raising something like a division of infantry.' As for the dislike of 'fancy regiments', 'from the military point of view, the desirability of getting people of kindred

[39] *Avtobiografiya*, pp. 186–9. 'The centre is here [in London] and should remain here,' Sokolov had written Brandeis. 7 April 1917. CZA, L6/90I.

[40] When conscription was introduced in Great Britain in 1916 Weizmann was duly called up, upon which he claimed exemption on the grounds that he was in the service of the Ministry of Munitions. This was entirely proper and legitimate and the exemption was granted without question, so far as is known. Weizmann to the Military Authorities, Woking, 31 August 1916. *Weizmann Letters*, vii, no. 269, pp. 289–90. In 1916 Weizmann was 41 years of age.

[41] Jabotinsky and Trumpeldor to the Prime Minister, 24 January 1917. PRO, CAB 24/9; Amery to Jabotinsky, 25 January 1917. JA, A1/3/5/1.

associations and qualities together has always [been] recognised, and I really don't see why you shouldn't have 'Jerusalem High-landers' just as well as Gordon Highlanders.'[42]

When fresh interdepartmental inquiries were made, the Foreign Office found that the War Office now no longer objected, but wanted the Foreign Office, who were still cautious, to make the first move.[43] In the end it was Milner who brought the subject up before the War Cabinet. There it was pointed out that so far as was known there were *not* likely to be a large number of recruits and that English Jewry generally disliked the scheme; but the decision was taken, none the less, to take a closer look at it.[44] The Secretary of State for War, Lord Derby, called in Jabotinsky (now a private soldier) and Trumpeldor, heard what they had to say, and was sufficiently impressed by the *political* arguments they offered not to turn them down.[45] In the Cabinet Office Ormsby-Gore drew up a position paper on 'Zionism and the suggested Jewish battalions for [the] Egyptian Expeditionary Force',[46] in which the two issues were explicitly and favourably linked and current thinking in the Cabinet Secretariat and Sykes's influence there clearly exposed. Its theme was 'the possibility of military co-operation with us by Jewish Nationalists all over the world'. Its central argument was that the 'Nationalist Jews', despite their slow start, formed a wholly serious movement, one that was steadily gathering strength not only in Palestine and Russia, but in the United States as well. The Zionists were anti-Russian, as were most other Jews, but, profoundly anti-German as well, knowing that 'the greatest stronghold of philo-sophic and social anti-Semitism' was Prussia. But they were deeply suspicious of the French too, both because 'the memory of the Dreyfus case dies hard' and because they held them to be 'an assimilitating people'. 'Why precisely the Zionists have become more and more pro-British since the war' was difficult to say, the paper's author admitted, 'but I am convinced there is no doubt of this fact. . . . The prospect of a division of Palestine into different spheres alarms them. . . . Their political idea is either [a] British

---

[42] Amery to Balfour, 29 March 1917. PRO, FO 800/204. The reference to Balfour's 'free expression' in favour of Zionism is plainly to his statement before the Imperial War Cabinet on 22 March 1917. See above, p. 215.

[43] Minutes by Graham and Balfour. Ibid.

[44] Imperial War Cabinet, minutes, 5 April 1917. IOLR, MSS. Eur. F112/134.

[45] Derby to Lloyd George, 9 April 1917. HLRO, Lloyd George Papers, F/14/4/34.

[46] GT 447, 14 April 1917. PRO, CAB 24/10.

Palestine or Palestine under the United States—preferably the former.' In sum, 'the important point is that the Zionist leaders regard the success of our arms as the only hope for Zionism.'[47]

The upshot was that, doubts remaining to the last about the uses of a Legion (temporarily defined as a 'Russian Jewish battalion') as a vehicle for recruiting Russian and Polish Jews in the East End of London,[48] and fully aware of the opposition within Jewry, it was decided to proceed with the scheme after all. The decisive grounds, the Foreign Office was informed on the Prime Minister's behalf, were political: 'The raising of a Jewish Legion for use in Palestine, if coupled with assurances from the British Government of their sympathy with the desire of many Jews to settle in Palestine and build up a community within it, might produce a very beneficial effect in making the Jews in America and Russia keener on helping to see the War through.'[49] Jabotinsky, it turned out, had been holding the wrong end of the stick throughout. He and his friends had conceived the Legion chiefly as an instrument whereby political support might be obtained for Zionism. It was granted as a consequence—and public affirmation—of political support offered Zionism on other grounds. But it was Weizmann's final and triumphant coming to the fore that provides the best illustration of the changed and sharpened British tactics, following a reordering of purposes and priorities by Lloyd George's new Government in the early part of 1917.

Shortly after the outbreak of the war Weizmann had chanced to meet C. P. Scott who, as the owner-editor of the *Manchester Guardian*, a newspaper that stood as did no other for the old, moralistic Gladstonian Liberalism, and as a man of immense energy and independent views, was one of the most influential journalists of his day. Weizmann courted him and won him to his cause. It was a firm, genuine, and disinterested conversion; and Scott thereafter was assiduous in his support both of Weizmann the man and Weizmann the representative of a form of Jewish nationalism of which he approved profoundly. It was Scott who had introduced him to Samuel, although no doubt Weizmann would have found his way to Samuel on his own sooner or later. More important by far were

[47] Ibid.
[48] Memorandum by Derby, 23 May 1917. PRO, CAB 24/14.
[49] Kerr to Graham, 5 May 1917. PRO, FO 371/3101.

Scott's talks with Lloyd George about Weizmann, and a number of meetings he arranged between the two men from November 1914 onwards, with Lloyd George as successively Chancellor of the Exchequer, Minister of Munitions, Secretary of State for War, and finally Prime Minister. Weizmann the gifted chemist with a new technique for the production of one of the components of cordite, Weizmann the temporary civil servant in trouble with, and apparently mistreated by some of his hierarchical superiors, and Weizmann the inventor whom HMG was honour-bound to reward financially comprised one set of matters which Scott repeatedly brought before Lloyd George both in Weizmann's presence and, more often, in his absence. The other set was of course the matter of Zionism itself.

Lloyd George's attitude to and understanding of Zionism was a great deal less clear-cut than Balfour's. It is more than probable that Asquith struck the truest note when he observed two years earlier that 'Lloyd George . . . does not care a damn for the Jews or their past or their future.'[50] But he did care about Palestine. No British politician of comparable stature in or out of government had shown as much interest in it as Lloyd George, at any rate since the Turks had entered the war.

Weizmann had several meetings with Lloyd George prior to 1917. Only in one, on 26 November 1915, was the matter of the Near East, Zionism, and the Jews taken up in a spirit of practical politics— Herbert Samuel joining in 'as a good Jew', Scott noted in his diary. Lloyd George (Minister of Munitions at this point) spoke of French ambitions and of the possibility of a three-Power condominium over the country, to which Samuel and Weizmann immediately objected. The Minister, Scott recalled, then

asked how many colonists the Jews expected to be able to supply and Weizmann said he thought half a million in 50 years. George evidently thought this a very small number, but W. pointed out that this kind of colonization was extremely expensive (it had cost so far about £200 per family per holding). . . .

George thought there might have been a rapid immigration from Russia encouraged by the Russian Government, but W. said Palestine c[ould] offer no solution to the Jewish q[uestion] in Russia with its six million Jews and Samuel pointed out that the country, though a very fine one, was small and

---

[50] M. and E. Brock (eds.), *H. H. Asquith: Letters to Venetia Stanley* (Oxford, 1982), p. 477. See above, pp. 95–6.

c[ould] not support more than about two and a half millions of population.[51]

A year and a quarter passed before Lloyd George, by then Prime Minister, discussed Palestine again with Weizmann. Had he been disappointed by what he had learned from him of Zionism? Or had he simply been content with what he had heard and taken the measure of whom he had seen? In any event, at the time Weizmann's sights were still on the great international conference that was to establish the peace that was to follow the war, and his immediate object was access to the great men in Whitehall and Westminster. Access to one led to access to another. Access to them as a class established him in his colleagues' eyes first as a man of parts, then as the man of the hour. If Lloyd George was content to listen and signify general, non-binding understanding of Weizmann's theses, that was an achievement in itself. And meanwhile Scott kept the connection alive, reminding Lloyd George of Weizmann and the Zionists from time to time and feeding Weizmann with such information as came his way and was relevant to his cause. Thus throughout 1915 and 1916. At no stage was political business, properly speaking, transacted. Matters of chemical technology apart, at no stage were either the meetings or the services Scott performed as go-between anything but private and unofficial. At no point did Lloyd George openly shunt his interest in Weizmann and the Zionists into established ministerial and official channels. When Sykes, a member of Lloyd George's Cabinet Secretariat, sought out Weizmann in January 1917, it was through the agency of James Aratoon Malcolm, London representative of the International Armenian Committee (the third side of the Arab-Armenian-Jewish triangle of protégés upon which Sykes hoped to build British power in the Near East). There is nothing to suggest it was Lloyd George who advised him to do so. There is no direct evidence that Sykes was aware of Weizmann's access to Lloyd George. If he did ask for permission to make semi-formal contact with the Zionists, it is probable that he asked it of Milner. Most

[51] C. P. Scott Papers, BL, Add. MSS. 50902, fos. 59–64. Weizmann's discounting of Erez-Israel as a haven for Russian Jewry was consistent with the set Aḥad Ha-'Amian view of the Jewish problem. Writing to Lucien Wolf in the following year, he defined the disjunction, as he saw it, in crystal-clear terms: 'This question is entirely independent of the Palestine question and the two things have no connection.' 3 September 1915. *Weizmann Letters*, vii, no. 271, p. 292.

likely it was his own idea to speak to them. Lloyd George was newly in power. The war was raging. Sykes had his general instructions; his instructions were in important respects of his own devising; and in any case he was accustomed (and, it seems, expected) to interpret them with reasonable freedom and imagination.

What then of Lloyd George? It could perhaps be said of him that in respect of foreign and imperial policy he was Mark Sykes writ very large: older, more experienced, vastly more powerful, of an even more original and imaginative cast of mind, perhaps the greatest political adventurer of all in Britain. Lloyd George liked informal contacts and sources of information. It has been said of him that he preferred to learn from people rather than from papers. He cultivated Scott, the great editor of the great newspaper most closely associated with his party, no less than Scott cultivated him. He was prepared to humour Scott, and at the same time was not in the least averse to learning from him. He learned from him of Weizmann, and there was something to learn directly from Weizmann too. His initial interest in Weizmann the Zionist seems to have been slight, if genuine enough. His interest in Weizmann the chemist arose out of the circumstance that Weizmann turned out to be a man who could tell him things of importance about his own Ministry. His interest in Weizmann's Zionism quickened, however, when, in 1917, he was fully in power and British forces were poised for the invasion of Palestine. His prompt use of bits and pieces of information gleaned from Weizmann, as when he advised Sykes, who was to leave for Cairo, to consider employing local Jews as 'motor-drivers and guides . . . intimately acquainted with Palestine', was character- istic.[52] But at no stage did he *negotiate* with Weizmann. Throughout, the form allowed and readily accepted by Weizmann himself was that of an effort by Weizmann (and others) to inform, to explain, to persuade, and to instruct: always rationally, sensibly, and on the basis of an assumption of common humanity and common interests—Herzlian diplomacy all over again, applied to the man or men at the top, as Herzl had always believed it should be. Thus with Lloyd George, thus with Balfour and Cecil, thus with Sykes, thus with the British establishment generally. That it was their task to persuade the British by logical, historical, political, and, if neces- sary, by moral argument to adopt Zionism, Weizmann and his colleagues did not doubt. When it began to appear that the British

[52] War Cabinet conference, 3 April 1917. PRO, CAB 24/9.

might indeed do so, they did not doubt that they had contributed much, perhaps everything, to the new view taken of their movement and to the new, apparent intimacy of the relationship into which they were now admitted. Nothing said to them, nothing shown them, suggested otherwise. And nothing illustrates the depth of their illusion that they were not merely involved in the formulation of British policy on the matter of Palestine and on Zionism in particular but were in certain vital respects its initiators as the energy they invested in seeking to show His Majesty's Government how necessary it was not only to reject the idea of 'international-izing' the country, but how immensely undesirable it was to subject it to a Franco-English condominium. Balfour 'gave me a good opening to put before him the importance of P.[alestine] from a British point [of] view, an aspect which was apparently new to him,' Weizmann noted after his long-awaited interview with the Foreign Secretary in March 1917.[53] The arrival of the Zionists at the brink of success was not without its irony.

In its two essentials, then, the British decision to couple Palestine with Zionism (the 'Palestine idea', as it had been called at an earlier stage) was one to which the Zionists themselves had made no direct contribution. The value of Zionism in the campaign for Jewish goodwill had been argued by the vociferously anti-Zionist Lucien Wolf and others, and had been accepted in London (although not in Paris) the year before. The idea that Zionism would have its uses in the coming effort to remove the 'danger' of a French presence in Palestine emerged spontaneously within the inner circle of British Government itself. In neither case had the Zionists themselves been consulted. In the former case the project was aborted before any such consultation became necessary. In the latter case no consult-ation was even possible: they could not be told of the terms of the Anglo-French Agreement of 1916 (they had to discover them for themselves); and they could not be expressly recruited by one ally to help revoke an agreement concluded with another.

What the Zionists had done, however, was to have produced

---

[53] Weizmann to Cowen, 26 March 1917. *Weizmann Letters*, vii, no. 325, p. 348. To Scott he had written: 'Mr. Balfour did not at first see the importance of the Zionist claim from the British point of view; I think I succeeded in explaining that to him.' Ibid., no. 323, p. 346.

meanwhile the seeds of a fresh leadership and a fresh policy of their
own. The process was not a parliamentary one. It was not the
outcome of clear-cut decisions at any level, least of all at that of the
central, formal institutions of the movement. Rather, it was the
paralysis of those institutions that had made it possible and, in some
minds, as we have seen, necessary, and this same paralysis at the
centre goes some way to account for the fact that the new leaderships
arose in one of the smaller, outlying branches of the movement (and
of Jewry). It was indeed the exceedingly small proportions of the
arena in which the new men fought for prominence that helps to
explain the part played by the determination, agility, and contingent
circumstances of the central figure in question. And while the
decision to take the Zionists aboard the British ship of state was
decisive for the *further* growth and strength of the new leadership, it
is the case that, in its initial stages, the rise of the new leadership
proceeded independently of the fact that in one way or another
Zionism was the object of close Governmental interest.

iii

Something of the terms and a great deal of the spirit in which official
Britain and the unauthorized—but now ever more independently
minded—Zionists in London were to move towards alignment in
1917 were set very early in that year. On 7 February, at Sykes's own
request, he met what he could have fairly considered as near an
encapsulation of the 'Great Jewry' by which he held such store and
of the Zionists he had long thought best fitted to speak for (and to) it
as could conveniently be put together in wartime London: Lord
Rothschild, James de Rothschild (Baron Edmond's son), and
Herbert Samuel could be rated major Jewish notables; Sokolov
could claim to speak for the Russian branch of the movement and to
retain some shaky institutional authority as an elected member of
the EAC; Gaster, Herbert Bentwich, and Cowen were all veteran
figures of English Zionism; Harry Sacher was one of its new men;
and Weizmann who, in some ways, fell into all three categories
without being in the top class in any one of them, was, as we have
seen, well on his way to supremacy all round. All these men felt from
the first that this was the confrontation they had been waiting for.
They had been enormously excited by the prospect of such a
meeting with Sykes. 'We may be called upon *very soon* to put our

Zionist aspirations into practice,' Gaster had written to colleagues in the United States the week before.[54] And in the aftermath none doubted, least of all Weizmann, that the movement had indeed reached a point of 'crisis'[55] and had never been closer than it was now to the 'heart of the matter'.[56] Indeed, they had cause to think so: it was not merely a meeting to exchange information; it turned out to be a meeting to discuss tactics as well. At the same time, in form as well as in substance, the conference was wholly unlike the straightforward political talks Herzl had held with Lansdowne and Joseph Chamberlain at the Foreign and Colonial Offices respectively a decade and a half earlier.[57] The conference was convened at a private home (Gaster's), not in Whitehall. It was declared unofficial: Sykes, Assistant Cabinet Secretary and principal agent for the British Government in matters relating to the Near East, was careful to stress that he attended only in 'his private capacity'. Both the fact that the conference had been convened and its proceedings were held to be secret. And in one central respect it was asymmetrical. Whereas the Zionists came primed to restate[58] their case and to make known their purposes, Sykes kept the key datum and his own main purpose to himself. The Englishman heard the Jews out on their 'irreconcilable opposition' to any form of condominium over Palestine, on their desire for British rule over the country, on their wish for a chartered company under the auspices of which 'a Jewish Palestine' would be developed, on the strength of Jewish national feeling in eastern Europe, and on the strategic importance of Palestine to Great Britain itself. For his part he expressed his sympathy with the 'idea of a Jewish Palestine' and went on to outline what he took to be obstacles to its realization. There were the Russians who were sceptical, but—their concern for

[54] Gaster to de Haas, 31 January 1917. WA. Emphasis in original.

[55] Aḥad Ha-'Am to Pevsner, 24 February 1917. *Igrot AH*, vi, p. 61. Aḥad Ha-'Am did not attend, but was kept well informed by Weizmann and others.

[56] Weizmann to Jabotinsky, 8 February 1917. *Weizmann Letters*, vii, no. 306. p. 329.

[57] See *Formative Years*, pp. 146–8.

[58] A written memorandum had been submitted to Sykes some days before the meeting. It is not clear which of a number of versions on which the Zionists in London had been working towards the end of 1916 was handed to him. It was possibly a version entitled 'Outline of a Programme for a new administration of Palestine and for a Jewish resettlement of Palestine in accordance with the aspirations of the Zionist movement' to be found together with the minutes of the conference with Sykes and connected documents among the Lothian Papers, SRO, GD40/17/42. Philip Kerr, later Lord Lothian, was Lloyd George's private secretary. But see *Weizmann Letters*, vii, p. 328 n. 3, and Appendix, pp. 543–4.

the Holy Places apart—not greatly interested in the country itself. There were the Arabs: there was certain to be a great national movement among them 'within a generation or so', they claimed all Syria and Palestine, and some had already commenced attacking Zionism. 'One would have to go very carefully with [them]. . . . Still, the Arabs could be managed, particularly if they received Jewish support in other matters.' There were the Italians who 'went on the principle of asking for everything the French demanded.' But they were not 'a very serious difficulty'. The serious difficulty was France.

He did not understand French policy, Sykes told the Zionists. Was their motive sentimental— 'clerical' or colonial ambition? Was it economic— a matter of railway concessions? The latter could be 'disposed of with money'; the former was more difficult, and nationalist pretensions were more difficult to deal with than clerical. The British Government would have to discuss the question with the French, but thus far no 'pledge' on the matter of Palestine had been given them. Indeed? He 'had been informed differently,' James de Rothschild interjected. Sykes repeated his assurance: 'The French have no particular position in Palestine and are not entitled to anything there.' After some talk on the structure of the future administration of the country, Rothschild reverted to the matter of an alleged British pledge to the French. Had one been given? Sykes avoided a direct reply: perhaps Samuel would say what 'had taken place'. But Samuel would not violate Cabinet secrecy. 'Sir Mark,' the minutes of the conference state, 'thereupon repeated that with great difficulties the British Government had managed to keep the question of Palestine open.'[59] Not a word was said of the May 1916 Anglo-French (Sykes-Picot) Agreement or of current British intentions. Samuel apart, the most the Zionists may have gleaned in the nine months since the conclusion of the Agreement, most probably as hints of Sykes-Picot had slowly passed along the London grapevine, was that some sort of Anglo-French joint or compromise arrangement was on the stocks—possibly the 'condominium' they now all so greatly feared.[60] But that British policy

---

[59] 'Memorandum of a Conference held on 7 February 1917.' CZA, L6/90I.

[60] See for example: Sacher to Weizmann, 1 February 1917, WA; Sieff to Weizmann, 2 February 1917, WA; C. P. Scott to Lloyd George, 5 February 1917, HLRO, F/45/2/4 [also WA]; and a day after the conference with Sykes: Lord Rothschild to Weizmann, 8 February 1917, WA.

on Palestine had been turned round none of them so much as imagined. When Sykes advised them to 'put the Jewish views' to the French directly, none grasped his purpose. Surely it was the business of the British Government 'to deal with the French and dispose of their pretensions,' Samuel had objected. But Sykes, avoiding a reply, repeated his request and in the end it was agreed to. Sokolov, 'who could speak for the Russian Jews', undertook to see Picot. Sykes himself would make the introduction.[61]

After that things moved rapidly. Sokolov, Sykes, and Picot met at Sykes's London home the next day. The atmosphere was cordial. Picot wanted to learn about Russian and Polish Jewry and why, 'if the motto was "Poland for the Poles", did not the Jews become Poles, just as the French Jews became Frenchmen and the English Jews Englishmen?' Sokolov explained, and shifted the conversation to Zionism and Palestine. How did the Jews propose to organize themselves as a nation in Palestine, Picot inquired. Sokolov told him (in very general terms) what they had in mind, and went on to assert that all obstacles would fall away if 'a great civilized Power' took control of the country. Which Government did Sokolov have in mind? Britain, said Sokolov, chiefly because the Zionists laid great store by the British principle of allowing other nationalities free cultural development. As for France, the Jews had always recognized its great contributions to civilization and knew France itself to be the 'centre of the idea of liberty and equality in Europe and the world'. Still, the preference was strongly for British suzerainty. That, rejoined Picot, would be for the Powers to decide. From the conversation that followed Sokolov gathered that at some time in the past the 'idea of internationalization of Palestine' had indeed been 'entertained', and that both Picot and Sykes, but Sykes especially, disliked the idea. Picot, the good diplomat, duly stressed 'that there was no possibility of France renouncing completely its aspirations in Palestine in favour of Great Britain' and that the French people—95 per cent of them, he said—favoured outright annexation of the country. But his more personal response to what Sokolov had had to say to him was not entirely negative, and he promised to do what he could in Paris 'to make known the Zionist aims'.[62]

The introduction having been made, Sykes, still urging Sokolov

---

[61] 'Memorandum', ibid.
[62] 'Notes [almost certainly by Sokolov] of a meeting', 8 February 1917. WA.

on, retired into the background. Sokolov met Picot on his own at the French Embassy the following day to consider what should now be done in practice. Sokolov wanted French moral and political support for the movement. Picot undertook to communicate the 'facts about Zionism' to the 'proper quarters' and to do his best to win such sympathy for it as might be 'compatible' with French interests. He was opposed to any effort to address French public opinion directly, but he did point out one respect in which France 'was specially disposed to take an interest in the Zionist movement. He referred to the cause of the small nationalities which in France had been taken up with [the] greatest ardour and was inspiring every citizen.' Sokolov was delighted. It was a matter for great satisfaction that 'the Jews were considered in France as one of the smaller nationalities which were now struggling for liberty,' he told Picot. 'This [alone] would be a guarantee that their cause would be treated in the same spirit of justice and equity which France would show other nationalities.' Picot drew back somewhat. The point was 'not yet quite established.' Not all were agreed that the Jewish question amounted to the cause of 'a small nationality'. Put in such terms it was sure to meet considerable opposition, 'more perhaps from French Jews than from true [*sic*] Jews.' But in any event, he summed up, sympathy apart,

it would be of great use to their cause if the Jews would make their devotion to the Entente more evident and more publicly known. He did not doubt for a moment the sincerity of their attachment to the cause of the Entente, but nevertheless he could assure them that the more the Jews, as Jews, especially in the neutral countries, brought their support for the Entente into prominence, the better their chances of success.

Sokolov duly assured the Frenchman of Jewish loyalty to the *entente* in its component countries. As for the neutrals, the simplest way to win their sympathy for the *entente*, he said, was to show clearly 'that the cause of Jewish liberty was intimately bound up' with the *entente's* success. On that there was no disagreement.[63]

Meeting next day to review progress, Sykes, Weizmann, and Sokolov decided they had reason to be well satisfied. Sykes, still unsure of his ground so far as the French were concerned, anxious to avoid real tension between the two Powers, let alone an explosion of

[63] 'Memorandum of interview', 9 February 1917. SRO, GD40/17/42.

ill will,[64] and perhaps still without wholly firm prime ministerial instructions as yet (these were to be formulated and registered in binding terms just prior to his departure for the Continent and the Near East early in April, as we have seen), preached caution, however. He warned the Zionists against 'too emphatic' a public exposition of the idea of British suzerainty over Palestine, lest it 'intensify the French opposition'.[65] Some discussion on the future administration of Palestine, on the scope and powers of the Jewish chartered company that would undertake the settlement work, and on the proposed borders of the country followed and the Zionists promised to collate and submit their views on the matter of boundaries in detail. On the central tactical issue of representations in Paris, Sokolov, following Picot's advice, would await (unspecified) 'events'. Sykes would inform him when the proper time for action in France, Italy and, perhaps, the United States too, had arrived.[66]

In the course of the second half of February and the month of March, as British policy crystallized, bits and pieces of information on Anglo-French Near Eastern policy and commitments filtered through to the Zionists—always enough to keep them alert and uncertain, never enough for them to grasp (certainly not with confidence) precisely what British purposes were. But the basic tactic agreed upon was not called into question and on 1 April, at Sykes's explicit request, Sokolov duly travelled to Paris to tackle the French authorities directly. Sykes himself followed some days later, keeping discreetly but impatiently in the background as Sokolov went about their joint business.

It was conducted in triangular form and went through two main stages. Sokolov was first received by Picot and told that in his, Picot's, view there could be no question of British suzerainty over Palestine, let alone American; that it was with the French the Zionists would have to deal; that there could be no question of a

---

[64] 'The main job that I feel will be mine,' he wrote Sir Reginald Wingate, the High Commissioner in Egypt as soon as he learned of his appointment as Chief Political Officer to the EEF, 'is to keep the Franco-British situation clear.' 22 February 1917. WA.

[65] Sykes had in mind the activities of the British Palestine Committee, an independent pro-Zionist ginger group, composed of both Jews and non-Jews, on which some of Weizmann's friends were prominent. It tended (as Weizmann discovered) to be suspicious of the Foreign Office and less than fully convinced of Sykes's own benevolent intentions. Weizmann promised to try to rein them in.

[66] 'Notes of meeting', 10 February 1917. CZA, L6/90I.

Jewish chartered company; that there would have to be some support for Zionism from French Jewry if a French Government was to take it up; but that the Zionist interest would none the less be taken into account and that, for example, a form of local autonomy would be granted Jewish settlements immediately—he would see to that on his own authority as French Commissioner on the spot. How far Picot's word on the subject was likely to be the last, Sokolov had no way of determining. Edmond de Rothschild, whom he consulted, thought not. But in any case, Picot had undertaken to introduce him to his superiors;[67] and meanwhile, Sykes, having arrived in Paris on his way to the Levant, set about coaching Sokolov for the next stage of his talks. He counselled caution, as before, and putting the emphasis on the principles and needs of the Zionists, rather than on the final disposition of the territory, a matter to be left to the Powers. And simultaneously, closing the triangle, he set about impressing upon Picot, directly, 'the importance of meeting Jewish demands' and the advantage of preparing the 'French mind for the idea of British suzerainty in Palestine by international consent'. 'I pointed out to him,' he reported to London, 'that our preponderant military effort, rights of trans-Palestine railway construction, rights of annexation at Haifa [all conceded under the May 1916 agreement], coupled with [the] general bias of [the] Zionists in favour of British suzerainty, tended to make such a solution the only stable one.' To none of this, the Foreign Office was agreeably surprised to note, was Picot overtly antagonistic.[68]

Sokolov, meanwhile, was asked to submit a written statement of Zionist desiderata: what facilities for colonization they desired, what the terms of the chartered company they wished established would be, what communal autonomy and language rights they envisaged; and he was given to understand that it was likely that the French Government would admit the *justice* of these demands. Sokolov thought that such an admission by France of the 'principle of recognition of Jewish nationality in Palestine' would be a firm step in the right direction. Sykes agreed. With a British occupation of Palestine in the offing, the concessions in Palestine already granted Britain under the Anglo-French Agreement, and now, if it could be obtained, French recognition of Jewish national aspirations, 'we

[67] Sokolov to Weizmann, 4 April 1917. WA.
[68] Sykes to Graham, 5 April 1917. Minute by Oliphant, 8 April 1917. PRO, FO 371/3045.

should be able,' he wrote the Cabinet Secretary for Lloyd George's benefit, 'to go into a Peace Conference fairly well equipped.'[69] On 9 April Sokolov was called to the Quai d'Orsay, seen by the Secretary-General flanked by the French Ambassador in London and Picot, and told that the Zionists' aspirations were indeed recognized as legitimate. No official statement was promised; and Sokolov did not press for one. The question of suzerainty over Palestine was not discussed. At the same time, it was made clear to Sokolov that he and his friends, for their part, were expected to do what they could to throw Jewish influence in Russia into the scale against the forces working for Russia's withdrawal from the war and, in Italy, to encourage the further consolidation of the *entente*. The three French diplomats would be glad too if Sokolov now travelled to Italy to learn for himself, and to inform them, what was thought there of Zionist aspirations. For the rest they would see. It was evident to him they had not yet entirely made up their minds about Zionism, but Sokolov was well satisfied: 'We are now accredited here in the same way as in England,' and again, 'It was more than the greatest of optimists could have looked forward to,' he wrote Weizmann. Sykes was jubilant.[70] As he had already concluded and had written to Balfour the day before, 'As regards Zionism . . . the French are beginning to realise they are up against a big thing, and that they cannot close their eyes to it.'[71] Lord Bertie, the British Ambassador in Paris, was less optimistic, however. He warned the Foreign Office, as he had done once before, that the prospect of inducing the French to give up what their 'uninformed general Public' took to be their 'special prescriptive rights' to Palestine remained exceedingly remote.

The influence of France [in Syria and Palestine] is that of the Roman Catholic Church exercised through French Priests, and schools conducted by them; and the Government of France is anti-clerical and for the most part free-thinking. Monsieur Ribot [the Prime Minister] is of the French Protestant Faith which in the eyes of the French Catholics as a body is abhorred next unto the Jewish Faith. Even if M. Ribot were convinced of the justice of our pretensions in regard to Palestine, would he be willing to face the certain combined opposition of the French Chauvinists, the French

---

[69] Sykes to Graham, 5 April 1917. Ibid. Sykes to Hankey, 7 April 1917. PRO, CAB 21/96.
[70] Sykes to Graham, 9 April 1917. PRO, FO 371/3045; Sokolov to Weizmann, 18, 19, and 26 April 1917. WA; Sykes to Balfour, 9 April 1917. Hull, SP 12/7.
[71] Sykes to Balfour, 8 April 1917. Ibid.

uninformed general Public and the Roman Catholic Priests and their Flocks?'[72]

Sir Ronald Graham, to whom he had written, agreed. He thought it 'rather remarkable' that even the internationalization of Palestine had been agreed to by the French. But meanwhile, the British Government was 'now more or less committed to *encourage* Zionism' and Sykes received his instructions direct from the Prime Minister and 'I am not sure what they were or how far he was to go.'[73] Seeing Lloyd George in Paris several days later, Bertie repeated his argument, adding that 'the Jews are not a combative race and that if we support the Zionist movement and establish Jewish Colonies there they will not be able to hold their own against the Arabs without British or French support, and what may be the effect on the feelings of the Arabs towards England if such support be given?' But the Prime Minister was unimpressed. His view 'seems to be,' Bertie noted, 'that we shall be in Palestine by conquest and shall remain and that the French will have to accept our Protectorate; and— which is quite true—that we are the only people fit to rule a mixed population of Mahommedans, Jews, Roman Catholics and all religions, and that we ought to substitute ourselves for the position hitherto occupied by the Turks and keep the peace between the several religions and political factions.'[74]

The fact was that Sykes, 'sanguine of temperament' though he was[75] and therefore always somewhat suspect in the eyes of the professionals, had struck a chord that Bertie and Graham had failed to note. On the one hand, minds had not yet been made up at the Quai d'Orsay about Zionism; on the other hand, the longstanding worry about American Jewish public opinion was very much alive and had been newly stimulated by a rumour that Germany itself might take up the Zionist cause. The particular fear at this point was that a combination of anti-British pressure by the Irish within the Democratic Party in the United States and some such new factor as German support for a Jewish cause likely to pull Jewish opinion and 'Jewish finance' wholly in the German direction, might seriously affect American presidential policy—virtually, but still not finally set on massive participation by the United States in the war on the

[72] Bertie to Graham, 12 April 1917. PRO, FO 371/3052.
[73] Graham to Bertie, 16 April 1917. Ibid. Emphasis added.
[74] Bertie to Hardinge, 22 April 1917. Ibid.
[75] See above, pp. 222–4.

side of the Allies. Picot, arriving from London and primed with information about the Jews, the Zionists, and Palestine was therefore listened to with attention,[76] and Sokolov was received with, as he himself put it, 'goodwill'.[77] But, he was told, first the Italians had to be sounded and, unexpectedly, the Vatican as well.

Sykes preceded Sokolov to Rome and paved the way. He told neither the curia officials he interviewed (among them Mgr. Pacelli, the future Pope Pius XII) nor the reigning Pope Benedict XV, of whom he had an audience, anything of the Anglo-French Agreement. He contrived, not least on the strength of his own Roman Catholic faith, to leave the impression that it might be no bad thing, from the Vatican's point of view, if the British, rather than the French, took control of the Holy Places. His glowing account of the nature of the Zionist movement was heard with diplomatic interest. His recommendation that Sokolov be seen was accepted.[78] Before moving on to Cairo he left written advice to Sokolov to visit Pacelli and, if he saw fit, to ask for an audience with the Pope as well. This was a considerable expansion of the visit, both in scope and time. Sokolov's main business—in Paris, to which he was due to return— had still to be rounded off. As April drew to an end and a great conference of Russian Zionists to be held in Petrograd was announced for the beginning of June (NS), it was thought intolerable in Weizmann's circle that the man best fitted to bring their message before Russian Zionism should have allowed himself to be diverted to Rome on less than essential, if not dubious business. Weizmann was fearful lest he lose the control he sought to exercise over Sokolov and that Sokolov compromise his (Weizmann's) insistence on an exclusively British orientation by

[76] Bapst (Copenhagen) to Paris, 10 March 1917; Jules Cambon to Ribot, 11 March 1917. AE, Guerre 1914–18, Sionisme II, vol. 1198. That concern to sweeten Jewish public opinion in the United States was the decisive factor in moving French diplomacy to take a kinder view of Zionism despite its known pro-British tendency is confirmed with precision by a passage in a despatch by Picot, writing from Cairo seven months later: 'The declarations [*sic*] made by Mr Balfour to Lord Rothschild on the subject of Zionism have aroused much emotion in Muslim and Christian circles and a feeling of deep bitterness against England. Without denying that *it was greatly advantageous to us last April to make concessions which gained the active sympathy of the Jews of America*, it seemed it would be best [now] not to reveal the action we had taken.' Picot to Pichon, 29 November 1917. SHAT, 7N2145. Emphasis added.

[77] Sokolov to Brandeis incorporated in Sykes to Graham, 9 April 1917. PRO, FO 371/3045.

[78] Sykes to Graham, 15 April 1917; and Sykes to Sokolov, 14 April 1917. Hull, SP 12/7.

some verbal concession to the French. But Sokolov had little choice but to follow the path indicated by the French and now carved out afresh for him by Sykes. Besides, he was less sure than was Weizmann that the British would end by having everything their own way. He greatly favoured a British orientation. He agreed with Weizmann that it seemed to offer the 'shortest path to our beloved target.' But there were other possibilities. Other Powers would have a say in these matters and might help or hinder the Zionists according to their interests or out of ignorance or out of pique because none had bothered to apply to them. Even if all went well, he reminded his colleague, good relations with others than the British would be necessary. 'One ought not to be a one-sided optimist.'[79]

It was the middle of May before he was clear of Rome, his purposes there achieved. Sonnino, the Foreign Minister, had preferred not to receive him, but did tell the British Ambassador, Rodd, that he 'was inclined to view [the Zionists] with sympathy [, that] . . . he had no objection at all to the proposal to found Jewish colonies in Palestine,' and that he thought such colonies might even be counted advantageous, having regard to the difficulties the Jews in eastern Europe constituted for the Governments in question. Sonnino agreed, however, to Sokolov being received by the Secretary-General of the Foreign Ministry (on 8 May) and being informed in friendly fashion that while Italy would take no 'initiative' in the matter, it would surely provide whatever moral and diplomatic support was feasible. And four days later the Prime Minister, Boselli, heard Sokolov's exposé of Zionist purposes and plans and repeated the Italian formula: no initiative, but moral support and diplomatic assistance for the Zionists so far as possible. That he had already been received amicably by the Pope stood him in good stead in what the Italians frankly regarded as the 'delicate' matter of the Holy Land.[80]

Like Herzl before him,[81] Sokolov was received cordially enough at the Vatican. In his reception at the hands of Pacelli, Cardinal Gasparri (the Secretary of State), and Pope Benedict XV himself in

[79] Sokolov to Weizmann, 27 April 1917. WA; and Sokolov to Weizmann, 12 May 1917. CZA, A18/26.

[80] Rodd to Balfour, 10 May 1917. HLRO, LlGP F/56/1/37; and 'Shetei sihot' (a verbatim account of Sokolov's conversations with Boselli and Di Martino), in S. Rawidovicz (ed.), *Sefer Sokolov* (Jerusalem, 1943), pp. 271–81.

[81] In 1904. See *Formative Years*, pp. 336–9.

turn there was barely a trace of the hostility which had informed the Roman Church in its approach to Jewry—resolute and organized Jewry above all—from its beginnings. And there was nothing at all of the revised and reinvigorated social and political anti-Semitism that had become an established part of the Church's ideological baggage in its fight against the forces of liberalism and modernism crowding at its gates. But there was a seriousness of tone and a precision of questions and statements which served as ample evidence of the special and peculiar nature of such a series of meetings between what neither side could help seeing as ancient, bitter enemies. What of the Holy Places? Sokolov was asked by Pacelli. The Zionists wanted no part of them, was the answer; it was the land beyond—for settlement and cultivation—that they were interested in. Ah yes, but there was a problem there and a division of opinion, Pacelli told him. Some churchmen thought in terms of discrete *places*; others in terms of the entire country. What was Sokolov's response to that? For we shall 'have to know in advance what it is you claim if there is to be no disagreement and competition in the future.'[82] Two days later, Gasparri, the Secretary of State, took up the same theme, while allowing himself some general comment on the relations between Church and Jewry as well. So far as the Jews were concerned, the Roman Church, he told Sokolov, had shaken free of its old medieval tendencies. It sought only to defend itself. When attacked by Jews there was of course resentment. Where Jewry as such concerned itself only with its own affairs it could, however, be sure of being treated with respect. For he, Sokolov, must know, that the Church opposed anti-Semitism, clerical no less than secular, and if there were complaints against clerics on that score they would assuredly be dealt with. Sokolov replied that he was pleased to hear that that was the case. The two men moved on. The condition of Jewry in general and in eastern Europe in particular was discussed; then the likely fate of Palestine at the hands of the Powers; then Zionism. The Church would welcome a new Kingdom of Israel, the Cardinal said. But the Zionists, Sokolov retorted, had no intention of founding one. 'You have nothing to fear,' was the reply. 'It was only a phrase. Call it what you will. You can be sure that we shall put no obstacles in your path. On the contrary. . . . I wish you every success.'[83]

---

[82] Conversation with Pacelli. Sokolov to Weizmann, 29 April 1917. WA.
[83] Sokolov to Weizmann, 1 May 1917. WA.

Sokolov's audience of Pope Benedict XV touched on the same topics: the Jews, their history, the scope and purposes of Zionism, the attitude of the Powers, and, most closely and particularly, the Holy Places. The small dimensions of the contemporary *yishuv* surprised the Pontiff, but, he told Sokolov, he regarded the enterprise sympathetically. Of the British interest in Palestine and Zionism he approved. Sokolov's assurances that the Zionists had no intention of encroaching on Christian Holy Places, which would in any case be under international guarantee, were accepted with satisfaction. 'What then can I do for you?' he asked. The Zionists wanted his moral support, was Sokolov's answer. 'Yes, yes,' the Pope replied by way of agreement. 'I believe we shall be good neighbours.'[84] At no stage were specific points of doctrine, Catholic or Jewish, touched upon; no opposition to a Jewish return to Erez-Israel *in principle* was mentioned (as had been the case when Herzl was received thirteen years earlier). Sokolov had reason to be content.

Still his essential business was in Paris. In France the opposition to undivided British control over Palestine—the 'Syrian party', as Sykes called it, the party that regarded Picot as a fool and a traitor because he had not insisted the year before on French control of the whole of the Mediterranean littoral down to El Arish—was certainly alive. Britain's professional diplomats in London as well as in Paris were as convinced as ever that the idea of prising Palestine out of French hands was 'utopian' and 'unrealisable' and that the French would 'never abandon their sentimental claims' to the country. It was all very well, they reflected with a kind of bitter embarrassment, to have the support of the Zionists and to reap the relevant benefits in America and elsewhere. It remained that the Zionist movement was 'based' (so it was now generally assumed at the Foreign Office) on 'a British Palestine' and therefore 'on a condition which [Britain] could not enforce'—and that for reasons, moreover, of which the Zionists could be told nothing. 'Are we wise [?],' the Permanent Under-Secretary wondered. 'Failure, when it comes, will be laid at the door of the F.O., and not without reason.'[85] That the Prime Minister insisted on Palestine being obtained for Great Britain and

[84] 'Memoriale: Audienza particolare.' 4 May 1917. CZA, L6/90II; and Sokolov to Weizmann, 7 May 1917. PRO, FO 371/3053.

[85] Minutes by Graham, 17 April 1917, on Sykes's report from Rome, no. 8, 15 April 1917; and by Hardinge and Graham, 21 April 1917, on Sykes's report no. 2, 15 April 1917. PRO, FO 371/3052.

that it was an important part of Sykes's mission to obtain it was known. How he proposed doing so and what the Zionists' role in his scheme was intended to be was still not fully understood, however. And Sykes himself, on arrival in Egypt towards the end of April, became of a sudden less sanguine about the prospects—principally because, taking stock of the situation in the field and the effective defence of the country (at Gaza in particular) put up by the Turks, he was less than confident that an advance into Palestine and Syria would succeed. If the expeditionary force was not reinforced, he warned London, and no more than 'local' successes were gained, then it would be 'necessary to drop all Zionist projects and all schemes involving negotiations with settled rural and urban Arab elements in Syria.' Any other policy would expose adherents to the British cause 'to greater rigours of oppression than heretofore' and make Britain 'morally responsible for [the] increase of their misery'. The Zionists in London and the United States should be warned of this danger and the 'Jabotinsky scheme' for a Jewish Legion should not be pursued. Otherwise, the wrath of the Turks would fall upon the Jews and the Arabs as it had fallen on the Armenians. The allies had already gone far to encourage Zionism in London and Paris and foster Arab and Syrian hopes in Cairo. They would have to endure the odium of having caused such misfortune 'to befall these people'. And 'the situation can only be made worse by a continuance of political action not based upon equivalent military action.'[86] In private he expressed himself in sharper language. He had hoped for great things. He now regretted coming. What he feared, if more energy and force was not put into the campaign, was 'a second Gallipoli'.[87]

Meanwhile, in London, the Zionists had learned, at long last and by a necessarily circuitous route, what some had come more or less to suspect: that the question of the final disposition of Palestine was anything but open. In mid-April Weizmann heard from Scott, who had it from a French journalist, of the fact that an Anglo-French Agreement had been concluded and, in outline, of its terms. He was panic-stricken. Weizmann had built everything on the association of Zionist purposes with Great Britain and British purposes with

[86] Sykes to Graham, 24 April 1917. WA. The wording of Sykes's telegram, as received and deciphered in London (PRO, FO 371/3052), is slightly different, but the sense is the same.

[87] Thus to Aaronsohn. Yoram Efrati (ed.), *Yoman Aharon Aaronsohn* (Tel-Aviv, 1970), pp. 251–3.

Zionism and had seen it as his function to persuade both parties of the uses of such a special relationship. On the Zionist side he had not been as successful as he had hoped. He had had little trouble on this score among colleagues either in England itself or in the United States. But he had not succeeded in Russia. Tchlenov, the effective leader of Russian Zionism at this point, continued to cleave to the policy of neutrality laid down by the EAC at the beginning of the war and with him did most of his associates.

For all that it was crucial to the whole pro-Zionist argument as it had now been adopted in Downing Street that not only American Jewish opinion but Russian Jewry and the Russian Zionists in particular were likely to be moved sentimentally and politically by a British decision in favour of the movement, the true state of opinion in Russian Zionism was not understood in official London and the question itself never thoroughly gone in to. Doubts had been voiced, by the Ambassador in Petrograd, for one, as we have seen: and Sykes had been infuriated by the implied questioning of Weizmann's, Sokolov's, and Jabotinsky's credentials as spokesmen for Russian Jewry.[88] It was then accepted, it seems, that in any case there was no way of taking really useful and valid soundings of qualified opinion in Russia given the turmoil obtaining there. It remains that Weizmann had no warrant for continually asserting (as in a message to Brandeis) that 'Russian Zionists fully approve' a Jewish Palestine under [a] British Protectorate as the 'only satisfactory solution',[89] or (as he told Robert Cecil) that 'Jews all over the world trust Great Britain and look to this country as a liberator of Palestine'.[90] Weizmann certainly knew the facts of the matter, but had to stick to his guns if his scheme was to advance; and in British ears at any rate his position was far from being an implausible one to argue. It had been heard in Whitehall in one form or another ever since the war had started. It was certainly what those most concerned with the subject wanted to believe. If there was a shadow of doubt in some minds, none were inclined to insist. 'I was much impressed, as indeed I have been on previous occasions, by the enthusiasm and idealism of M. Weizmann,' Lord Robert noted in his own memorandum of the conversation with Weizmann on 25 April; 'but of course I am not in a position to

---

[88] See above, p. 220.
[89] Weizmann to Brandeis, 23 April 1917. *Weizmann Letters*, vii, no. 351, p. 371.
[90] 'Note of interview', 25 April 1917. Ibid., no. 356, p. 375.

express any opinion as to how far he represents Jewish feeling in this matter.'[91] In sum, the question just where Russian Jewry, the Zionists among them, stood on the issues of greatest concern to the Allies was never settled to anyone's full satisfaction, but nor did it ever entirely evaporate. It may be that the pressure of events and other diplomatic business was too great for the matter to be chased to a conclusion. It may be that it was felt intuitively that it was not of cardinal importance anyway. It is assuredly the case that the tendency to see Weizmann as the most effective general agent and contact man available for a large part of Jewry, certainly for the Zionists, was growing steadily. For that reason, if for no other, it made sense to trust and support him.

But what if there was not going to be a 'British Protectorate' after all? What if the division of the country had long been settled by formal agreement and the British part was definitely to be minimal? It was to argue the case for a *British* Palestine once more that Weizmann had seen Cecil at the end of April—after applying first to Samuel (who was too discreet to do more than confirm that there had been an agreement and that 'from the British point of view' it was a satisfactory one) and then to Sir Ronald Graham (who could tell him no more than had Samuel and passed him on to Cecil,[92] Acting Foreign Secretary in Balfour's absence). He was still told nothing of the Anglo-French Agreement, for all that he himself referred to it in some detail. Nor did he elicit a response either to his argument in favour of British military control of Palestine or to his political argument founded on where Jewish sympathies were said to lie. Nor did Cecil so much as hint that it was now firm policy to evade the relevant terms of the Agreement and reassure Weizmann that he was preaching to the thoroughly converted.

In the event, Weizmann, who had come to Cecil, it was noted, in a 'fine rage',[93] was neither comforted nor reduced to despair. Always resilient, he informed both Scott and Brandeis that it was his impression that the 'arrangements' between the British and the French were 'vague', perhaps only 'provisional', at any rate not 'binding'. In practice, he was sure that what should be done, and all that could be done, was to press harder than ever, at as high a level as possible and with American help, 'to clear this matter up' and to

[91]   PRO, FO 371/3053.
[92]   Weizmann to Scott, 26 April 1917. *Weizmann Letters*, vii, no. 357, pp. 379–80.
[93]   Ormsby-Gore to Sykes, 8 May 1917. Hull, SP, DDSY (2) 11/40.

see that Britain was set on the only course that, so far as he was concerned, made sense for either party. For his part, he had no intention of doing otherwise or working towards any other goal. 'I shall have no standing at all,' he told Cecil, 'if I depart from a line of action which is vital to the Jewish interests[:] it would compromise my organisation and would ruin me.'[94]

In these circumstances his dread lest Sokolov unwittingly sell the pass by allowing the French or anyone else to think that his negotiations in Paris implied that the Zionists might favour—or acquiesce in—a 'French alternative' after all[95] is readily understandable. But in fact, he had nothing to fear, as an increasingly upset and offended Sokolov repeatedly informed him. When Weizmann learned that a full conference of Russian Zionists was to be held in Petrograd at the beginning of June—only the second[96] such conference to be held openly on Russian territory since the movement's foundation twenty years earlier—he pressed Sokolov to leave immediately for Russia. It was now urgent to try to bring Russian Zionism, now plainly about to be reconstituted in the newly free and democratic Russian state, to drop neutrality and declare for the British. The Foreign Office too thought it a good idea and even briefly considered supplying Sokolov with an authorized statement of British sympathy for Jewish national aspirations. And finally, in Weizmann's view, departure for Russia would put an end to Sokolov's dangerous journey among England's Latin allies. 'Cancel your appointments and leave straight for [London],'[97] he telegraphed Sokolov peremptorily (through British diplomatic channels), and Sokolov reluctantly but obediently cut short his stay in Rome and forwent a promised audience of the King of Italy. But he still had to return to Paris to confront the French with the need to take a clear stand of their own on Palestine, the Jews, and Zionism itself.

Back at the Quai d'Orsay, Sokolov reported that he had duly sounded the Italians and had found them favourably disposed and that he had seen the officials of the curia and the Pope himself and

[94] Weizmann to Scott, 26 April 1917; and Weizmann to Brandeis, 27 April 1917. Ibid., no. 357, pp. 378–82, and no. 362, p. 386.

[95] Weizmann to Sokolov, 27 April 1917. Ibid., no. 360, p. 384.

[96] A conference of Russian Zionists was held publicly in Minsk in 1902 with special police authorization. On the circumstances, see *Formative Years*, pp. 178 ff.

[97] Weizmann to Sokolov, 14 May 1917. *Weizmann Letters*, vii, no. 386 and n. 2, pp. 408–9.

been told that no conflict between the interests of the Church in Palestine and the purposes of the Zionists obtained either. Two possible obstacles to a stronger and more explicit statement of position by the French Government had thus been removed. Moreover, there was now a positive reason for support to be expressed: he was being asked to proceed to Petrograd to attend the conference of Russian Zionists to speak for the Allied cause and argue the Jewish interest in it—and so, in practice, if not in so many words, argue for Russia's continued participation in the war. But to do so effectively he must arrive with authority to assert the sympathy of the Allies for the Jewish national cause itself. He therefore asked to be received by the Prime Minister and to be provided with an official, written 'communication' in which the sympathy of the French Government for Jewish national aspirations in Palestine would be clearly stated.

The French were no less concerned than the British at the ever more serious prospect that Russia might leave the war. Like the British, they had been watching Jewish public opinion in Russia, if only sporadically and imperfectly,[98] and while unsure just what weight to ascribe to the Jews of Russia, the feeling that in some ill-defined way they were to be reckoned with had taken hold as never before. None the less, they were cautious. Picot, now in Cairo, was asked to provide a review of the whole question.[99] His response was that as the British had already given their support for the 'constitution of a sort of Jewish nationality under the suzerainty of a Great Power', the question was no longer an open one. Indeed, so far as France was concerned, it was no longer one of determining whether such a project was desirable, but whether it would serve current French purposes 'to quarrel openly [*rompre en visière*] with all the Jewish elements, proclaiming ourselves opponents of their claims and thus risking having unshakable enemies one day at the gates of Syria.'[100] Evidently, Picot by this time seems to have been convinced that the British would end by seizing Palestine and

---

[98] For what seems a typical example of the kind of information fed into the machine, see a French intelligence report on an unidentified 'meeting of the Jewish proletariat' in April 1917 at which a resolution demanding an end to the war was voted. No place or precise date was given, but the item was incorporated in the regular fortnightly bulletin of information obtained from secret sources issued by the Deuxième Bureau (No. 2, 5 May 1917). SHAT, 7N678.

[99] Jules Cambon to Picot, 30 April 1917. AE, Guerre 1914–1918, Sionisme II, vol. 1198, fo. 185.

[100] Picot to Ribot, 5 May 1917. Ibid., Sionisme III, vol. 1199, fo. 2.

keeping it regardless of their undertaking to the French, and the logic of his position—if such it was—inclined him to making the best of the situation. It is likely that the Prime Minister's own approach was much the same. Ribot had long been a member of the colonial lobby in French politics and had had a special interest in the Levant. But he had greater things to worry about with the war going very badly for his country and with his British counterpart telling him at the St Jean de Maurienne conference in April that Britain proposed to take Palestine for itself.[101] Jean Gout, the official mostly closely concerned with the affairs of the Levant at the Quai d'Orsay itself and reckoned to know a great deal about the Jews, took a more moderate line. Asked for his views, he restricted his comments to an operative question, namely how best to approach the matter of Jewish national aspirations and how to deal with those who were most prominent in articulating them. His view, as we have seen, was that, indeed, even intelligent and educated Jews retained something of the 'dreams of the old ghettos', and that such people did have some influence on 'ignorant governments'. But he by no means ascribed to them the same quality and power implied by Picot. He thought something should be conceded them in Palestine: not an 'independent nationality', but the 'possibility' of some sort of corporate existence 'within the framework of the existing nationalities.'[102]

In the circumstances, then, given that the Zionists evidently had the support of the British and that their representative had been well received in Italy, it was beginning to be awkward for the French to refuse some friendly gesture in their direction. It might even be 'useful to our cause in Palestine', the Director of Political Affairs at the Quai d'Orsay observed somewhat vaguely in putting forward his proposal that Sokolov be received by Ribot after all and that the written statement asked for be approved and issued. But the decisive and most explicit argument hinged on the influence Sokolov might be expected to bring to bear on 'his coreligionists' in Russia.[103] Sokolov was then received by Ribot and, on prime ministerial authority, a written statement was provided in the form of an official letter to Sokolov over Jules Cambon's signature. It began in the

---

[101] War Cabinet 126, 25 April 1917. PRO, CAB 23/2.
[102] Gout to de Margerie, 7 May 1917. See above, p. 196.
[103] Memorandum by de Margerie, 22 May 1917. AE, Guerre 1914 1918, Sionisme III, vol. 1199, fos. 33–4.

customary diplomatic way with a brief recapitulation of the nature, aims, and justice of Zionism as Sokolov himself had outlined them. It went on to state that

The French Government, which entered the present war to defend a people that had been unjustly attacked and which pursues the struggle to ensure the triumph of right over might, cannot but feel sympathy for your cause, the triumph of which is bound up with that of the Allies.[104]

In the event, the decision to issue it (two days before the conference opened) came too late for Sokolov to leave for Petrograd. But the central purpose of his journey to France and Italy had been attained.

iv

What were the aspirations and what was the political thinking of the Russian Zionists *in Russia* now that Russian Jewry had been swiftly and dramatically released from the iron frame of law and administration in which they had been bound for a century and a half? The conference, called for 6 June 1917 (24 May OS), was in one cardinal respect an immense success. Within a little more than two months of the decision to convene it, the dwindling pre-war Zionist movement —no more than 26,000 paid-up members in 1913 in the largest (six million strong) Jewish community in the world—had sprung to organized life: 550 delegates elected by some 140,000 voters in close to 700 towns and villages,[105] along with three times as many guests, gathered in Petrograd in the wake of a whole series of great meetings of resuscitation held all over the country, even (by express permission of the military authorities) in the armed forces. It was the greatest demonstration of Jewish national sentiment ever known in Russia. But in the circumstances of war and revolution it was inevitable that the enthusiasm and the spirit of renewal that infused it owed more to the prospect of a free and democratic Russia and the conviction that Russian Jewry, along with the other subject nations of the old Empire, could now reorder its affairs within it than to the hope that specifically Zionist purposes in Erez-Israel were about to be realized. It was the policy laid down at the Russian Zionists'

---

[104] Jules Cambon to Sokolov, 4 June 1917. CZA, A18/24. A summary of the entire episode was prepared by Gout and despatched to the Embassies concerned, 30 August 1917. AE, Guerre 1914–1918; Sionisme III, vol. 1199. fo. 136.

[105] Some two-fifths of Russo-Polish Jewry being in areas occupied by German forces, the effective strength of the community in 1917 was now greatly reduced.

Helsingfors conference held in the wake of the first revolution that was now chiefly recalled and reasserted.

The principal theme of the conference was a call for equal national rights for the Jews in Russia itself in conjunction with loyal Jewish participation in the movement for a democratic, secular, multinational Russian state.[106] It would be necessary, it was argued, to join with other Jewish groups to convene a general (i.e. not exclusively Zionist) conference at which the precise foundations on which the organization and representation of Russian Jewry would be considered and laid. And while in principle—and indeed ultimately—all action in the Diaspora could be no more than, as Tchlenov put it, a 'substitute' for the full national life to which Jews aspired in their own ancestral home, they must now seize the present opportunity of becoming masters of their own fate in the lands in which they resided and where, in their great majority, they were likely to remain. This was Tchlenov's view and this was his own finest hour as the leader of Russian Zionism: a militant from its earliest days, the only Russian member of the EAC to have remained in Russia during the war and the revolution, popular, respected, immensely prudent. The Zionists, he said in his opening address, were realists. They were concerned with the here and now of Jewry no less than with an ideal future for it. They wanted a national centre in Erez-Israel as an integral part of the *whole*, complex Jewish organism. They wished to neglect no part of it that was vital to the strength and vitality of the Jewish people in its entirety. Other delegates pursued these themes and elaborated upon them. None took issue with Tchlenov directly. Ussishkin did sound a somewhat different note when he argued that the central question to be put before the people was whether they did—or did not—wish to return to their own homeland. It was to the Return of the Jews and to their work there, in Erez-Israel, that all attention should be concentrated and, when the time came, it was the duty of all Russian Jewry, non-Zionists no less than Zionists, to put the Jewish people's demand for the right to return before the Powers. No one argued with Ussishkin and something of his point of view was reflected in the final resolutions, notably a clause calling explicitly for a referendum throughout Jewry on the matter of Erez-Israel. But two other notable figures, Yizhak Gruenbaum, speaking very much in the

---

[106] On the Helsingfors conference of December 1906, see *Formative Years*, pp. 467–74.

spirit and terms he had adopted at Helsingfors, and Julius Brutzkus,[107] followed on after Tchlenov. They called for the recognition of Russian Jewry as a national entity possessed of rights of internal self-government in all areas of national life and made a series of very specific institutional proposals for the realization and enjoyment of those rights.[108]

On the question that Weizmann had been feverishly pressing the conference to take a stand,[109] it was the supremely cautious Tchlenov, once again, who set the tone. He did not refer to Weizmann, Sokolov, and their circle in London directly. He said nothing at all about the idea of 'a Jewish Palestine under [an] English Protectorate' to which, so they had assured him, the 'authorities [were] very favourable',[110] an assurance which Weizmann expanded a few days later into the unambiguous statement that 'England is ready to take Palestine under her protection to enable the Jews there to establish themselves and live independently.'[111] Tchlenov confined himself to expressing the sympathy and gratitude of the Jews to the English on the general grounds that 'no other Christian people has ever shown so much feeling and understanding for the suffering of the Jewish people', and that it was the British Government which, in 1903, 'had offered to the homeless people an autonomous home in one of the colonies.'[112] He then went on to recall that the Jews had other debts, that there were Jews in all armies, that among those debts was a great historic one to Turkey, and that Jews were now serving with distinction in the Ottoman army among many others.[113] The implication, that sides should not be taken in the present conflict and that the policy of neutrality laid down by the central institutions

[107] On Gruenbaum and Brutzkus, see *Formative Years* pp. 471 ff. and 259–60.

[108] The proceedings of the conference are summarized and the resolutions given in Izḥak Ma'or, *Ha-Tenu'a ha-ẓionit be-rusiya* (Jerusalem, 1973), pp. 434–51. For a useful and detailed account by Y. Gruenbaum himself, see his *Ha-Tenu'a ha-ẓionit be-hitpathuta*, iv (Jerusalem, 1954), pp. 97–109.

[109] James de Rothschild, Weizmann, and Cowen to Tchlenov, 27 April; Weizmann to Tchlenov, 29 April; Weizmann to Rosov, 16 May; and Weizmann to Tchlenov and Rosov, 4 June 1917. *Weizmann Letters*, vii, nos. 359, 364, 390, and 417, pp. 383–4, 387–9, 412, and 429–30.

[110] Rothschild *et al.* to Tchlenov, 27 April 1917. Ibid.

[111] Weizmann to Tchlenov, 29 April. Ibid.

[112] A reference to the offer of a large tract of land for a self-governing Jewish settlement in present-day Kenya. See *Formative Years*, pp. 154 ff.

[113] Zionist Liaison Office, Copenhagen, Bulletin no. 43. 24 July 1917. ML, GP/55/43.

of the Zionist Organization at the onset of the war still had to be adhered to, was clear to all who heard him. Tchlenov made no more than a passing, almost apologetic reference to the Turkish expulsion of large numbers of settlers and none at all to the massive ill-treatment of those members of the *yishuv* who had chosen and managed to stay put. Ussishkin, for his part, avoided saying anything at all about the state of the *yishuv* in wartime on the somewhat disingenuous grounds that there was not enough hard information to form an opinion. The upshot was that with neither Weizmann, nor Sokolov, nor Jabotinsky (now in the British army), nor Boris Goldberg (a Russian member of the GAC, in England for most of the war, who had been provisionally slated to substitute for Sokolov) present, and with none of the leaders of Russian Zionism attending the conference differing from Tchlenov on essentials there were no spokesmen of the first rank to voice the counter-argument. Certainly, there was no one in Petrograd who had any idea of the intricate moves that had by now brought Zionism and British imperial policy within an ace of intersection.[114] Only Grossman, who had returned to Russia on the outbreak of the revolution, and a handful of other 'activists' were there to speak in favour of a Jewish Legion, namely of armed Jewish participation in the conquest of Erez-Israel, to what proved to be a largely hostile audience. He demanded that the dead of Gallipoli be honoured and that the conference send a formal message of appreciation to Jabotinsky, and he argued that this was not a time to speak of the ways and means of settling Erez-Israel, but rather of ways and means of obtaining it. But Grossman's intervention was an episode. It led only to a brief, if fierce debate. It was reflected nowhere in the conference's formal resolutions.

Was it then the case, as a member of the Rothschild family in London had told Sir Ronald Graham, that the effect of the emancipation of the Jews in Russia had been to ring down the curtain on Zionism?[115] It was not implausible. It was the same idea that Lucien Wolf had expressed (in stronger language) when he told another Rothschild that 'the Revolution had knocked the bottom out of the Zionist argument that their plan is the only solution.' The

---

[114] Sokolov did sum up the moves and achievements of the past few months in a triumphant letter to Rosov. But dated 6 June 1917, it could not have reached Petrograd until after the conference had dispersed.

[115] Shemu'el Tolkowsky, *Yoman zioni medini*, edited by Devorah Barzilay-Yegar (Jerusalem, 1981), entry for 17 May 1917, p. 80.

further consequence, Wolf thought, was that the Allied Governments had now been 'relieved . . . of any absolute necessity to deal
with the Zionist question at all.'[116] Weizmann knew nothing of this
latter conversation, but he was worried when Graham turned to him
for enlightenment, and with good reason. In one form or another the
old questions were being asked once again. Where did Jewish
sympathies lie? What were the true concerns of the Jews? How
influential were the Zionists within Russia itself and where did *their*
sympathies really lie? The information reaching London from the
Foreign Office's own sources was at least partly at variance with the
picture Weizmann had painted so effectively and consistently since
the war began. 'Everyone unites in affirming that [the] Jews are
working against England and are strongly in favour of Germany,'
the British Consul in Odessa reported. 'England is represented as
Russia's worst enemy. Jewish agitators, all young, pervade every
meeting in the towns and villages.'[117] 'Suppose the British Government were to authorise an official statement expressing their
readiness to establish a Jewish State in Palestine,' a member of the
Political Intelligence Department of the Foreign Office asked Wolf
point-blank in the latter half of May 1917. 'Do you think this would
make the Jews more friendly to England?'[118]

But if such questions arose periodically and nagged at some
minds, there was, of course, as before, no way of answering them
decisively. There could only be varying impressions and conclusions
derived from the steady trickle of raw data and argument, some of it
tendentious, some not, into the Foreign, War, and Cabinet Offices
since the beginning of the war. Most of it, as we have seen, pointed
in a particular direction; and what was decisive was the resulting
cumulative effect. There were now more than enough Ministers and
senior officials in London who had accepted not only the general
argument that the Jews did matter politically in various important
ways, but the twin theses on Zionism as well—namely, that it
embodied the trend most apt to provide a key to Jewish sympathies
and that, in the main, it was, or could be rendered pro-*entente*, indeed
pro-British. In brief, the balance of opinion lay with those whose
answers to these questions were much the same as Sykes's. Besides,

[116] Wolf to Leopold de Rothschild, 22 March 1917. Graham's informant was
Anthony de Rothschild, Leopold's son.
[117] Buchanan to Foreign Office. 10 May 1917, PRO, FO 371/2996.
[118] Memorandum by Wolf on a conversation with R. A. Leeper, 21 May 1917.
CZA, A77/3B.

the evidence that, *pace* Wolf, Zionism was not dead in Russia and had in fact largely revived was genuine enough and abundant; and Weizmann made it his urgent business to draw the Foreign Office's attention to such bits and pieces of data as came his way: for example, that at a conference of representatives of the some two million Jews of southern Russia pro-Zionist resolutions had been passed and the strongly anti-Zionist, socialist Bund defeated by a vote of over nine to one.[119] One way or another, at the top of the bureaucratic pyramid the tendency to ascribe substantial influence to Zionism never seriously weakened and the evidence supporting the accepted view was studied with satisfaction. 'It is certain,' Graham minuted on reading a report on the Petrograd conference, 'that our best card in dealing with the Russo-Jewish proletariat is Zionism'.[120]

Weizmann, with his inexhaustible resources of energy, his personal presence, his undeviating confidence in the validity of his own position and arguments, and his corresponding talent for sweeping away to the furthest corners of his own mind all such thoughts and recollections as were inconsistent with them, probably did more than anyone, even Sokolov, to persuade the British that the Zionists would, in the final analysis, serve their purposes. In part, it was the brilliance of his *attack* that helped wear down lingering doubts. In part, it was the evidence that he had the ear, even the co-operation, of the American Zionists—for all that careful observation would have revealed that the increasing tendency of the Americans, not excluding Brandeis at this stage, to deal with him rested chiefly on his ability to convey the impression that he had the backing not only of the better part of European Zionism but of the British Government as well long before either the one or the other had been truly secured.[121] In part, it was his curious double status. He presented himself and was accepted as a Russian-Jewish nationalist and referred to as such, the capital M (for Monsieur) which traditionally marked the foreigner in official British correspondence being sometimes appended to his name. At the same time, of his manifest loyalty to Great Britain, his devotion to both its wartime and its imperial causes, and his profound and transparent con-viction that the interests of the Jews coincided with those of his

---

[119] Weizmann to Graham, 13 June 1917. *Weizmann Letters*, vii, no. 432, p. 441.

[120] 27 June 1917. PRO, FO 371/3053, fo. 313.

[121] See for example, Weizmann to Brandeis, 23 April 1917. *Weizmann Letters*, vii, no. 351, pp. 371–3.

adopted country to the benefit of both, none had cause to doubt and none doubted. Perhaps in the final analysis, it was his capacity—together with Sokolov in some cases, alone in others, but at any rate as the now leading member of the team in London—to produce desired political results when called upon to do so. For so doing he and Sokolov not only demonstrated goodwill and efficacy but seemed to validate the fundamental assumption on which the association of the Zionists with British interests ultimately turned: that which Lord Robert Cecil had termed 'the international power of the Jews'. In mid-summer 1917 Weizmann was granted a signal opportunity to demonstrate his ability to tap it.

On 22 May Balfour, in Washington at the tail end of his mission to the United States, was informed by Lansing, the American Secretary of State, that the Administration was inclined to support a peace initiative directed at Turkey and proposed by a former Ambassador to that country, Henry Morgenthau. The United States was not at war with the Ottoman Empire and on the whole did not take kindly to projects to dismember and divide it among the Allies—projects of which it knew something, but not all. The idea of persuading the Turks to withdraw from the war—a move which necessarily entailed abandoning all plans to deprive them of their Near Eastern (as opposed, perhaps, to their remaining European) possessions—was attractive to the Americans on grounds of general principle. It was not unattractive to limited but important political circles in France where the burden of the war was increasingly felt to be more than society could bear, the idea that that burden might be reduced tended to be welcomed *a priori*, and interest in the Near East itself was slight. In Britain too, over and above the long-established 'pro-Turk' school of strategic and diplomatic thought, there were many whose thinking was along similar lines. A series of proposals put up directly by dissident Turkish leaders on the one hand and would-be, usually self-appointed non-Turkish intermediaries on behalf of the ruling circle in Constantinople on the other had been looked at since quite early in the war. Thus far nothing had come of any of them.

Balfour made no immediate objection.[122] It was understood that the project had President Wilson's support, and Balfour was not disposed to enter into debate with the Americans. There could

[122] Balfour to Foreign Office, 23 May 1917. PRO, FO 371/3057.

certainly be no question of expressing reservations openly on the explicit grounds of the *entente's* territorial ambitions in the Levant— the more so as the French, who were to be informed too, seemed likely at this point to look at the project with some favour. Besides, the British campaign in the Near East was not going well (the EEF having been repulsed at Gaza) and there was a real danger that the whole intricate series of negotiations with the French, the Russians, and the Italians on the disposition of Asiatic Turkey would turn out to have been no more than a futile exercise. The skin of the bear had been shared out before the hunt had properly begun and it might be necessary to treat with the Turks after all. In that case, however, it followed that it was indeed essential that the range of possibilities be explored, albeit with the utmost care and in total secrecy, it being assured that no suspicion of weakness on the Allied side register with the Turks and that the emissary himself be motivated by absolute loyalty to the Allies. On all these scores it was not long before doubts about Morgenthau's prospective mission set in in London, and even in Washington, and the question was raised how, if it could not be stopped, it might be rendered harmless. Morgenthau's good Turkish connections—specifically with the CUP—were thought to tell against him. His vanity and his 'boundless desire to play a big role',[123] as the Foreign Office judged it, and his 'fantastic' idea of conniving with well-placed Turks to secure passage for Allied submarines through the Straits to destroy the German warships that had been moored in Constantinople since the beginning of the war did him no credit.[124] The impression gained, without much justification as it happend, that he was talking to too many people about his projected mission diminished it further. As time passed, the State Department itself became worried, and the Foreign Office, at a loss for a way to intervene, began positively to pray that his projected visit to Europe would fall through. At the end of May the Americans, unwilling wholly to abandon the scheme, resolved none the less to reduce it to minimal dimensions and obscure its true purpose: it was to be presented as a no more than philanthropic mission of relief for Palestinian Jewry. At the same time the British and the French were asked to send representatives to meet Morgenthau at Gibralter, half way to his destination, to discuss the

[123] Minute by Oliphant, 24 May 1917. PRO, FO 371/3057/104218.
[124] Barclay to Foreign Office, n.d. (30 May?), and minute by Hardinge, 31 May 1917. PRO, FO 371/3057.

real political questions with him in strictest privacy and, in effect, to take him, so far as possible, in hand themselves.[125]

It was Morgenthau himself who, unwittingly, brought the Zionists into the affair. He had not been as free with information about his project as was suspected in Washington and London, but he had spoken to Jacob de Haas, a close associate of Brandeis (as of Herzl many years earlier), probably with the cover story that had been allotted him in mind. The Zionists in America were not sure what Morgenthau was really up to; they were only sure they did not wholly trust him. He had been very helpful to the *yishuv* in its struggle to survive after the outbreak of war. He had interceded with the Turkish authorities on their behalf and he had provided a channel for the transmission of economic aid. But he was a strong and open opponent of Zionism as such, and a fairly typical member of the class of American Jewish notables of German (as opposed to Russo-Polish) origin who, by virtue of their wealth, their earlier arrival in the United States, and their command of the major Jewish institutions, still constituted a collective obstacle to the growth of Zionism in the country. What then followed is somewhat obscure. It is likely, but not certain, that Brandeis, warned by de Haas, engineered the inclusion of Felix Frankfurter in Morgenthau's entourage to keep an eye on him and alerted Weizmann, in turn, to what was impending. Morgenthau himself, falling in readily enough with the mission's cover plan, then suggested—either on his own initiative or at Frankfurter's urging—that he be met at Gibraltar by a Zionist representative, possibly Weizmann. With a request sent to the British to arrange such a meeting and an explicit presidential stipulation that Morgenthau might not 'commit the United States Government in any way but must refer all proposals' to Washington,[126] the American chapter of the venture was then effectively closed.

Meanwhile, in London, torn between mounting dislike of what seemed to be in store and fear lest he cause offence to 'the sensitive American mind', Cecil had taken the plunge and instructed Spring Rice to seek at least a postponement of the mission.[127] The move had failed. Lansing remained confident that with Morgenthau's mission ostensively restricted to 'Jewish matters' and the ex-Ambassador

[125] Barclay to Foreign Office, 30 May 1917. Ibid.
[126] Spring Rice to Foreign Office, 12 June 1917. PRO, FO 371/3057.
[127] Minute by Cecil, and priority telegram to Spring Rice, 14 June 1917. Ibid.

himself being under clear instructions to initiate nothing of a political nature, no damage to anyone would ensue.[128] The British were not soothed. They knew that the true and original purpose of the mission had leaked out—to the Armenians and the Zionists, among others—and their fear of diplomatic embarrassment and their distrust of Morgenthau personally had been raised to very high temperature by the arrival of an enraged Weizmann on their own doorstep.

On 10 June at the Cabinet Office, 'very much excited and very angry', as Ormsby-Gore noted, Weizmann[129] protested the various unofficial moves then in course (among them Morgenthau's) to sound out the Turks on a separate peace. He warned of the dangers he envisaged. He denounced Morgenthau personally. The former American Ambassador to Constantinople was 'notoriously pro-German and he acted with and on behalf of an international ring of Jewish financiers in Hamburg, Berlin, Vienna, Paris, and New York,' Weizmann told Ormsby-Gore. 'This international ring was violently hostile both to Great Britain and to Zionism and had always been one of the most valuable assets to Germany.' What Morgenthau was after was an 'inconclusive peace' which, in turn, would give German capital and German Jews 'an ascendant importance throughout the Turkish Empire and particularly in Palestine.'[130] Two days later he turned up at the Foreign Office and, still 'in a state of some agitation', it was recorded, said much the same things to Graham.[131] Morgenthau was 'extremely pro-Turkish and, as a Jew, represented international finance, Conjoint Committees, and anti-Zionism.' In sum, Weizmann argued, the Morgenthau mission was a German move.[132]

Weizmann's picture of a great enemy intrigue had no foundation in fact. If the springs of Morgenthau's activity did lie, as virtually everyone thought, in an inflated ego and frustrated political-diplomatic ambitions, it is beyond question that his conscious

[128] Spring Rice to Foreign Office, 16 June 1917. Ibid.

[129] The meeting at the Cabinet Office had been arranged by Malcolm, the Armenian nationalists' representative in London, who was equally dismayed, and the two men went together.

[130] Memorandum by Ormsby-Gore, 10 June 1917. Hull, SP 12/8.

[131] Minute by Graham, 13 June 1917. PRO, FO 371/3057. Weizmann went to the Foreign Office alone. Malcolm followed him later the same day.

[132] See also Weizmann's long letter to Graham, 13 June 1917. *Weizmann Letters*, vii, no. 432, pp. 438–42; and Graham's minute after an earlier conversation with Weizmann, 9 June 1917. PRO, FO 371/3057.

purposes were wholly decent and humanitarian. But Weizmann could see nothing but a 'silly and ridiculous' project that struck at the heart of his own design for the future of the movement. Peace with Turkey at that point, or even feelers towards a compromise settlement, with the EEF's operations hardly begun, would almost certainly mean the collapse of all hope for a radical revision of the political and territorial order in the Near East. It seemed to point to nothing less than the relegation of all hope of attaining that recognized territorial-political status which the Zionists had been working for since Herzl's time to an infinitely distant future. Weizmann had no doubt that such peace moves as Morgenthau could be expected to initiate, if ever followed up, would leave the Zionists out in the cold. In his extreme agitation, it never occurred to him to sit prudently on his hands in confident anticipation that Morgenthau was unlikely to succeed. He was even impervious to the argument, put to him by at least one critical observer,[133] that no Jewish leader should presume to impede a move intended, after all, to limit the fighting and shorten the war. Determined to stop Morgenthau, he offered to go out to Gibraltar to intercept him; and with the State Department intent on lending an expressly Jewish aspect to the mission and Morgenthau himself having proposed that Weizmann meet him, the offer was accepted in London with alacrity. The official British mind was still somewhat divided on the question whether all possible trails leading to a separate peace with Turkey should or should not be explored—*even* by such as Morgenthau.[134] But once the original plan of sending out a senior diplomat well versed in Turkish affairs to meet him had been dropped—largely for fear that it might look as if it was Great Britain that was intent upon a separate peace[135]—Weizmann's candidature for the task could not fail to secure approval.

In the event, Weizmann, with Frankfurter's help, was triumphantly successful. He and the French representative who accompanied him met the American party at Gibraltar as planned on 4 and 5 July. Facilities were provided by the Governor.

---

[133] A. S. Yahuda. For Professor Yahuda's account of his meetings with Weizmann in Spain and a bitter refutation of Weizmann's version of that and other episodes in his autobiography *Trial and Error*, see A. S. Yahuda, *Dr. Weizmann's Errors on Trial* (New York, 1952), pp. 14–16 and *passim*.

[134] For example: minute by Drummond, 8 July 1917. PRO, FO 371/3057.

[135] Foreign Office to Spring Rice, 27 June 1917. Ibid.

Morgenthau was asked to outline his view of conditions in Turkey and his own plans and intentions. He was then closely questioned. Did he really think the time had come for the Allies to begin negotiations with the Turks, and if so on what grounds? On what conditions, if at all, were the Turks likely to be prepared to leave the war? Why precisely had he tried to enlist the Zionists in support of his mission? But to none of these question were clear answers forthcoming and it seems that Morgenthau was eventually forced to admit not only that he no had clear mandate from his own Government, but that he had no solid, least of all up-to-date, information on Turkish intentions either. When that point had been reached it proved not too difficult to persuade him to abort his mission there and then, to travel neither to Egypt nor to Switzerland, and to make do instead with a face-saving visit to General Pershing in France. The Zionists, he was then told, would have nothing to do with such efforts as his to gain a separate peace—not, at all events, on their own account and independently of the Governments concerned. He was asked firmly to remember this; and Morgenthau, if Weizmann's account of the conversation is anything to go by, seems meekly to have promised to do so.[136] The operative conclusion in the joint report signed by all four participants (Weizmann, the French Colonel Weil, Frankfurter, and Morgenthau himself) stated roundly that 'the time is not now ripe to open channels of communication with Turkish leaders.'[137]

Success was therefore complete, the Foreign Office delighted. Weizmann's private report was circulated, by Balfour's special instruction, to the Cabinet. Weizmann himself was confirmed in the Office's collective mind as an efficient operator and a 'shrewd observer', a man to be trusted and held in high regard.[138] In retrospect, it is true, the episode itself came to be dismissed as one of small consequence: 'first in order, but not in importance' of what was to be a series of attempts by a variety of people to examine the chances of a separate peace with a dying empire once the new Government in Petrograd had released the Allies from old commitments regarding Constantinople.[139] But neither the good impression

---

[136] Weizmann to Graham, 6 July 1917. Ibid.

[137] 6 July 1917. *Weizmann Letters*, vii, no. 454, pp. 465–7.

[138] Minutes by Graham and Balfour, 13 July. Graham to Hardinge, 23 July 1917. PRO, FO 371/3057.

[139] Memorandum on Turkish peace overtures, 20 November 1917. PRO, CAB 21/59.

Weizmann had made on his British sponsors nor his own rising sense of mastery of diplomatic tactics were in any way affected.

v

All that now remained—so far as the Zionists in London were concerned—was for the British Government finally to make a binding, public commitment to their cause. They had begun to press hard for it in June. What they wanted, Weizmann told Graham, was 'an open expression' of the British Government's 'sympathy with, and support of, Zionist aims', one that should 'publicly recognise the justice of Jewish claims in Palestine.'[140] There was no question of asking for more, even if it had been thought that the Government would agree. A few, notably those grouped in the British Palestine Committee, wanted a more specific reference to a Jewish desire for political independence. But Sokolov had spoken not only for Weizmann and himself, but for all those within the now dominant circle of activists in London, when he explained to Brandeis, a few months earlier, that

I think we all agree that we don't want Palestine to be handed over to us as an independent state. The responsibilities are too great and the risk of failure too terrible. The country is, or will be, too important strategically for a small race to depend on unless backed in some way by stronger Powers. It would hardly be favourable for unprotected Jewish nationa[l] aspirations, were Palestine to become the battle-field of the world.[141]

The British could not very well go further themselves, not, at any rate, without getting French approval and not before the defeat of Turkey was assured. Such was Balfour's view.[142] What the Foreign Office was disposed to recommend was 'something on the lines of the French assurance'. That having been given, French 'susceptibilities' would be unaffected. It would, it was known, satisfy the London Zionists themselves and serve 'to secure Zionist political support which is so important to us in Russia at the present moment.'[143]

In the course of July and August, drafts of a public statement that would both satisfy the London Zionists and be acceptable to the British Government were discussed, worked over, and discussed

140 Graham to Hardinge, 13 June 1917. PRO, FO 371/3058.
141 Sokolov to Brandeis, 7 March 1917. WA.
142 Minute by Balfour, n.d. (mid-June 1917). PRO, FO 371/3058.
143 Minute by Graham, 19 June 1917. Ibid.

again with British officials. It was to be a long process extending into the autumn and not concluded until the very eve of the publication of the final version in November. The simple, original proposal for the operative statement, namely that 'His Majesty's Government accepts the principle that Palestine should be reconstituted as the national home of the Jewish people', submitted to Balfour over Lord Rothschild's signature on 18 July 1917,[144] failed to survive the process intact. But on the principle underlying it as understood in London by both sides there was no wavering and no serious argument. It was accepted that Great Britain was 'committed' to the Zionists, even if the terms of the commitment were still undefined and the criteria by which they should be determined remained obscure.

The general political grounds for assuming a commitment to the Jewish national movement in its Zionist form were now well established, however. The process by which the French were to be eased out of Palestine and their claim to it watered down was in train. A decision to restart the invasion of the country and send General Allenby out to manage it having been taken in June, the question of how the country was to be disposed of was once again both open and necessarily on the Government's agenda. No one suggested that the well-established arguments for weaning American and Russian Jewries away from pro-German and neutralist sentiment had lost anything of their validity and urgency—least of all when it was noted in London that Germany too had begun to take an interest in Zionism as part of *its* play for Jewish opinion.[145] Finally, the Zionist notables with whom the British had been dealing had proved themselves politically effective and trustworthy. All in all, Sykes, upon his return to London and finding that much, in his view, had gone wrong in his absence, had some reason to be pleased that at least Zionism, among the many movements and projects he had sponsored, had 'held good'.[146]

Only one last obstacle to public adoption of the Zionist movement and the Zionist purposes (in however attenuated a form) remained.

---

[144] PRO, FO 371/3083.

[145] England wants Palestine for itself, it was argued in the *Vossische Zeitung*, 1 August, and proposes to gain it 'through the furtherance of the Jewish movement.' Cited by Townley (The Hague), reporting to Foreign Office, 3 August 1917. Graham minuted: 'An interesting article—it foreshadows Germany encouraging Zionism in a Palestine remaining Turkish.' PRO, FO 371/3053.

[146] Sykes to Clayton, 22 July 1917. Hull, SP 11/61.

It was the rediscovery in Downing Street that the Jews themselves were divided and that the most articulate opposition to such an act of adoption came from the ranks of the notables of English Jewry itself. These were not voices that could be comfortably ignored, the more so as promises to take their views into account with the utmost consideration had been given repeatedly. The problem was that the division in Jewry being, as would soon be found, unbridgeable, it would be for the British Government itself to decide for one or the other party.

7

The Solomonic Judgement

i

It had now been clear for some years to all British Ministers and officials who had in any way to deal with Jewish questions that on the twin matters of Palestine and Zionism the Jews themselves were deeply and bitterly divided. Those Englishmen in high places who had not discovered it for themselves were taught as much by the protagonists. Neither Lucien Wolf nor Chaim Weizmann—representative figures for these purposes—seem to have overlooked any opportunity to drive their respective messages home. Each lavished such arguments and data as he thought might help fortify the position he claimed as spokesman for the true Jewish interest. Each was ready to disparage and undercut his rival with only minimal regard for the proprieties. The relevant Foreign Office files bulge with confidential correspondence and reports on internal Jewish affairs submitted by Wolf on his own authority, along with his acid comments on those he disagreed with. Weizmann, as we have seen, had no more compunction about denigrating his political opponents, going so far in some cases as to impute not merely misguided but unworthy motives to them. It all stood in sharp contrast to the ancient rules of prudence, discretion, and absolutely minimal intermingling of Jewish affairs with those of the sovereign power prescribed by tradition and ingrained in the public servants of Jewry by centuries of practice. No doubt the spirit and energy, if not passion, with which the conflict was pursued, to say nothing of a measure of mutual personal dislike, go far to account for these undignified proceedings. But ultimately they hinged on the desire shared by both parties—precisely that against which the Jewish

Sages and their latter-day devotees had always advised[1]—to assimilate Jewish purposes to those of the sovereign power. And there was a sense in which, because both Zionists and anti-Zionists sought the ear and sympathy of the authorities, neither had an alternative course of action. The cumulative effect on British officialdom, in any event, was greatly to heighten awareness—and wariness—of the divisions in Jewry. 'When Jews fall out,' the Foreign Office's principal authority on Jewish questions, Lancelot Oliphant, observed on one occasion, 'it is none too easy for Christians to decide whether the Zionists or anti-Zionists are in the wrong.'[2] When Jabotinsky's scheme for a Jewish Legion came up again early in 1917, the difficulty about it, another official observed, was that 'it raises the whole Zionist question. This is a matter upon which the most representative Jews are utterly divided and it seems to me that H.M.G. may be laying [in] stores of trouble, if they encourage a scheme which commits them to Zionism.' The Permanent Under-Secretary agreed: 'I think there is a good deal in what Mr. Clerk says and I imagine the Gov[ernment]t ought to be careful not to identify itself with either Jewish faction.' Balfour himself, at this point, did not think otherwise.[3]

Initially, the anti-Zionist school, represented formally by the CFC and informally by the majority of Jewish notables in and out of politics, had the advantage. Their purposes were indisputably philanthropic and meritorious and they formed a recognizable— and recognized—part of the social and institutional mosaic of the United Kingdom. The Zionist movement, in contrast, was in all essential respects foreign: its chief spokesmen were outsiders, at best newcomers. Its fundamental purposes, however they might be defined, were ultimately political. It followed that a British Government owed a friendly ear to the anti-Zionists on grounds of morality and humanity, and by virtue of the fact that their cause was one that had been adopted by British nationals of goodwill and some considerable standing *unless* countervailing political considerations obtained. To the Zionists, on the other hand, so long as no clear and

---

[1] 'Seek not acquaintance with the ruling power' runs a classic Mishnaic injunction; and another: 'Be wary of the ruling power for they bring no man nigh to them save for their own need, they seem to be friends such time as it is to their gain, but they stand not with a man in his time of need.' Avot ('The Fathers'), i, 10 and ii, 3.

[2] 10 December 1916. PRO, FO, 371/2817 fo. 163.

[3] Minutes by George Clerk, Lord Hardinge, and Balfour, 30 March 1917. PRO, FO 371/3101/65760.

persuasive political grounds for attending to them were adduced, it owed nothing. The erosion of the anti-Zionists' advantage was in fact largely consequent upon such clear and persuasive political grounds for taking up their rivals having arisen. But not alone. It has much to do too with the collapse—as it seemed at the time—of their principal cause, that of Russian Jewry.

The major positive demands of the Conjoint Foreign Committee, it will be recalled, all had to do with the wartime and post-war condition of Jewry in central and eastern Europe, above all in Russia. Again and again, the British Government had been pressed to make it its business, so far as possible, to induce the foreign Governments concerned to accord their Jewish subjects a full measure of human rights and the basis for a decent existence. To this end, in the course of 1916, after a great deal of internal debate and much correspondence on the subject with the authorities, a carefully worded outline of the views and requests of the Committee was submitted to the then Foreign Secretary, Lord Grey. It was drawn up with particular attention to the 'magnitude' and 'extreme delicacy' of what the CFC chiefly had in mind: nothing less than the 'total abolition of the existing disabilities' under which Russian Jewry had laboured; and it was argued, not for the first time, that it was in the Allied Governments' own interest to prepare to deal with this and other issues before the war ended and before the peace conference it was supposed would follow the war was convened.[4] The memorandum was then passed to the French for their comments. There was a half-hearted attempt at the Quai d'Orsay to look at it; the matter then dropped from sight and no response from Paris seems ever to have emerged.[5] But nor was there any from the Foreign Office itself—until, a full three months later, they returned a dusty one. It would not be possible to express 'any official opinion' on the CFC's 'report . . . regarding Jewish questions arising out of the war,' the Committee was informed. Nor could the new Foreign

---

[4] D. L. Alexander, C. G. Montefiore, and L. de Rothschild to Viscount Grey, 1 October 1916. BD, C11/3/2/1. The problem of Russian Jewry apart, the memorandum referred the Government to the 'unfulfilled Treaty obligations' of Romania in regard to its Jewish population, the question of the rights of those Jewish subjects of the Central Powers who might fall under Russian and Romanian rule at the end of the war, and 'the future of the Jews of Palestine.' The last item amounted to a recapitulation of the proposal made the Foreign Office by the CFC in March 1916. (See above, pp. 188.)

[5] Granville to Briand, with enclosure, 21 October 1916; internal memorandum, 27 October 1916. AE, Guerre 1914–1918, Sionisme, vol. 1198.

Secretary (Balfour), they were told a few weeks later, 'hold out hopes of an understanding [between the Allied Governments] being arrived at now or in the immediate future' on the matters they had dealt with. Nor was Wolf encouraged to persist and visit the Foreign Office to discuss them all over again.[6]

The Committee's memorandum had not had a friendly reception upon receipt in October 1916. Sympathy for east European Jewry had never been common. In some quarters the only response evoked by the request to aid them was that the Jews having demonstrated pro-German feelings, they deserved as good as they got; at the very least it would now be virtually impossible to help them.[7] But the insurmountable obstacle to any serious effort on their behalf, even where there was goodwill, was the entrenched view that it was politically imposssible to take up their cause with the Russian Government anyway. It had never been thought possible to do so with vigour. In the present state of near-collapse in Russia (all this was just prior to the February Revolution) it could not be done at all. The arguments for and against had, of course, long been familiar to both sides. 'The disappointing decision of the Foreign Office,' Wolf noted after a final exchange in January 1917, 'had not been unanticipated.'[8] It was plain that there was nothing to be done for the time being. And then in March, after the revolution and the emancipation of Russian Jewry decreed formally by the new Russian Provisional Government, the subject tended to drop naturally—if only temporarily—from view. Not so the matter of Zionism, to which the Committee and those most closely associated with it now tended to bend their energies—as much, it seems, for lack of any other central cause to fight for, or fight against, as out of profound and passionate conviction.

They had never made a secret of their views, as we have seen.

The attitude of the leaders of the Anglo-Jewish community [Wolf informed the Foreign Office at the end of 1916, not for the first or the last time] is that they have no objection to the plans of the Zionists in Palestine, so long as they do not prejudice the cause of Jewish emancipation in other countries. In their view, the Zionist scheme is not, and cannot be, a solution to the so-called Jewish Question, and many of us think that it is bound to be a failure in other respects. But they do not urge this view.

[6] Oliphant to Wolf, 5 January; de Bunsen to Wolf, 20 January 1917. ML, AJ/204/3.
[7] Minutes by unidentified official, 6 January and 2 March 1917. PRO, FO 371/3092.
[8] Note, n.d. ML, AJ/204/3, p. 77.

Their essential concern, he explained, lay elsewhere and was of a different order.

All they ask is that the Zionists shall not postulate a Jewish nationality outside Palestine, which does not exist, and which, if it did exist, would prove an obstacle to their being true nationals of the countries in which they live; and, in the second place, that they shall not seek to promote their schemes in Palestine by asking for rights and privileges not shared by other races and creeds, in order to hasten their numerical preponderance in the country. Such special rights and privileges would obviously compromise the agitation now being carried on for equal rights for the Jews of Russia and Rumania.[9]

Naturally enough, as reports of a possible British commitment to the Zionists multiplied, alarm grew. When Wolf and his colleagues learned of Sokolov's journey to Paris in April 1917 and of his having told Jewish notables there something of his purposes and of British support being assured, they were in a panic.[10] Had a *fait accompli* been engineered behind their backs? They lost no time lodging enquiries and protests. 'Was the report accurate?' they asked the Foreign Office. Did the Government propose to carry its negotiations with the Zionists to an agreement without ascertaining *their* views? Did it understand that, if so,

a great injustice would be done the Anglo-Jewish community, and a very serious mischief might result, . . . more especially as the gentlemen with whom His Majesty's Government have so far been in negotiation are all foreign Jews, having no quality to speak for the native Jews of the United Kingdom with whom, for the most part, they do not co-operate in the affairs of the community.[11]

The Foreign Office was immediately on its guard. 'This shows how warily we must walk in encouraging Zionism.'[12] True, nothing had been settled finally and it was easy enough to assure the CFC that no binding agreement with the Zionists had been concluded.

---

[9] Wolf to Oliphant, 1 December 1916. PRO, FO 371/2817.

[10] Bigart, secretary of the Alliance Israélite Universelle, to Wolf, 16 April 1917; and resumé of Sokolov's statement to members of the Alliance, 14 April 1917. CZA, A77/3B. Bigart had sent the text of the resumé to Wolf in confidence, authorizing him to communicate its contents to his principals, the presidents of the Board of Deputies, Alexander, and of the Anglo-Jewish Association, Montefiore. Wolf seems not to have hesitated to pass it on to the Foreign Office along with his letter of protest.

[11] Wolf to Oliphant, 21 April 1917. PRO, FO 371/3092.

[12] Minute by D[rummond?], 25 April 1917. Ibid.

This was done. The difficulty lay in formulating the Government's intentions for the future. The Government, the CFC was told, was 'sincerely anxious to act in all matters affecting the Jewish community not only in its [the community's] best interests but with due regard to the wishes and opinions of all its sections.' From these 'guiding principles', it was assured, there would be no departure.[13] Ten days later the increasingly anxious Committee was explicitly (and reluctantly) given the further promise that its views would be taken into account.[14] In fact, even if the will in Downing Street to ignore 'the whole of Jewish opinion' had been stronger—and it was growing all the time—it was soon materially impossible to do so.

Contrary to established practice (and much against what it knew to be officialdom's express desire to avoid scandal and open controversy),[15] the Conjoint Committee resolved in mid-May 1917 to make the entire subject and the central differences between the two schools matters of public knowledge. It chose to do so, moreover, not only in terms as sharp as might be commensurate with its dignity, but in the way best calculated to attract attention in the circles to which its members attached most importance, namely by issuing a formal statement in *The Times*. In its way, it was an act of desperation. It was certainly an attempt to stop the rot, make a stand, and counter the steady growth of sympathy for Zionism in English Jewry by showing where its established leaders stood. Above all, it was intended to meet the publicists and polemicists of Zionism on the ground where they had evidently been making most progress: among the members of the non-Jewish social and political élite—the élite on whom the notables of Anglo-Jewry had always chiefly relied and of which, in greater or lesser degree, they thought themselves a part. It was not their first essay at meeting the Zionists on public, neutral ground. Claude Montefiore and Lucien Wolf had already expounded their views in articles in the *Fortnightly Review* and in the *Edinburgh Review* which were, at least in part, answers to a notably successful collection of Zionist essays published on behalf of the Weizmann-Sokolov circle by the highly reputable publisher John Murray. It may be that what was particularly galling to the opposition was that in *Zionism and the Jewish Future* the case for

[13] Graham to Wolf, 27 April 1917. Ibid.
[14] Memorandum by Cecil, 8 May 1917. PRO, FO 371/3092.
[15] Minute by Oliphant, 2 May 1917. Ibid.; and Wolf to Montefiore and Alexander, 8 May 1917. CZA, A77/3B.

Zionism had not only been set out in the plainest language the various authors could muster, but that here and there the contempt—or pity—in which many of them chose to hold their opponents was barely disguised. 'The claim to be Englishmen of the Jewish persuasion—that is, English by nationality and Jewish by faith,' wrote Gaster, 'is an absolute self-delusion.'[16]

There is no mistaking the intense emotion the controversy had generated in what had once been a notably confident, in fact complacent circle. 'I had a long talk with my friend, Claude Montefiore, yesterday [the day before the decision to go to *The Times* was taken],' Milner recorded. 'It must, of course, be borne in mind that he is tremendously anti-Zionist. . . . He begged me, almost passionately, to be very careful how we commit ourselves to Sokoloff or Weizmann.'[17] And Montefiore himself wrote Milner after the same interview, that he would beg him

to trust your own fellow citizens, who, at all events, are Englishmen through and through, and whose sons are serving in England's armies, rather than foreigners who have no love for England, and who, if the fortunes of war went wrong, would throw her over in a trice, and hurry over to Berlin to join the majority of their Colleagues. In [the] old days they puffed up Turkey no end; now, of course, Turkey for the time being, is run down.[18]

The formal decision to publish a 'Statement on the Palestine Question' was taken by the Committee on 17 May, Montefiore, it seems, pushing hardest for its adoption. Six of the fourteen regular members of the CFC approved it. Two opposed the decision. One abstained. The rest were absent. Of the seven co-opted members, six voted for the resolution; one was absent. Headed 'The Future of the Jews', the Committee's statement appeared in full in *The Times* a week later. The result, by the generally staid standards of the Anglo-Jewish community, was an explosion. It was not so much the content that shocked. The Committee's argument was no more than a rehearsal of its long-established views, familiar to all *cognoscenti*: Judaism was a 'religious system' and the attempt to invest it with national and *a fortiori* political significance was anachronistic; Zionism entailed the risk that the Jews be held 'strangers in their native lands' and their hard-won position as citizens and nationals

---

[16] Harry Sacher (ed.), *Zionism and the Jewish Future* (London, 1st edn. June 1916, 2nd edn. January 1917), p. 93.

[17] Milner to Cecil, 17 May 1917. PRO, FO 800/198.

[18] Montefiore to Milner, 17 May 1917. CZA, A77/3B.

of those lands be undermined; and there was a fatal inner
contradiction between the Jews' claim for equality in the lands of
their present dispersion and the demand for a special status for them
in Palestine.[19] It was the twin facts of publication in the general
press and an internal dispute exposed before all and sundry that
jarred, and that it had been done in the name of two of the
premier institutions of the community and in a manner that
positively invited the opposing school to respond in kind. The
Zionists did indeed reply—and with a vigour that might have been
anticipated—again in *The Times*. Lord Rothschild wrote to dismiss
the central thesis of the Committee as untenable: he could see no
reason why 'an autonomous Jewish State under the aegis of one of
the Allied Powers can be considered for a moment to be in any way
subversive to the position or loyalty of the very large part of the
Jewish people who have identified themselves thoroughly with the
citizenship of the countries in which they live.' The Chief Rabbi,
referring to the Committee's 'extraordinary statement', informed
The Times that he could not 'allow your readers to remain under the
misconception that . . . [it] represents . . . the views of Anglo-Jewry
as a whole.' And Weizmann stated roundly that while 'it may
possibly be inconvenient to certain individual Jews that the Jews
constitute a nationality' they were just that: a fact 'attested by the
conviction of the overwhelming majority of Jews throughout all
ages', a conviction which non-Jews had always shared.[20] All this led
to a fresh body of notables, headed by Lord Swaythling (Edwin
Montagu's brother) and Israel Gollancz, describing themselves as
'Jews of British birth and nationality', to write in support of the
Committee.[21] Finally, the editors of *The Times* themselves plunged
into what they termed 'this important controversy'. On the question
of Jewish nationhood, they agreed with Weizmann. They were sure
that what the Chief Rabbi had had to say on the score of the
representative quality of the Committee could not be ignored. On
the issue of loyalties, they sided with Rothschild. 'Only an
imaginary nervousness suggests that the realization of territorial
Zionism, in some form, would cause Christendom to round on the
Jews and say, "Now you have a land of your own, go to it!"'
Generally, the newspaper argued, betraying the hand, or at the very

[19] *The Times*, 24 May 1917.
[20] Ibid., 28 May 1917.
[21] Ibid., 1 June 1917.

least the opinions, of its foreign editor, Henry Wickham Steed, there was a good deal to be said for Zionism.

It had fired with a new ideal millions of poverty-stricken Jews cooped up in the ghettos of the Old World and the New. It has tended to make Jews proud of their race and to claim recognition, as Jews, in virtue of the eminent services rendered by Jewry to the religious development and civilization of mankind.[22]

This was not at all what the Committee had hoped for; and its miscalculation was confirmed a fortnight later (15 June) when the Board of Deputies of British Jews, as near a representative body as there was in the community, voted its disapproval of the original statement and its disquiet at the fact of publication. The Board's representatives on the CFC were called upon to leave it, which they did. The CFC thereupon collapsed and—in name, at least—vanished from the scene.[23] True, the majority had been a narrow one: 56 in favour of the resolution, 51 against. The decisive issue for most delegates was less what the Committee had argued in *The Times* than its unauthorized conduct—the parent bodies not having been consulted—and the resulting scandal. Analysing the result for the Foreign Office's benefit, Wolf could point out, with some justice, that the distribution of votes had shown that 'not only are the English-born and well-to-do classes all on the side of the Conjoint Committee, but that a large portion of the foreign and poor elements are also on that side.'[24] It was a defeat for him and his friends, none the less; and by the same token, it could be and was represented as a victory for the Zionists. But above all, it served to raise the temperature of the debate within Anglo-Jewry and to make it more difficult than it might otherwise have been for the Government, as it approached the day a public, formal, and binding decision on Palestine and the Zionists had finally to be taken, to avoid taking a stand towards those elements in Jewry who were fearful precisely of what they were now certain the Government was about. On strict construction, Sir Ronald Graham at the Foreign Office had cause to observe with evident satisfaction that 'this vote signifies the dissolution of the Conjoint Committee and it will no longer be

---

[22] Ibid., 29 May 1917.
[23] It was reconstituted under a slightly different name ('Joint Foreign Committee') and with reduced authority early in 1918. Lucien Wolf remained its secretary.
[24] Wolf to Oliphant, 18 June 1917. PRO, FO 371/3053.

necessary to consult that body.'[25] But the larger body of *opinion* the Committee had represented could not be ignored. None could deny that it was *their* Government that was about to take the decision. However half-hearted, the promise given them that they would be consulted when the time came had in one way or another to be honoured, the more so as they had a vigorous figure, one of their own number, within the Government itself to speak for them.

ii

The Zionists had first submitted the precise wording they proposed for the official statement of support for their movement in mid-July.[26] They had expected results within a matter of weeks. The Foreign Office had duly submitted Lord Rothschild's draft (in slightly amended form)[27] to the Cabinet Office for approval, but having neglected to make the explicit request that it be brought speedily before the Cabinet nothing happened. A month went by. In mid-August, the impatience of the Zionists now palpable and their own deeply ingrained sense of good bureaucratic order offended, the Foreign Office pressed for action, whereupon the machine did come to life.[28] Milner took it upon himself to consider the precise text and, in the event, proposed further amendment of the formula.[29] On 3 September 1917, at a routine meeting of the War Cabinet, the three formulas—and the subject as a whole—were finally before the British Government in formal session.[30]

[25] Minute by Graham, 20 June 1917. Ibid.

[26] See above, p. 269.

[27] It ran: '1. His Majesty's Government accepts the principle that Palestine should be reconstituted as the National Home of the Jewish people. 2. His Majesty's Government will use its best endeavours to secure the achievement of this object and will discuss the necessary methods and means with the Zionist Organisation.' The Foreign Office, with Balfour's approval, proposed that the end of the formula be rephrased to read: '. . .and will be ready to consider any suggestions on the subject which the Zionist Organisation may desire to lay before them.'

[28] Nicolson to Longhurst, 17 August; and Longhurst to Nicolson, 20 August 1917. PRO, CAB 21/58.

[29] Milner thought the terms 'reconstituted' and 'secure' much too strong; and proposed the fundamental substitution of the phrase '*a* home *for* the Jewish people' for the original '*the* National Home *of* the Jewish people'. Ormsby-Gore to Hankey, 23 August 1917. Ibid. (Emphases added.)

[30] War Cabinet 227. Neither Lloyd George (away from London, ill) nor Balfour (on holiday) attended. Bonar Law presided. Cecil attended as Acting Foreign Secretary. As it happened the first item on the agenda was that of the designation of the Jewish Legion. It was recorded, that in view of the objections of 'a very influential

There was no review or discussion, however, of the chief positive reasons for supporting the Zionists: there was no reference to British strategic interests in the Near East, let alone of Anglo-French rivalry there; there was no mention of developments in Russia; and the Cabinet was reminded of the weight of Jewish opinion in the United States only in the wake of a semi-technical suggestion that a decision be postponed. Plainly, all present were sufficiently familiar with the subject. With one exception, none of the Ministers questioned the wisdom of the policy proposal *per se*. The only general reservation made (and accepted) was that 'a question raising such important issues as to the future of Palestine, ought in the first instance, to be discussed with our Allies, and more particularly with the United States'. It was resolved, accordingly, that the 'views of President Wilson should be obtained before any declaration was made.' (The possibility that *other* Allies be consulted was noted, but passed over.) The only objection to the policy of support for the Zionists as such, and to the terms of the declaration that would announce it, came from Edwin Montagu, recently appointed Secretary of State for India, present at the War Cabinet by special invitation. It was he therefore who determined the subject of such debate as there was; and that subject was his charge that by supporting and promoting Zionism the English Government would be betraying English Jewry.

With Samuel, the loyal Asquithian Liberal, out of office, Montagu was now the only Jew of ministerial rank in the British Government. He had never hesitated to tell his colleagues of the depth of his opposition to Zionism and of his horror—there can be no other term—at the prospect of the British Government taking it in one way or another under its wing. He had done so, as we have seen, when the idea was first launched on Cabinet waters (by Samuel) almost three years earlier; again when Wolf's formula had been under consideration;[31] and now, as the policy conceived by Sykes

deputation of [English] Jews' and their fear that despite the distinction with which English Jews were serving in the British forces, 'the whole reputation of English Jews as fighters' would be staked on the performance of such a regiment, it was resolved that it would have no distinctive title. It would be designated only by a number. The Cabinet then moved on to consider what it plainly saw as the linked question 'of the attitude to be taken up towards the Zionist movement as a whole.' PRO, FO 371/3083.

[31] See above, pp. 96–98; and 170–1.

was at long last nearing its public inauguration, he struck out once more.

Montagu brought his views before his colleagues in two formal Cabinet papers (one of them entitled, with characteristic vehemence, 'The Anti-Semitism of the Present Government'), in a letter to Lord Robert Cecil which he had circulated to the Cabinet as well, and by word of mouth at two of the three Cabinet meetings at which the topic was discussed. (He was on his way to India when the last, decisive meeting of the Cabinet was held.) He never wearied. He went to immense pains to drive his argument home. He got his brother Lord Swaythling to supply the Cabinet with a large quantity of published anti-Zionist polemical material written by Montefiore, Wolf and others. He spoke and wrote privately to the Prime Minister. He collected and offered evidence of every kind to show that Jewish opinion was not, *least of all in England*, pro-Zionist; that, appealing to the authority of Gertrude Bell, the concept of an independent Jewish Palestine had to be 'ruled out' on local political and demographic grounds; that if it was true that the French were in sympathy with the Zionists, it was only because they wanted to be rid of their Jews; that what one Chief Rabbi had argued another had denied; that the effect of such a declaration by the Government would be the driving out to Palestine of the Jewish citizens of 'every country'; and that, above all, the entire concept of Zionism was fatally flawed because 'there is no Jewish nation.'[32] In substance, his arguments were identical with those he had put to Asquith in March 1916. But they were still more remarkable for the eloquence, the passion (if not hysteria), and the pathos that now informed them. A passage from his private appeal to the Prime Minister is characteristic:

I don't want to make difficulties. . . . I accepted office [as Secretary of State for India] because I placed (as indeed I do) India far above everything else in my field of vision. It seems almost inconceivable that I should have to give it up for something wholly unconnected with India at all, and yet what am I to do? I believe firmly that if you make a statement about Palestine as the national home for Jews, every anti-Semitic organisation and newspaper will ask what right a Jewish Englishman, with the status at best of a naturalized foreigner, has to take a foremost part in the Government of the

[32] 'The Anti-Semitism of the Present Government', 23 August 1917. PRO, CAB 24/24; Montagu to Cecil, 14 September 1917. PRO, CAB 24/27; and 'Zionism', 9 October 1917. PRO, CAB 24/28.

British Empire. Palestine is not now British. It belongs to our enemies. At the best it can never be part of the British Empire. The country for which I have worked ever since I left the University—England—the country for which my family have fought, tells me that my national home, if I desire to go there, therefore my natural home, is Palestine. . . . Among your many colleagues you have none more desirous of serving you. I would ask you most respectfully to give me your advice in the difficult circumstances in which I find myself.[33]

The great strength of Montagu's argument lay in the fact that it was not with the Zionists themselves that he was conducting it. He seems neither to have had nor to have sought any contact with them. He evidently disliked them for what they were and what they stood for. He feared them for the threat to his kind he was sure they embodied. But it was with his ministerial colleagues he chose to quarrel and it was from them that he demanded a reply, an explanation, and—if possible—retreat. Asquith had been surprised and amused when the two cousins, Herbert Samuel and Edwin Montagu, had argued the point early in 1915. For Lloyd George, Balfour, Milner, Cecil, and their officials, it was less amusing: a real matter of policy was at state. Besides, the ground was now very familiar.

Fortified by a remarkable Foreign Office paper in which Montagu's view of the Jewish people, their nature, their history, and their collective aspirations was courteously refuted, point by point, with a precision of analysis and historical data which cannot but have put the Secretary of State for India to shame (in the eyes of his more knowledgeable colleagues, at any rate),[34] the attack was beaten off. It was 'urged' in Cabinet, with confidence, that the

[33] Montagu to Lloyd George, 4 October 1917. HLRO, LlGP F/39/3/30. At no point, so far as is known, did Montagu threaten to resign in so many words. But the appeal to the Prime Minister for 'advice' was preceded by a reference to the likely effect in India if he did resign: Lloyd George, it would be said, had succumbed to the anti-progressive forces and had driven Montagu out of office. Montagu was in fact known as a man of liberal views where India was concerned. Consulted by Lloyd George, Balfour had written about the proposal to appoint Montagu to the India Office: 'Montagu is very able: he knows a great deal about India; he would be very popular I am told with the Indians. *Per contra* he would be disliked by the Anglo-Indians—partly because he is too much (in their opinion [])] of a reformer, partly because he is a Jew.' 16 July 1917. PRO, FO 800/199/38. I have found no record of the Prime Minister's response to Montagu's plea. So far as policy was concerned, he remained unmoved. And Montagu remained in office.

[34] 'Note on the Secretary of State for India's Paper on Anti-Semitism of the Government', by 'R. McN.' (Ronald McNeill?), n.d. (end of August? 1917). PRO, FO 371/3083.

conditions of the Jews in lands where they did not enjoy equal rights would only be improved by 'the existence of a Jewish State or autonomous community in Palestine'; that the position of Jews 'in countries like England' where such rights were possessed would be unaffected; and that while it was true that 'a small influential section of English Jews were opposed to the idea,' 'large numbers were sympathetic to it.'[35] When the subject was brought up in Cabinet for the second time, on 4 October, the Prime Minister presiding and Balfour present and in charge, the counter-attack was pursued.

Balfour's ever firmer personal views and sympathies and the cumulative effect of what had been to put to him and to his subordinates by Zionists and non-Zionists, Jews and non-Jews, virtually since the war began, were now all compounded in a characteristically concise and clear-minded statement of position. While the movement was

opposed by a number of wealthy Jews in this country [Balfour was recorded as having told his colleagues, it did have] behind it the support of a majority of Jews, at all events in Russia and America, and possibly in other countries. He [Balfour] saw nothing inconsistent between the establishment of a Jewish national focus in Palestine and the complete assimilation and absorption of Jews into the nationality of other countries. Just as English emigrants to the United States became, either in the first or subsequent generations, American nationals, so, in the future, should a Jewish citizenship be established in Palestine, would Jews become either Englishmen, Americans, Germans, or Palestinians.

What was at the back of the Zionist Movement was the intense national consciousness held by certain members of the Jewish race. They regarded themselves as one of the great historic races of the world, whose original home was Palestine, and those Jews had a passionate longing to regain once more this ancient national home.[36]

The Cabinet passed to the question of the Allies, barely touched on at the earlier meeting. So far as the French were concerned, all was well, Balfour assured them. Cambon's letter to Sokolov[37] was produced and read, and the Cabinet was satisfied. On the attitude of the Americans there was still uncertainty. The Zionists had assured the Foreign Office, on the strength of what they had heard from

[35] War Cabinet 227. Minutes. Loc. cit.
[36] War Cabinet 245. 4 October 1917. PRO, CAB 21/58.
[37] See above, p. 255–6.

Brandeis, that Wilson was favourable to the movement. Colonel House, on the other hand, had informed the British directly that the President was not.[38] It would all have to be looked at again. Back then to the Jews. Montagu rehearsed his argument and his fears and repeated that 'the Cabinet's first duty was to English Jews'. And Curzon now joined the discussion, entering objections to the proposed statement of policy on 'practical grounds', namely the poverty of Palestine as a country of settlement—'a less propitious seat for the future Jewish race could not be imagined'—and the question of the existing inhabitants. How was it proposed to get rid of *them*? And, anyway, how many Jews were in fact willing to return? The proponents of the policy agreed to make a small tactical retreat. A new formula intended to go some way towards meeting both Montagu's and Curzon's strictures was submitted by Milner. It would be 'clearly understood that nothing shall be done to prejudice the civil and religious rights of the existing non-Jewish communities in Palestine, or the rights and political status enjoyed in any other country by such Jews who are fully contented with their existing nationality and citizenship.' No final decision would be taken until both the views of President Wilson and of Jewish leaders, both Zionists and 'representative persons in Anglo-Jewry opposed to Zionism', had been ascertained.[39]

It can hardly be doubted that this promise to sound leading Jewish opinion was something more than a gesture, an attempt to appease Montagu until he was safely on his ship bound for India. He was, after all, a senior member of the Government. He could not be ignored. Besides, and perhaps still more to the point, his appeal to his colleagues and his protest had been peculiarly personal and the matter—historical, ideological, speculative, even theological in its nature—went far beyond the normal ken or competence of a

[38] Following the 3 September Cabinet, Cecil had asked Colonel House (through Wiseman) to ascertain Wilson's view. The answer was that 'the time is not opportune for any definite statement further perhaps than one of sympathy provided it can be made without conveying real commitment.' Weizmann, meanwhile, had asked Brandeis to approach Wilson and a fortnight after House's telegram, Brandeis informed Weizmann that 'From talks I have had with the President and from expressions of opinion given to closest advisers, I feel I can answer you that he is in entire sympathy with declaration ... as approved by Foreign Office and Prime Minister.' Cecil to House, 3 September. Yale, WP, 466/123/4326; House to Cecil, 10 September. PRO, CAB 24/26; Weizmann to Brandeis, 12 September. *Weizmann Letters*, vii, no. 496, pp. 505 6; and Brandeis to Weizmann, 26 September 1917. PRO, CAB 24/26.

[39] War Cabinet 245. Loc. cit.

British Cabinet. Montagu had been allowed to say his piece and submit his papers. No one had agreed with him, not even Curzon. No one, it cannot but seem, had wanted to agree with him. But nor did anyone feel free to ride over him rough-shod, nor over those he termed the English-born Jews to whom the Government owed its first loyalty in this connection. And nor had Montagu himself drawn back in the face of the wall of argument raised against him. A choice had therefore to be made. As it happened, it was in the nature of a philosophical and historiographical choice, and it speaks volumes for the quality of government in Great Britain at the time that the Cabinet did not hesitate to undertake it. There only remained the question by what method it would proceed. Meanwhile, the focus of the Cabinet's attention had been shifted from the substance of the policy proposal before it to one of its possible, but inherently tangential implications.

iii

At this point, Hankey's well-oiled Cabinet Secretariat took over. A list of ten 'representative Jewish leaders' was drawn up, in consultation with Montagu (for the non-Zionists) and Weizmann (for the Zionists). Lord Rothschild and the Chief Rabbi figured on the Zionist list along with Weizmann himself and Sokolov. Claude Montefiore and Stuart Samuel, the new president of the Board of Deputies, were on the list of presumed non- or anti-Zionists. (In the event, Stuart Samuel turned in a mildly pro-Zionist reply.) Herbert Samuel was added on grounds of general standing and known views, as was Montagu.[40] Montagu apart (he, of course, was fully informed and had had his say), each was informed confidentially that 'at the instance of the Foreign Secretary' the question of a formula setting forth the attitude of the Government towards the Zionist movement in general and the future of Palestine in particular was under discussion. Milner's version was set out for them; each was asked, 'in view of the apparent divergence of opinion expressed on the

---

[40] But not Rufus Isaacs, Lord Reading, on the face of things perhaps the most distinguished Jew of all in the United Kingdom: Lord Chief Justice as the time, soon to be Ambassador in the United States, later to be named Viceroy of India. In fact, Reading was kept informed by Montagu and Claude Montefiore of what was transpiring (see for example Montefiore to Reading, 11 October 1917. IOLR, MSS. Eur. F118/58). He sympathized with their views and sustained them. But he was extremely cautious, refraining from direct involvement and avoiding the assumption of a *public* position.

subject by the Jews themselves', to comment upon it. Within less than two weeks, the Secretary's letter had been sent out, the replies collected, and with some supplementary material (chiefly on Jewish national sentiment in Russia and the state of the Zionist movement in the United States) the whole brought together in the shape of an orderly, 18-page Cabinet paper.[41]

The Foreign Officed acted with equal dispatch to determine President Wilson's attitude. The Germans, House was told, had been 'making great efforts to capture the Zionist movement', and with that in view, the Cabinet had decided to take up the matter of 'a message of sympathy with the movement' once more. The Foreign Secretary would be grateful therefore if House would again apply to the President for his opinion.[42] Balfour had indeed referred to the Germans in his presentation to the Cabinet on 4 October . Reports of their awakening interest in Zionism had been coming in sporadically all year. A report from Berne of a meeting said to have taken place in Berlin between Foreign Secretary Kühlmann, Jamal Pasha, and 'a leading Zionist' (unnamed) was thought important enough early in October to circulate to the Cabinet.[43] That Weizmann had reason to make the most of what he had gleaned on the subject is evident. How seriously anyone in the Foreign and Cabinet Offices took these reports is less clear. That the Germans would wish, or feel free to go beyond an anodyne expression of sympathy for the Jews was inherently incredible: the territory in question was Turkish, the Turks were their allies. The most they could promise the Zionists was an effort to press the Turks to soften their position. There was no hard evidence that they had attempted to do so. There was no real likelihood that if they did they would succeed. And with British troops now moving into Palestine in full force, what the Turks were prepared to do for the Jews was rapidly ceasing to be an interesting question in any case. What might count was the gesture: an expression of German sympathy for a Jewish cause might have a propaganda effect in Russia, perhaps even in the United States, irrespective of the probability of its ever being translated into effective action. But as the basis of an argument for restarting, or accelerating consideration of the planned British

---

[41] 'The Zionist Movement', G. 164. 17 October 1917. PRO, CAB 24/4.

[42] Balfour to House (via the British intelligence channel), 6 October 1917. Yale, WP 666/1/6.

[43] Goodhart to Balfour, 2 October 1917. PRO, CAB 21/58.

declaration, fear that the Germans might pre-empt the British served admirably—in London itself, no less than in Washington. House duly informed the President of the new British request and this time, perhaps because the subject of Zionism had been linked in this way to Germany, he seems (there is no certainty) to have recommended approval. Wilson for his part was ready enough to comply. He 'concurred in the formula', he informed House; and Sir William Wiseman on 16 October was able, at long last, so to inform London.[44]

It only remained to get the subject back onto the Cabinet's agenda. At least two attempts to do so in the course of October failed. The Zionists pressed hard—where necessary discreetly, where possible publicly.[45] The Foreign Office itself wanted the matter settled. 'Further delay will have a deplorable result,' Graham minuted for Balfour's eyes, 'and may jeopardise the whole Jewish situation.' Uncertainty about British intentions was

growing into suspicion, and not only are we losing the very valuable co-operation of the Zionist forces in Russia and America, but we may bring them into antagonism with us and throw the Zionists into the arms of the Germans who would only be too ready to welcome the opportunity. . . . We might at any moment be confronted by a German move on the Zionist question and it must be remembered that Zionism was originally if not a German at any rate an Austrian idea.[46]

Graham reviewed the context for what would be the last time. The French had stated their sympathy, in more 'definite' terms than

[44] Wilson to House, 13 October 1917. A. S. Link (ed.), *The Papers of Woodrow Wilson*, xliv (Princeton, 1983), p. 371; Wiseman to Drummond, 16 October 1917. Yale, WP 666/1/22. House was not sympathetic to Zionism and far from fond of Jews as an ethnic, let alone political, category. It is virtually certain that Wilson's first negative response was fuelled by House's advice. It was Brandeis's standing with Wilson and evident British pressure that most probably led him to drop his opposition.

[45] A week before the final decision in the Cabinet, a list of some 300 synagogues and other communal bodies in Great Britain which had passed a resolution in favour of the 'reconstitution of Palestine as the National Home of the Jewish people' was transmitted to the Foreign Office by Weizmann, and promptly used by the Office to demonstrate that Anglo-Jewry was by no means opposed. Weizmann to Graham, 23 October 1917. *Weizmann Letters*, vii, no. 531, p. 539; Graham to Balfour, 24 October 1917. PRO, FO 371/3054; and Balfour to Lloyd George (enclosing Graham's memorandum), 25 October 1917. HLRO, LlGP F/3/2/34.

[46] Graham to Balfour, 24 October 1917. PRO, FO 371/3054. When the memorandum was retyped the next day for transmission by Balfour to the Prime Minister, the last clause was corrected to read '. . . if not a German *Jewish* at any rate an Austro-*Jewish* idea.'

even the British envisaged. The Italians approved. So did the Vatican. So did President Wilson. And now, above all, there was Russia.

Information from every quarter shows the very important rôle which the Jews are now playing in the Russian political situation. At the present moment these Jews are certainly against the Allies and for the Germans, but almost every Jew in Russia is a Zionist and if they can be made to realize that the success of Zionist aspirations depends on the support of the Allies and the expulsion of the Turks from Palestine we shall enlist a most powerful element in our favour.[47]

More than three months had passed since the Zionists had submitted their draft: they had 'reasonable ground for complaint',[48] Balfour minuted the Prime Minister. The following week, on 31 October, room was at last found on the agenda and the subject brought before the Cabinet for final settlement. Once again, none of the Ministers questioned the fundamental datum on which all depended: the power of the Zionist idea in Jewry itself. No one questioned Lloyd George's plans for the post-war disposition of Turkish territories in the Near East. No one raised the question of the effect the attempt to implement those plans might have on relations with France. All that was water under the bridge. The reservations the Cabinet had to consider were two. Those expressed by Montagu; those expressed by Curzon. The views of the Jewish notables had long been circulated. Curzon too had prepared and circulated a paper on 'The Future of Palestine'. The Cabinet had only to make up its mind.

The 'representative Jewish leaders' polled by Hankey had gone over ground that was now thoroughly familiar. The tally, the Secretary had found, was six in favour of a declaration of intent, four (with Montagu) against. There had been characteristic emphases. Herbert Samuel argued in its favour chiefly on strategic grounds: 'the best safeguard [of Egypt] would be the establishment of a large Jewish population [in Palestine], preferably under British protection.' For Joseph Hertz, the Chief Rabbi, it would 'mean the realisation of Israel's undying hope of a restoration'. Lord (Lionel Walter) Rothschild would welcome a declaration because 'it would show that His Majesty's Government is benevolently disposed

[47] Graham to Balfour, 25 October 1917. HLRO, LlGP F/3/2/34.
[48] Balfour to Lloyd George, 25 October 1917. Ibid.

towards and would lend its potent support to the aspirations of the great mass of the Jewish people;' and went on to argue that only a fraction of Jewry in England or anywhere else opposed them. The new president of the Board of Deputies, Sir Stuart Samuel, expressing himself with extreme caution, agreed that English Jewry favoured a National Home for Jews in Palestine *under proper safeguards*. But it would have to be economically viable and the Holy Places in Jerusalem were best internationalized, 'or at any rate not . . . placed under entirely Jewish control', if non-Jewish opinion was to be conciliated. Weizmann and Sokolov brought up the list of those in favour, Weizmann concerned chiefly to discredit the anti-Zionists, Sokolov to improve the text of the draft declaration: especially the substitution of 'Jewish people' for 'Jewish race'.

The Zionists, naturally enough, struck notes of warmth, satisfaction, and gratitude. Through the comments of their opponents there ran an unmistakable undercurrent of injury and outrage. 'In replying to your letter,' Sir Philip Magnus began, '. . . I do not gather that I am expected to distinguish my views as a Jew from those I hold as a British subject.' The Jews did not need 'the offer of a national home in Palestine to excite their ardour or stimulate their courage' in the present war, he assured the Government. They were not fighting for 'distinctly Jewish ideals'. They were fighting for 'the attainment of the self-same objects which His Majesty's Ministers have so unmistakably defined' for everyone else. Claude Montefiore

deprecate[d] the expression 'a national home'. For it assumes that the Jewish race constituted a 'nation', or might profitably become a nation, both of which propositions I deny. . . . The idea of a 'home' for the Jews was started by the late Dr. Herzl, . . . because (as he himself told me) he believed—*(a)* That anti-Semitism was eternal, and that it was hopeless to expect its removal. *(b)* That the Jewish problem in Russia was insoluble in Russia. I told him that *(a)* was a libel upon (1) the Jews and (2) human nature, and that even *(b)* was too pessimistic. I was not wrong. For if the Revolution in Russia holds and reaction does not set in, the Jewish problem *has* been solved in Russia.

But that said, if for some reason unknown to him, the Government believed it to be in the British interest to publish such a declaration, 'I would, of course, subordinate my Jewish feelings, wishes, and interests to the interests of England and the Empire.' L.L. Cohen, chairman of the philanthropic Jewish Board of Guardians, said much the same. Montagu's views were very well known.[49]

There was no real discussion this time. Everyone, said Balfour, plainly confident that minds were made up,

> was now agreed that, from a purely diplomatic and political point of view, it was desirable that some declaration favourable to the aspirations of the Jewish nationalists should now be made. The vast majority of Jews in Russia and America, as, indeed, all over the world, now appeared to be favourable to Zionism. If we could make a declaration favourable to such an idea, we should be able to carry on extremely useful propaganda both in Russia and America.

True, there was what was defined as 'the difficulty felt with regard to the future position of Jews in Western countries'. Balfour, as if speaking to an invisible audience, over the heads of those present, disagreed. Far from 'hindering the process of assimilation in Western countries'—as they evidently feared—the establishment of a Jewish National Home would accelerate the process. And he offered the parallel of an Englishman leaving for the United States to establish his home there: he would have no difficulty becoming a full national of the United States. Whereas in Jewry's present position, assimilation was often felt to be incomplete, now 'any danger of a double allegiance or non-national outlook would be eliminated.' It was a telescoped argument (telescoped, at any rate, by the minutes-taker); and no sort of answer to the carefully drafted arguments submitted by Montagu, Magnus, Montefiore, and Cohen in turn. But there were none present to debate with him.[50]

There remained the 'immediately practical questions' Curzon had expounded in a typically incisive and well-informed paper circulated several days earlier. In the first place, the phrase 'national home' was exceptionally vague and open, as he easily showed, to varying and conflicting interpretations. In the second place, it was far from clear that the policy to be pursued was capable of successful

---

[49] 'The Zionist Movement', 17 October 1917. PRO, CAB 24/4.

[50] War Cabinet 261, 31 October 1917. PRO, CAB 21/58. Montagu was in India when he learned of the decision. He wrote in his diary: 'It seems strange to be a member of a Government which goes out of its way, as I think, for no conceivable purpose that I can see, to deal this blow at a colleague that is doing his best to be loyal to them despite his opposition. The Government has dealt an irreparable blow at Jewish Britons, and they have endeavoured to set up a people which does not exist.' S. D. Waley, *Edwin Montagu* (London, 1964), p. 141.

realization. Curzon reviewed the size and poverty of Palestine, the condition and nature of its population, the attention paid it by the major religions, and what he took to be the contrast between the meagre, at any rate modest, prospects for the Jews within it even in the best of circumstances and the 'romantic' and idealistic aspirations' to which the Zionists were attached. If it was only a matter of securing a European (not Jewish) administration and of equal civil and religious rights, including the right of land purchase and settlement, for the Jews, then 'there was no reason why we should not all be Zionists.' But if, as was evidently the case, more was implied in the policy proposed, then, in his judgement, it was not one that would in fact 'provide either a national, a material, or even a spiritual home for any more than a very small section of the Jewish people'.[51]

But Balfour, fortified by a paper rushed to him by Sykes and setting out a vastly rosier picture of Palestine and what the Zionists had done—moreover, given the chance, could do[52]—conceded no more than that he understood that the experts differed. His information was that if Palestine were 'scientifically developed', it could sustain a very much larger population than in the past under Turkish rule. And as for the meaning of the words, 'national home'

to which the Zionists attach so much importance, he understood it to mean some form of British, American, or other protectorate, under which facilities would be given to the Jews to work out their own salvation and to build up, by means of education, agriculture, and industry, a real centre of national culture and focus of national life. It did not necessarily involve the early establishment of an independent Jewish State, which was a matter for gradual development in accordance with the ordinary laws of political evolution.

Curzon restated his reservations, but did not insist. 'He recognized,' so it was recorded, 'that some expression of sympathy with Jewish aspirations would be a valuable adjunct to our propaganda.' He would be content if the language of the declaration was 'guarded'. No doubt he recognized too, that it was not 'practical considerations' the Cabinet had in mind at all, only diplomatic and political ones: the winning of the war, opinion in America, the fate of Russia. What would and could be done in Palestine, when the country was

---

[51] 'The Future of Palestine', 26 October 1917. IOLR, MSS. Eur. F112/124.
[52] Undated and unsigned, but submitted to Balfour on 30 October 1917. PRO, FO 371/3083, fo. 113 ff.

in British hands, was not of immediate—and therefore not of serious—concern to the Cabinet. Curzon admitted 'the force of the diplomatic arguments in favour of expressing sympathy'. He agreed that 'the bulk of the Jews held Zionist rather than anti-Zionist opinions.' He no more agreed with Montagu than did Balfour.

It was settled. The phrase 'Jewish race' in Milner's draft declaration was altered to 'Jewish people' and the unwieldy last clause was shortened. The new text was approved. Balfour was authorized to publish it.[53]

From that point on, the question why it might be politic to issue the declaration faded, giving way to what would prove to be the larger question what practical meaning it might be politic to lend to it.

[53] War Cabinet 261. The well-known final text of the 'Balfour Declaration', published two days later, states that 'His Majesty's Government views with favour the establishment in Palestine of a national home for the Jewish people, and will use its best endeavours to facilitate the achievement of this object, it being clearly understood that nothing shall be done which may prejudice the civil and religious rights of existing non-Jewish communities in Palestine, or the rights and political status enjoyed by Jews in any other country'. Ultimately, the origins of the phrase 'national home' lay in the definition of the central purpose of the Zionist movement adopted at Herzl's First Congress of Zionists in 1896: 'Zionism aims at the creation of a home for the Jewish people in Palestine to be secured by public law.'

PART FOUR

Into the Arena

8

London, Petrograd, Jerusalem

i

The Balfour Declaration was an act of British foreign and imperial policy in wartime. The authors of one of the volumes of the official history of the Great War put the point bluntly and correctly: 'The development of the war, which was ever engaging more nations and affecting more interests, the imperative pressure of Allied needs, and the international power of the Jewish race, had made desirable the recognition of Jewish aspirations for a "National Home" in Palestine.'[1] As such, it was an act designed primarily to achieve advantages in the short term. That for the Zionists it represented a promise of great things to come was incidental to its main and immediate purpose, the more so as the advantages expected in the short term proved disappointing. The 'international power of the Jewish race' turned out to have been vastly overrated. The Zionist trend in Jewry was revealed as substantially weaker than official London had come to believe. The state of affairs in Russia (to which, as we have seen, the greatest importance had been attached) was transformed overnight by the Bolshevik *coup d'état* and the outbreak of civil war. Jewish opinion was thereby rendered in all significant respects irrelevant to the very central question, as the British saw it, of Russia's continued membership in the anti-German alliance; and the Russo-Polish Jewish community itself was now to be subjected to pressures, strains, dilemmas, and dangers so harsh as to cause the literally distant issue of the Jewish national enterprise in Ereẓ-Israel to recede rapidly from the circle of its immediate and vital concerns. It was at this point that the process whereby Russian Jewry was to be broken and in great part isolated from other communities began,

[1] Lt.-Gen. Sir George Macmunn and Capt. Cyril Falls, *Military Operations: Egypt and Palestine, August 1914–June 1917*, (London, 1928), p. 219.

and the weight and role of the Russian element in Jewry as a whole drastically diminished.

True, as anticipated, a great wave of sympathy and gratitude to Britain did sweep through the Jewish world, notably in Russia, but in the United States too—never to be wholly extinguished even in the bitter years that were to ensue a generation later. Reports of the impact of the news of the Declaration and of celebrations and pro-British demonstrations virtually throughout the Jewish world flowed into London in November and December 1917.[2] In Odessa, in a zone still comparatively free, the British Consul was glad to report that on 29 November a crowd estimated at no less than 150,000 had packed the street outside the Consulate and that 'a procession some two miles in length marched past the Consulate playing repeatedly [the] British and Jewish national anthems.'[3] There were even murmurs of satisfaction in Zionist circles in Germany, and a faint attempt by both the Germans and the Turks to counter them by friendly statements of their own. But the sea-change in Jewish national opinion had been rendered irreversible and British military intelligence was happy to conclude (correctly) that there was nothing the Germans could, or the Turks would, do to 'win' Zionism for themselves. Jewish 'assets' and 'world-interests' were reviewed and the conclusion that the 'trump cards are still in the hands of the Allies' asserted with confidence.[4] What was necessary and urgent, it was thought, was to make the most of the achievement; and the Foreign Office and the Government's propaganda machine set out to devise 'the best method of obtaining full political advantage from the new situation created by the Declaration'[5] and only regretted that 'so much time ha[d] been lost'—hoping that 'with skilful management of the Jews in Russia the situation may still be restored in the spring.'[6] But time had been lost and so had, or so it was

---

[2] See e.g. the otherwise generally hostile Spring Rice, writing to Balfour, 21 December 1917. PRO, FO 800/209.

[3] British Consul, Odessa, to Foreign Office, 30 November 1917. PRO, FO 371/3054.

[4] 'Attitude of Enemy Governments towards Zionism', 15 February 1918. PRO, CAB 21/58. For a contemporary Turkish analysis of the Zionist issue, chiefly an attempt to account for the way in which an insignificant movement came to be part and parcel of the enemy's schemes for dismantling of the Ottoman Empire, see an Ottoman Foreign Ministry confidential report, 'Filistin meselesi: Siyonizmin davası', 16 March 1918. OFMA, 332/17.

[5] Minute by Graham, 3 November 1917. PRO, FO 371/3083.

[6] Minute by Hardinge, ibid.

believed, an opportunity. 'This is very satisfactory and the News Dep[artment]t is making full use of it,' Graham minuted on reading the report from Odessa. 'The regrettable feature is that our Declaration did not come some months earlier.' Hardinge agreed: 'It might possibly have made all the difference in Russia.'[7]

The other proposition on which British policy on Zionism had been founded—the use that might be made of it in the long-maturing effort to bury (or at least modify) the Sykes-Picot Agreement—was still solid enough. Yet it could not now seem as compelling as it had been thought to be a year or so earlier. The British now held Palestine. It availed the French nothing to celebrate the taking of Jerusalem by 'English, French and Italian troops', as was announced, with a *Te Deum* sung at Notre Dame, the President of the Republic and the Cardinal Archbishop of Paris presiding, as if it had been a joint venture.[8] The conquest of Palestine had not been one, and had never been so intended. The French in Palestine consisted of little more than two battalions of second-rate colonial troops, the Italians of a few hundred bersaglieri and carabinieri. Allenby's army was a British one, and by the autumn of 1918 British military occupation of the country (and much of the land beyond) was complete and not to be relinquished for thirty years. The result was growing confidence in London that the French had now no choice ultimately but to renounce their claims to political rights in Palestine.[9]

There was, however, the difficulty that the French themselves, by and large, continued to proceed on 'the supposition that the

---

[7] 11 December 1917. Ibid. (The telegram from Odessa took ten days to reach London.)

[8] The capture of Jerusalem, said the Cardinal in his allocution, was an event 'of which the Church could not fail to rejoice. The great enterprise of the Crusades had been resumed in the course of the present war and crowned with success, the infidels had been chased from the tomb of Christ, the cradle of our civilization.' He had been gladdened too by the fact that 'at the side of the English and the Italians, French soldiers had come to the Holy Places to affirm the ancient rights of protection possessed by the eldest Daughter of the Church.' *Echo de Paris*, 17 December 1917. The British were more cautious. Allenby had been careful to ask what flags, 'if any' should be hoisted upon occupation of Jerusalem. His query was brought before the War Cabinet itself which decided, that 'in view of the unique character of the city and the many difficult political and diplomatic questions that were raised in connection with it,' no flags at all should be flown. War Cabinet 282, 26 November 1917. IOLR, MSS. Eur. F112/141.

[9] See for example, War Cabinet 308, 31 December 1917. Minutes. IOLR, MSS. Eur. F112/141.

Agreement of 1916 still held good,' as Curzon informed the War Cabinet in October 1918.[10] So while in London all agreed with Lloyd George, who 'had been refreshing his memory about the Sykes-Picot Agreement, and had come to the conclusion that it was quite inapplicable to present circumstances, [and that it] was altogether a most undesirable agreement from the British point of view,'[11] the question how the French were to be brought round to that view remained. That it would be a delicate operation was accepted. That Zionism would serve as one of the tools to be employed was accepted too. The plan, in very general terms, was to argue that the original proposal of an international administration for the country would be, as Curzon put it, 'profoundly unacceptable' not only to 'the native population' but to the Zionists as well 'who are returning in large numbers to Palestine',[12] and that the logic of support for Zionism in principle required support and sympathy for Zionism in practice. That would be one argument. The other major argument concerned the identity of the *single* Power that would assume responsibility for the country. Here the British had to be more careful. They could not openly name themselves.[13] 'The policy of His Majesty's Government at the Peace Conference,' ran a cautious, confidential formulation of the Foreign Office, 'is to support the establishment of a Palestinian State under a mandatory, who may be Great Britain.'[14] It was therefore exceedingly convenient that the Zionists were pressing the British candidature forward with all the strength they could muster and at every appropriate opportunity, and were seen as having been particularly and vitally successful in doing so in the United States. They were thought, in effect, as the author of a General Staff paper put it, to have prepared the way (largely through the influence Brandeis was believed to exert over Wilson), 'for the acceptance by the Government of the United States of the policy eventually determined upon by Great Britain.'[15] Mark Sykes was not alone in thinking that, so

[10] War Cabinet 482A, 3 October 1918. Minutes. Ibid., F112/132.
[11] Ibid.
[12] 'Bases of policy concerning German colonies and Turkish possessions.' GT 6015. 16 October 1918. Ibid., F112/125.
[13] See e.g. Foreign Office to Reading in Washington, 18 April 1919. PRO, FO 609/99.
[14] Foreign Office to Barclay (Bucharest), 19 February 1919. PRO, WO 106/189.
[15] 'Notes on Zionism' prepared on the basis of an analysis of the Zionists' own internal (partly intercepted) correspondence, p. 3. PRO, WO106/189.

far as British policy in the Levant was concerned, 'Zionism is the key to the lock',[16] and that

the important point to remember is that through Zionism we have a fundamental world force behind us that has enormous influence now, and will wield a far greater influence at the peace conference. If we are to have a good position in the Middle East after the war, it will be through Zionist influence at the peace congress that we shall get it.[17]

It was true, finally, that there was some sympathy in London for Zionism *per se*, namely as the means whereby the Jews would be incorporated as one more working part into the whole new clockwork mechanism of states and nationalities, justice to be done to them as to all others, and conflict between Jew and gentile, as between other nations, if not eliminated, at least radically and dramatically reduced. Thus at all events in Europe, but so too, eventually, on Europe's Asian periphery. In practice, Balfour was not prepared to go beyond what he himself recognized to be the cloudy concept of a 'national home', but he, at any rate, made no secret of his special interest in Zionism and of his belief that it was inherently right and deserving of support.[18] 'Our justification for our policy,' he observed on one occasion (when Roman Catholic opposition began to be voiced and the evident contradiction between support for Zionism and the unambiguous application of the principle of self-determination in Palestine was cited),

is that we regard Palestine as being absolutely exceptional; that we consider the question of the Jews outside Palestine as one of world importance, and that we conceive the Jews to have an historic claim to a home in their ancient land—provided that home can be given them without either dispossessing or oppressing the present inhabitants.

I think the opposition offered by so many Roman Catholics to the Zionist policy is very little to their credit, and cannot be easily reconciled with the tenets of their religion. Those of them who are only animated by the fear

---

[16] Sykes to Hankey, 14 November 1917. PRO, FO 371/3057.

[17] Sykes to Wingate, 3 March 1918. PRO, FO 800/221, fos. 404–5.

[18] Reporting this, the French Ambassador in London remarked that Balfour's attitude to Zionism was 'characteristic of the English Minister's dilettante and eclectic spirit.' Paul Cambon to Pichon, 18 January 1919. AE, Palestine 1918–1919, vol. 12, fos. 59–61. When a voice of opposition to the Government's policy was raised within the British official establishment and the Prime Minister's own loyalty to it seemed to be in question, Lloyd George wrote to Balfour to reassure him that 'I have always been a strong supporter of *your* policy.' 27 August 1918. HLRO, LlGP, F/3/3/30. Emphasis added.

that the Christian Holy Places may fall into Jewish hands can be easily consoled. For these should be permanently safeguarded for Christendom by the League of Nations. But I suspect that the motive of most of them is not so much anxiety about the Holy Places as hatred of the Jews: and though the Jews undoubtedly constitute a most formidable power whose manifest-ations are not by any means always attractive, the balance of wrong-doing seems to me on the whole to be greatly on the Christian side.[19]

But all these views, attitudes, considerations, and beliefs were, in the nature of such things, ephemeral. They relied on intangibles and speculation. They took the form of assessments grounded (perhaps inevitably) on incomplete and, in some cases, shaky information. They were enormously influenced, if not largely determined, by the shattering impact of the war. They related to political and strategic assets that were fated to erode and waste. And if only because, as Balfour rightly observed, the Jewish case was in its very nature exceptional, the policy compounded of these ideas, plans, and purposes was exceptionally dependent on their acceptance and adoption by a handful of individuals in key places. More, these ideas, plans, and purposes were not of the class that regular and established officials of the institutions of the Empire tended to rely upon. Such men, concerned with day-to-day and direct government and administration in remote places, tended to be drawn to, and to accept as valid, concepts, aims, and rules of a wholly different order. In this sense, the strictures of Curzon, ex-Viceroy of India, had pointed from the beginninng to the nature of the counter-theses that would soon emerge and multiply within all the ministries and services concerned. The fluidity of thought and personnel in wartime government would in any case now begin to give way to that preference for limited purposes and minimal movement which is perhaps the salient characteristic of a peacetime government in which regular soldiers and established civil servants, rather than first-rate political leaders and star-class, temporary officials set the determining climate of ideas. The sudden death of Mark Sykes of influenza in mid-February 1919—Sykes, the man who had done more than anyone to establish the idea of a community of interests between imperial Britain and the Jewish national movement as both feasible and beneficial—was thus not only a critical loss so far as the Zionists were concerned, but, in its way, an omen.

[19] Balfour to Lloyd George, 19 February 1919. HLRO, LIGP, F/3/4/12.

ii

The great question that now confronted the Zionists was what they were to make of the opportunity that seemed to have opened up before them. On the face of things, they needed only to break it down into linked and straightforward questions of fact, assessment, and interpretation: what were—or, more precisely, what would be—British intentions, how far did these accord with the Zionists' own purposes, in what degree and under what conditions might it be possible to extend the scope of the 'National Home' narrowly constructed so as to bring it into line with those purposes, how strictly would they need to trim their sails to the prevailing wind from London, and, perhaps most profoundly, how independent in mind and action should they and dare they be? One of the salient aspects of the Zionist movement as it was now to evolve, however, was that no agreed answer either to the central question facing it or to that question's constituent parts could ever be contrived. This had a great deal to do with imperfect information imperfectly distributed, with marked differences of temperament and degrees of confidence and self-assurance, and with the people concerned being often differently placed and subject to strikingly different environmental influences. It had still more to do with widely varying demands of and for Zionism itself. The long process whereby both the possibilities and the limits of the opportunity granted them would be discovered and understood was thus shot through with internal disagreement as much on fundamental strategy as on immediate tactics. Such disagreement was compounded by the wartime collapse of the central institutions of the movement, and the necessary making of policy in the immediate post-war period was rendered inseparable from the drive to substitute new centres and new men.

The official leadership of the Zionist movement—the EAC headed by Warburg in Berlin with its branch liaison office in Copenhagen—had managed to keep abreast of developments in London, but only with difficulty, always at some delay, and to little practical purpose. It was not until the end of July 1917 that the four members of the EAC still resident on the continent of Europe (Warburg, Tchlenov, Jacobson, and Hantke) were able to meet in Copenhagen and hear a detailed report on what had transpired at the meeting more than five months earlier between the London-based Zionists and Sir Mark Sykes.[20] In fact, so full a meeting of the EAC was an event in itself. Most of its sessions in the last stages of the war were attended by no more than two full members, some by one alone. The importance of the Copenhagen office as a means of communication, dissemination of information on all branches of the movement to all branches, and, on occasion, as a forum for direct consultation, was therefore capital. What it did not provide was a base of operations. But then, on the one hand, the policy of neutrality decided upon by the official leadership meant abstention from political action so strict as to be almost complete, and on the other hand, the rebels in London had resolved to go their own way in defiance of their elected leaders in any case. Still, the result was less than clear-cut. Sokolov, despite his having allowed himself to be converted from gamekeeper to poacher, provided not only a limited and shadowy legitimacy to his own and Weizmann's activities, but also a link of sorts, through Copenhagen, with his erstwhile colleagues in Petrograd and even Berlin. And since Warburg and Hantke had not attempted to assert their authority over Sokolov and Weizmann as they had over Jabotinsky and Grossman, the acquiescence of Berlin in the London-based rebellion was slowly established, if never actually confirmed. It seems to have been clear to Warburg and his colleagues that they could not have succeeded had they tried. They could see for themselves that sporadic attempts to do so by the Russian Zionist establishment—people who were much closer to Weizmann and Sokolov in spirit and language than they could ever be—had remained without effect. There was only this difference, that whereas the men in London, Weizmann especially, refrained consistently from direct exchanges of views and information with the people in Berlin, they had no compunction about communicating directly with their colleagues in Petrograd—to press them, as we have seen, to bring Russian Zionism round to full support for the pro-British line and (if on the whole less energetically) to put the Russians in the picture so far as developments in London and Paris were concerned. Naturally enough, as the pace of negotiations in London quickened in the summer and autumn of 1917 and as the desire of the British

[20] EAC minutes, 29–31 July 1917. CZA, L6/164I. Sokolov continued to refrain from leaving Allied territory. The sixth member of the EAC, Levin, was still in the United States.

Government to bring Russian Jewry round to support for continued participation in the war became ever more evident and urgent, the attention each side paid the other greatly intensified. In essentials, however, it was a dialogue devoid of symmetry and of equality of esteem.

Although a great deal of thought was given in Petrograd to what Weizmann and Sokolov were about, and the reluctance to support them publicly, and so deviate finally from the policy agreed upon by the Actions Committee early in the war, remained strong, the response to the insistent voices from England was not wholly negative. Plainly, something of importance was transpiring in London. What it was precisely, how important it might be, and what might come of it were all questions, however, on which it was hard for the Zionists in Petrograd to take a stand. The demands and requirements they thought their friends in London should lay before the British as a basis for the proposed unambiguous alignment of the movement on the side of the Allies were worked out in some detail, none the less, and transmitted. They wanted assurances of free immigration into Erez-Israel, Hebrew language rights, 'the whole territory of Palestine' to comprise Galilee, Samaria, Judea, and Transjordania, and of internal self-government for the Jewish population of the country. But the terms and language in which these demands of the Russian Zionists were formulated revealed nothing so much as their growing, underlying feeling that their primacy and influence in the movement had been largely lost, overtaken by events, and that they themselves had been overtaken by new men. Their formulations were exceedingly and uncharacteristically cautious: these were only such general concerns and suggestions as, in the circumstances, they allowed themselves to make, they assured London. Precise presentation and elaboration would be left to 'your discretion and good judgement'. In case their proposals were found, on examination, to be 'inconvenient or not acceptable', colleagues in London should know that Tchlenov (already on his way to Britain) was explicitly authorized 'conjointly with [Sokolov] and Weizmann to alter, draw up and finally redact the same.'[21]

In fact, Weizmann certainly, and even the milder Sokolov, had no intention at any time of accommodating their policy to the

---

[21] Aleinikov, Brutzkus, Boris Goldberg, Idelson, Yanovsky, and Rosov to Sokolov, 10 September 1917. CZA, A18/40/5.

reservations, concerns, and demands of Tchlenov and his party. So far as these two men were concerned, the overwhelming and decisive circumstance was that the British Government had accepted *them* as the effective representatives of Zionism; and from that datum it was only a step to the (still unspoken, but to their minds self-evident) conclusion that it was upon them personally that the British connection with Zionism depended. The advance of Zionism in Great Britain, Sokolov sought to make plain to Tchlenov even before his arrival, had been in official circles, not in the public at large or in the press or within the Jewish establishment.[22] It was a function of diplomacy, not of open (let alone mass) politics.

Tchlenov's mind was not put at rest. While he and his friends conceded that 'much' had been done in London, it was far from clear to them what 'exactly' had been achieved. 'Excuse my frankness,' he wrote to them, just prior to his arrival, but it did appear to him (and to Jacobson too) that Sokolov and Weizmann were now 'so steeped in diplomacy' that they had become incapable of speaking (and reporting) plainly. He and the other Russians therefore very badly wanted it made 'absolutely clear' to them just what rights it was intended to offer the Jews in Erez-Israel. Had the Charter they still insisted upon been discussed with the British or had it not? Just what did the British—and the London Zionists themselves for that matter—think of the Arab question and of the related problems of majority and minority that were likely to arise in the new protectorate? And there were many other questions, such as that of French intentions, about which the Zionists in Petrograd has not been seriously informed at all. Finally, as had been repeatedly pointed out, and as the Zionists not only in Russia but in Berlin too were acutely aware (while those in London, it was implied, were not), the country was still largely under Turkish rule and it was at least conceivable that the war might end with the Turks still in place. How then, in such circumstances, could they be expected to come out in *public* support of the British orientation, as Weizmann and Sokolov continually insisted they do? The least they asked for, therefore, were clear and 'binding' pledges from the British. They asked, notably, for explicit recognition of the 'Jewish character' of the country and for a promise of internal autonomy for the Jews within it before Zionism was committed to British causes.[23] Failing

---

[22] Sokolov to Tchlenov, 22 August 1917. CZA, L6/90I.

[23] Tchlenov (from Bergen, awaiting passage to England) to Sokolov and Weizmann, 24 September 1917. CZA, A18/4/2/8.

that, they wanted to keep the movement's options open. In fine, they were at one with Warburg and Hantke in thinking that it would be at the peace conference to come that the demand for Jewish rights and the claim to Ereẓ-Israel were best raised and had highest hopes of success. They were encouraged to hold that view by the friendly promise of the Russian Provisional Government to ensure that they would be heard before any decisions on Palestine were taken. They were fortified by the rise of Jewish national consciousness throughout Europe and by both the immediate and the anticipated effects of the emancipation of Russian Jewry.[24]

By the time Tchlenov arrived in England (on 25 October) it was evident, for all that he was treated with courtesy, that events had indeed passed him by. On the morrow of the publication of Balfour's Declaration he could only confide glumly to Gaster (who had long since been dropped from the circle of those consulted by Weizmann) that he was dissatisfied. The policy pursued by Weizmann and Sokolov was 'one-sided, dangerous and ultra-British, instead of being . . . Jewish.' The Russians favoured an 'international solution' such that the 'English/Entente Zionists' would be in harmony with the 'Central Power Zionists'. The Declaration, he feared, 'might lead to schism and danger' in and for the movement. Only if no 'international solution'—even one which left Turkey as the suzerain power—could be engineered would an 'English solution' be acceptable, and even then with reservations. But, as Gaster recorded Tchlenov as telling him,

Weizmann, Sokolov, Sacher and the hangers-on were now rabid Englishmen and did not see anything else but from an ultra-patriotic point of view, which struck him [as] rather ludicrous in the mouth[s] of these Russian Jews who had no long-standing connection with this country and simply played up to the G[o]v[ernmen]t and to a particular gallery. They had forgotten that Zionism was neither English nor does it affect many English Jews. It was the ideal of the continental masses and above all of the Russians. But, he [Tchlenov] added plaintively, what am I to do? They will not listen to me and even try to shut me up and warn me not to hinder their work by incautious speech![25]

---

[24] EAC minutes, 10 October 1917. CZA, L6/64I; EAC report for March to October 1917 (by Warburg and Hantke), n.d. CZA L6/18III.

[25] Notes by Gaster [4] November 1917. ML, Gaster Papers. Tchlenov pursued much the same arguments, in milder form, in Weizmann's political committee, to which he was admitted on arrival in England. See for example entry for 6 November 1917 in Tolkowsky's diary, op. cit., pp. 203–10.

Tchlenov took ill suddenly and died in London at the beginning of February 1918. But he had not been alone in his reluctance to follow Weizmann and Sokolov in the direction they were taking the movement, or in his distrust of their judgement and his resentment at their having arrogated authority to themselves to speak for all. Nor had he been alone in his suspicion and forebodings at the contrast between the indeterminant language of the positive promise contained in the Declaration and the precision of the negative terms in which—within the same complex sentence—that promise was circumscribed. Nor were these doubts and distrust removed by events and the passage of time. A year later Avraham Idelson, perhaps the clearest mind, certainly the most articulate, among the members of the front rank of Russian Zionism,[26] and an altogether stronger man than Tchlenov, could be found summing them up before the established leaders of Russian Zionism in firmer language than ever. It was clear to Idelson that the British had had their own very good reasons for responding to Zionist 'demands', but that the latter, having failed to press their case, now had to make do with 'a polite and no more than encouraging letter'. The Declaration was assuredly of great moral importance, but its practical value was very doubtful. In consequence, a great opportunity had been lost. Erez-Israel was now in British hands anyway. The need for Jewish support had waned. It was the Arab world, 'an enormous political factor', to which Great Britain would have to attend, now that it had become 'an Arab power'. And though Balfour was no Plehve or Stolypin, a British and not a Russian Minister, and the promise would surely be redeemed, it would be done minimally, no more than the letter of the promise required—amounting in practice to no more perhaps than some sort of Aḥad Ha-ʿAmian cultural centre for the Jews in the half-recognized ancestral Land. For all these reasons, Idelson argued, now that Britain's material control of the country was absolute, the Zionists' best course was quite the contrary of what Weizmann and his friends had in mind: it was to do all they could to make the issue an *international* one *before* Britain's formal authority there had been generally confirmed. That there was opposition to Britain in this respect was clear. It might be that the stronger the opposition by other powers to British suzerainty and

---

[26] On Idelson, editor of *Razsvet*, Russian Zionism's most important journal at this time, and the leading spirit behind the Helsingfors Programme of 1906, see *Formative Years*, pp. 464 ff.

the more equally balanced the competing forces, the greater the chance of expanding and consolidating Jewish rights in the country.[27]

That said, such scepticism—certainly when coupled to so ingenious a readjustment and reformulation of the old policy of neutrality—was confined to the higher reaches of the movement. The electric surge of emotion and anticipation that went through the greater part of Russian Jewry in all its variety of belief and political tendency upon the publication of Balfour's Declaration was vastly more powerful and its effects longer-lasting (except on the extreme left where, on very different grounds, suspicion of imperial Britain and fear of anything that might divert 'Jewish workers [from] . . . their struggle against the criminal ambitions of the international bourgeoisie, the Jewish one included,' were entrenched).[28]

Once again, as in Herzl's time, the enthusiastic popular response to the achievements, real or illusory, of distant, self-appointed spokesmen for the Jewish interest agitated the prudent *cognoscenti*, all too conscious of weakness, of paucity of means, and of the evident obstacles to progress on the ground, and fearful lest matters get out of hand and be followed by collapse. Once again they had no choice but to put a good face on things, the more so as their own position and that of their constituents was weakening steadily as revolution, civil war, the German occupation of large parts of the old Empire, rapidly multiplying attacks on Jews as such, and general turbulence was destroying not only their movement but their society as a whole. Besides, they were themselves, in their hearts, by no means immune to the promise the Declaration seemed to hold out—for all its deliberate imprecision—and to the striking departure from all previous political practice represented by a world power openly and explicitly championing a Jewish national cause. Despite their fears and their memories of countless false starts, they had no wish, as they explained, 'to cool down the tremendous enthusiasm' the Declaration had evoked and damp down the general aspiration to move in great numbers and with firm economic plans in mind to Erez-Israel.[29] To that end the Russian movement's Palestine Department was reorganized and strengthened and charged with

---

[27] 'O real'noi tsennosti deklaratsii Bal'fura' (On the real value of the Balfour Declaration), exposé before the Russian Zionist Central Committee, 6 October 1918, Petrograd. *Sbornik Pamyati A. D. Idelsona* (Berlin, 1925), pp. 261–71.

[28] From a manifesto by the Bund, 2 December 1917. CZA, A77/3B.

[29] Goldberg to Jacobson, 2 January 1918. CZA, Z3/892.

co-ordinating the expected flow of settlers, the channelling of resources, and the collection and distribution of accurate information on conditions and possibilities for all concerned.[30]

In the event, they had a great deal less to do than they had hoped for. In western Russia, the very heart of the Pale but now under German occupation, local Zionists looked to Berlin perforce for guidance.[31] By May 1918 the Central Committee of the Russian wing of the movement, meeting in Moscow, with its eye plainly on the ever firmer consolidation of the Bolsheviks in power, resolved on a prudential retreat from political action and renewed emphasis on economic and philanthropic activity. It reaffirmed the 'neutral orientation'. It recognized its inability to lead from the centre by establishing 'provincial central offices' in Kiev and Minsk.[32] In July it was still possible to review the progress made since the great Zionist assembly in Petrograd the year before, and to note with satisfaction that the number of local associations had risen to 1,200, that groups of pioneers (*haluzim*) had been forming for immediate settlement, that 60 per cent of the vote for the planned Jewish national assembly (never in fact allowed to convene) was pro-Zionist, and that there were good grounds for estimating the total membership of the movement in Russia at a quarter of a million. Nevertheless, the concluding note was one of deep foreboding. 'Our movement has grown and proliferated,' was the summing-up for the benefit of the EAC, but a crisis was 'imminent'.[33] Perhaps most telling of the weakening and isolation of the great Russian wing of the Zionist movement in the course of the single year 1918 was a discussion held in its Central Committee on the questions who, how, when, and if at all its representatives should join the Zionist Commission that Weizmann was leading to Erez-Israel—a discussion conducted in a fog of unresolvable dilemmas and uncertainties and lack of solid information. Ussishkin, Goldberg, and Rosov were all slated to go. But would it be possible to leave Russia? Would Weizmann still be in the country when they got there? What were the functions of the Commission? And, most fundamentally, what precisely could they and should they be charged to do in the light of the greatest uncertainty of all, namely, what the British were

[30] Goldberg to Ruppin, 11 February 1918. CZA, Z3/892.
[31] Kaplan (Minsk) to Hantke, 30 March 1918. CZA, Z3/892.
[32] Central Committee to Copenhagen, 19 May 1918. CZA, Z3/892.
[33] Petrograd to Berlin [11 July 1918]. CZA, Z3/892.
[34] Central Committee, minutes, 3 June 1918. CZA, F30/128.

prepared to grant the Jews? Would it be political autonomy broadly conceived or no more than a Charter? No persuasive answers to these questions were propounded. No decision was taken. No Russian Zionist of standing joined the Commission on its initial journey.[34]

iii

The steady and accelerating enfeeblement of the Russian wing of the movement helped greatly to free Weizmann's hand as he propelled his way to the overall leadership. With Tchlenov dead, with the other principal members of the Russian leadership cut off ever more decisively as much from the west[35] as from their own constituents, with Sokolov being slowly reduced to (and increasingly perceived as) Weizmann's junior rather than senior colleague,[36] and with Jabotinsky as good as out of the way because in uniform and soon to embark for Palestine with his regiment, there were virtually no effective competitors. The American wing of the movement was as yet too new and too remote and still too uncertain of itself—even of its precise purposes—to make its full weight felt. When in February 1918 it conceded leadership to the London group it had, in any case, moved by considerations of efficiency as much as by anything else, made it a specific condition that affairs be governed by a single responsible leader: Weizmann. The Americans, unlike the Russians, were well satisfied, at any rate at this stage, with what he was judged to have accomplished. 'Things in England are in wonderfully good shape,' Felix Frankfurter reported back to Washington for Brandeis's benefit. 'The political work there has been handled with an effectiveness that just challenges admiration to us all for its persistent skill and far-sighted statesmanship.'[37] But the first fully public and therefore crowning confirmation of Weizmann's new status as the man of the hour was the appointment of a 'Zionist Commission' and its dispatch to Palestine under official British auspices with Weizmann as president and far and away its most considerable member. Here was an end to waiting in ante-rooms, to

[35] In September 1918 Goldberg complained from Petrograd that a full year had passed since he had last had a letter from London. 26 September 1918. CZA, L6/31/II.
[36] See for example the always alert Tolkowsky's comment on Sokolov's irresponsibility, in unstated, but implicit contrast with Weizmann's thoroughness and absolute seriousness. Tolkowsky, op. cit., p. 379.
[37] Frankfurter to de Haas, 1 April 1918. CZA, A264/26.

relying on intermediaries to make his contacts for him, to being of a status and authority so uncertain even towards the end of 1917 that Balfour's letter of 2 November could not, so the Foreign Office thought, even be addressed to him. He was sent off to the Levant with Balfour's special blessing, with letters of recommendation to Allenby,[38] with an Assistant Cabinet Secretary (Ormsby-Gore) as military member of the Commission and its liaison officer to the occupation forces in Palestine, and, after some hesitation in Whitehall,[39] an audience of the King. There might be concern in Petrograd and Copenhagen about the Commission's competence and Weizmann's intentions;[40] in effect, he was to all intents and purposes his own master, and almost as close to mastery of Zionism as he could reasonably hope to be.

The idea of such a Commission had first come up in the discussions of the Zionist Political Committee that had formed around Weizmann in London in July 1917. This was not an elected body. It was not a recognized, statutory institution of the Zionist Organization or even of the local English Zionist Federation. Strictly speaking, it was no more than an invited, informal group, almost a club, established explicitly to serve Weizmann in an advisory and consultative capacity and implicitly to bolster his authority. The only members of established reputation in Jewry were Sokolov and Aḥad Ha-ʿAm and their presence was therefore crucial. But it was Weizmann who dominated the discussions. It was he who gave its deliberations such coherence as it had. And if, at the same time, and not infrequently, it was ignored by him (a state of affairs in which Sokolov and the junior members generally acquiesced, but which Aḥad Ha-ʿAm stiffly resented)[41] the cumulative result was to confirm and reconfirm him as the strong (and perhaps truly indispensable) man. It was therefore characteristic both of the uses and the weakness of the Committee that it considered in advance of the November Declaration how the Zionists might in practice establish themselves in Ereẓ-Israel once the British were in place, and that its original idea—that a body be formed to act as a sort of semi-governmental Jewish authority—was hopelessly over-ambitious. Materially, the Zionists, as they would

---

[38] From Lloyd George and Balfour, both dated 1 March 1918. CZA, A264/26.

[39] Balfour to Stamfordham, 2 March 1918. PRO, FO 800/204.

[40] Rosenblüth (speaking for Victor Jacobson) to Oettinger, 3 March 1918. CZA, A18/17/16.

[41] Aḥad Ha-ʿAm to Weizmann, 4 September 1917. *Igrot AH*, vi, pp. 83–4.

soon grasp, had neither the men nor the resources for large-scale settlement and administration of any kind. Politically, a 'state within a state' was wholly incompatible with anything the Government in London—and *a fortiori* its representative in the Near East—had in mind for Palestine, or with what international law was taken to lay down in respect of territories under wartime military occupation, or with political and demographic realities on the ground in the country itself. But it was accepted in official London that the Declaration had to be followed up with real steps, that Weizmann and his friends would be severely criticized if nothing were done, that existing Jewish settlements were indeed beset, as the Zionists had argued, with urgent problems of wartime and post-war relief, livelihood, and security, and that, in sum, the formation and despatch of a Zionist mission to Palestine to 'work under [the] guidance of . . . [the] military authorities' was 'inevitable as a natural development of [the] Zionist movement'.[42]

The terms of reference of the Commission (as it was to be called) were carefully whittled down by the Foreign Office. It was to form a 'link' between the British authorities and the Jewish population of the country. It was to deal with relief work and to help the *yishuv* back on its feet after the wartime dislocation. It was to try to foster good relations with the Arab population. It was to investigate possibilities for further economic development of the *yishuv* and of the country in general. It was to see whether a university could be established in Jerusalem. And to these stated ends and subject to military exigencies it would be free to travel. Military operations still being in progress (Allenby's army held to a static, east-west line across the country just north of Jerusalem until his breakthrough in September 1918), the Commission would be composed exclusively of nationals of the Allied countries. In the event, the Russians were unable to join, the Americans were dissuaded from doing so by a State Department insisting that the United States was not at war with Turkey and that its nationals should not be involved in a military occupation of Turkish territory, the only French member was Sylvain Lévi, a distinguished scholar and a loyal and active member of the Alliance Israélite Universelle but no Zionist, and the Italian member, a late arrival, was a worthy but politically obscure naval officer, Angelo Levi-Bianchini. The result was to focus the spotlight still more powerfully on Weizmann. He towered above his

[42] Foreign Office to Clayton, 11 December 1917. Hull, SP, DDSY 2/11/79.

colleagues. He dominated their proceedings. It was he who conducted all the Commission's essential business with the British, Arab, and Jewish leaders. He had some cause to ask his wife rhetorically after a while, 'What will happen when I leave? Who is to replace me?'[43]

The Commission did useful work. It re-established firm contact between the *yishuv* and the rest of Jewry and with the Zionist movement in particular. It organized relief. It carried out some initial surveys of the country with a view to development and settlement. It set up functional departments (agriculture and settlement, education, land, finance, immigration, statistics) for which the Zionist Organization's Palestine Office established under Warburg by Arthur Ruppin[44] provided the nucleus and to some extent the model. Ruppin's assistant, Ya'akov Thon was co-opted. Ruppin himself, although a German national, was eventually allowed to return and join in the work. It was a small affair; but, in retrospect, it may be said to have functioned as the embryo of the Jewish 'state within a state'—the institutions of Jewish self-government, crowned eventually by the Jewish Agency for Palestine —that were to follow in due course after all.

For the time being its real importance lay elsewhere, however: in the fact that its seemingly triumphant arrival immediately brought to a head those issues, tensions, and conflicts that were to cloud the newly established relationship between Great Britain and the Zionists virtually at birth and ultimately destroy it. It revealed a fatal initial disjunction between the purposes, concerns, and perspective of those who governed the Near East on behalf of official London and those who ruled in official London itself. It proved, over time, that there was more than one framework of political and moral reference in which British officialdom would be operating, and varying and incompatible views of where British national interests lay. It served immediately to demonstrate that Sykes's expectation of a British system of overlordship founded on the three mutually reinforcing pillars of Arab, Armenian, and Jewish nationalism was a mirage.

On the morrow of the publication of the Balfour Declaration, Sykes, from the Foreign Office in London, had telegraphed Clayton,

[43] Weizmann to Vera Weizmann, 17 June 1918. *Weizmann Letters*, viii, no. 213. p. 209.
[44] See above, pp. 67 ff.

the Chief Political Officer of the EEF, that 'it is most urgent to my mind that you get your Arab Committee in Cairo into being once more and impress upon them the vital necessity of Jewish and Armenian good-will.'[45] Clayton's response was cautious, not hostile, but the difference between the respective mental worlds he and Sykes inhabited must have come across very clearly to anyone reading it with care. He was at pains to emphasize 'how absolutely military the whole situation' still was and that Jerusalem and Jaffa were still within range of enemy guns. Beyond that, he could, he said, 'see [Sykes's] arguments regarding an Arab-Jew-Armenian combine and the advantages that would accrue if it could be brought off.' He and his colleagues on the spot would indeed try to do so, but only

very cautiously[;] and, honestly, I see no great chance of any real success. It is an attempt to change in a few weeks the traditional sentiment of centuries. The Arab cares nothing whatsoever about the Armenian one way or the other—as regards the Jew the Bedouin despises him and will never do anything else, while the sedentary Arab hates the Jew, and fears his superior commercial and economic ability.

He was in no position, he said, to estimate the weight the Zionists carried, especially in America and Russia, 'and of the consequent necessity of giving them everything for which they ask.' But it was clear to him that in so doing there was the risk of Arab unity 'becoming something like an accomplished fact and being ranged against us.' Clayton did not go so far as to say that he thought Arab distrust of 'the Jew' was well founded and that 'the Jew' was indeed, as 'the Arab' thought, namely 'prone to extract his pound of flesh'. But he did think that 'We have therefore to consider whether the situation demands out and out support of Zionism at the risk of alienating the Arabs at a critical moment.'[46]

Clayton expected little of the Arabs as military allies of the British, and does not seem to have thought of them at this stage as reliable political allies in the future. What he wanted to avoid were the 'dangers and difficulties' he feared were in the offing. He was a politically sensitive man and aware that he and his colleagues in the Levant were 'apt to become local' and lose their grasp of 'the whole situation'.[47] Allenby, the Commander-in-Chief, and General Arthur

---

[45] 14 November 1917. Hull, SP, DDSY 2/11/73.
[46] Clayton to Sykes, 15 December 1917. Hull, SP, DDSY 2/11/83.
[47] Ibid.

Money, who took over as Chief Administrator of Palestine[48] some weeks after the arrival of the Zionist Commission, had a much simpler—it could be said, reduced—view of the matter. Allenby's mind was on the campaign. Money went by the book, and the book laid down that it was the duty of an occupying power to maintain the *status quo ante bellum* subject only to military requirements. Neither was much interested in 'the whole [political] situation'. Allenby could not be troubled with it except sporadically. Money was outside the political-diplomatic net altogether: unlike Clayton, who continued to serve as Chief Political Officer, he had no direct line to or contact with the Foreign Office. What he was chiefly intent upon was keeping his sphere of operations and responsibility trouble-free, and in this he naturally had the warm support of Allenby. The fact that the arrival of the Commission and its continued presence in the country promptly gave rise to a series of Arab protests, demonstrations, warnings of disaffection, and street-disturbances on a rising scale of intensity did nothing to commend it or the movement it represented (and in a sense personified) to General Money. The fact that the Commission was intent upon introducing *change* into the system (such as it was) by which Palestine had been governed and its society and economy ordered necessarily put it at cross-purposes with one who was determined to stray as little as possible from what was implied by the 'Laws and Usages of War'. The fact that Money himself was wedded to a vulgar form of stereotypical thinking when it came to foreign nations and races—and to Jews in particular—gave an additional twist to his *a priori* hostility because it rendered it not only fiercer and somewhat nastier, but also almost entirely uncomprehending. An entry in his diary after his first meeting with Weizmann late in April 1918 gives the flavour of his thinking:

We very naturally are not too keen on [the Zionists'] policy as tending to upset the Arabs in Palestine. . . . The trouble about all these Jewish schemes is that, however skilfully ruled, they are rather open to the suspicion of having some financial end in the background, as the Jew is not in the habit of going to out of the way parts of the world solely for the benefit of his health.[49]

---

[48] The military government of Palestine was defined formally as Occupied Enemy Territory Administration (OETA). When the British pushed into Syria the title was amended to OETA (S[outh]).

[49] Quoted in Bernard Wasserstein, *The British in Palestine*, (London, 1978), p. 25.

Money's outlook was shared by many, perhaps most, of his colleagues, subordinates, and successors, civilian as well as military. It was of the age.[50] It did not determine the fate of the new Anglo-Jewish alliance. But it coloured it and injected it with a poison that was never eradicated.

Still, the credentials of the Commission, having been provided by the central Government in London, were impeccable. In such circumstances no firm line of resistance to the Zionists could be openly or even covertly defined, let alone cleaved to. In practice, therefore, the conduct of the men on the spot, the new rulers of Palestine, tended to oscillate between, on the one hand, bursts of outright opposition and of resentment at being compelled to take on what could not fail to appear to them as an egregious burden and, on the other hand, minor concessions and compromises, attempts to bring Arabs and Jews together (despite scepticism in that regard), and pressure on Weizmann to hold back the more enthusiastic, radical, and determined of his colleagues and followers. In the case of the long, passionate fight to establish Hebrew as an official language—a cardinal issue of principle to the Zionists, an additional potential irritant to the nationalist Arabs, a plain deviation from the *status quo ante bellum*—OETA eventually conceded the point. Hebrew was admitted, although in the junior position after English, French, and Arabic.[51] The foundation of a university was agreed to as well, but not much more. A series of meetings between Arab notables and

[50] See above, pp. 102–4. There were exceptions to what the Zionists tended ever more strongly to perceive as the rule of British anti-Semitism laced with romantic Arabophilia, at any rate where Palestine was concerned. The most notable in these early years was Colonel Richard Meinertzhagen, appointed Chief Political Officer in September 1919. Beginning (like Sykes) as what might be termed a simple-minded anti-Semite, he became an open, fervid pro-Zionist and developed views on Jews and Arabs that were as fierce as any, but the precise reverse of those common among his colleagues. 'The Jew [is] virile, brave, determined and intelligent,' he wrote Lloyd George on one occasion. 'The Arab [is] decadent, stupid, dishonest.' *Middle East Diary 1917–1956* (London, 1959), p. 17. The entire subject of such stereotypical thinking and its influence on political, diplomatic, and strategic policy in the Middle East is at once familiar, important, and badly in need of close investigation. Whether such investigation can itself ever be free of such thinking remains an open question.

[51] Cox, Assistant Administrator, OETA(S), to military governors of Jerusalem, etc. 17 July 1919. CZA, A18/38/1. The rules laid down were very precise: where identical texts were to be published in vertical order, 'English will be above French which will be above Arabic which will be above Hebrew. . . . When written in the same line or in parallel columns the order from left to right will be English, French, Arabic, Hebrew. If Arabic and Hebrew alone are used, Arabic will be to the right of Hebrew.' Upon Britain's assumption of the formal mandate for Palestine, French was dropped. Otherwise these rules were followed to the end (in 1948).

members of the Commission were arranged in Cairo, Jerusalem, and Jaffa, culminating in a visit by Weizmann to Britain's principal Arab protégé, the Emir Feisal, at the latter's camp near Ma'an early in June 1918.

In general, on these Jewish-Arab occasions, courtesy reigned and the tone was cordial. Weizmann emphasized repeatedly that there was no question of a Jewish Government being established, that the Zionists' immediate interest was in British rule, and that the Zionists would certainly respect the legitimate interests of others. There was no attempt by either side to explore the other's views and purposes, especially remoter purposes, in depth. The differences between local Arab notables in Palestine and other figures in the Arab world—such as Syrian exiles in Cairo or, more particularly, Feisal of the Hedjaz—who, having their eye on greater prizes, were prepared to be conciliatory for the time being in respect of Palestine—tended to be taken at face value by the Zionists. The Arabs for their part had still to make their assessment of Jewish power and influence in London and other major capitals. As the full extent of the British commitment to France under Sykes-Picot and the consequent uncertainty about the future of Syria began to be realized, the uses of the Zionists as allies in the coming effort to enlarge and bolster the British presence in the Levant at France's expense were not to be dismissed. So here at least something of what Sykes had had in mind seemed to be in the making—to his and Clayton's satisfaction.

Weizmann himself was delighted by friendly words and undismayed by others. He had taken note of local Arab hostility very soon after his arrival in Palestine. Making no effort to probe it, he had first put it down to 'misconception of our real aims' (which he had tried to remove by defining them for the notables' benefit in appropriately moderate terms). That having failed and the Arab spokesmen being, as it seemed, convinced that 'Palestine was and would remain a purely Arab country', he felt it was for the British to bring the Arabs of Palestine

to realise the actual position and the intentions of the Government, and that this work of education can be carried out only by the Authorities themselves. It is of no use for us to attempt it, because the Arabs, as far as we can tell, are not in a frame of mind in which any explanations offered by us would receive serious attention. What is necessary is that the exact meaning and scope of Mr. Balfour's Declaration should be authoritatively explained to them, and that it should be made perfectly clear to them that this declaration represents the considered policy of H.M. Government, and that it is their duty to conform to it.[52]

So much for the Palestinian Arabs. With Feisal he was in another world, more familiar and more to his taste, the world of high politics, of men of power and recognized and effective authority. 'I feel I do not need to concern myself with the [Palestine] Arabs any more,' he had written to his wife a month earlier; 'we have done everything that was required of us, we have explained our point of view publicly and openly: *c'est à prendre ou à laisser*.'[53] He had not much liked the Arab notables he had met in Jaffa and Jerusalem; and he had tended to distrust them. Feisal was different: 'the first real Arab nationalist' he had met, 'a leader!' Not interested in Palestine and contemptuous of the Palestinian Arabs 'whom he doesn't even regard as Arabs!' It was Damascus he wanted and the whole of 'northern Syria'. 'He talked with great animosity against the French,' Weizmann noted, and 'expects a great deal from collaboration with the Jews'.[54] Generally, the views he had formulated in London long before he set out for the Levant seemed to be amply confirmed. 'The centre of gravity is in the Hedjaz,' he had told the Political Committee in November 1917.[55]

Weizmann was thus encouraged (and he encouraged others)[56] to distinguish very sharply between the wider Arab national movement led, as he thought, by Feisal and the uncomprehending and troublesome Arab notables of Palestine. The former would be the ally of the Zionists. The latter would have to be dealt with by the

---

[52] Weizmann to Ormsby-Gore, 16 April 1918. *Weizmann Letters*, viii, no. 161, pp. 128–30.

[53] Weizmann to Vera Weizmann, 30 April 2 May 1918. Ibid., no. 181, p. 171.

[54] Weizmann to Vera Weizmann, 17 June 1918. Ibid., no. 213, p. 210. The French themselves, as Weizmann would have been the first to recognize, had no reason to welcome an Arab-Zionist *entente*. But in fact they took a cooler (and more penetrating) view of the meeting. 'For all that the president of the Zionist delegation was received with great courtesy, the Emir was very reserved,' Picot's assistant informed Paris. 'To the advances made him, he replied that his father alone was qualified to deal with political questions; but he added that personally he was in favour of co-operation between all the elements which wished to chase the Turks out of the Arab lands [*pays arabes*].' Coulondre to Foreign Ministry, 13 June 1918. AE, 1918–1940, Série Y, Internationale, vol. 377, fo. 14. The last two words of the telegram were not particularly emphasized, but could well have been.

[55] Tolkowsky, op. cit., p. 230.

[56] Brandeis among others. See Weizmann to Brandeis, 23 June 1918. *Weizmann Letters*, viii, no. 215, p. 213.

British. He had done what he could in that respect. 'At the top' matters were improving, he assured Sokolov after a while. They were less satisfactory 'below, i.e. the military governors and their offices—and it is they who mainly run the country—do not understand us, and many of them do not wish to!'[57] But that was a problem that could only be solved, ultimately, in London. And there, he felt, the position of the Zionists was strongest of all. Certainly, the view from London could be very different.

As political advisor on Near Eastern affairs [Sykes wrote Lloyd George on 2 September 1918] I have had full opportunity of seeing how things have been run for the last eight months, and I think that on the whole it may be considered that the military-political developments have been fairly satisfactory. Our Arab, Syrian, and Palestinian policy has not landed us in any great difficulties and has on the other hand given us a considerable return in prestige, booty and enemy casualties. We have friendly populations, native allies, and good material and moral assets for a peace conference.[58]

Weizmann left Ereẓ-Israel in September. The Zionist Commission continued to function, its status still imperfectly defined, for several years. All—British, Arabs,and Jews—were uncertain what to make of it. But while its future was outside the bounds of reasonable calculation, it became, for the present, a focus of attention, and therefore of somewhat shadowy authority, for the modernist-Zionist part of the *yishuv*. It served as a channel of communication between the *yishuv* and the military authorities and thus acquired a certain representative function as well. It became— by sheer inertia, as it were—an accepted part of the country's political and institutional landscape and, as such, strongly symbolic of the metamorphosis the country was undergoing as Turkish rule was replaced by British. In brief, it reflected with some precision the evident imprecision of British goals, promises, outlook and, above all, practical intentions.

In certain respects, Weizmann returned to London (early in October 1918) with mixed impressions and feelings. The new *yishuv* had delighted him ('strong and healthy young generation of fresh and beautiful children, speaking, singing and playing in Hebrew . . . [in] modest, but clean villages').[59] Parts of the old *yishuv*, especially

[57] Weizmann to Sokolov, 23 June 1918. Ibid., no. 217, pp. 214–15.
[58] Sykes to Lloyd George, 2 September 1918. Hull, SP, DDSY 2/11/107.
[59] Weizmann to Brandeis, 25 April 1918. *Weizmann Letters*, viii, no. 175, p. 163.

the Jewish Quarter of the Old City of Jerusalem, had revolted him ('nothing but filth and infection. The indescribable poverty, stubborn ignorance and fanaticism—the heart aches when one looks at it all!')[60] His conclusion, so far as the work of settling and organizing the *yishuv* in all its aspects was concerned, was that if the task was formidable, it was not an impossible one. His leadership and outlook had been accepted in the main by the Zionists of the *yishuv.* For their part, they would serve, as they had always been expected to serve, as the nucleus of the greater enterprise that was to follow. They were few, but there would be others. In any case there was the will; there was a foothold. What was needed were the funds. These, now that there was little to be expected from Russia, would have to come largely from the United States: close to half a million pounds sterling, urgently, in the first instance in the interim period before the status and governance of the country had been settled at the Peace Conference, much more later on. To that end he applied to Brandeis to assume the relevant responsibility and considered travelling to the United States to press the case himself.

But the key to all things at this stage was a political one, and manifestly it was the British who held it. He recognized that the 'general attitude in the Army' was not satisfactory, for all that he had set himself to 'explain and preach Zionism' at every opportunity.[61] Yet he was far from despairing. He had found a sympathetic ear in Clayton and in Wyndham Deedes, another senior intelligence officer, and of course in Ormsby-Gore.[62] And, all told, he had got on well with Allenby.[63] He had grounds for concluding that the higher the level at which he operated and the more politically minded the officials and officers concerned, the easier it was to find a common language and to identify common interests. In this sense, his experience in Palestine only strengthened his conviction that the *locus* of the key to all major questions remained London. His own growing confidence in the strength of his own position there—and therefore in his ability to turn that key—is illustrated in a remarkably vigorous 5,000-word letter to Balfour in which he sketched what he took to be the outlines of the situation in

---

[60] Weizmann to Vera Weizmann, 18 April 1918. Ibid., no. 163, p. 133.

[61] Weizmann to Aḥad Ha-'Am, 3 August 1918. Ibid., no. 245, pp. 249–50.

[62] 'It is my firm conviction,' Ormsby-Gore wrote Sykes from Tel-Aviv, 'that the Zionists are the one sound firmly pro-British, constructive element in the whole show.' 9 April 1918. Hull, SP, DDSY 2/11/96.

[63] Clayton to Sykes, 4 April 1918. Durham, SA, CP, G/15 513/1.

Palestine, presenting a long catalogue of misfortunes, errors, and built-in obstacles to the success of what he assumed British policy to be.

There had been the damage done to British prestige by the failure to keep up the momentum of the military advance, the injury to Zionism consequent on local British equivocation on Balfour's own Declaration, the fatal contrast between doubtless well-meaning but innocent British officials and corrupt former (Arab) servants of the Turks through whom the country was being administered in practice, the continual retreat before ever more arrogant and demanding Arabs by 'nervous' British administrators 'knowing as they do the treacherous nature of the Arab', and the growing disappointment, even 'despair and bitterness', of 'our own people' to whom Weizmann and his colleagues had done their 'level best to explain the situation.' Palestine, in sum, was being handed over to the Arabs, and the *yishuv* with it; and 'the question now at issue,' he summed up, '. . . is what the British occupation of Palestine is going to mean.' Had the capture of Jerusalem merely been the capture of 'a city of dirt and squalor, a home of physical and moral disease, and sorry domain of a corrupt Arab municipality', or 'the centre of a nation's traditions and hopes, a city whose name sends a thrill of reverence and aspiration through millions of hearts'? What was happening in the country bore upon what would transpire at the Peace Conference, Weizmann argued. He himself would be going to the United States to rally American Jewry—and, he was sure, non-Jewish opinion too—behind Anglo-Zionist purposes. A congress of representative Jews in Palestine was also being planned. Such voices, 'I venture to think,' he put it to Balfour, 'will not pass unheard at the Peace Conference. But the possibility of formulating a clear, strong and representative demand will exist only if the Jewish people knows that during the period of British occupation the foundations of the National Home have been laid in Palestine.'[64]

[64] Weizmann to Balfour, 30 May 1918. *Weizmann Letters*, viii, no. 208, pp. 197–206. In the event, Weizmann's journey to the United States did not materialize. The Americans, impressed by what they had heard of his achievements in Palestine advised him to stay there. They agreed that he might 'from time to time have business in England', but the main thing was for him to remain with the Commission in Palestine and 'develop an administration to which America will as freely as possible contribute technical experts.' Aaronson (speaking for Brandeis *et al.*) to Weizmann, 24 September 1918. Yale, WP, 666/11/282.

A reminder? A warning?[65] At the very least, an attempt to pull the vehicle back onto the rails upon which he believed it had been mounted. Feisal and 'the real Arab movement . . . developing in Mecca and Damascus' provide the solution so far as the Arabs and larger British interests in the Levant were concerned, he assured Balfour in a second message some weeks later. To this 'those who know the local situation fully' (i.e. the real experts in Cairo, as opposed to the temporary administrators in Jerusalem) agreed. There was still the Sykes-Picot Agreement, an obstacle as much to Arab as to Zionist aspirations, a focus of 'political intrigue which obscures the true vision and runs counter to the principle of real self-determination' and to which Picot and his circle 'cling for dear life'. Plainly, Weizmann was trying to tell Balfour, it would have to be abrogated. And venturing still further into territory in which his grasp of matters, let alone his *locus standi*, was exceedingly imperfect, he pointed out to the Foreign Secretary how ill co-ordinated were the various local centres of policy, military and civilian, and how unfortunate was the absence of a single authority and clear lines of communication and instruction from London.[66] Here was a man who now saw himself as more partner than supplicant.

[65] If so, it failed. 'It is very interesting but hardly optimistic,' was Balfour's only marginal comment on Weizmann's letter. [17 July 1917]. PRO, FO 371/3395, fo. 144.

[66] Weizmann to Balfour, 17 July 1918. *Weizmann Letters*, viii, no. 232, pp. 228–32.

9

On the Threshold

i

By the end of September 1918 the conquest of Palestine by British forces was complete—almost simultaneously with the breaking of the Hindenburg Line on the Western Front. Within a little more than a month the Great War was over. Ten weeks later, on 18 January 1919, the long-awaited Peace Conference—at which all but the very shrewdest and best-informed believed, and had long anticipated, that all great questions would finally be discussed and settled, justice done, and a new, improved international order instituted—was convened in Paris. If this was not to be, it was not least because it was indeed the greatest assembly of statesmen, diplomats, historical, economic, statistical, demographic, and military experts, all with their attendant secretaries, printers, drivers, guards, and other minions, ever convened. Under the Council of Ten representing the five 'Principal' Allied Powers, greater and lesser councils, secretariats, commissions, and committees (territorial, 'new states', *ad hoc*, drafting, and negotiating) proliferated. Some thirty official delegations representing states attended the Conference. Countless other groups and individuals representing, or claiming to represent, nations that had not yet, but hoped to achieve statehood were in attendance. The consequent confusion and complexity were intensified and multiplied several times over by the incompatible purposes of the major delegations, by the secrecy in which much of the Conference's business was inevitably (and necessarily) conducted, by the absences for long periods of the Big Three (Wilson, Lloyd George, and Clemenceau), by the relative efficiency and coherence of some delegations (the British, notably) as opposed to the lack of solid preparation and the internal disorder pervading others (among them the French), by problems of language and mentality, and by the plain logistical difficulty of housing, feeding, and bringing together in the right combinations and at the right times several hundred privileged, preoccupied, often overworked and not unnaturally self-important servants of their respective countries. Finally, the ability of the assembled delegates to deal thoroughly and comprehensively with the political ills of the world was further vitiated by two additional, near-fatal character-istics of the business laid before them. Some topics were plainly of central—and therefore overriding—importance and urgency, chief among them being that of the strategic situation and future military capabilities of Germany. By the same token, others were perceived as correspondingly marginal to the concerns of the major powers and treated accordingly—which is to say, either delegated to 'experts' or relegated to a later date (and, often, a later, continuation conference). The treaty of peace with Turkey, soon to be a dead letter anyway, was not signed at Sèvres until August 1920, long after the Peace Conference proper at Paris had dispersed. The second characteristic of virtually all topics listed for consideration—and the list tended to grow as the Conference proceeded—was their sheer intricacy: intricacy of substance (demography, history, topography, and other such features of the European landscape in particular); intricacy of conception and design (as in the case of Wilson's insistence on a League of Nations as a cure for international conflict, the Covenant of the League being incorporated as an integral part of the several treaties of peace).

In these circumstances, that the question of Palestine was never seriously taken up in Paris is anything but surprising. But in fact, to all intents and purposes, the central issue in its regard, whether its future would be governed by the terms of the Sykes-Picot Agreement or not, had been disposed of before the Peace Conference ever convened. Three weeks after the end of hostilities, in the course of a major conference of the Allied Governments in London (2–4 December 1918), Clemenceau was persuaded privately by Lloyd George to agree to Palestine and Mosul being allotted to Great Britain when the expected distribution of spoils of war in the Near East took place.[1] The meeting was *tête-à-tête*. No written record of what transpired was made; or at any rate, none survived. A great

---

[1] *DBFP*, First series, iv, p. 251.

deal of wrangling on the subject between the two ensued a year later.[2] But there was never any doubt on either side—at all events at the highest level—that a deal on some such lines had been concluded and that Sykes-Picot was dead or dying, however long it would take *all* the French parties, administrative corps, and schools of opinion concerned to admit it. The fury of the French colonialist and Catholic lobbies when news of the deal leaked out and the lack of regular documentation notwithstanding, no French Government sought seriously, in the end, to deny, let alone break it. There remained (and still remains) the question what it was that Clemenceau had obtained, or thought he had obtained, as the counterpart of the concessions made to the British in the Levant. Probably it was a promise of British diplomatic and strategic support for France in the arena on which his eyes had always been fixed unerringly and unblinkingly, namely that in which the Franco-German conflict, as he believed, would continue to be played out. But that was not a promise Lloyd George could allow himself to commit to paper, least of all in the terms Clemenceau would assuredly have wished to have it stated. As for the Levant itself, Clemenceau had never had much interest in or regard for it.[3] Much later, at the San Remo Conference, in April 1920, when the matter of Palestine was at last taken up for final disposition in earnest, Clemenceau's successor complained only mildly that he was 'not precisely informed as to what had transpired during the discussions which Mr. Lloyd George had held with M. Clemenceau on this subject.' He would rely perforce on his British colleague to provide 'precise information'. To which Lloyd George's prompt reply, neatly encapsulating the two chief British arguments for abandoning Sykes-Picot, was that

[b]oth he and M. Clemenceau had agreed that any régime of an international character would almost certainly lead to trouble, and that therefore it was preferable that the mandate for Palestine should be committed to a single Power, and that Power should appropriately be Great Britain, as the conqueror of Palestine.[4]

---

[2]   See, for example, the bitter exchange of messages in October 1919 between Clemenceau and Lloyd George following the formulation, by the British, of modalities for the occupation of Syria, Palestine, and Mesopotamia by the two powers. Lothian Papers, SRO, GD40/17/1343.

[3]   And he was impervious to its charms. 'Syria, Palestine, Jerusalem, they're all a kind of lice heap,' he observed in extreme old age. Jean Martet, *Clemenceau* (London, 1930), p. 258.

[4]   *DBFP*, First series, viii, no. 15, pp. 163–4.

If the Jewish interest in the country and the Balfour Declaration specifically were touched upon at all at that very private meeting between Clemenceau and Lloyd George, which is doubtful, it could not have been more than tangentially and as an afterthought. Later, in their fierce exchange of messages in October 1919, where Lloyd George referred to the 'understanding' arrived at in December of the previous year, he did add, somewhat piously, that 'the sentiments of the inhabitants of Palestine, whether Arab or Zionist, appeared to favour a British Mandate.'[5] But that was all. What the ever stronger British determination to abandon, and the ever weaker French determination to uphold Sykes-Picot did not of themselves entail was an answer to the question of precisely what arrangement would replace it. The mandates system had yet to be worked out, and within the inner circle of British Government itself not all were as intent on control of Palestine as was Lloyd George. Balfour, for one, with a sharper eye for the the difficulties which seemed bound to ensue, had not entirely given up the idea of the Americans being talked into assuming the mandate.

Meanwhile, in any event, the Zionists wished to have their day in court to plead their case before the Conference along with so many others. There were none in the Zionist camp itself who objected to that, nor did the British oppose the idea. Still convinced (and encouraged to continue to believe) that Sykes-Picot constituted a major obstacle to their purposes, the London Zionists were pressing strongly everywhere and at every opportunity (at Weizmann's urging) for a British administration in Palestine; and that was certainly, so the British thought, to the good. The support of the Zionists added a mite of respectability to what otherwise had the look (especially when set against the lofty purposes to which the English-speaking allies in particular were publicly committed) of a very old-fashioned imperial exercise. For those whose minds were set upon control of Palestine for the purely strategic reasons formulated early in the war, the Zionists thus had their uses, even when the prospect of the Zionists *in* Palestine was now regarded with ever increasing apprehension and dislike. From the point of view of those, like Balfour, who were genuinely attracted to the idea of the re-establishment of the Jews in Palestine *per se* (however apprehensive they might now be about the burden Britain might be assuming), it was judged right and proper to grant them a formal hearing in any case.

[5]   Lloyd George to Clemenceau, 18 October 1919. SRO, GD40/17/1343/10.

The London Zionists took their expected appearance before the great men of the Council of Ten, along with the prospects of lobbying for their cause among the major and minor figures assembled in Paris, with great seriousness, and with a strong sense that it might be in their power to help tip the balance of relevant if imperfectly identified forces finally and decisively in the desired direction. They proceeded with enormous energy and determination. By the middle of December 1918 they had installed a delegation in Paris, headed by Sokolov, with Weizmann following on. A long series of conversations and presentations with and before everyone who was thought actually or potentially of influence and was prepared to listen to them ensued: President Wilson and Colonel House, Pichon and Berthelot, Masaryk and Huysmans, Nubar Pasha (the leader of the Armenians) and Edmond de Rothschild, Léon Bourgeois and, of course, as many of the notables and functionaries of British diplomacy present in Paris, from Balfour and Milner down the heirarchic line to Arnold Toynbee and Harold Nicolson, as could find time to see them. The vexed question was, what precisely should they be asking for?

Broadly, there were two schools of thought. One, in which American Zionists, representatives of the *yishuv*, and some of the Russians in touch with London (among them Jacobson) were prominent, believed that the demands and purposes of Zionism should be defined in large, confident, and explicit terms. The Jewish people had something important to say and deserved to be heard. The occasion was uniquely one for claiming ancient rights, one on which traditional caution and moderation were inappropriate and timidity likely to be fatal—not least because it was an occasion that would never recur. It was a school of thought comprised chiefly of those who tended to think in general—even somewhat abstract— terms, people who had not been involved in step-by-step negotiations with any of the victorious Powers during the war and were free of the burden of words heard and spoken and the other hostages to fortune steadily (and on the whole willingly) accumulated by those who had. The other school, of whom the London Zionists led by Weizmann and Sokolov were now, very naturally, the leading exponents, sought always to define and redefine their purposes in terms of what they believed possible and feasible and, not least, in close accord with their own increasingly set views on the international conjuncture that was most likely to favour the Zionist enterprise. They thought habitually, if not always explicitly, in terms of a continually amended compromise between what was desirable *a priori* and what the political traffic was likely to bear in practice. And it was their view that everything turned ultimately on the British connection; it would be the British, ultimately, who would determine—who already were determining—how far Zionist purposes and claims could be pressed. In the final analysis, the difference between the two schools was one of approach to the business of politics, and to diplomacy in particular. Did you set your goals and proceed towards them subject to modification in the light of circumstances? Or did you examine the circumstances and set your goals in the light of what was most likely to accord with your findings? In practice, the line distinguishing the two approaches (or, as some might term them: philosophies) one from the other can rarely be sharp. Thus with the Zionists. But it was none the less the latter school that tended to dominate the movement at this stage of its history.

The first formulation of the Zionist demands took shape as a compromise between what the first school thought of as 'asking too little' and the second school assessed as demands that were 'maximal' and unlikely to be met, at any rate in full.[6] The Peace Conference would be asked to recognize 'the historic right of the Jewish people to Palestine and their right to reconstitute Palestine as their National Home.' The political, administrative, and economic measures to be instituted would be, explicitly, 'to assure the development of Palestine into a Jewish commonwealth'. Under British trusteeship, the Chief Executive Officer of the country would be a Jew, and the majority of the members of the executive and legislative councils would be Jews as well, although the civil, religious, and representative rights of non-Jews would be protected. The means whereby the country's economy might be developed, its administration organized, and its land laws reformed were outlined. A Jewish Council for Palestine elected by a Jewish Congress representative of all Jewry to function, in effect, as the partner of the administration in all fields of public life— education, immigration, settlement, finance, and public works—was envisaged.

All this, embodied in a carefully worded 41-page document,[7] was

[6] Weizmann to Hacohen, 21 January 1919. *Weizmann Letters*, ix, no. 108, pp. 101–2.

[7] Memorandum of the Zionist Organisation relating to the Reconstitution of Palestine as the Jewish National Home, January 1919.

submitted to the British delegation to the Peace Conference for its approval at the end of January 1919 and promptly rejected as 'extravagant'. It was judged to have gone much further than anything previously demanded by 'responsible' Zionists. It was sure to cause distrust among Christians and Muslims by its insistence on 'a racial and religious test' to be applied to the Chief Executive or Governor, and by its demand for what its British critics considered 'gross over-representation of the Jews' in the country's future executive and legislative councils. The phrase 'Jewish commonwealth' was objected to particularly. 'It is clear,' the otherwise outstandingly friendly Ormsby-Gore minuted, 'that it involves steps towards the creation of what is practically and virtually[,] if not nominally[,] a Jewish Government in Palestine.' It was not Weizmann's fault, of that Ormsby-Gore was certain. Weizmann, he asserted, had hitherto been 'moderate and reasonable'; but he had been 'pushed along by the Jewish Jingoes of America and neutral countries who having been given an inch want an ell.' The Jews, it was agreed on all sides, would be unwise to put forward such proposals. In any event, His Majesty's Government, so Sokolov was informed, could not make itself in any way responsible for them.[8] The Zionists were of course free to do as they saw fit. But they must under no circumstances suggest that their proposals had been approved by the British Government. They could, if they wished, ask for Great Britain as the future mandatory power. But that too had to be on their own initiative; and they should know that if they and the Peace Conference insisted upon a constitution for the country as outlined in their memorandum, the British Government, for its part, was most unlikely to accept the duty of administering it.[9] In sum, the Zionists, Balfour laid down a few days later, 'must present their own case in their own way'. He would take no responsibility for advising them as to what they should or should not submit to the Peace Conference. Finally, to remove all doubt, all that had been said to them on this score was to be regarded, so Sokolov was carefully informed, as 'entirely unofficial and personal'.[10]

[8] Minutes by Ormsby-Gore, Mallet (the latter quoting Balfour), and Forbes Adam, 22, 23, and 27 January 1919. PRO, FO 608/98.

[9] Ormsby-Gore (citing Mallet and Drummond) to Sokolov, 24 January 1919. Ibid.

[10] Ormsby-Gore to Sokolov, 28 January 1919. CZA, A18/32/1. 'Now what is a Commonwealth?' Curzon, a greater critic of the Zionists, had remarked, on learning

In the face of this crushing rebuff there could be no argument. The memorandum on 'the reconstitution of Palestine as the Jewish National Home' was scrapped. Herbert Samuel was hastily called in to help produce a more acceptable redaction. A new, blander title was formulated. The text was cut by two-thirds. The proposals that had caused greatest indignation were wholly eliminated or drastically watered down. The Peace Conference would now be asked to recognize no more than 'the historical title of the Jewish people to Palestine and the right of the Jews to reconstitute *in* Palestine their National Home.' The mandate, still to be entrusted of course to Great Britain, was, the Zionists asked, to operate 'under such poltical, administrative and economic conditions as [would] secure the establishment there of the Jewish National Home and *ultimately* render *possible* the creation of an autonomous Commonwealth'. Jews would be 'entitled to [no more than] fair representation in the executive and legislative bodies and in the selection of public and civil servants'. The Jewish Council would, in effect, be a consultative body, hardly more.[11] All this was very much better in the eyes of the British officials to whom, once more, a draft was submitted and who now pronounced it 'moderate'.[12] The new text, first in English then in French, was formally deposited with the Conference's secretariat in February. The summons to the Council of Ten, they were informed, would be for a day at the end of the month.

ii

The summoning of the 'Zionist Mission' (as it was officially termed) to appear before the Council of Ten was fraught with immense— and for the Zionists exceptionally encouraging—symbolic import. Yet like so much in the tortuous, necessarily incomplete process by which modern Jewry has moved from being object to subject, it was an event flawed in a number of subtle but characteristic ways. The

what the Zionists had in mind. 'I turn to my dictionaries and find it thus defined: "A State." "A body politic." "An independent Community." "A republic." . . . What then is the good of shutting our eyes to the fact that this is what the Zionists are after and that the British Trusteeship is a mere screen behind which to work for this end.' 26 January 1919, PRO, FO 371/4153.

[11] Statement of the Zionist Organisation regarding Palestine, 3 February 1919. CZA. Emphases added.

[12] Mallet, with Hardinge's and Balfour's approval, 30 January 1919. PRO, FO 608/98. Minutes by Forbes Adam, 11 February, by Ormsby-Gore, 12 February, and by Mallet, n.d. PRO, FO 608/99.

reservations (old and new) that Zionism aroused both within Jewry and outside it and the still uncertain and transitory status of its current institutions and principal functionaries were all in evidence. The very membership of the delegation was determined in part by forces moved by unfriendly if not hostile intent—with the immediate result that it was very imperfectly representative and spoke, as we shall see, in two conflicting voices. It remains that the invitation to the hearing constituted the first general, formal, and public recognition of the Zionist movement as an acceptable and legitimate component of the international political arena. It entailed unprecedented, virtually full, international recognition of the Jewish national cause as one worthy of attention (and some sympathy) by the most spectacular gathering of the Powers to be convened in modern times. 'We are going to the Peace Conference to have our demands confirmed,'[13] Sokolov told the Zionist Conference convened in London on the eve of his and Weizmann's departure for Paris. And if, strictly speaking, his was a total misconception of what could (and what would) transpire, in a larger, looser sense, Sokolov's (and Weizmann's) conviction that it would be an event to set a seal upon the final emergence of Zionism from the furthest and more obscure corners of the world of high and serious politics to within measurable distance of its centre had a great deal to be said for it.

It was with this in mind that Weizmann and his friends in London now, for the first time, made a serious effort to provide themselves with such credentials as would put their *locus standi* as spokesmen for the movement beyond all reasonable doubt. To do so they had to try to resurrect official, institutional Zionism from the ashes to which the war in general and their own rebellion in particular had reduced it. But if they were not to lose control of events, if they were not to see the pre-eminence they had acquired for themselves diminished, and if they were to avoid the appearance of Zionism as anything but a movement closely associated with the victorious Allies, they had to do so in circumvention, if not defiance, of the calls (notably from Russia) unambiguously to rejuvenate the old leadership and the old institutions in full by means of an authoritative gathering of representatives of the movement in *all* countries, to be held, of

---

[13] *GAC Minutes*, 14 February 1919, p. 13.

course, in Copenhagen.[14] That they were able to achieve their purpose without great difficulty followed from the fact that the number of possible answers to the questions who was now to lead the movement not only *de facto* but *de jure*, how tactical decisions were to be taken, and where, and by whom, had been severely limited by the larger political circumstances. The defeat of Germany had put the seal on the elimination of Warburg as anything more than titular leader of the movement and had entirely removed the possibility of resuscitating the movement's old pre-war headquarters in Berlin. Plainly, the role of Central European Zionism, indispensable and immensely influential if never quite dominant in the movement since Herzl's time, would now be greatly reduced. Warburg, Hantke, Bodenheimer, and others—enemy aliens all—were not yet free to travel to Paris and London, even had they wished to, even had Weizmann been glad to have them at his side. Even Nordau, in exile in Madrid throughout the war, and no friend of the Central Powers, for whom a special effort had indeed been made to secure his admission to England, was refused entry outright.

The meaning and positive value of the Balfour Declaration were, of course, as clear to the people in Berlin as elsewhere, and Warburg and Hantke put as good a face on things as they could muster.[15] At war's end they resigned themselves to the inevitable, and at a formal

---

[14] As demanded by the Central Committee of the Russian Zionist Organization. Goldberg to the EAC, Berlin, 14 November 1918. CZA, Z3/893. 'Messrs. Weizmann and Sokolov are Zionist leaders, yet none of these gentlemen holds a formal brief for the representation of the Zionist portion of the Jewish people,' was the comment of Nordau, remote in his Madrid exile, but not out of touch and still very much the Grand Old Man of Zionism. 'It is absolutely necessary to offer the Zionist masses a possibility to appoint men of their confidence who shall have the authority to speak in their behalf to the Great Powers,' he wrote privately to the editor of the *Jewish Chronicle* in London. 'Dr. Weizmann represents, perhaps, the English Zionists, but they are at present a very small, if exceptionally influential fraction of the world's Judaism and Zionism. Mr. Sokolov, although a member of the [EAC], has no special mandate [such as] is indispensable at this turning [point] of our history, and the [EAC] itself is at present, and has been for the last four years, a myth. Justice Brandeis may claim to be the man of confidence of the very important American Jewry, but this ought to be confirmed expressly by that Jewry. The Russian, the Austro-Hungarian, the Romanian, the South African, the Canadian, the Argentine, not to speak of the Dutch, Swiss, French, Italian and Turkish Jews, are to be left in the cold. Yet they have a right to speak and to be heard.' Nordau to Greenberg, 21 November 1918. CZA, L8/142.

[15] See for example their summary of developments in the movement attached to a circular letter from Copenhagen, 24 June 1918. CZA, L6/18 III.

meeting of the (rump) EAC in Copenhagen explicitly surrendered their now shadowy authority. With Jacobson's approval, Warburg and Hantke agreed that Weizmann should be co-opted onto the EAC[16]—an irregular procedure which occasioned some grumbling, but was none the less generally accepted as reflecting the real state of affairs; and they completed their personal surrender by signing a curious and equally irregular document in which they granted their Russian colleague Jacobson 'unlimited' and 'irrevocable' power to act on their behalf in all matters coming under the competence of the EAC. Finally, all present resolved that henceforth the headquarters of the EAC would be in London.[17] Thus, with the Russian branch of the movement ever less capable of functioning effectively, at all events as a united and coherent body, and with the American branch geographically and psychologically remote from the central arenas of activity and both ill suited and too diffident to play a role commensurate with its size and resources, the London centre of Zionism was rendered supreme in all but name.

With his elevation at long last to a position of formal authority equal to that of Sokolov and Jacobson, Weizmann's own position as master of the London centre was further strengthened, and much of the ambiguity that long clouded it (and so greatly irritated him) removed. He was increasingly deferred to, even by his former seniors, even when they disagreed with him, partly because none competed with him for sheer energy, drive, and force of personality, partly because in London, at any rate, it was hard for them, newcomers to the 'new political conditions' (as Jacobson termed them) in which all had now to operate, not to recognize that he had the advantage. Weizmann is 'practically the only man,' Jacobson felt he must concede, 'who knows the whole situation and who is capable of seeing and understanding things.' He had hoped to have been useful in London, he wrote his friends in Copenhagen a few weeks later; 'but you must understand that I came too late, when the work here had already received its definite shape, when the relations had been established and the whole system and method of work laid down.'[18]

Still, the absolute supremacy Weizmann craved for eluded him for

---

[16] Along with Julius Simon.
[17] EAC minutes, 29 November 1 December 1918; and 'Deed of Power', 1 December 1918. CZA, L6/93.
[18] Jacobson to Copenhagen, 16 December 1918 and 8 January 1919. CZA, L6/48.

the time being. None seriously contested his demand for a reconstruction of the institutions well in advance of the convening of the next full Congress—planned tentatively for the latter half of the year (but, in the event, not assembled until the summer of 1921). Least of all did anyone propose to compete with him for his role of principal spokesman for the movement in British official circles. But the full centralization of responsibility and the vesting of the leadership in his hands alone—bringing an end to what he bitterly called 'the double-headed eagle' system under which he and Sokolov spoke jointly for the movement[19]—this was more than his most senior colleagues were prepared to grant him. And Weizmann had no choice but to retreat (not for the first time) from a rash threat of resignation and refrain from pressing too vigorously for Warburg's (indeed, Herzl's) crown at this stage lest his 'fellow-Jews in Russia' charge him, as he himself put it, with effecting 'a *coup d'état*' and of committing 'the crime of throwing out Sokolov'.[20] But he hardly needed to go so far. At the two men's urging, a conference of Zionist activists was convened in London on the eve of their summons to the Peace Conference. As an instrument whereby they would be provided with as broad an approval of their role as spokesmen for the movement as was possible within the limits they had set themselves and Weizmann would obtain at least implicit recognition as the leading figure in the movement as a whole, it proved entirely adequate—Weizmann's and Sokolov's status being confirmed and reconfirmed, numbers of delegates referring to them unhesitatingly as 'our leaders'.

The London Conference sat from 23 February 1919 (with an interruption while the delegates waited to hear what had been achieved in Paris) until 12 March. Strictly, it was no more than an informal gathering: neither a meeting of the GAC, nor of the 'annual conference', least of all a properly constituted Congress of Zionists. Nor was it an assembly of all or most of the notables: Warburg, Hantke, Bodenheimer, and Nordau were barred from coming, as we have seen. The two most prominent of the new men were absent: Brandeis remained in Washington, despite Weizmann's pleas to

[19] 'Report by Dr. [Stephen S.] Wise', National Executive Committee, Zionist Organization of America, 9 February 1919, pp. 8–9. Zionist Archives, New York, de Haas Collection, micr. reel 5, 535–77. See also Wise's earlier report, 22 January 1919. CZA, S30/2513C.
[20] Ibid., p. 9; Tolkowsky, pp. 339–400.

come; Jabotinsky was in Ereẓ-Israel with his regiment. Of the old guard, not all who were free to come made the journey. Jacobus Kann remained in Holland. Aḥad Ha-ʿAm, in London all the while, did not attend. But Ussishkin, unquestionably the central personality in Russian Zionism now that Tchlenov was gone, was present.[21]. So was Shmarya Levin (with Weizmann, Sokolov, Jacobson, and Julius Simon all present, thus bringing the number of members of the new EAC attending up to five). Motzkin, Frankfurter, Fischer, de Haas, Rosov, and Cowen participated. There was a strong and confident delegation from Ereẓ-Israel itself. There was one of religious Zionists (the Mizraḥi), another of Zionist socialists (Poʿalei Ẓion). All told, close to eighty Zionist activists and loyalists of all ranks and from a dozen countries attended. It was as large and comprehensive (if only very loosely representative) an assembly as could, in the circumstances, be reasonably expected to gather. The only serious flaw in its proceedings—certainly the greatest source of disquiet and tension among the delegates—lay in the fact that what all now took to be the central and immediate business of the movement, the terms on which the matter of Zionism was to be presented to the Paris Peace Conference, had been settled before the Conference ever convened. This carried with it the minor result that much time perforce was spent on the technicalities and finances of settlement, land purchase, immigration to, and education in Ereẓ-Israel—all subjects considered in confident and hopeful spirit, but not the stuff of what was intended (and expected) to be an essentially political conference. It carried the major result that such political debates as were held tended to proceed along very general, essentially speculative lines devoid of the underpinning of such hard facts and specific information on the true intentions of the Powers and the political and social realities in Ereẓ-Israel itself as could have rendered them fully constructive and lead to specific operative conclusions.

Had Weizmann and Sokolov asked less, or no more, than the Powers could reasonably be expected to grant? Should the claims of the Jews be cast in terms of *right* or in terms of *interest*? Had it been politic, or had it been an error, to separate the claims and needs of Zionism from the immediate claims and needs of the mass of Jewry

---

[21] But very nearly prevented from coming to London by the inexplicable but certainly false belief of British military intelligence, reporting from Constantinople, that Ussishkin was a German agent. PRO, FO 371/4167, fos. 223–4, 296–7.

(notably to national/minority rights) in eastern Europe, the latter being left to one side—indeed, implicitly discounted, as Weizmann wanted? Should so much trust be placed in England? If not, in whom? Had it been right or wrong of the London Zionists to bow to British pressure and withdraw the movement's demands as originally phrased and submitted? In sum, once again, had a unique opportunity to state one's case and stake one's claim to freedom and equality among the other nations been seized; or had it been allowed, unpardonably, to slip from the movement's grasp and dissipate; and what resources could Zionism really muster to pursue and achieve such ends as it was determined to set itself? These were the questions which troubled the delegates and were repeated in different forms and in varying degrees of intensity throughout. To none of them were clear and well-founded answers forthcoming. 'Neither Mr Sokolov nor I had the courage to ask for more,' Weizmann remarked at one point; and anyway, he continued, the immediate task before the Zionists was to remake themselves, to mobilize new forces, to find great sums of money, and 'build a large and disciplined organization'. It was an enormous undertaking, he conceded, a matter of five or six years' work in itself. And in the meantime? 'I would advise you,' he told the delegates, 'not to bite off more than you can chew.'[22] But the difficulties Weizmann had described would be of little interest to future generations before whom we would all be called to account, one of the more restless and dissatisfied delegates countered.

They will say that we had been granted a stupendous opportunity which we then proved unfit to meet. Why should you not conceive instead that the [Jewish] people is in fact fully behind you and that its strength and wealth are yours to employ? We cannot and must not make concessions, for [if we do] we are liable to lose everything.[23]

In the end, none were prepared to insist upon an attempt to change the terms of what would be put before the Council, nor to repudiate Weizmann and Sokolov either before their journey to Paris or upon their return. None questioned the position the two men had won for themselves in the diplomatic arena. None disputed the command of detail and the familiarity with the pathways of British and French bureaucracy they had acquired. None was

[22] *GAC Minutes*, p. 69.
[23] Jean Fischer. Ibid., pp. 69–70.

remotely in a position to dispute even so egregious an assertion of influence on British policy and strategy as Weizmann's bald statement that it was he and his friends 'who had discovered Palestine for England';[24] or his mistaken impression that United States policy on Zionism hinged on the belief that a 'Jewish National Home' was a means of siphoning off potential immigrants;[25] or that 'the Italian question is more dangerous than the Arab question'.[26] A few cautious proposals to take stock and reconsider the terms of the submission to the Peace Conference[27] were made—but promptly defeated. None so much as hinted (and very probably none thought) that the Zionist notables assembled in London should express anything but confidence in Weizmann's, Sokolov's, and—as was decided—Ussishkin's ability and fitness to represent them. The idea that the composition of their delegation to the Conference might be determined, even in part, by other than the Zionists themselves occurred to nobody.

iii

On the whole, the Zionists gathered in London, even those newly arrived and critical of Weizmann and Sokolov, expected things to go smoothly at the Peace Conference. Everything they had been told pointed that way.

> The situation in Paris is quite satisfactory [was the message Jacobson passed on to the Liaison Office in Copenhagen]. Our friends [have] had the opportunity to approach responsible representation of all the Great Powers. It seems that the English, American and Italian representatives are absolutely in favour of the Zionist claims, as formulated in our last [i.e. second] statement and find them very 'modest and moderate'. Most of them told our friends—they find our memorandum 'the most statesmanlike document' of all presented to the Peace Conference.[28]

'Absolutely in favour' was certainly too strong. The compliment on the 'statesmanlike' quality of their revised memorandum should not have been taken wholly at face value. But the grounds for optimism, so far as Britain's allies were concerned, were not unfounded. President Wilson had finally granted the American Zionists a

[24] Ibid., p. 10.
[25] Ibid., p. 13.
[26] Ibid., p. 14.
[27] By Jacob de Haas, among others. Ibid., p. 22.
[28] Jacobson to Copenhagen, 16 February 1919. CZA, L6/48.

statement of his 'deep and sincere interest in the reconstructive work [of the Zionist Commission] in Palestine at the instance of the British Government'[29] (without however, going quite so far as to endorse the idea of a Jewish National Home on behalf of the United States unambiguously). In mid-January in Paris, with British encouragement, the President agreed to receive Weizmann in person. True, while the Zionist had prepared himself with care, the President, with royal impatience, was in no mood to hear his visitor out. On the other hand, he did agree readily enough with Weizmann on what Weizmann judged the essentials, namely that Palestine should go to the British, if only they could be persuaded to take it over, and that it must certainly not be left in the hands of the French.[30] The Italians, for their part, had long since informed Sokolov officially of their support for a *centro nazionale ebraico* in language that was virtually identical with that of the Balfour Declaration.[31] The Japanese, in somewhat more forthright terms than used by any of the other Powers, had expressed their approval.[32] The danger of conflicting claims being pressed by the Arabs seemed to have passed: the Zionists had learned that Feisal, in *his* appearance before the Council, had specifically excluded Palestine from the regions to be incorporated in the future Arab state. ('Palestine, in consequence of its universal character,' the official minutes did indeed report him as stating, 'he [Feisal] left on one side for the consideration of all parties interested. With this exception, he asked for the independence of the Arab areas enumerated in his memorandum.')[33] This left the French.

Contact with French officialdom and with the French political class generally had been sporadic and half-hearted throughout the war, as we have seen. Apart from the inhibiting atmosphere in post-

[29] In the form of a 'New Year's Greeting to the Jewish People' addressed to Stephen Wise, 31 August 1918. CZA, A264/28.

[30] Memorandum by Mallet, 14 January 1919. PRO, FO 608/98, fo. 143; H. G. Nicolson, *Peacemaking 1919* (London, 1944), p. 237. Mallet gives 14 January as date of the interview, Nicolson gives 13 January.

[31] Imperiali (Italian Ambassador in London) to Sokolov, 9 May 1918. CZA, L6/90II.

[32] 'The Japanese Government gladly take note of the Zionist aspirations to establish in Palestine a national home for the Jewish people and they look foward with a sympathetic interest to the realization of such desire upon the basis proposed.' Chinda (Japanese Ambassador in London) to Weizmann, 6 January 1919. Naoki Maruyama, 'Japan's response to the Zionist Movement in the 1920s', *Bulletin of the Graduate School of International Relations, International University of Japan*, ii, 1984, pp. 28–9.

[33] Secretary's Notes, 6 February 1919. PRO, CAB 28/6.

Dreyfus France so far as Jewish questions were concerned, this had much to do with the weakness, bordering on invisibility, of the Zionist movement in the country, and the relative and contrasting prestige and influence within French Jewry of its two major institutions, the Consistoire and the Alliance Israélite Universelle— both explicitly and implacably anti-Zionist. On another score, even when, urged by Sykes, the London Zionists had made a serious attempt to enlist official France among the powers favouring Zionism—or at least not unfriendly to it—Weizmann personally had remained suspicious of it, and above all fearful lest involvement with the French spoil the connection with the British to which he attached overriding importance, in the sense that he conceived it as the pivot on which the entire Zionist enterprise must now turn. Besides, while it was known, if only in a general way, that there were conflicting currents of opinion in Paris, there was very little first-hand knowledge and nothing like the near-intimacy that had developed in the Zionists' relations with certain sections of the British political establishment. One result was a failure to grasp to quite what degree French policy on the Near East was a matter of mixed motives and cross-purposes and how significant was the fairly consistent inability of the French to resolve them by the imposition of supreme and binding authority in the manner of the English for whom, in analogous circumstances, the immensely powerful War Cabinet system of government provided an effective machinery of ultimate rule. When it began to percolate through to the Zionists some time in advance of their appearance before the Peace Conference that the French did not perhaps now insist on the maintenance of the Sykes-Picot Agreement and that there might only be the question of the northern borders of Palestine to settle, they jumped to the conclusion that at least the formal exposition of the Zionist case they had planned would encounter no opposition from that quarter.[34] Weizmann, Sokolov, Ussishkin (the three official spokesmen)[35] and the small band of assistants gathered around them in Paris were therefore stunned by the news, delivered on the very eve of their testimony before the Council, that they would be flanked by at least one other Jewish notable, selected (and, it could be assumed, briefed) by the French Foreign Ministry and

[34] Jacobson to Copenhagen, 16 February 1919. CZA, L6/48.
[35] De Haas had been slated to speak for the American Zionists, but the summons came too late and he was unable to reach Paris in time.

known to all for his hostility to virtually everything they stood for.

The fact was that French policy towards the Zionists, as on all questions relating to Jewry, was no clearer nor more settled at the beginning of 1919 than it had been two and three years earlier. There had never been instituted so comparatively thorough an attempt to weigh all the perceived factors and think the issue through to a conclusion as there had twice been in London, first under Grey, then under Balfour. Public statements, while not unfriendly, had appropriately been few in number, issued reluctantly, and always carefully ambiguous in form and content. Early in 1918, pressed both by André Tardieu, his representative in the United States, and by Baron Edmond de Rothschild to follow up the British Declaration of 2 November 1917, a sceptical Clemenceau had passed the matter on to his equally sceptical Foreign Minister. Pichon agreed to receive Sokolov and did authorize a communiqué which, so Sokolov was informed, had been issued explicitly 'with a view to defining [the Government's] attitude towards Zionist aspirations looking to the creation of a national home for the Jews in Palestine.' But all that was stated in the communiqué (of 9 February 1918) itself was that the Minister had been 'happy to confirm that there is complete agreement between the French and British governments in matters concerning the question of a Jewish establishment [*sic*] in Palestine'.[36]

The ambiguity in the French position certainly derived in part from their reluctance to take the Zionists entirely seriously and their somewhat easy initial assumption that the British did not either. It was part and parcel of a somewhat less serious view than the British tended to have at this time of the weight to be ascribed to the Jewish factor in international politics generally[37]—less serious, more precise, and on the whole more hostile. There were voices that spoke in tones much like those of the British and did argue forcefully for accommodation. André Tardieu, as Clemenceau's special 'High Commissioner for Franco-American Wartime Affairs', impressed by the public response in American Jewry to Balfour's Declaration and the capture of Jerusalem, had sought to persuade his Government

---

[36] The arguments for receiving Sokolov in friendly fashion are set out in a minute (probably drafted by Jean Gout), 1 February 1918. AE, Guerre 1914–1918, Sionisme, vol. 1200, fos. 124–5; on Rothschild's intervention, see L. Stein, *The Balfour Declaration* (New York, 1961), pp. 590–1.

[37] See above, pp. 245–5.

that 'Judaism and Zionism were [now] identical from the international point of view'; that the notables, 'the great Jews'—
Morgenthau, Schiff, Strauss, Marshall, and their like—formerly
hostile, had now no choice but to follow the popular trend; that the
Jews had 'great influence' over the American Government itself; and
that in sum, therefore,the question whether it was politic for France
to allow this 'force to turn, now or later, against us'—by default, and
as a consequence of the common impression that France was hostile
to it—was one that required an answer.[38] It was true, as the Foreign
Ministry had argued,[39] that the attitude of 'our own [French] Jews'
was lukewarm at best and that 'our Muslims' were likely to be very
discontented. But was it wise to allow purely 'internal' considerations to determine policy, especially when the country's two
principal allies had made their position clear, and France, in
consequence, was likely to be out of step with them? And then again,
looking to the future, 'in favour of which belligerents would the force
represented by Judaism play at the peace conference [when], for the
first time, the Jews would be representing not only international, but
[their own] national interest?' France should take care not to give
'certain American Jewish elements' an excuse for indifference to the
French claim to Alsace-Lorraine on the grounds that France was
indifferent to the Jews' own right to self-determination.[40]

A year later, however, with the war over, the capitulation of
Germany accomplished, and the Peace Conference run not as a
forum in which genuine negotiations between the belligerents were
to be conducted but as a congress of allies in which the terms of a
dictated peace were to be drawn up, no such argument could, or
needed to be, advanced—not, at all events, so insistently. Jewry as
an international force and Jewry as a force suspected of pro-German
sympathies, even if believed in, could be discounted. The Jews as a
factor of some weight and influence in the United States might be
deserving of attention, but the Peace Conference was not long
underway before it was recognized that on the central issues
dividing the French from the Americans it was entirely improbable
that Jewish influence on President Wilson and his entourage—if it
could be said to exist at all—would or could be effectively exerted.

---

[38] Tardieu to Clemenceau and Pichon, 17 January 1918. AE, Guerre 1914–1918,
Sionisme, vol. 1200, fos. 85–8.

[39] Pichon to Tardieu, 26 January 1918. Ibid., fos. 205–6.

[40] Tardieu to Pichon, 30, 31 January 1918. Ibid., fos. 111–14.

The French (of all schools) were reluctant to find themselves out of step with their major allies. They were aware that they had made a commitment of some sort to the Zionists. Most (but not all) of those concerned had as good as given up the idea of incorporating the northern half of Palestine within their future Syrian domain and of retaining a share, perhaps a principal share, in the governance of the rest.[41] The energy and confidence with which the British had set themselves to take over Palestine immediately upon entry into the country,[42] the collapse of much of what had been taken to be the French position in the Levant, and the sense that France might be too exhausted to compete with its ally had all left their mark. 'As for the entente cordiale, it was created and maintained with a view to the war which has just ended,' one particularly clear-sighted member of the diplomatic service reflected. 'Will it survive the peace? It is not certain. . . . In a word, I do not believe that France is in a condition to participate effectively in a division of Turkey. That is why I was never in favour of our 1916 agreements.'[43]

Still, few in the Foreign Ministry, let alone in the colonialist lobby proper, had entirely given up hope of saving something from the wreckage, the more so as all, from Clemenceau down, found themselves increasingly drawn into Near Eastern quarrels with the British and their Arab protégés in Syria—which led them back time and again to Sykes-Picot, still the foundation of their central claims. In this context, in a variety of ways, they came up against the Zionists and judged them repeatedly to be at one and the same time committed to, manipulated by, and dependent upon the British. In short, the context in which Zionism was now principally and increasingly regarded by Paris was no longer the wider one of high wartime politics, but the limited and specific one of the division of the Near Eastern spoils. In this latter context they were perceived as in no sense useful to French causes, but as irritants and nuisances (if not parasites upon the British)[44] in a situation that was exceedingly

---

[41] 'La Question syrienne et la revision eventuelle des accords de 1916', 24 January 1919. AE, Gout papers, vol. 7, fos. 107–27.

[42] See for example Picot to Gout, 31 December 1917. Ibid., vol. 9, fos. 45–8.

[43] A. de Fleuriau, deputy to the Ambassador in London, to Gout, 29 January 1919. Ibid., vol. 9, fos. 64–5.

[44] 'The only reason for fearing Zionism lies in the powerful support for it in England and America,' is a characteristic observation for internal official consumption, embodied in a handwritten, plainly spontaneous, unsigned memorandum retained in a military intelligence file headed '1919 Syrie Marine'. SHAT, 7N1640.

aggravating on many other counts, and, in terms of their own absolute, local resources *in the Levant itself,* so weak as to be almost negligible. Finally, through such internal debate and correspondence as was conducted, informing and colouring the fundamental —and, it might be said, the visceral—approach to the Zionists, there ran a distinct thread of complacent dislike and contempt.

The Zionist regiment [i.e. the Jewish Legion] . . . has finally arrived in Egypt [the chief French diplomatic representative in Cairo reported]. It is composed of about a thousand men, most of whom [to judge by their] physical characteristics, seem to belong to the class of street pedlars, rather than the solid race customarily seen in British uniform. Small, of poor bearing, these soldiers are for the most part of the Polish Jewish type. By the same token, the parade through the streets of Cairo yesterday was not as impressive as the British authorities and the Zionist Federation doubtless had hoped, although nothing had been neglected to obtain such a result. The members of the [Zionist] Maccabi sports association had been mobilized and, dressed in a uniform which resembled nothing so much as that worn by scullions, formed a sort of guard of honour.[45]

But in any event, he reported a few weeks later (quoting no source), the great majority of these Jewish troops 'had no desire to go and fight for the liberation of the Promised Land.' For this and other reasons, there might be something to be said, he advised Paris, for the indifference with which sensible Egyptians observed the evolution of the Zionist programme, namely that

It would be wisest . . . to let things be, not to intervene: for many here are persuaded . . . that neither love of their fellow-men nor devotion to the cause will impel the Jews to come in their masses and settle in a country devoid either of stock exchange or commerce[.] It is said, besides, that if that were ever to happen, it would contain the germ that would ruin Zionism: for wolf does not eat wolf and one diamond does not wear down another.[46]

In Paris, nevertheless, it was thought wise to keep an eye on this new, imperfectly known, certainly doubtful quantity. To that end the addition of a French member to the Zionist Commission

---

[45] Defrance to Pichon, 11 March 1918. SHAT, 7N2145.
[46] Defrance to Pichon, 3 April 1918. AE, Guerre 1914–1918, Sionisme, vol. 1201, fos. 85–6. However, the relatively junior Coulondre, Picot's assistant, reported both more accurately and more favourably on the arrival of the battalions of the Jewish Legion, their service at the front, and the success of their campaign to recruit from among the young men of the *yishuv.* Coulondre (Cairo) to Foreign Ministry, 19 June 1918. SHAT, 4N61/2; and 30 June 1918. AE, 1918–1940. Série Y Internationale, vol. 377, fos. 17–18.

(Sylvain Lévi, of whom more will be said) had been approved by the Quai d'Orsay, and some satisfaction had been registered at his exercising, as was believed, a moderating influence on Weizmann and the other commissioners—'as could be expected, given his patriotism and the soundness of his judgement'.[47] For whatever was finally settled between the Powers in this matter of Palestine and the Zionists, it was clear in Paris that there could be no question of the Jewish 'establishment' in Palestine going beyond very modest dimensions. 'The Government of the Republic,' the Foreign Minister summed up on the eve of the Zionists' summons to the Peace Conference,

gave its consent to the creation of a Jewish national, moral and intellectual home in Palestine as early as 1916; it has never declared itself in favour of the constitution of Palestine as an independent Jewish state, nor the formation of a sovereign Jewish organism in any part of that region. The best solution to the Jewish question and the one most likely to ensure the conciliation of the contradictory aspirations which are now apparent in Palestine would, in his view, be the recognition of Zionism in the form of autonomous Jewish communities living within the framework of the international state provided for by the [Sykes-Picot] agreements of 1916.[48]

In sum, the approach to Zionism—barely a policy—of those specifically called upon by their functions to deal with it implied not so much a determination to fight (let alone crush) the Jewish national movement as a strong conviction that it needed to be diminished. Other voices in other quarters concerned with greater matters and only fleetingly and obliquely with those which pertained to the Jews tended to be drowned out.[49] For a while the Foreign Ministry would have its own way. And to its ends, at this very late stage, its chosen instrument was Sylvain Lévi.

Lévi was unusual among those Jews who had achieved a place of

[47] Ibid.

[48] Pichon to Constantinople, 12 January 1919. AE, Levant 1918–1929, Palestine, vol. 12, fo. 46.

[49] The tone and content of a paper on the subject prepared at this time in the Prime Minister's office differ markedly from views and papers originating in the Foreign Ministry: 'Between the French and Arab zones and Egypt under British protectorate, Palestine forms an enclave, the importance of which cannot be measured by its territorial extent. The competition of which the Holy Land has always been the object will be allayed by the restoration of the Jewish people to their native land.' 'Plan de reglement des questions d'Orient', 12 December 1918, p. 15. Clemenceau Papers, SHAT, 6N72.

high distinction in the French socio-official hierarchy (as an eminent scholar and a professor at the very prestigious Collège de France) in that he retained a consistent and genuine interest in Jewish affairs. But, perhaps as one who had lived—and in a sense continued to live—through the Dreyfus Affair, he was exceedingly sensitive to the question of his primary loyalty: it was consciously and unreservedly to France, to the French nation of which he saw himself a part, and to French culture, language, and civilization of which he was both a distinguished representative and an ardent protagonist. In practice, his devotion to his country was so complete, so unswerving, and so uncritical that (like the wretched Captain Dreyfus himself) it rendered him an extraordinarily pliable tool in the hands of any institution of central government that chose to call him to its service. Where the affairs and interests of Jewry (as he understood them) could be adjusted or subordinated to, or made compatible with, the interests of the French state as these were laid down for him by authority, all was well. Where actual or potential conflict was registered or suspected or, worse, appeared actually to threaten the delicate balance between that primary loyalty to the French Republic he believed incumbent on all French Jews to bear and such historical and philanthropical concerns with Jewry—particularly non-French Jewry—as drew him to action from time to time, there his agitation was intense. And there his utility to the official establishment as a figure publicly associated with Jewish causes was at its greatest.

Lévi's opposition to Zionism stemmed from just such considerations and perceptions. As a minor *philanthropic* exercise in the resettlement of unfortunates from eastern Europe it might pass— particularly if the *yishuv* could be satisfactorily integrated into the campaign to establish the French language ever more firmly as the *lingua franca* of the Levant, and Paris as the sun around which all local educational and cultural institutions ultimately revolved. Anything beyond that, anything explicitly national, anything independently political (unless tied to France with iron bands), and, above all, anything that smelt of Jewish statehood even in the distant future was perceived as wrong-minded in principle and hugely dangerous in practice. In sum, Zionism as the Zionists (of all varieties) understood it was to be fought. The more he learned of it, the stronger this conviction grew. And in his ever fiercer struggle with the Zionists his most effective ally, so Lévi seems to have thought, was his own Government, notably the Ministry of Foreign Affairs. Thus the circle of his Jewish concerns and sympathies was fitted to the square of his patriotism. And the depth, not to say violence, of his feeling on the matter of Zionism was abundantly (and characteristically) evident in the numerous memoranda with which he peppered the Foreign Ministry at this time.

In the privacy of these written confidential statements and reports, Lévi consistently and ever more furiously took the Zionists to task. He denounced them for their orientation: 'sectarian fanaticism temporarily tied to English political interests'.[50] He denounced them for their deficiencies as a movement on the grounds that their American version was 'essentially an internal phenomenon, a specifically Jewish aspect of American bluff and American idealism',[51] while their French section was 'essentially a group of foreign Jews living in France, led by Jewish and non-Jewish dilettantes', to allow whom to speak at the Peace Conference would be to deal truly patriotic French Jewry's 'most intimate sentiments' an injury.[52] He denounced them, too, for their methods: for allegedly tempting the 'ambitious' Herbert Samuel into their camp, for example, by holding out to him the chance of 'honours' as 'His Britannic Majesty's first proconsul in the Zionist State'.[53]

For its part, the Quai d'Orsay's firm, somewhat contemptuous determination to use him when appropriate, to drop him when not, is equally evident. Its officials had him sent to the United States charged with the mission of bringing Jewish opinion around to a more friendly attitude to France.[54] They judged his performance as a member of the Zionist Commission very satisfactory, and regretted his departure and their failure to find a replacement for him for the very good reasons that he had been found to have provided the Ministry with inside information on the affairs of the Zionists and, more generally, to have helped uphold the 'moral interests of

[50] 'Palestine juive et Société des Nations', February 1919. AE, Levant 1918–1929, Palestine, vol. 12, fos. 177–9.

[51] Ibid.

[52] Memorandum, 26 February 1919. Ibid., vol. 13, fos. 48–9.

[53] 'Sionisme et Palestine', 8 February 1919. AE, Série Y Internationale, vol. 377, fos. 196–208.

[54] For Lévi's detailed report on his journey to the United States from the end of October to the beginning of December 1918, see AE, Levant 1918–1929, Palestine, vol. 12, fos. 109–61.

France' in the Levant.[55] But they recognized him as a dutiful rather than an independent figure, no more than a shadow (*reflet*) of the more formidable Baron Edmond de Rothschild so far as his basic ideas and lines of conduct in public affairs were concerned. At no point were they prepared actually to be guided by him, still less to be drawn by his zeal into what seemed to them to be mere internal Jewish quarrels. His suggestion that the Government sponsor a committee of Jewish notables to act as a kind of counterweight to the London Zionists (seen by him as little more than a Jewish appendix to the British Foreign Office) was rejected out of hand—partly on just such grounds, i.e. lest it draw them into a Jewish quarrel, and partly because, in practice, French policy on Zionism and Jewish affairs generally could not be made nearly so clear-cut as Sylvain Lévi and his friends would have liked it to be. 'The Government cannot go back on its promises,' was Jean Gout's verdict on his proposal, 'and appear to give its confidence solely to the reactionaries [in Jewry]'.[56] So while Lévi, carefully briefed, was the Quai d'Orsay's obvious candidate for an appearance before the Council (there could be no question of leaving the arena wholly to Jewish spokesmen who were stamped indelibly in French eyes as protégés of the British), there was some fear in the Ministry lest the extremism of his views and the intemperance with which he was liable to express them upset the balance which it sought to achieve and project upon the scene. There followed the suggestion that someone less fervently anti-Zionist but reliably French be called to speak with him. Only one suitable candidate came to mind. Late on 26 February, André Spire was summoned urgently by telephone to present himself at the Ministry the following afternoon to testify.[57]

Spire had in common with Sylvain Lévi that he was certainly no foreigner and had a firm place in the French socio-bureaucratic

[55] Gout to Berthelot, 7 February 1920. AE, Levant 1918–1929, Palestine, vol. 14, fos. 76–7.

[56] Memorandum by Lévi, 9 February 1919. Ibid., vol. 12, fos. 227–30; Gout to Berthelot, 26 February 1918. Ibid., vol. 13, fos. 50–1. 'I would add,' Gout wrote in a postscript, 'that if I am in favour of studying Jewish questions with a view to the position to be taken by the French Government, I would regard it deplorable [*fâcheux*] even on internal political grounds, to entrust the task to Jews alone. Besides their bringing to it their petty, clannish spirit, the [general] public would never agree that in questions which are of interest to all Frenchmen (Palestine, relations with Poland, Romania, Greece, the Ukraine, etc.) the Government be guided by the Jews alone.' Ibid.

[57] [Berthelot?] to Gout, 23 February 1919. Ibid., vol. 13, fo. 30; unsigned record of summons by telephone, 26 February 1919. Ibid., fo. 46.

hierarchy. He came from a family established in Lorraine for several hundred years. He had entered the civil service through a door that virtually guaranteed advancement: as *auditeur* at the Conseil d'État. He duly rose to the not inconsiderable rank of Inspector-General at the Ministry of Agriculture. He was a poet of some talent. He was a man of firm convictions and considerable courage. An ardent Dreyfusard, he had fought a duel at the time of the Affair to uphold Jewish honour. And unlike Lévi, Spire was a man of a wholly independent cast of mind of which he was both conscious and proud. He thought a denial of Jewish identity despicable and he was revolted by the attempt of the well-established Jews of France to draw a self-protective line between themselves, the *Israélites*, and the newcomers from eastern Europe, the *Juifs*.[58] He felt increasingly drawn to Jewish issues and concerns and, in the years leading up to the War, to Zionism. He was a founder member of the League of the Friends of Zionism set up soon after the publication of the Balfour Declaration. He was Weizmann's and Sokolov's one sure native ally in Paris at this time.

For all these reasons, all parties expected him to make a statement favourable to Zionism. What was particularly wanted of him by the officials of the Quai, however, was to offer it in a moderate and, so far as possible, pro-French form. Spire, by his own account, promptly warned them that this was neither realistic politically nor, from the Zionists' own point of view, desirable: on objective grounds a British administration might well be thought better for them. There was, of course, some argument on that score and an attempt to exert pressure. Spire stuck to his guns. Meanwhile, time was pressing: Spire's briefing took place only minutes before the Council session was due to begin. He promised no more than that he would speak very briefly indeed, and that was accepted.[59]

The French—like the British before them—had been drawn by their larger purposes into an internal Jewish quarrel after all. What

[58] 'I did not yet feel myself a Jew in the way that rising anti-Semitism forced me bit by bit to become;' he wrote retrospectively of his time at the Conseil d'État at the height of the Affair, 'but rather an *israélite*, a Jew with a small j, ... one of those hybrids whom the great scholar Sylvain Lév[i]—professor at the Collège de France, President of the Alliance Israélite Universelle at the end of his life, a good and sensitive man, but one who preferred to look to the Faubourg Saint-Honoré [i.e. to the Rothschilds] rather than to the rue des Rosiers [the Parisian Jewish 'ghetto'] whence his own parents had emerged— wished to be named Jewish-Frenchmen.' A. Spire, *Souvenirs á bâtons rompus* (Paris, 1962), pp. 36–7.

[59] Ibid., pp. 105–8.

was of greater consequence, they had done much to bring the conflict between Zionists and non-Zionists to a head once more.[60]

iv

The summons to appear before the Council of Ten was for the afternoon of 27 February in the Minister's room at the Quai d'Orsay. No objection to the proposal that the Zionists be called had been voiced. The British had explicitly promised them an invitation, and it was well in accord with the formal decision taken in London immediately after the war, when Clemenceau, Lloyd George, and Orlando agreed, amongst many other things, to invite representatives of 'nations in the making' to state their respective cases before the Conference.[61] The Armenians had just preceded the Jews, to the

---

[60] The much more formidable and better organized English wing of the anti-Zionist front had had, in contrast, to take a more moderate line. The reformed and renamed Joint Foreign Committee of the Board of Deputies and the Anglo-Jewish Association, but led as before by Lucien Wolf, avoided open opposition to what was now settled government policy. They continued to press, however, somewhat surreptitiously, for an administration in Palestine that would avoid the grant of 'political or economic privileges or preference . . . in favour of any race or religious community.' And while calling for the recognition of Hebrew as an official language, the Sabbath as the Jewish day of rest, and other such communal rights to be extended to the Jews of the country on a par with the other communities, they were adamant against any system of administration that appeared to imply Jewish nationhood above and beyond the strict territorial limits of the country. Thus they deprecated, as they informed the Foreign Office, 'any permanent scheme of external Jewish control or interference such as might impair the growth of a healthy system of local self-government.' ('Statement of Policy on the Palestine Question', 4 February 1919. PRO, FO 608/98, fos. 259–60.) This had always been their position, and their reasoning was unchanged. 'The Committee,' as Wolf put it afresh for the internal consumption of its members, 'are in a sense the custodians of the interests of seven million of Jews in Eastern and South Eastern Europe who base all their hopes of comfort and happiness on the enjoyment of equal rights with their non-Jewish fellow citizens, and on the abolition of all political and economic privileges. If then, the Jewish Nationality in Palestine should claim and exercise any form of economic preference, the whole case for the emancipation of the Jews of Poland and Rumania would be compromised.' ('Memorandum on the Zionist Proposals', 5 December 1918. CZA, A77/3 C.) But they had already shot their bolt. Minds both in Whitehall and among the members of the British delegation to the Peace Conference were made up and uninterested in the Conjoint Committee. The response of one of the officials handling these matters gives the tone: 'It is surely better in the interests of the "National Home" policy that the whole movement should be left for the present in Dr. Weizmann and his organization's hands. Otherwise we shall have confusion and divided counsels at the last minute.' (Minute by Forbes Adam, 14 February 1919. PRO, FO 608/98 fo. 257.)

[61] The original formulation, submitted to the three leaders for their approval in London 2 4 December 1918, spoke of 'new nations born since the beginning of the war and nations in the making [*Nations en gestation*]'. It was then pointed out that this did

accompaniment of heavy coverage and applause in the Paris press. So had two distinct schools of Arabs: the Hedjazi and the Syrian. The Zionist occasion promised, however, to be less spectacular than the one on which Feisal, with T. E. Lawrence in attendance, had appeared. None of the Zionists, all sober men in dark suits, could compete with the Hedjazi prince in his bedouin robes. None of the heads of Government would be present to hear them. Still, the Council, composed that afternoon of Balfour, Milner, Lansing (the American Secretary of State), Pichon, Tardieu, Sonnino (the Italian Foreign Minister), and Makino (the Japanese Foreign Minister) was a very considerable gathering. Ormsby-Gore, now the chief British authority on Zionism, was among the experts in attendance, as was Jean Gout, who of all French officials knew most about the subject.

The actual proceedings turned out to be formal, not to say stiff. The Jews were invited to make their statements, one by one. The members of the Council were content to listen in silence. There was no interrogation, no give and take, no discussion either with the Zionists or, after their departure, within the privacy of the Council. A single question was put to them—and that, more or less by arrangement, by Lansing. All was over in about an hour and a half. No decision or resolution was taken; none so much as proposed. After hands had been shaken and courtesies exchanged (Sonnino was the only one to have made a point of demonstrating friendliness), the Jews left and the Council went straight on to the other business on its agenda: notably questions relating to the Åland Islands and Transylvania.

Yet for the Zionists themselves it was unquestionably—as Sokolov told the Council in so many words—a 'solemn hour' for which the Jewish people had waited eighteen centuries.[62] Weizmann and Sokolov, with Tolkowsky and Spire at their side, had been in a fever of preparation all of the previous day: who would say what; in what order; for how long. The juniors on the team were terrified lest the notoriously long-winded Sokolov and even Weizmann, neither of

not suit e.g. the Polish case. The wording was then changed to read: 'Nations that had arrived at independence since the beginning of the war and nations in the making will be authorized to state their case [*exposer leur cause*] verbally and in writing before the inter-Allied Conference.' AE, Série Y Internationale, vol. 15, fos. 226–9.

[62] Secretary's Notes, Peace Congress: Paris. 27 February 1919. PRO, CAB 28/6, fo. 247.

whom were prepared to speak other than extempore, would ramble, and fail to end their statements properly and on time, and the great occasion be fumbled. Written presentations were prepared for them, and eventually and reluctantly grudging consent to use them, if only as notes, was extracted. So was a rough division of the responsibility. There was some discussion when Ussishkin, co-opted at almost the last moment to represent Russian Jewry, announced that he would speak in Hebrew. Would this be seen as provocative? In the event, Ussishkin had his way and no harm was done: perhaps because he undertook to speak very briefly. The alarming news, delivered very late in the day, that Sylvain Lévi would be joining them had led to frantic efforts to find him, speak to him, and reach an understanding with him if only it were possible. But he was at the opera that evening—in Baron Edmond de Rothschild's box, as the Zionists grimly noted—and unavailable. An exceedingly brief, inconclusive encounter with him some hours before the Council session raised the temperature on both sides. All the Zionists elicited from Lévi was his irritated protestation that they were very wrong to suspect him of hostile intentions. Their own anxieties remained unappeased. They knew perfectly well that he had been in and out of the Foreign Ministry all week, and felt in their bones that he had been groomed for, and would indeed be playing, the role of spoiler.[63]

Thus, there were no real surprises. Sokolov spoke first—the weight of two thousand years of exile, pain, and affliction plainly on his shoulders, as Weizmann was to put it later—placing the occasion and the demands of the Zionists in a large perspective. The delegates had come to the Conference to claim their historic rights to Palestine, he told the Ministers, a country in which the Jewish people had created an immensely influential civilization. It was its loss that had reduced them to a nation possessed of neither land nor national power and condemned to a long and continuous martyrdom. True, there were small groups of contented Jews in the west who lived freely and peacefully, and the Jews were properly grateful to France, Great Britain, Italy, and to the United States for the rights, liberty, and sympathy they had been granted in all four countries. But the problem of the great mass of Jewry in the east and its craving for a full national existence remained. During the war, sustained by promises made to them, the Jews had supported the Allies as best they could; and 'now that a victory of great ideals and

63 Tolkowsky, pp. 423–6.

of justice had been gained, the hour of deliverance of this unhappy people [has] struck.' Sokolov went on to present the needs and demands of the Zionists as embodied in the document they had prepared and circulated. Chiefly, their call was for recognition of the Jews' 'historic title' to Palestine, the right to reconstitute a National Home within it, and the vesting of the 'sovereign possession' of the country in the League of Nations, Great Britain being entrusted with its government as the League's mandatory.

Weizmann followed. A central element of his argument was in essence that which Herzl had employed when appearing before the Royal Commission on Alien Immigration in 1902. The matter of Zionism and Palestine had to be seen, he warned, in the context of the catastrophe that had befallen Russo-Polish Jews and the river of emigrants that had flowed to the west before the war and would now 'increase enormously'. But since the western states' 'power of absorption' could be expected to decrease, and their Governments would henceforth 'scrutinise every alien' asking for entry as never before, 'the Jews would find themselves knocking about the world, seeking a refuge and unable to find one'. This was a problem 'no statesman could contemplate . . . without feeling impelled to find an equitable solution'. What was wanted was both 'peace'—i.e. less conflict and less tension—and a means of transforming 'Jewish energy into a constructive force, instead of its being dissipated into destructive tendencies or bitterness'.

The means, of course, was Palestine. Weizmann went on to outline the country's possibilities, its 'empty spaces' in which four to five million 'at least' could be settled 'without encroaching on the legitimate interests of the people already there', and the intense desire of the Zionists to take the enterprise in hand. He recalled the passages in the Zionists' formal memorandum which specified the terms on which they believed the mandatory system should be founded. He concluded, saying that he spoke 'in the name of a million Jews who, staff in hand, were waiting for the signal to move.' If the leaders of Jewry 'found themselves unable to tell their people to wait'—i.e. if the craving of the Jews of eastern Europe for security and national self-expression went out of control—a catastrophe would ensue. The support of the Great Powers was indispensable. The leaders of Zionism relied upon them to render it.

Sokolov and Weizmann each spoke for about ten minutes, Ussishkin and Spire, who followed, more briefly still. Ussishkin

(Sokolov translating his Hebrew into French) asserted the support of Russian Zionism and Russian Jewry (on the strength of resolutions adopted in south Russia) for the position stated and the claims submitted by the two previous speakers. Spire spoke for the French Zionists (admittedly 'not in the majority amongst the Jews of France'), and of his conviction that France, 'which had ever defended the rights of the oppressed,' would now support the Zionists' claims—a view that was 'only natural,' he said firmly, for a French Jew to express.

It was Sylvain Lévi's turn. His statement was immensely long (it took some forty minutes to deliver) and laboured. He read from a prepared script, translated (by Pichon's instruction) sentence by sentence into English. To the Zionists' dismay, then fury, he began with a condescending appreciation of the accomplishments of the new *yishuv* (with heavy emphasis on the roles of Baron de Rothschild and the Alliance Israélite Universelle—Zionism, he managed to imply, having been consequent upon their efforts). He went on to break the larger subject down, 'difficulty' by 'difficulty', by way of arguing that, while he was not opposed to the resettlement of Jews in Palestine, the methods and purposes of the Zionists were unacceptable. The country itself, small, poor, and harsh in climate, was 'disproportionate' to the millions who might wish to go there from eastern Europe. The people in question, 'the masses' who might wish to return to Palestine, had indeed been subject to persecution and ill-treatment. For that very reason they could be expected to carry with them 'highly explosive [i.e. revolutionary] passions, conducive to very serious trouble in a country which might be likened to a concentration camp of Jewish refugees.' The Peace Conference should be aware too that it would be a motley crowd, drawn from many countries: 'aspirations would not suffice to create a national entity . . . the fusion of all these people would take time.' The Zionists' idea of forming an International Jewish Council to act as 'guardian and political ruler of Palestine' was 'ingenious'. But he, Lévi, as a Frenchman of Jewish origin, feared the results. It was dangerous to allow citizens of one country to govern and exercise rights of citizenship in another. True there was a precedent for such dual citizenship, but it was a German one and as such 'a sad beginning' for the Jewish revival. Most shocking, in his view, was the claim of special privileges for the Jews when they, in proper accord with the spirit of the French Revolution, had long and rightly, and in part successfully, claimed no less, but no more, than equality of rights in the countries of their residence. Finally, he wished to place on record the part France had played in 'the organisation of the Jews in Palestine. Whatever country might eventually be appointed as mandatory in Palestine, he trusted that France would be permitted to continue her beneficent education work, by maintaining the schools which had been of such inestimable value to the peoples of Palestine.'

The official minutes are silent on the tension that followed and the dilemma in which the Zionists were placed. Other sources make no secret of them. Should they respond? Should they let what Lévi had said pass? 'Did I say anything that could have shocked you?' Lévi whispered to Spire as he sat down. 'Much,' was the reply. Relief came in the form of a question by Lansing. Would Weizmann 'clear up some confusion which existed in his mind as to the correct meaning of the words "Jewish National Home". Did that mean an autonomous Jewish Government?' Weizmann leapt at the opportunity. So far as Lansing's question was concerned, the answer was no. The Zionists did not want autonomous government. That might come later, when the Jews formed the large majority and were 'ripe to establish such a Government as would answer to the state of the development of the country and to their ideals.' What they wanted now was 'merely to establish in Palestine, under a mandatory Power, an administration, not necessarily Jewish, which would render it possible to send into Palestine 70,000 to 80,000 Jews annually.' And the right to establish schools, develop institutions, and generally 'build up gradually a nationality, and so make Palestine as Jewish as America is American, or England English.'

He then set upon Lévi. Of course, the enterprise raised problems and difficulties. If it had not been so there would have been no need to submit it to the Conference. But if the Jews were left in Russia the difficulties would be greater. The Jewish Council for Palestine the Zionists proposed would not be political; its functions would be economic and financial. The fear that the Jews would be accused of double allegiance was groundless. It was true that the Jews of Russia lived in an atmosphere that was not conducive to 'quiet thinking'. But the Jewish settlements which Lévi had spoken of in glowing terms had been created by just such Russian Jews. As for the country itself and its capacity to absorb numbers of immigrants— that surely would vary and increase as it was transformed by settlement and investment. There were precedents: Tunisia, for example; and Palestine was better endowed. Once again: such difficulties were as nothing compared with those faced by the Jews in eastern Europe, the overwhelming majority of Jews in all Europe. He, Weizmann, spoke for them; and they shared the views he had endeavoured to express that afternoon.

It was over. As the Jews emerged from the Ministry building, Lévi extended his hand. The Zionists refused it. They were unforgiving. 'You betrayed us,' Lévi was told, first by Weizmann, then by Sokolov. But they were well pleased with their own performance and with the impression they were sure they had made on their listeners. 'It was a marvellous moment,' Weizmann wrote his wife; 'the most triumphant of my life! . . . a most brilliant victory!' Tolkowsky, the secretary to the Zionist delegation in Paris, and a most precise and sober observer of its affairs, did not think otherwise. It had been a day 'worthy of being remembered in the history of the Jewish people,' he noted that evening in his diary.[64]

The argument between the Zionists and Sylvain Lévi continued to reverberate for some days both in the Jewish press in forthright terms[65] and, more subtly and with the influential hand of the Quai just visible, in the major newspapers of Paris. The terse official communiqué reporting the appearance of the Zionists was printed verbatim, along with a line or two at most on what the Zionists had had to say. Lévi's objections were commonly reviewed in some detail, with no little attention paid to his experience, academic prestige, and undoubted private virtues. Only one newspaper took the trouble to present the case for the Zionists as the Zionists themselves conceived it.[66] None of the Paris newspapers referred to Tardieu's announcement to the press immediately after the Council

[64] The chief sources for this account are the official British minutes (Secretary's Notes, Peace Congress: Paris. 27 February 1919. loc. cit.); Tolkowsky, op. cit., pp. 425–9; Spire, op. cit., pp. 108–10; Weizmann's report to the London Conference, 5 March 1919, *GAC Minutes*, pp. 52–5; Weizmann to Vera Weizmann, 28 February 1919. *Weizmann Letters*, ix, no. 123, pp. 116–19; and Sylvain Lévi's own hostile account as recorded by the equally hostile Lucien Wolf in his diary, 1 March 1919. CAHJP, 525/5, pp. 54–6. Broadly, all six versions tally.

[65] See for example *La Palestine nouvelle*, 1 March 1919; and *L'Univers israélite*, 14 March 1919.

[66] See for example, *Le Temps*, 28 February and 1 March 1919; *Journal des débats*, 1 and 2 March 1919; and *Le Petit parisien*, 28 February, 3 and 4 March 1919. *Le Matin* carried an extensive interview with Sokolov on 28 February 1919.

session to the effect that all five Powers had now agreed to entrust Palestine to Great Britain.

It remained, none the less, that to all intents and purposes, minds—the minds that counted—had indeed been made up, and that the appearance of the Zionists before the Council had set a public seal on their legitimacy and political respectability. Henceforward the Zionist movement would be a part, however small, however controversial, however welcome to some and unwelcome to others, of the established furniture of the international political arena. And it was the French, as it happened, by finally withdrawing—in some cases smothering—their objections and reservations to the principle (as opposed to the details) of the re-entry of the Jews into Palestine on the terms the British (not the Jews themselves) had laid down, who completed the long drawn out, immensely convoluted process. Two days after the Council session, Tardieu, acting as much in Clemenceau's as in his own name, briefed the Commissariat for Franco-American Affairs in New York on the principles upon which France was moving towards a peace settlement. 'We do not insist upon maintenance in full of the Franco-British Accord of 1916,' he informed his colleagues for their information and as guidance in their relations with the press. France would continue to insist on its interests in Syria. But 'so far as Palestine is concerned, we will not object to a British mandate and we will keep the promises made to the Zionists.'[67] All told, then, Weizmann had some cause to sum up before the Zionist Conference, on his return to London, on an immensely optimistic note.

There will be discussions [in Paris] on many details. But the principle of a Jewish National Home has been accepted. . . . And meanwhile we can say to the Jews, to the Jews of the world, that the Jewish National Home in Erez-Israel is a fact. Now it depends on us alone.[68]

[67] Prime Minister's Office to French Commissioner, New York, 2 March 1919. SHAT, 13N12.
[68] *GAC Minutes*, 5 March 1919, p. 55.

10

The End of the Beginning

The arrival of the Zionists at the very threshold of success was marked by a profound irony in that it coincided with the beginning of the ruin of European Jewry. Formal civil emancipation was shortly to be granted the Jews before long everwhere: willingly enough in post-revolutionary Russia, in Czechoslovakia, and in the briefly independent Ukrainian republic; with resignation in the Baltic states; grudgingly and under pressure in Romania; with huge ill will in newly united sovereign Poland. But in a matter of years it would be revoked almost everywhere, explicitly or in substance, in whole or in part; at the very least, it would be subject to ever more vociferous contestation. Long before the slate had been wiped clean again and the old liberal dream entirely replaced by fear and darkness as a matter of high policy by the German state, the signs that terrible things might be in store for the Jews were multiplying. It was beginning to be apparent that the collapse of the old European empires had not greatly benefitted them after all, and that the effect of the dissolution of the outer political and administrative framework within which they had conducted their lives for centuries was likely to be catastrophic. They had now to contend with new rulers of new states, the rulers of a notably narrow cast of mind, the states founded on a principle of territorial nationality from the compass of which the Jews were necessarily excluded. The new frontiers and the new, largely artificial political loyalties imposed upon them (why should the Jews of east Galicia declare for the Poles rather than for the Ukrainians, let alone for themselves, when the Poles were in the minority?) tended to balkanize the hitherto fairly compact mass of Ashkenazi Jewry and raise new barriers to old roads of escape. Finally and most ominously, they were exposed as never before in the modern era to violence and molestation at all levels of intensity and on all scales of magnitude—from petty but continuous (and therefore exceptionally unnerving) jostling by hooligans in the streets and the universities to mindless butchery, notably in Poland and the Ukraine, on a scale unknown for three centuries.[1] The cumulative result was unprecedented destitution, disorientation, and despair, and the Jews were revealed, not for the first time, as catastrophically weak and defenceless.

The affairs of the Zionists were shot through with other ironies and paradoxes, among them the fact that what had transpired amounted, as shall be argued, to an unspoken vindication of the methods and purposes of the Herzlian political-diplomatic school by men who had fought Herzl in his lifetime and continually argued his failings as a leader and as a Jew long after his death. But mostly they were trivial. Not so this grant to Zionism—and through it to the Jewish people—of its first effective ticket of entry into the international arena at the moment when the cornerstone of the great

---

[1]   The intensity and dimensions of the killings and depredations to which the Jews of Poland and the Ukraine were subject immediately after the world war, in the course of the civil war in Russia, and during the fighting between Soviet Russia and independent Poland, defy summary. None can estimate the numbers (probably thousands) beaten up, shorn of their beards, plundered, killed by a mob, or in extreme cases summarily shot or hanged on patently false charges by officers and men of the new Polish army. But it is the massive slaughters in the Ukraine that, in retrospect, cannot but seem to have been so many plain indicators both of the jeopardy into which eastern European Jewry was now placed and the freedom with which their enemies, if so willing, could now deal with them. The most cautious contemporary estimates of the numbers killed outright in the years 1918–21, before Soviet control was finally established, are 30–50,000. Later calculations put the total, including those dead of injuries, at at last twice the latter figure. The Jewish quarters of over 500 towns and villages were ravaged, some several times over, chiefly, but not exclusively by Ukrainian nationalist formations and by troops fighting for the White counter-revolutionary cause. In one notorious case 1,500 Jews of all ages and both sexes were deliberately bayonetted and cut to pieces with sabres in the small town of Proskurov in February 1919 by a brigade of Zaporozhian cossacks. (The use of firearms had been explicitly forbidden the men for these purposes by their commander, lest shots fired at the Jews in one part of the town give warning of what was transpiring in another.) But except in one respect, Proskurov was much like so many other places, a relief worker from Kiev reported. It was much like Uman, for example, another small town where 400 Jews were killed some months later. Except this, that whereas at Uman the cossacks had butchered Poles and Jews indiscriminately, 'at Proskurov,' the relief worker reported, 'only Jews were massacred, the Poles and the other Christians having observed the most strict neutrality.' Comité de délégations juives, *Les Pogromes en Ukraine* (Paris, 1927), annexes, p. 52. See also E. Tcherikower, *Di Ukrainer pogromen in yor 1919* (New York, 1965), pp. 121–9; and N. Gergel, 'The Pogroms in the Ukraine in 1918–21', *YIVO Annual of Jewish Social Science*, vi, 1951, pp. 237–52.

structure of events that would lead to the disintegration and destruction of European Jewry was being laid. For it had, of course, been out of Europe, especially eastern Europe, that Zionism had emerged in the first place. It was on the afflictions of its Jewry that Zionism's *raison d'être* hinged. It was to their regeneration and rehabilitation that Zionists of all schools had always been dedicated. And, by a last ironic twist, the historical conjuncture at which the myth of the power of the Jew had—uniquely—borne them (and the Zionists in particular) some useful fruit would be the very one at which their true, ancient, endemic, and ultimately fatal impotence was set to be exposed as never before. The question how they were to deal with the catastrophe unfolding before their eyes would face the Zionists to the end.

They did not, under their new leaders, ignore events in eastern Europe. They could not have had they wanted to: their offices in London, Paris, and Copenhagen were flooded with reports of insecurity and deep uncertainty in inner Russia and persecution on its periphery. Nor did they refrain from drawing the attention of the western Powers to the fate that had overtaken the Jews in the new Poland in particular or from pleading for intervention on their behalf and protection from their new masters. Nor did they question their right and duty to speak out on the subject.[2] But the old fear that a panic rush by the Jews to escape their rulers and persecutors was incompatible with the short-term and tactical interests of the movement informed their every move. If the hammering of the Jews culminated in a great expulsion (as some Poles threatened) or even a voluntary, but large-scale migration, 'we shall', in Weizmann's language, 'have all the miserable refugees who will be driven out of Poland, Galicia, Rumania, etc., at the doors of Palestine. We shall be swamped in Palestine and shall never be able to set up a community worth having there.'[3] So did a determination to keep the issue of Palestine distinct from that of European Jewry, at all events so far as the discussions and decisions at the Peace Conference were concerned. 'The Zionist Organization as such was not an organization concerned with these European problems though individual Zionists may have their views upon them,' Sokolov insisted in Paris.

---

[2] See for example Weizmann's interview with Sir George Clarke at the Foreign Office, 28 November 1918. SRO, GD40/17/1160.

[3] Weizmann to Wickham Steed, 30 November 1918. *Weizmann Letters*, ix, no. 45, p. 50.

'The Zionist Organization existed for Palestine only and the Zionist question was geographically limited to Palestine.' But while the British accepted this, the French did not. They wanted the question of Palestine 'relegated to a Committee to be set up to consider Jewish affairs in Poland, Galicia, Roumania, etc.' as well. It was Sokolov's hope, therefore, that the British would use their influence to prevent this being done, namely 'to prevent Zionism being included in other Jewish questions.'[4] The British were accommodating.

The roots of the dilemma in which the Zionists found themselves ran deeper than mere fear of procedural and conceptual muddle at the Peace Conference such that what they took to be their own simple and straightforward cause be drowned in a host of other, complex, embittered, and geographically and politically remote causes. It ran deeper than Weizmann's nightmare (with *its* roots leading all the way back to pre-Herzlian Ḥibbat Ẓion) of the *yishuv* being 'swamped' by more immigrants than it could handle and the resources of both the movement and the country being revealed as irremediably inadequate. The fact was that the war and the collapse of the European empires had recast the terms of the Jewish Problem not only in the sense that the afflictions of the Jews were greater and their conditions more perilous than before, but in the sense that outside the Soviet Union, eastern Jewry seemed to be emerging— and was certainly thought by others to have emerged—as a political factor of some momentary and limited (if always somewhat shadowy) consequence in its own right.

The rules for survival in the old multinational empires had been relatively clear. The Jews, by and large, neither competed for power nor were seen as the allies of any of the nations except, indirectly, and then specifically by virtue of their passivity and lack of national-political ambition, of whoever was in power at the time: Russians, Germans, Magyars, or, locally, the Poles. True, on the *margin* of otherwise coherent, Ashkenazi, Yiddish-speaking Jewry, there were such as did seek active alignment with Russians, or Germans, or nationalist Poles. Usually such desire for alignment with any of the more powerful nations of central and eastern Europe was bound up with an assimilatory flight from Jewry and Judaism themselves. But the overwhelming majority of Jews sought no allies, refused to look forward to a time when mighty Russia or conveniently complex—

---

[4] Note by Sir Louis Mallet, 20 January 1919. PRO, FO 608/98, fos. 152–3.

because supremely multinational—Austria-Hungary might founder, and wished chiefly to be left in peace. Thus they troubled none of the parties fighting to retain, or to attain, national supremacy or independence or both. And thus that great part of Jewry that constituted in all significant respects (by virtue of their culture, language, history, descent, and even, to a large extent, territorial concentration) the Jewish *nation* in Europe played no significant part in the pre-war jockeying for territorial power. It was seen by none, not even by itself, as a candidate for full, which is to say political, national self-determination, and found that there were times and places when even the old, and always profound cultural-religious-historical hostility with which it was regarded by rulers and ruled alike was so far mitigated by political calculation as to be partially (and temporarily) replaced by benevolence. The Jews were the only true Austro-Hungarians, it was said of them, the only ethnic category upon whom the Emperor Franz Joseph could really rely.

Even in Imperial Russia, where hostility to the Jews had long been a principle of state policy openly proclaimed, the full potential consequences of such a policy had always been mitigated in practice not only by the nagging desire of the Autocracy to retain a place among those who regarded themselves as the civilized powers of Europe, but by its knowledge that, seen in the context of the multiplicity of nations it sought to govern, the relative passivity of the Jews was a boon. The failure of the Autocrat and his servants to resolve the contradiction had the twin effects of driving ever greater numbers of Jews into the ranks of their active enemies and of leading ever more Russians to see that official anti-Semitism was not the least of those state policies that was self-destructive of the regime. More, the battering of the Jews, while perhaps less intense, less systematic, and more sporadic than it might have been had the Autocracy's policy towards them not been touched by ambivalence, was none the less sufficiently brutal and long-lasting to turn ever more Jews in Russia *and* outside it to thoughts of national Jewish action—of which Zionism was only one notably radical variety. No government did so much as the Russian—at least from 1881 onwards—to move its Jewish subjects towards a *political* state of mind.

What moved their now quondam subjects a very great step further, however, was the coincidence at the end of the war of the grant, or at least the promise of a grant, of full civil rights and equality throughout central and eastern Europe *and* the establishment of the principle of nationality as the basis for such rights, and for political arrangements generally, as the one accepted and acceptable basis for public life throughout the continent. On the one hand, this provided a boost to those tendencies within Jewry, all hitherto minoritarian, some subterranean, to seek an equal place in the sun through the acquisition of collective national rights and status in some form and in some degree. On the other hand, the drive by the hitherto subject nations in whose midst the Jews lived towards full political independence and control over the territories allotted to them, or claimed by them, was for the most part too intense and too impatient for the pretensions of the Jews to be considered with understanding, let alone generosity, or even at all. In the new world of minor national states—with newly independent Poland serving as the paradigm case—the ever stronger claim by Jews (but not the Jews alone) for limited, but still formally and internationally recognized *rights* and to a special communal regime as a distinct national group, precipitated a conflict with their majoritarian neighbours and would-be masters of a wholly unprecedented—because political—kind. The inner driving force, so far as the claim for minority—in effect, national—rights in the successor states of central and eastern Europe was concerned, was very similar to that which fuelled Zionism: fear for the future of the Jewish people as a coherent, historically and culturally continuous body of men and women battered physically and being pulled apart by hostile foreign cultures and, so far as the problems and afflictions of the Jews themselves were concerned, irrelevant political ideologies. Where, then, would the drama of modern Jewry be played out: in Poland, say, or in Palestine? And where should the adepts of the modern Jewish national tendency direct their attention and energy: to London, Paris, and Jerusalem, or to Warsaw—and perhaps, Proskurov? Of one thing there could be no discussion: the *people* were in Poland and in the lands contiguous to it; and there (none thought otherwise) they were likely, overwhelmingly, to remain. Thus the largest question and the greatest ambiguity overshadowing the Zionists' affairs (faithfully reflected in the direction Weizmann and Sokolov had taken) were still those pinpointed by Aḥad Ha-'Am a generation earlier. Was the Zionists' essential business with the moral, spiritual, and cultural afflictions of Judaism at this time; or was it rather with the material afflictions of the Jews themselves? If the latter, would the Zionists have anything, example and precept apart, to offer the mass of impoverished and persecuted Jewry directly? If the former, was there not added reason to take a moderate line so far as the National Home was concerned, to avoid precipitating a rift with the British—in a word, to concentrate on 'practical' Zionist purposes, albeit in a new form and in vastly improved circumstances? In that event short-term and long-term purposes, available resources, political possibilities, and instinctive preferences could all be matched, and the problem of eastern European Jewry *in situ* left safely in the hands of its own local leaders whose interest in the progress of Zionism, when not hostile, was mixed and now much reduced.

It was perhaps in the nature of such things that to neither question was a clear answer ever forthcoming in the sense that the ambiguity in Zionism, as Weizmann and his supporters seemed to have conceived it, and certainly directed it, was ever cleared up. They chose to limit their purposes, to refrain from sweeping measures and a dramatic strategy. They chose, if only by default, not to take up the cause of all Jewry and not to put themselves—or seek to put themselves—at the head of the entire people. In that the Zionist position and creed had always represented a departure from, and a rebellion against, the settled patterns and customs of Jewish life and behaviour, this was not unnatural. In that the deepest roots of Zionism lay in the deterioration of the social and economic conditions of the Jews—in the steady loss of physical security, in the mounting threats against them, in their continuing and pervasive impoverishment—the failure of the new leaders of the movement to consider its purposes in the light of the Jews' contemporary condition and with a view to its direct and, if possible, immediate cure marked them as disciples of Aḥad Ha-'Am after all. The tactics of Herzl had been applied with such success as he himself would have applauded and envied. Of the ultimate, underlying purpose which had moved Herzl, the source both of his strength and special quality as a leader and of the unique potency of his posthumous reputation—the will to submit the Jewish people to rapid and sweeping change—Weizmann and his school fought shy.

ii

A preference for limited, ostensibly realistic purposes to be determined by considerations of prudence and a sober calculation of means, rather than by intuition, imagination, and an eye fixed upon ultimate ends, accorded well with the conventional wisdom of Jewish public life. It had been strengthened immeasurably and made a matter of all but explicit doctrine for the Zionist movement by the force which Weizmann—relying on what he judged to be the lessons of the war years—lent to it. It was confirmed and, so it seemed, rendered mandatory by the means by which the Zionists had finally broken through into the world political arena, namely by their crucial links with and dependence upon Great Britain. And here again, Weizmann, to a degree unknown in Zionism since Herzl and unknown in Jewish public life generally for centuries, emerged unquestionably as the central, pivotal and—as many now thought —indispensable figure, decisive as much for style and doctrine as for short-term tactics and overall policy.

Weizmann set himself four tasks in the immediate post-war years: to consolidate the British connection; to make the most of such possibilities as now seemed to be open to the Zionists in Erez-Israel; to have his own leadership confirmed and consolidated and the old guard and the wartime opposition to his policy removed from office and influence; and, a fourth task, to redefine Zionists purposes and targets in terms compatible with the first three. The purposes and policies he pressed for, if accepted, and the consolidation of his primacy in the movement were, of course, mutually reinforcing. He continued to believe, and taught others to believe, that Zionism was uniquely dependent upon the British for immediate entrenchment in Erez-Israel and for expansion and progress thereafter. He saw himself, and taught others to see him, as uniquely capable of pushing the enterprise forward in tandem with the British. All were now encouraged to believe, and it seems Weizmann himself had come to believe, that the link with the British and the Balfour Declaration in particular had been, in the final analysis, of his making. He had, so great numbers of his followers were convinced, long studied and now knew, understood, and admired the British— a famously exotic and unfathomable race—as did none other.[5] In

---

[5] His only true competitor at this stage was Jabotinsky, who, in some ways, thanks to his service in the British army, had a clearer, less sentimental insight into the English national character (and was in any case a man of richer imagination than Weizmann). But Jabotinsky never attained Weizmann's *entrée* and status in British officialdom and public life, and when he concluded that the British might end by betraying the Jews, he set out to fight them in a manner that Weizmann, as much intermediary for the Zionists as their representative, could not, to the end of his life, countenance.

sum, for at least the decade that followed the war, the thesis that the new alliance with Great Britain was crucially dependent upon, if not indistinguishable from, Weizmann's *persona* was hardly less than authoritative.

In all this Weizmann relied upon, and was indeed granted, a very large measure of British support. He was increasingly, in British eyes, the man they were prepared to work with, the man who could be trusted to listen to what they had to say, a man who was sure to press for no more than what was sensible and moderate, the man whose loyalty to Great Britain was in no more doubt than his loyalty to his own people, and who was besides—hence his uses—their proven and immensely effective leader. It followed that he deserved to be listened to in turn and, so far as possible, supported even when his purposes were regarded with scepticism or outright disfavour.[6] Hence the symbolic moves from time to time to bolster his position: the relative frequency with which—still representing no state or Government—he was received at the highest political level, his audience of the King prior to his departure to head the Zionist Commission in 1918, the plan (never implemented, in the event) to award him a knighthood, and many other such marks of respect and favour.

That Weizmann by 1919 had established himself in London as the Government's indispensable channel to the Zionist movement and, to some extent, beyond it to world Jewry as a whole, may not implausibly be judged his supreme political achievement. Unquestionably, it was on this that his position in the movement, and in Jewish public life generally, ultimately turned. And as the balance of official and political opinion in London shifted slowly, but ever more steadily, into line with the critics of the association with the Zionists in the Near East, so Weizmann's position became at once more difficult and—in the eyes of those who relied upon him on either side—more valuable.

iii

The basis for the British retreat from association with the Zionists was laid, as we have seen, almost as soon as the fact of association

---

[6] Allenby, for example, a man whose attitude to Zionism was at best ambivalent, had high praise for Weizmann 'for his moderate views [which had] gone a long way to ameliorate the political conditions in Palestine' and for his 'schemes for the future of Zionism ... [which were] bold and progressive; but, as outlined to me ... practicable.' Letters to Lloyd George, 24 December 1919 and 14 April 1920. HLRO, F49/13/2.

was proclaimed and acted upon. It had still to gather speed. For the time being, on the letter of Balfour's promise to the Zionists—yet who could say, authoritatively, what it had been intended to convey?—the British continued to stand firm. They had their way with the French, who were resigned, finally, to giving in to the British on the matter of Palestine as a whole and on the issue of the new territory's northern borders in particular, because they judged their own control of Syria to be conditional upon it.[7] As for the phenomenon of Zionism itself, there too the final note struck in Paris was one of resignation. 'France,' it was said at the Quai d'Orsay with something of that sly elegance for which its papers were often distinguished,

having made certain pledges to the Zionists and incapable of indifference to any work of liberation, must maintain a benevolent attitude towards them; but since Zionism does not love France and cannot serve her [interests], its partial failure will cause her no distress [*elle ne s'affligera pas de son échec partiel*].[8]

So then, with French resistance worn away, the allocation of Palestine to Great Britain could be formally and relatively smoothly resolved upon at the San Remo Conference of the Allied Powers in April 1920. Its direct fruit, the peace treaty with Turkey (the Treaty of Sèvres of 10 August of that year, almost as intricate a document as the Treaty of Versailles), duly repeated the wording of the Balfour Declaration and laid down that the mandatory power would be 'responsible for putting [it] into effect'.

The British had their way too, Balfour leading them with great determination, in the face of all efforts—notably by the Americans, but from within their own house as well—to apply to Palestine the now almost sacrosanct principle of national self-determination. The sentiment which that principle expressed was certainly 'unimpeachable', Balfour admitted. But the fact was, he reminded his colleagues, that in the case of Syria it was abundantly clear that there had never been a serious intention of consulting the inhabitants: 'Whatever the inhabitants may wish, it is France they will certainly have.' As for Palestine, the contradiction between the

---

[7] Thus Clemenceau to Gouraud, High Commissioner in Beirut, 30 November, 1919. SHAT, Fonds Clemenceau, 6N291.

[8] 'Le Sionisme', a 10-page, somewhat hasty, and in part inaccurate review of the matter and history of Zionism from Herzl's founding of the movement to the Peace Conference, n.d. but probably drawn up in April or May 1919. AE, Levant 1918–1929, Palestine, vol. 12, fos. 1–10.

letter of the Covenant and the policy of the Allies was more flagrant
still.

For in Palestine we do not propose even to go through the form of consulting
the wishes of the present inhabitants of the country, though the American
[King-Crane] Commission has been going through the form of asking what
they are. The four Great Powers are committed to Zionism. And Zionism,
be it right or wrong, good or bad, is rooted in age-long traditions, in present
needs, in future hopes, of far profounder import than the desires and
prejudices of the 700,000 Arabs who now inhabit the ancient land.

In my opinion this is right. What I have never been able to understand is
how it can be harmonised with the [Anglo-French] Declaration [of
November 1918 promising the inhabitants of Syria and Mesopotamia self-
rule], the Covenant, or the instructions to the [King-Crane] Commission of
enquiry.

I do not think that Zionism will hurt the Arabs; but they will never say
they want it. Whatever be the future of Palestine, it is not now an
'independent nation', nor is it yet on the way to become one. Whatever
deference should be paid to the views of those who live there, the Powers in
their selection of a Mandatory do not propose, as I understand the matter,
to consult them. In short, so far as Palestine is concerned, the Powers have
made no statement of fact which is not admittedly wrong, and no
declaration of policy which, at least in the letter, they have not always
intended to violate.[9]

Still, the tide was turning, and the body of Ministers, military
commanders, diplomats, and administrators who remained true
believers in both the uses and the virtues of the alliance with the
Zionists dwindled steadily. Arab feeling 'against our Zionist policy
has now reached fever heat, and . . . [the] Zionist claims become
more and more exorbitant,' Curzon complained to his colleagues in
April 1919.[10] 'It appears to be taken for granted that Great Britain is

---

[9] 'Syria-Palestine-Mesopotamia', 11 August 1919. Balfour Papers, BL, Add. MSS.
49752.
    [10] 'Note . . . by Earl Curzon', 22 April 1919, Enclosure 2 in No. 1. IOLR, MSS.
Eur. F112/1278. 'The feeling of the Arabs against the Jews is so intense,' British
officials were telling the Zionists in Palestine to their faces at this time, 'that the
Zionist demands now must be carried out on the point of the bayonet if at all; that
neither Britain nor any other nation can undertake the job.' Robert Szold to Felix
Frankfurter, (n.d. but probably) early in May 1919. 'The attitude is prevalent . . .
shared by the highest authorities, and likely to lose us everything,' Szold continued.
'. . . It may strike your mind as fantastic, and indeed it struck mine, when Jabotinski
suggested . . . two months ago that the logical development of the present attitude is
the prohibition of Jewish immigration. But now, though I know such prohibition will
not come, it is no longer inconceivable.' CZA, A264/7.

to be the tutelary power in that country,' a Foreign Office official of middle rank, much concerned at this stage with Jews, Zionists, and Palestine, complained.

I venture to think [he continued] that we shall never in any circumstances, be the controlling power. Jewish aspirations, as may be seen from . . . [various papers] emanating from the Zionist Organization, are unlimited, and the Jew will control his controller not only in Palestine, but in every quarter of the Globe.[11]

Sir Ronald Graham, his senior, once an enthusiast for the Declaration, tended now to agree, though cautiously and in the knowledge that Lloyd George and Balfour took a different view.[12] The Director of Military Intelligence, after a tour of the region in April and May 1920, reported that 'Our policy is one fraught with extreme danger.' Should the Jews be given 'unwarranted ascendancy over the other inhabitants' there would be serious local trouble and even 'rebellion throughout our Eastern Empire. All this was stated to me quite openly by the Grand Mufti, who went so far as to to talk about a Jehad.' As for his own kind, 'British officials of our administration in Palestine and British officers of the Troops of Occupation are unanimous in expressing their dislike of any policy favouring the Jews.'[13]

But always, long after Balfour had departed the scene, there was the commitment that bore his name, a sort of verbal monument which all who ventured into the wild country of Near Eastern politics were destined to come upon. The grounds on which it had been originally assumed were soon largely forgotten by almost all concerned, and on both sides. When in 1922 the Colonial Office

[11] Minute by George Kidston, 27 February 1919. PRO, FO 371/4170. The *Protocols of the Elders of Zion* had been received by the Foreign Office and circulated within it in at least two versions by 1919. They had been labelled 'Zionist Protocols'. Kidston was among those who were, in his own words, 'convinced of their absolute genuineness [and] regard them as the key to the activities of the [Turkish] C.U.P., Bolshevism, Spartacism, [and] *hoc genus omne*.' He was careful to distinguish the 'Zionis[m]' of the *Protocols* from the 'modern Zionis[m] of Drs. Weizmann [and] Sokolov which centres in Palestine. While the object of both movements was 'domination of the Jewish race in the world in fulfilment of the Scriptures', the Weizmann Zionists would postpone further action until the centre in Palestine was secure. Minute by Kidston, 4 July 1919. PRO, FO 371/4230. See also Bayley to Drummond, 19 October 1918. PRO, FO 371/3414, fos. 353–451.

[12] Minute by Graham, 28 February 1919. Ibid.

[13] Major-General Sir William Thwaites to Foreign Office, 11 June 1920. PRO, FO 371/5261, fos. 178–99.

(responsible for Palestine from March 1921), sought to review the entire problem, it discovered—it was so informed by the Foreign Office—that 'Upon the origins of the Declaration little exists in the way of official records; indeed, little is known of how the policy represented by the Declaration was first given form;' and Ormsby-Gore had to be applied to to add what he remembered to the 'very meagre' material available.[14] But the Declaration itself, its single convoluted sentence incessantly repeated and relied upon as much with hostile as with friendly intent, took on the character of a sacred text, a litmus test of honour, wisdom, or political ability— depending upon one's point of view—such that as Britain would deal with it, so Britain would be cursed or blessed. In 1918 a list of 'pledges given by [Great Britain] to foreign Powers or Nationalities' drawn up for the Cabinet listed the Jews, along with France, Russia, the Poles, the Albanians, and many, many others. 'We are bound only by the limited assurances given to Lord Rothschild in Mr. Balfour's letter,' it stated firmly.[15] But bound they were; so it was believed, and so it was held, for a time. In the Government's first full post-war statement of policy on Palestine in 1922 it was boldly affirmed that the Declaration 'is not susceptible of change.' Qualifications and reservations (additional to those embodied in the now famous single sentence of the Declaration itself) multiplied, beating up against and slowly eroding both the positive promise made the Zionists in 1917 and its 1922 corollary, that 'it is necessary that the existence of a Jewish National Home in Palestine should be internationally guaranteed and that it should be formally recognized to rest upon ancient historic connection.'[16] But it was 1939 before promise and corollary were finally washed away and the decision to end Britain's special relationship with the Jewish national movement finally made, proclaimed (in all but so many words), and acted upon.

Viewed from the British side, no mere summary of the stages of the wasting of that relationship can do justice either to its intricacy

[14] 'Palestine', memorandum drawn up by Ormsby-Gore, 24 December 1922. IOLR, MSS. Eur. F112/266. Balfour too was consulted, but, stressing his 'defective' memory and, regretting the death of Sykes ('who had the whole thing at his fingers' ends'), was unable to help. Balfour to E. Marsh, 19 February 1923. SRO, TD/84/84/5.
[15] 'Synopsis of our obligations to our Allies and Others' [by Harold Nicolson?], 6 February 1918. IOLR, MSS. Eur. F112/123.
[16] *British Policy in Palestine*, Cmd. 1700, June 1922, p. 19.

and protean quality or to the depth and force of ideological and emotional capital invested and subsequently lost in it both by those who favoured and those who fought it. The opponents of Britain's adoption of Zionism and *a fortiori* the opponents of Zionism *per se* had only the bitter satisfaction of seeing the Balfour-Sykes policy collapse within much less than a lifetime and their strictures—both the well-founded and those that served as self-fulfilling prophecies—borne out by events. For the dwindling class of supporters there was no joy to be had at all. Harold Nicolson, as faithful an observer and man of these times as any, sentimental and realistic in turn, an enthusiast for Balfour's policy although hardly a particular friend of the Jews,[17] recorded on hearing of Mark Sykes's death, that

I mind dreadfully. He is a real loss. It was due to his endless push and perseverance, to his enthusiasm and faith, that Arab nationalism and Zionism became two of the most successful of our war causes. To secure recognition of these his beliefs he had to fight ignorance at the F[oreign] O[ffice], suspicion at the I[ndia] O[ffice], parsimony at the Treasury, obstruction at the W[ar] O[ffice], and idiocy at the Ad[miral]ty.[18]

When in May 1939 the House of Commons debated the proposal (embodied, as Nicolson put it, in what was 'known to the Jews as the Black, and to the Gentiles as the White, Paper on Palestine')[19] to reverse the policy proclaimed twenty-two years earlier, he wrote:

My mind goes back to those distant days of 1917, when, in a dark basement of the Foreign Office, Mr. Dunlop and I were charged with the task of drafting and redrafting the Balfour Declaration. . . . That document is represented today by the champions of Arabia Deserta as some wartime improvisation, some flurried expedient, devised to placate the Hebraic denizens of Wall Street. . . . [But] it was not of the strong Jews that we were thinking; it was of the millions of weak Jews who lived, not in Kensington Palace Gardens or on Riverside Drive, but at Cracow and Galatz.[20]

On 15 May 1948 he noted in his diary:

The end of the Palestinian Mandate and the birthday of the independent State of Israel. All the pleasure I might have felt at this realisation of the

---

[17] 'Although I loathe anti-semitism, I do so dislike Jews,' he observed some time in 1945. Harold Nicolson, *Diaries and Letters 1939–45* London, 1967), p. 469.
[18] Entry for 17 February 1919. H. Nicolson, *Peacemaking 1919* (London, 1944), p. 263.
[19] Cmd. 6019, May 1939.
[20] *Spectator*, 26 May 1939, p. 900.

hopes of Zionism is clouded by the fear of war and the humiliation we have suffered.[21]

There would, of course, be disappointment and bitterness enough on the Zionists' side. If anything, it would be deeper because the asymmetry of power, dependence, and purposes was so immense; because for years their high hopes had been crossed and undermined by a misconception of what the British had been about from the beginning; because by and large they had yielded to the complacent temptation to see themselves as the true begetters of the policy proclaimed in November 1917; because their subsequent reliance on Great Britain seemed absolute, and abandonment and betrayal that much more fearful; and because the steady disintegration of the Jewish condition in central and eastern Europe, the impunity with which the crushing of the Jews had been made a matter of public policy in one member of the society of nations after another, and the barring of almost all the old roads of escape,[22] had rendered the Jews' incoherence and weakness as a nation manifest and plainly well beyond the power of the Zionists to correct. Yet in one central and decisive respect things were otherwise with them. The movement had passed through a crucial phase in its progress towards its ultimate goal. By 1919 the social rehabilitation of Jewry through its political reconstruction, while not within reach, was now at least within sight. Henceforward it would never be wholly lost from view.

iv

'Zionism aims at the creation of a home for the Jewish people in Palestine to be secured under public law' was the wording of the 'Basel Programme' of 1897. The institutional structure Herzl had asked for was a public 'Charter' laying down the rights, duties, and sphere of free operations of the autonomous Jewish community-to-be. His strategy, at its broadest, was to enter into a political alliance with one or more of the major Powers—preferably, but not necessarily, the Power in actual political and military control of the

---

[21] *Diaries and Letters 1945–62* (London, 1968), p. 139.

[22] By the late 1920s restrictive immigration laws enacted in the United States in 1921 and 1924 had reduced the number of Jewish immigrants into that country to one-tenth of the pre-war rate. By the early 1930s the number had been reduced to one-twentieth.

country, and always on the basis of give and take and sober calculation of interest on *both* sides. His tactic was to penetrate the world of high politics and to attain a status and recognition within it amounting, in the course of time, to a form of candidature for full membership. His underlying operating principle was that of the primacy of politics; and its corollary was that social reconstruction in Ereẓ-Israel or elsewhere *devoid* of political instruments, armature, and status would lead nowhere. A failure to re-enter the world of politics as subject (rather than object) and without a positive will to work for national ends on the basis of such national resources as could be mobilized to advance them would expose the Jews and their achievements in Ereẓ-Israel, however worthy and however substantial, to the untrammelled will of their rulers once again. The Zionists must work for the political reconstruction of Jewry because a thorough-going rehabilitation of the Jews was conditional upon it. It and it alone would provide the dignity, security, and cohesion which those who wished both to preserve the Jewish people and engineer a great accommodation to the conditions of the time thirsted for. These were the immediate, but also the deeper purposes of Zionism. In the final analysis ends and means were one and the same: the re-entry of the Jews as such into the world of politics and power. Some would say: the re-entry of the Jews into history.

All this was either explicit or implicit in Zionism as Herzl had sought to fashion it. Much of it had now, ten to fifteen years after his death, been acted upon; much of it had now been achieved. The *entente* with Great Britain had been founded—very precisely and more truly than the Zionists themselves realized at the time—on Herzl's principle of give and take (his beloved *do ut des*) and calculated interests. The League of Nations mandate embodying the Balfour Declaration, laying down the mandatory power's responsibility for securing the Jewish national home and facilitating Jewish immigration and settlement—all in co-operation with a specially established 'Jewish agency' to be recognized as a public body for such purposes[23]—was nothing if not the 'Charter' which Herzl had

---

[23] Under the terms of the mandate, it was laid down *inter alia*, that 'The Mandatory shall be responsible for placing the country under such political, administrative and economic conditions as will secure the establishment of the Jewish National Home . . . and the development of self-governing institutions, and also for safeguarding the civil and religious rights of all inhabitants of Palestine, irrespective of race and religion . . . (Article 2.)

'An appropriate Jewish agency shall be recognized as a public body for the purpose

wanted and his opponents, Weizmann among them, had scoffed at.

It is true and deeply characteristic of the peculiarity and fragility of the wartime *entente* into which the British and the Zionists had entered that the process of its erosion began, as we have seen, virtually at birth. Yet that *entente*, for all its fragility, was the saving of Zionism both as movement and doctrine. It provided (at the Peace Conference) public recognition of the Jewish people as legitimate participants in the affairs of the world political community and of the Zionists themselves as Jewry's representatives *par excellence*. It provided the Zionists with that open and seemingly secure, and therefore hugely promising, foothold in Erez-Israel they had craved for from the beginning and which the Turks, from the beginning, had denied them. It thus saved the movement from the apparently ineluctable decline into which it had fallen in the last years before the war, and given it an unprecedented opportunity finally to show its worth and prove its theses. It was the occasion— and the means—whereby the movement came to be equipped with fresh leaders and fortified institutions. And the reinvigoration of Zionism was completed, and, as it were, crowned by its specific content: the reunion of Jewry with Erez-Israel.

There is probably no people for whom the distant yet recorded past is so central to their being and practice as a collectivity as the Jews. Yet it is a past they had to carry entirely in their minds. No object or artefact embodied or even obliquely represented it. Nothing of consequence survived in concrete form to be set by one generation before the eyes of another: no Parthenon, no great cathedrals, no Crown of St Stephen, no Stone of Destiny, no great national, original documents. Their books, on which all turned, have been so many copies, few older than some centuries, none older

of advising and co-operating with the Administration of Palestine in such economic, social and other matters as may affect the establishment of the Jewish National Home and the interests of the Jewish population in Palestine, and, subject always to the control of the Administration, to assist and take part in the development of the country.

'The Zionist organisation, so long as its organisation and constitution are, in the opinion of the Mandatory, appropriate, shall be recognized as such agency . . . (Article 4.)

'The Administration of Palestine, while ensuring that the rights and position of other sections of the population are not prejudiced, shall facilitate Jewish immigration under suitable conditions and shall encourage, in co-operation with the Jewish agency . . . close settlement by Jews on the land, including State lands and waste lands not required for public purposes.' (Article 6.)

than, perhaps, a millennium. There was only the Land itself and the little it contained, but largely forbidden to them and in any case out of sight, remote, unreal. Whether it was indeed essential to turn the people back towards it and whether the past of the Jews should and could, in some way yet to be worked out, be rewoven into their present and future on the basis of such a Return, had been debated furiously by the Zionists in the last year of Herzl's life. The radicals' argument was that a break with the Land, and therefore, finally, with the last, tenuous, concrete link to the past, was justified if that was what the rescue and reconstruction of European Jewry required. It was rejected, never to be seriously revived. Now its defeat was absolute, and no error or failure by the proponents of the accepted doctrine—the protagonists of the Return—would reduce the vast prestige they had garnered by virtue of their triumph. For the significance of the Return, over and beyond its meaning for individuals and for the overt programme of the Zionists, was the provision of the Land itself as the Jews' visible and tangible symbol of their past. No attempt to stem, cancel, or even reverse the process of Return by those who opposed the re-entry, by right and in great numbers, of the Jews into Erez-Israel could ever entirely stop the flow of moral energy its onset precipitated into the ancient, tired body of Jewry. And the Zionists, by virtue of their having been its protagonists and the instrument whereby it was, at long last, set in motion, were now the moral guardians not only of the process of Return but, in a sense, of the Land itself. Nothing would strengthen the movement, enlarge its membership, electrify its activities, and lend authority to its leading spokesmen so greatly as its coming to preside over this last great effort to erect a bridge for Jewry between past and future.

But if a window of opportunity had opened up for the Zionists during the war years—one which some, not all, were glad to clamber through—it had been in its way a fluke, an event none could have soberly predicted, let alone engineered. To be sure, it was what the Zionists had needed if they were to progress or even survive. It was what, in a sense, they had long prepared themselves for and some had even consciously awaited: the collapse of the wall the Turks had set up against them along with a vast redistribution of power, influence, and territory, both in Europe and the Near East, in the course of which, somehow or other, they would find a way to break through and advance their cause.

What they would now be able to make of their opportunity depended, however, on matters of a different order: on men, on money, on the ability to mobilize consistent political support in the face of a mounting and ever more ominous array of opponents. And these in turn depended ultimately on the strength of Zionism within Jewry—always limited, even if growing—and on the strength, resources, and morale of Jewry as a whole. It was precisely these, the moral and material resources of the Jewish people, that were now set for decline. Thus the Zionists emerged from the Great War with prospects that were at once brilliant and exceedingly dark—and entered, without as yet realizing it, in a perilous race against time.

Select Bibliography[1]

The primary materials available for a study of the Zionist movement in the years leading up to the Great War, the years of the war itself, and those of its immediate aftermath are now more than abundant. The pre-war years were those in which the Zionist Organization was consolidated and, to some extent, bureaucratized, with the result (among many others) that a great deal of documentary evidence on its activities accumulated. Once the war started and the matter of Zionism began to percolate into the central political and diplomatic arena, it affairs and its activities began to be observed and dealings with Zionists recorded by the relevant bureaucracies of the Powers as well, chiefly, of course, that of Great Britain. Later, the new, intrinsic importance in international political terms of particular events and developments in Zionism, notably the process of its alignment with Great Britain, led to an extensive secondary literature as well. But two general comments are in order. In the first place, the earlier, pre-war period in which the movement was led first by Wolffsohn, then by Warburg, was one which many have been (understandably) tempted to pass over, or even dismiss, as an almost intolerably dull interlude between the years of heroic frustration associated with Herzl and the years in which the Zionists finally found their way to the starting post in the race for political independence. The earlier period (1907–14) is thus much less well served than the later (say, 1914–19). The archival sources are still, almost exclusively, such as originated within the Zionist movement itself. The secondary literature is particularly sparse, although some useful additions have been made to it in recent years.

Secondly, while the later period has given rise to a large body of memoirs, narrative accounts, historical analyses and interpretations, and, of course, innumerable pieces of polemical literature, much of it is so unreliable as to be unusable except by the historian of, for example the *debate* on the origins of the Balfour Declaration as opposed to its true roots in British, or for that matter, Zionist policy. The most notable—certainly the saddest—case in point is that of the memoirs of the man who was long thought of as the very

---

[1] For works and documents of a general nature on Zionism and the Zionist Organization, and their roots in Jewish society, especially in eastern Europe, see the Select Bibliographies appended to the *The Origins of Zionism* and its sequel *Zionism: The Formative Years*.

maker of the Declaration. As acquaintance with the documents deposited not only in the Public Record Office in London and in the Central Zionist Archives in Jerusalem, but in the exceedingly important Weizmann Archives in Reḥovot themselves make clear, Chaim Weizmann's autobiography *Trial and Error*, (London, 1949) is useless to the historian—at all events, the political historian—except as an indication of what the author (and his entourage) recalled and wished to have recalled in his somewhat bitter old age. It is principally for this reason that I resolved from the first to put virtually all secondary literature to one side, to use memoirs very sparingly, if at all, and to construct my account so far as possible on the basis of truly contemporary sources: private and institutional documentation and correspondence, diaries, the press.

For the entire period covered by this book (roughly: 1907–19) the most important of such sources may be divided into two classes. First and foremost are the immense collections preserved and easily available in the Central Zionist Archives (CZA), Jerusalem. They include the files of the Zionist Central Office, first in Cologne (under Wolffsohn), then in Berlin (under Warburg), the files of the Copenhagen wartime liaison office, and the files of certain territorial offices, among them the sadly incomplete papers of the pre-revolutionary Russian Zionist Organization (supplemented, however, by the Zenzipper Collection). The importance of these collections lies as much in the files of incoming correspondence (from Vilna and Petrograd, for example) as in the minutes of regular meetings of the EAC and the GAC, the outgoing correspondence, and the very useful, if irregular series of confidential circulars (news letters and instructions) to the outlying territorial organizations instituted under Wolffsohn and kept up to the end. Of equal (and for many topics even greater) importance are the collections of private, chiefly political papers of major figures whose activities spanned the entire period—Nordau, Sokolov (an immense collection that has barely been tapped), Zangwill, Jacobson, Ruppin, Gruenbaum, and Motzkin among many others. The CZA holds a large and valuable collection of pamphlets and photographs and complete runs of the more important Zionist periodicals, among them, of course, the indispensable *Die Welt*, founded by Herzl as the movement's own weekly, and its Hebrew-language analogue *Ha-'Olam*. The latter is particularly useful for its Russian-Zionist perspective and its coverage of events in Turkey as they impinged on the Zionist enterprise in Ereẓ-Israel before the outbreak of the Great War.

Four other archival institutions in Israel must be noted. The Weizmann Archives (WA), Reḥovot, contain not only Weizmann's own letters and other papers but a great deal of related material collected posthumously with exceptional assiduity and care. The Israel State Archives (ISA), Jerusalem, hold some useful material on the Ottoman period, that portion of

Herbert Samuel's papers that relates to Palestine, and a large collection of copies of material relevant to the subject of this book but held in the original in foreign state archives. The Jabotinsky Archives (JA), Tel-Aviv, do for Jabotinsky and his associates, on a smaller scale, what the Weizmann Archives do for Weizmann. The Central Archives for the History of the Jewish People (CAHJP), Jerusalem, hold important collections of papers, of which those of the Alliance Israélite Universelle (in microform) and of David Mowshowitch (a close associate of Lucien Wolf) are especially noteworthy.

In London, the Mocatta Library (ML) at University College London holds the records of the Anglo-Jewish Association, the Conjoint Foreign Committee (most of which bear the hand of Lucien Wolf), and the private papers of Moses Gaster. The archives of the Board of Deputies of British Jews (BD) hold a great deal of material which is parallel or complementary to that held in the Mocatta Library.

Only a minute portion of these enormous accumulations of documents has been systematically selected, annotated, and published. However, verbatim reports of the debates at the regular Zionist Congresses (the last one to be convened before the war was the Eleventh in 1913, the first to be convened after it was the Twelfth in 1921) were always published and made available, usually within six months or so of the session. For the mood, general concerns, rumblings of discontent, and face-to-face confrontations between leaders and led—such as the parliamentary debates of the Congresses always conveyed, often with rare precision—the Congress Protocols are of unique interest. These, of course, were public debates. The minutes of the meetings of the GAC are of equal or greater value for the confidential discussions of immediate policy and tactics which took place continually in that forum and in which the leadership had to give a much more precise and detailed account of its stewardship than in the Congress. An annotated edition is in preparation for publication in Hebrew translation, but only two volumes have been published thus far: Y. Freundlich and G. Yogev (eds.), *Ha-protokolim shel ha-vaʿad ha-poʿel ha-zioni*, i, February 1919–January 1920 (Tel-Aviv, 1975); ii, February 1920–August 1921 (Jerusalem, 1984). Similarly, a number of projects for the publication of the letters and papers of major figures have been planned from time to time—Jabotinsky's letters in abbreviated form, for example: ʿEri Jabotinsky *et al.* (eds.), *Igrot Zeʾev Jabotinsky*, i, (Tel-Aviv, 1972)—but, with two notable exceptions, left incomplete or never properly begun. The selected letters of the most acute of observers and critics of Zionism from inside the movement and the man to whom Weizmann was, for a time, closest are of enduring interest and value: A. [L.] Simon with Y. Pograbinsky (eds.), *Igrot Aḥad Ha-ʾAm*, i vi (Tel-Aviv, 1956 60); and a new, enlarged edition is in preparation.

But unquestionably, the fullest, most richly annotated, and—because complete—uniquely valuable series is the one devoted to the man who emerged as the central figure in the period in question: M. W. Weisgal (general editor), *The Letters and Papers of Chaim Weizmann*, Series A, Letters (23 vols., London and Jerusalem, 1968–80.) The scrupulous work of editors and staff and the energy with which the whole project was pursued from beginning to end make it a rare monument of its kind. Volumes v–ix comprising just under two thousand meticulously annotated letters, cover the period 1907 to mid 1920. The seventh volume, for the period August 1914–November 1917, edited by Leonard Stein with Devorah Barzilay-Yegar and Neḥama A. Chalom, is a particularly fine piece of scholarship. One can only regret that nothing comparable has ever been attempted for Nordau or Sokolov, serious editions of whose papers would go far to put our understanding of the evolution of the Zionist movement at its centre on an entirely solid basis.

ZIONISM AND ZIONISTS UNDER WOLFFSOHN AND WARBURG

The chief primary sources for this period are, once again, the files of the Zionist Central Office, the flag-bearers among the movement's periodicals (*Die Welt* and *Ha-'Olam*), and the private papers of Wolffsohn and Warburg themselves—all to be found in the Zionist Central Archives. But this is the period of Zionism's decline and one in which it had begun to fall into a place in Jewry that betokened one moderately important movement and trend among others. There is therefore much to be learned about it from the observations of others, including its critics. The records of such institutions as the Anglo-Jewish Association and the Alliance Israélite Universelle are instructive in this respect. So is the general Jewish press, particularly the *Jewish Chronicle* (London), virtually a newspaper of record for the entire Jewish world, providing some of the best and most regular reporting of events and commonsensical reflection on the principal issues of the day. Of the diaries and memoirs of well-informed and perceptive figures in the movement, Richard Lichtheim's autobiography, *She'ar yishuv* (Jerusalem, 1953), and Arthur Ruppin's diary, *Pirkei ḥayai*, 3 vols. (Tel-Aviv, 1968), are outstanding. An instructive contemporary contrast to these clear-minded men of action, representatives of German Zionism in its heyday and at its best, is provided by the letters of Shmarya Levin, *Igrot Shemaryahu Levin* (Tel-Aviv, 1966), all high feeling, spirit, and ideas of the most general order as might be expected of the less rigorously inclined of the Russian Aḥad Ha-'Amians.

Secondary sources are exceedingly sparse. The standard work has long been Adolf Böhm, *Die zionistische Bewegung* (Berlin, 1920; revised edn. Tel-Aviv, 1935), undoubtedly worthy, but inevitably out-of-date. Wolffsohn's career as leader can be followed, however, in considerable detail in a respectful and thoroughly documented account by Mordechai Eliav, *David Wolffsohn: ha-ish u-zemano* (Jerusalem, 1977). Warburg's stewardship, on the other hand, has yet to be investigated systematically: there is only a brief, old-fashioned, and somewhat sentimental account backed up by a selection of letters and papers: Ya'akov Thon, *Otto Warburg* (Jerusalem, 1948). Only Weizmann, still a minor figure in this period, has been examined very thoroughly, chiefly for clues to his later eminence, in Jehuda Reinharz, *Chaim Weizmann: The Making of a Zionist Leader* (New York, 1985). Jabotinsky, much the most colourful of the figures of second rank in the Wolffsohn-Warburg era, still awaits the biographer who will bring him fully to life. Meanwhile students must make do with the official biography, Joseph B. Schechtman, *Rebel and Statesman—the Jabotinsky Story: The Early Years* (New York, 1956), besides which there are Jabotinsky's own writings and autobiography (see below). Nordau too awaits his biographer, but something of the views of the Grand Old Man of Zionism in his post-Herzlian semi-retirement can be gleaned from the limited collection of papers published as B. Netanyahu (ed.), *Max Nordau: ketavim zioniim* (Jerusalem, 1960) of which volume 3 covers the years 1905–14. The most compact, sober, and reliable of contemporary accounts of settlement work in Erez-Israel are Ruppin's own reports to the EAC and the Congress, a few of which are available in print in A. Ruppin, *Sheloshim shenot binyan be-Erez-Israel* (Jerusalem, 1937).

P. A. Alsberg, 'Ha-orientaziya ha-medinit shel ha-hanhala ha-zionit 'erev milhemet ha-'olam ha-rishona (1911–1914)', *Zion*, xxii: 2–3, 1957, and the same author's 'Ha-she'ela ha-'aravit be-mediniyut ha-hanhala ha-zionit lifnei milhemet ha-'olam ha-rishona', *Shivat Zion*, iv, 1956, are helpful introductions to the attempt to restore politics and diplomacy to Zionism on the eve of the war. The latter article, dealing with the Zionist Executive's effort to come to grips with the problem of relations with the Arabs, can be usefully supplemented by N. J. Mandel, *The Arabs and Zionism before World War I* (Berkeley, Calif., 1976), and by a discussion of attitudes towards the developing conflict in the *yishuv* as reflected in the local press, Y. Gorni, 'Shorsheiha shel toda'at ha-'imut ha-le'umi ha-yehudi-aravi ve-hishtakfuta ba-'itonut ha-'ivrit ba-shanim 1900–1918', *Ha-Zionut*, iv, 1975.

The Zionist country organizations as they evolved in the years before the war have, in the main, suffered much the same neglect as the major concerns, institutions, and personalities of the movement at its centre. That said, two serious academic studies deserve notice and emulation not least because both set Zionism in the larger communal perspective: Stuart A. Cohen, *English Zionists and British Jews: The Communal Politics of Anglo-Jewry, 1895–1920* (Princeton, 1982); and Jehuda Reinharz, *Fatherland or Promised Land: The Dilemma of the German Jew, 1893–1914* (Ann Arbor, 1975).

ZIONISTS AND ZIONISM IN THE GREAT WAR AND ITS AFTERMATH

The most important single guide to the immense archival sources now available to the student of the history of the British-Zionist connection as it took shape during the Great War and in its immediate aftermath is Philip Jones (ed.), *Britain and Palestine 1914–1948* (Oxford 1979), produced under the auspices of the British Academy. It indicates, often in considerable detail, the major holdings of relevant material in a number of countries, but chiefly and best, of course, in the United Kingdom itself. There is no precise analogue for the other major Power with a voice touching on the destinies of the Zionists in this period, France—partly, no doubt, because the Franco-Zionist connection was very different in quality, direction, and intensity. But numerous useful clues to the content and location of relevant French official documents will be found in Bernhard Blumenkranz (ed.), *Documents modernes sur les Juifs; XVIe–XXe siècles* (Toulouse, 1979).

In London, the Cabinet and Foreign Office papers at the Public Record Office (PRO) are of course absolutely indispensable for an understanding not only of the process whereby British policy shifted and was finally resolved upon and then began to shift again in respect of the Zionists, but the climate of ideas and opinion in which the matter of the Jews in general and the Zionists in particular was taken up and considered by the decision-makers. These must be supplemented by the private papers of Ministers and senior diplomats (many to be found in the FO 800 series at the PRO), the Lloyd George and Samuel papers at the House of Lords Record Office (HLRO), the Balfour papers (additional to those at the PRO), C. P. Scott's diary, and the Northcliffe papers in the British Library (BL) Department of Manuscripts, and the Curzon and Reading papers at the India Office Library and Records (IOLR). A third collection of Balfour's papers is preserved at his home in Whittinghame, available through the National Register of Archives (Scotland) in Edinburgh. The Scottish Record Office (SRO) in Edinburgh holds the papers of Lord Lothian (who, as Philip Kerr, was Lloyd George's private secretary), which include several files on matters relating to Palestine and the Zionists. Two other exceptionally important British collections outside London are those of the Sykes papers held by the Hull University Library and the Clayton papers held by the Sudan Archive at the University of Durham. Finally, still further afield, but of interest for the light they throw on wartime Anglo-American relations as these impinged on the developing connection with the Zionists, there are the papers of Sir William Wiseman, Controller of British Intelligence in the United States during the war, held by the Yale University Library.

In Paris, the major deposits of relevant material in state archives are two. One is at the Foreign Ministry (now entitled Ministère des Relations Extérieures) where both the relevant subject files and the collections of private papers (known as 'papiers d'agents') are indispensable, if in some cases so slim and the style of the internal correspondence so elliptical as to be disappointing. The second is the enormous collection at the military archives, the Service Historique de l'Armée de Terre (SHAT) at Vincennes, where not only general staff and military intelligence (Deuxième Bureau) papers, but copies of Foreign Ministry correspondence (often absent from the files at the Quai d'Orsay itself) and certain collections of private papers (notably those of Clemenceau and André Tardieu) are preserved. Jean-Claude Devos, *et al.* (eds.), *Inventaire sommaire des archives de la guerre, série N 1872–1919* (Troyes, 1974), published by the SHAT, is an exceedingly useful guide to readers in these remarkable archives.

The official British and French documents must, of course, be read in conjunction with the material deposited in Israel and in the Jewish archives in London referred to above. Of the very small number of diaries and other papers of close observers and participants in these affairs to have been published, the outstanding example is the diary of Shemu'el Tolkowsky, who served as secretary to the London Zionist Committee, published with an excellent apparatus as Devorah Barzilay-Yegar (ed.), *Yoman ẓioni medini; London, 1915–1919* (Jerusalem, 1981). Yoram Efrati (ed.), *Yoman Aharon Aaronsohn, 1916–1919* (Tel-Aviv, 1978), and M. and E. Brock (eds.), *H. H. Asquith: Letters to Venetia Stanley* (Oxford, 1982), deserve mention for such views of affairs at the periphery in one case and at the centre in the other which they provide as would be hard to come by from an examination of the official documents alone. In the same class are two autobiographies: Jabotinsky's, *Avtobiografiya* (Jerusalem, 1958), and that of André Spire, *Souvenirs à bâtons rompus* (Paris, 1962); and the wartime recollections of Meir Grossman, 'Reshit ha-ẓionut ha-aktivistit', *Ha-Uma*, 9 June 1964; and id., 'Ha-pegisha ha-rishona' and 'Kabalat-panim anglit le-"ben-brit"', *Ha-Mashkif*, 6 August and 3 October 1948.

Access to most of the relevant British and French documents for this period has been free only since the 1960s. It is therefore all the more interesting and impressive that much the most successful study of Zionist diplomacy in this period was written before all the files were available for study. Leonard Stein, *The Balfour Declaration* (New York, 1961), though inevitably dated in many respects and somewhat weakened by the author's disinclination to impose his judgement at any point, remains required reading. Following on and leading the new crop of historians who have had the benefit of access to virtually all the documents has been Mayir Vereté, whose seminal article 'The Balfour Declaration and its Makers', *Middle Eastern Studies*, vi: 1, 1970, blew the first great hole in the cloud of myth and misinformation in which the subject had always been, and to some extent still is, enveloped. Other works which are instructive either for the material their authors have unearthed or for the light they have thrown on particular aspects of the subject are Isaiah Friedman, *The Question of Palestine, 1914–1918* (New York, 1973), and Ronald Sanders, *The High Walls of Jerusalem* (New York, 1983), on the origins of the Balfour Declaration; Bernard Wasserstein, *The British in Palestine* (London, 1978), on the military and civilian government of that country in the first decade of British rule; Evyatar Friesel, *Ha-mediniyut ha-ẓionit le-aḥar haẓharat Balfour* (Tel-Aviv, 1977), on Zionist policy after the issuing of the Balfour Declaration; Elie Kedourie, *The Chatham House Version and other Middle-Eastern Studies* (London, 1970), on the deeper springs of British policy as it evolved in the Near East after the first World War; Christopher M. Andrew and A. S. Kanya-Forstner, *France Overseas* (London, 1981), for a close analysis of French colonial policy in this period; Ruddock F. Mackay, *Balfour, Intellectual Statesman* (Oxford, 1985), for a fresh look at the most complex and perhaps most intriguing of major figures on the British side—while still leaving the relevant chapters in Balfour's official biography, Blanche E. C. Dugdale, *Arthur James Balfour*, 2 vols. (London, 1936), as illuminating documents in their own right; and Roger Adelson, *Mark Sykes: Portrait of an Amateur* (London, 1975), which largely replaces the earlier Shane Leslie, *Mark Sykes: His Life and Letters* (London, 1923). There is also much to be learned from the most recent, still incomplete biography of Lloyd George by John Grigg, of which the third volume, *Lloyd George: From Peace to War, 1912–1916* (London, 1985) is valuable for its picture of the radical changes the British system of government underwent; and the fourth volume of Martin Gilbert's official biography of Winston Churchill (London, 1975), which covers the years 1916–22.

Finally, although this book is not concerned with the 'Palestine Problem' as such, it does certainly deal with the international political circumstances that did much—some may think everything—to precipitate it. Inevitably, much of the published literature on the topics with which the book does seek to deal has been coloured—in many cases tainted—by attempts to ensure that the accounts offered conform to contemporary views of the Problem and the Arab-Jewish conflict. It may be appropriate, therefore, to mention at least one study of the Problem, as good as any and much better than most, written moreover just as its profoundly intractable and tragic nature had begun to be apparent, yet before the true circumstances of its birth had been forgotten: the *Palestine Royal Commission Report* of July 1937 (Cmd. 5479, London, 1937).

Index

'Abd al-Hamid, Sultan 13, 18–19, 25, 71
    see also Turkey
Admiralty 158, 371
Aḥad Ha- 'Am (Asher Ginsberg) 14, 21,
    27–8, 32–3, 59–61, 66, 68–9, 71, 120,
    159–63, 165, 176, 181, 191, 308, 312,
    336, 363–4
Ahmed Riza 16, 24
Albanians 370
Aleppo 83
Alexander, D. L. 178
Alexandretta 95, 101, 201
Alexandria 127, 139, 143, 146
Al-Karmil 73
Allenby, General E. H. H. 269, 299, 312–
    13, 315–16, 321
Alliance Israélite Universelle (AIU) 16–
    17, 25, 31, 107, 118 n., 191, 195, 198,
    313, 340, 354
Allied Powers:
    on Jews and Zionism 109, 117, 133,
        137, 284, 368
    major conferences (including Peace
        Conference) 178, 244, 255, 300, 321,
        322, 324–32, 335, 336, 337–9, 340–7,
        350–7, 360–1, 367, 372, 374
    policy and declarations by 83, 89–92,
        98–102, 114–15, 118, 174, 178, 207,
        209, 273, 281, 332, 343–68, 372, 375
    see also France; Great Britain; Russia;
        United States
Alsace-Lorraine 94, 342
America *see* United States
Amery, L. S. 155, 212, 222
Anglo-French (Sykes–Picot) Agreement
    199–206, 213, 223, 228, 236, 239,
    243, 250, 252, 299, 300, 318, 323,
    325–7, 343, 345, 357, 368, *map* 2
Anglo-Jewish Association (AJA) 107, 175
Anglo-Palestine Company (and Bank)
    22, 70, 126
anti-Semitism 11, 39–40, 73, 102, 179,
    181, 215, 248, 282, 290, 362

Arabs 14, 70, 73, 125, 136, 315, 317, 339,
    368, 371, 373
    and British Government 193, 245, 308,
        318, 320, 322, 327
    national feeling and aspirations of 72,
        77, 79, 80, 82, 314–17, 323, 338, 371
    and Zionists 71, 72, 74–85, 88, 239,
        315–20
Armenia and Armenians 78, 83, 90, 100,
    103, 126, 209–10, 314–15, 350
Asquith, H. H. 95, 98, 204, 206, 208, 209,
    233, 282, 283
Austria-Hungary 10, 16, 35, 36, 104, 125,
    135, 146, 362

Balfour, Arthur J. 98, 177, 209, 214–17,
    219–20, 222, 233, 235–6, 244, 252,
    262, 267, 269, 272, 274, 283–4, 287–
    9, 291–3, 301–2, 308, 312, 321–3,
    327–8, 330, 341, 351, 367, 369–71
Balfour Declaration 280–93, 297–9, 307–
    9, 312–14, 318, 322, 327, 329, 338–9,
    341–2, 349–50, 365–73
Balkans 82, 125, 207
Baltic lands and states 109, 358
Bark, P. L. 111
Basch, Victor 183
Basel Programme 31, 372
Basra 101
Beiliss case 40
Beirut 5, 22, 94, 101, 212
Bell, Gertrude 282
Benedict XV, Pope 192, 246–7, 249
Ben-Gurion, David 156
Bentwich, Herbert 178, 237
Berlin, Congress and Treaty of 105, 107,
    173
Berlin as centre of Zionist activity 20, 27,
    56–7, 69, 72–3, 82, 84, 120, 125–6,
    136, 152, 158, 164, 265, 287, 303–4,
    333, 310
Berthelot, P. 328
Bertie, Lord 192–3, 203, 223, 244–5

Bialystok, pogrom in 106
Birzheviya Vedomosti 142
Board of Deputies of British Jews 107, 175, 279, 286, 290
Bodenheimer, Max I. 130, 333, 335
Böhm, Adolf 11
Bolsheviks 140, 297, 310
Boselli, Paolo 247
Bourgeois, Léon 328
Brandeis, Louis D. 67, 131, 164, 219, 251–2, 261, 264, 268, 285, 300, 311, 321, 335
Briand, A. 192, 205
Brindisi 147
British Palestine Committee 242 n.
Brutzkus, Julius 258
Buchanan, Sir George 192, 198, 220
Bund 41, 46, 261
Bunsen Committee, de 98–102, 209, _map_ 1

Cairo 74, 79, 250, 315, 318, 323, 344
Cambon, Jules 255, 284
Cambon, Paul 244
Cecil, Lord Robert 186, 189–90, 207, 222, 235, 251–3, 262, 264, 282–3
Central Powers 89, 115, 135–6
Chamberlain, Austen 207
Chamberlain, Joseph 238
Christianity, Christians 37, 74, 79, 80–2, 194, 299, 330
  see also Vatican
Churchill, Winston 208
Clayton, General G. 314–316, 318, 321
Clemenceau, Georges 216, 325–7, 341, 343, 350, 357
Cohen, L. L. 290–1
Cologne offices _see_ Zionist movement
Colonial Office 369
Committee for the Eastern Jews 130
Committee for French propaganda among Jews in neutral countries 183
Committee of Imperial Defence 98
Committee on the Terms of Peace 207, 212
Committee of Union and Progress _see_ Turkey: regime and politics
Congress of Zionists _see_ Zionist movement
Conjoint Foreign Committee (CFC) 107–9, 172–82, 183–5, 188, 225–6, 265, 272–80
  see also Wolf

Consistoire _see_ France: Jewry and Jewish organizations in
Constantinople _see_ Turkey
Copenhagen offices and meetings _see_ Zionist movement
Cossacks 110, 111, 359 n.
Council of Ten _see_ Allied Powers: major conferences
Cowen, Joseph 155–6, 178, 237, 336
Cracow 371
Crewe, Marchioness of 161
Crewe, Marquess of 171, 187, 189, 192
Curzon, Lord 207, 212–14, 285–6, 289, 291–2, 300, 302, 368
Czechoslovakia 358

Daily Graphic 108
Daily News 176
Daily Telegraph 28
Damascus 74, 79, 94, 319, 323
Dardanelles 100, 143
  Zion Mule Corps at 146–8
Deedes, Henry Wyndham 321
Deganiya 139
Delcassé, Théophile 148
Democratic Party (US) 116, 245
Derby, Lord 231
Diaspora _see_ Jewish people
Disraeli, Benjamin 95
Djemal Pasha 125, 154, 287
Dreyfus Affair 231, 340, 346
Duma, Russian 39, 110, 142

EAC (Engeres Aktions-Comité) _see_ Zionist movement
East Africa ('Uganda') project 5, 8, 21, 150
Easter Island 207
Edinburgh Review 276
Egypt, 94, 139, 143, 147, 149, 189, 201, 344
El-Arish 216, 249
English language 312, 354
Enver Pasha 100
Erez-Israel/Palestine 5–7, 10, 12–16, 20, 22, 24, 27, 30–3, 43, 46–7, 60, 85, 154, 157, 174, 178, 181, 226, 242–4, 249, 256, 291–2, 297, 307–12, 320, 336, 365, 374–5
  and Allied policy 85, 92, 101, 136, 145, 202, 210–15, 222–3, 231–9, 259, 308, 313, 317, 324–7, 329–31, 339–72

campaign in 210, 213, 227, 231, 250, 263, 266

immigration to and Zionist enterprise in 57, 61–4, 68, 71, 75–9, 85, 120, 130, 134–5, 151, 160, 281–5, 305–6, 357

Turks, Arabs, and Jews, relations between, in 75–85

see also Allenby; Allied Powers; Anglo-French Agreement; Arabs; de Bunsen Committee; League of Nations; *yishuv*

European Jewry *see* Jewish people

European Parliaments, appeal to 49

Feisal, Emir 318–19, 323, 339, 351

Filastin 73

Finland 106

Fischer, Jean 336

Fisher, Lord 95

Foreign Office, British 49, 172, 181, 208, 211, 219, 249, 253, 267, 273, 313, 348

and Jewish Legion 155, 231

and Jewish questions 105–6, 108, 167, 183, 186, 271, 283

and Palestine question 187–8, 222–3, 225, 268, 275, 280, 288, 298, 300, 323, 369–71

Fortnightly Review 108, 276

France 37, 89, 96, 114, 146, 182–3, 208, 244, 254, 256, 370

aspirations and policy in the Near East 92, 93, 94, 96, 100, 136, 184, 187–8, 192, 193–7, 211, 212, 223, 239, 240, 249, 318, 326–7, 339, 350–7, 367

attitudes to Jews 102–3, 187–93, 340–50, 357

Foreign Ministry 194–5, 205, 221, 244–5, 255, 273, 340–5, 347–50, 352, 356, 367

Jewry and Jewish organizations in 97, 112, 115, 118, 123, 185–6, 195, 288, 299, 340, 346–7, 349, 352, 354

and Zionists 141, 148–9, 195, 241–4, 253–5, 288–9, 339–45, 361

Frankfurter, Felix 264, 266, 267, 311, 336

Freemasons 104

French language 317

French Revolution 354

Fresco, David 24

Friedemann, Adolf 11

GAC (Grosses Aktions-Comité) *see* Zionist movement

Galatz 371

Galicia 11, 135, 360–1

Galilee 61, 66, 69, 202, 305

Gallipoli *see* Dardanelles

Gapon, Father 104

Gasparri, Cardinal Pietro 247–8

see also Vatican

Gaster, Moses 178, 224, 227, 237, 238, 277, 307

Gaza 250, 263

see also Erez-Israel/Palestine: campaign in

Gegenwartsarbeit 10

George V, King 312, 366

Georges-Picot, François *see* Picot

Germany 18, 37, 94, 114–15, 127, 213, 245, 265, 325–6, 333, 342, 358

and Jews 102, 103, 113, 116, 118, 123, 125, 127–8, 136, 192, 264, 310, 354, 361

and Zionists 51, 57, 124, 125–6, 131 n., 149, 196, 231, 269, 287–9, 298, 333

Gibraltar 263–4, 266

Goldberg, Boris 133, 259, 310

Gollancz, Israel 278

Goremykin, I. L. 49

Gout, Jean 196, 203, 255, 348, 351

Graham, Sir Ronald 222, 245, 259, 260, 261, 265, 268, 279, 288, 299, 369

Great Britain:

approaches to and policy on Jewish questions 102–7, 113–19, 169–75, 280–93, 316–17, 368–9

and Zionists 232–42, 250–3, 259–70, 286–93, 297–302, 327–31, 364–72

see also Allied Powers: Anglo-French Agreement; Balfour; Balfour Declaration; de Bunsen Committee; Erez-Israel/Palestine: and Allied policy, and campaign in; Foreign Office; Grey; Jabotinsky; Jewish Legion; Samuel; War Cabinet; Weizmann; Wolf

Greece, Greeks 103, 222

Greenberg, Leopold 83, 120, 155

Grey, Sir Edward 92–3, 95, 106, 115, 171, 187, 189, 192, 193, 198, 206, 273, 341

Grossman, Meir 40 n., 137, 141–2, 144, 150–3, 229, 259, 304

Gruenbaum, Yizhak 257

Gruzenberg, Oskar 40 n.

Haas, Jacob de 264, 336
Hague, The 9, 52
Haifa 101, 201, 202, 211, 243
Hakham Bashi 24, 73
Haldane, Lord 95
Hall, Captain W. R. 202
Hamadan 105
Hamburg 26, 53, 54, 265
Hankey, Sir Maurice 210, 286, 289
Hantke, Arthur 57, 124, 125, 130, 133, 149, 165, 191, 303, 304, 307, 333, 334, 335
Ha-ʿOlam 44, 85
Hardinge, Lord 205, 299
Hauran 212
Hebrew language 11, 15, 28, 44, 48, 59, 65, 66, 81, 97, 137, 143, 184, 305, 317, 352, 354
Hebron 22, 65
Hedjaz 221, 319, 351
He-Haver 142
Helsingfors conference and Programme 10, 46, 47, 51, 53, 142, 257, 258
Henriques, H. S. Q. 178
Hertz, Chief Rabbi Joseph 278, 282, 286, 289
Hervé, Gustave 148
Herzl, Theodor and his school 4–6, 8–10, 12, 17–19, 21, 22, 23, 28, 29, 32–4, 43, 45–8, 50, 54–6, 58, 60, 67, 108, 120–2, 124, 144, 146, 151, 155, 156, 157, 159, 164, 165, 195, 224, 235, 238, 247, 264, 266, 290, 309, 333, 335, 353, 359, 361, 364–5, 372–3, 375
Hibbat Zion 8, 58, 62, 68, 224, 361
Hilmi Pasha 24, 77–8
Hindenburg Line 324
Holy Land 30, 62
    see also Erez-Israel/Palestine
House, Colonel E. M. 285, 287, 288, 328
Hungary 36, 37
Huysmans, Camille 328

ICA (Jewish Colonization Association) 17, 25, 31, 64
Idelson, Avraham 308
India 197
Iraq 80
Isaacs, Rufus *see* Reading, Lord
Islam 6, 7, 74
Israel 101, 371

    see also Erez-Israel/Palestine
ITO (Jewish Territorial Organization) 8, 25
Italy 82, 83, 84, 89, 92, 103, 141, 146, 147, 192, 222, 244, 246–7, 253, 289, 338–9, 352
Izzet Bey 19

Jabotinsky, Vladimir (Ze'ev) 25, 55, 120, 127, 137, 142–4, 147–53, 156, 160–2, 165, 191, 223, 228–32, 250–1, 259, 271, 304, 311, 336, 365 n.
Jaffa 22, 65, 72, 73, 82, 315, 318
Japan 339
Jerusalem 5, 22, 65, 66, 69, 74–8, 96, 126, 143, 159, 318, 321, 323, 363
    and Allied Powers 201, 202, 211, 290, 313, 315, 341
Jewish Agency for Palestine 314
Jewish Board of Guardians 290
Jewish Chronicle 134, 155
Jewish Colonial Trust 20, 22
    see also Anglo-Palestine Company
Jewish Legion 133, 140, 143, 146–50, 152–3, 155–6, 161, 228–33, 250, 259, 272, 280–1, 344
    see also Zion Mule Corps
Jewish National Fund 43, 64, 130
Jewish People, condition of 3–4, 24–5, 35–43, 48–9, 61–2, 105–7, 109–114, 122–9, 173–5, 273–4, 310, 358–64
Jewish World 108
Jordan 101
Judea 61, 69, 305
Judenzählung, German 123 n.
Jusserand, Jean Jules 115–18

Kadet Party 40
Kann, Jacobus H. 22, 26, 29, 55, 135, 165, 336
Katzenelsohn, Nissan 50, 57
Katznelson, Berl 66–7
Kerensky, A. F. 140
Kiev 106, 310
King–Crane Commission 368
Kitchener, Lord 95, 100, 148
Klee, Alfred 148
Krivoshein, A. V. 110
Kuban 141
Kühlmann, Richard 287
Kuhn, Loeb and Company 117
Kurds 83

Ladino 15, 24
Land Oberost 127
Lansdowne, Lord 238
Lansing, Robert 262, 264, 351, 355
Latvia 127
Lawrence, T. E. 83, 351
League of the Friends of Zionism (Paris) 349
League of Nations 325, 353, 368, 373
  Mandate for Palestine 371, 373–4 and n.
Legion *see* Jewish Legion
Leontes (Litani) 212
Lévi, Sylvain 313, 345–9, 352, 354–6
Levi-Bianchini, Angelo 313
Levin, Shmarya(hu) 21, 57, 59, 131, 156, 164–5, 336
Levontin, Zalman D. 22
Liberalism, British 49, 107, 232
Lichtheim, Richard 68, 126
Lithuania 61, 127
Lloyd George, David 93, 95, 98, 192
  208–11, 213, 215, 217, 222, 227, 230, 232–5, 244–5, 249, 282, 300, 320, 324–7, 350, 369
Lodz 53
London 84, 91, 132, 334, 360, 363, 366
  Zionist Conference in 332, 335–8, 357
Lowther, Sir Gerard 104 n.

Ma'an, meeting at 318
Macaulay, T. B. 94
Maccabi 344
'McMahon Letters' 204 n.
Magnus, Sir Philip 290–1
Makarov, A. A. 51–2
Maklakov, Vassily 40
Malcolm, James Aratoon 234
Manchester 29, 159
Manchester Guardian 176, 232
Mandate for Palestine *see* League of Nations
Marshall, Louis 342
Masaryk, Thomas 328
Mecca 323
Mediterranean Sea in Allied strategy 101, 195, 249
Mendelssohn, Moses 78
Mesopotamia 77–8, 201, 212, 368
Milner, Lord 215, 231, 234, 277, 280, 283, 285, 286, 293, 328, 351
Minsk 47, 51, 310
Mizraḥi 56, 57, 336

Money, General Arthur 316–17
Montagu, Edwin 96–8, 102, 171, 187, 190, 281–3, 285–6, 289, 291–2
Montefiore, Claude G. 108, 116, 177 n., 178, 191, 276–7, 282, 286, 290–1
Morgan, J. P., & Company 116, 117
Morgenthau, Henry 126, 262–7, 342
Morocco 96
Moscow 15, 23, 310
Mosul 328
Motzkin, Leo 12–13, 20–1, 68, 112, 132–3, 139, 165, 336
Mufti of Jerusalem 369
Munitions, Ministry of 158
Muslims 70–1, 75–6, 79, 80, 81, 82, 94, 107, 330, 342

Nazim, Dr 16
Near East, plans for disposition of *see* Allied Powers
Negev 202
Netherlands, The 132
New York City 115–16, 265, 357, 371
Nicolson, Sir Arthur 49, 199, 204–5
Nicolson, Harold 328, 371
Nissenboim, Rabbi Y. 127 and n.
Nordau, Max 9–10, 13, 15–18, 22, 27, 29–34, 56, 58, 78, 120, 129 n., 130, 159, 195, 333, 335
Nubar Pasha 328

Odessa 38, 62, 127, 298, 299
OETA 316–17
Oliphant, Lancelot 172, 205, 272
Orlando, V. E. 350
Ormsby-Gore, W. G. 222, 231, 265, 312, 321, 351, 370
Ottoman Empire *see* Turkey

Pacelli, Mgr. Eugenio 246–8
Pale of Settlement 39, 46, 106, 110–111
  see also Jewish People
Paléologue, George Maurice 114–15, 197
Palestine *see* Erez-Israel/Palestine
Palmyra 101
Paris, especially Zionist activity in 84, 91, 112, 132, 148, 265, 275, 340, 356–7, 360
Pasmanik, Daniel 11
Peace Conference at Paris *see* Allied Powers
Persian Gulf 100, 201

Pershing, General 267
Petrograd 114, 116, 172, 304–5, 310, 312
  Zionist Conference in 246, 253, 256–9
Pichon, Stéphen 328, 341, 351, 354
Picot, François Georges 198–9, 201–6,
  211–13, 219, 240–3, 246, 249, 253,
  255, 323
  see also Anglo-French Agreement
Plehve, V. K. 47, 308
Po 'alei Zion 51, 336
Poland, Poles 6, 11, 35, 61, 127–8, 146,
  358–61, 363, 370
  see also Jewish People
Political Committee, London 312, 319
Political Intelligence Department 260
Primrose, Neil 116
Proskurov, pogrom in 359 n.
Protocols of the Elders of Zion 369 n.
Provisional Committee for General Zion-
  ist Affairs 131, 177
  see also United States: Zionists in

Razsvet 44
Reading, Lord (Rufus Isaacs) 171, 186,
  190, 192, 286 n.
Ribot, Alexandre 244, 255
Romania 6, 35, 37, 43, 105–6, 107, 180,
  273 n., 358, 360, 361
  see also Jewish People
Roosevelt, Theodore 216
Rosenbaum, Shimshon 21
Rosov, Israel 25, 133, 310, 336
Rothschild, Lord 116, 176, 216, 237, 269,
  278, 280, 286, 289
Rothschild, Baron Edmond de 64, 192,
  205, 225–6, 243, 328, 341, 348, 352,
  354, 370
Rothschild, James de 225, 237, 239
Rothschild family 108, 111, 116, 191, 259
Royal Commission on Alien Immigration
  353
Royal Fusiliers 229
  see also Jewish Legion
Royal Society 159
Rukhlov, S. V. 111
Ruppin, Arthur 21, 67–73, 82, 120, 126,
  154, 314
Russia and Russian autocracy 10–11, 23,
  25, 33, 35–9, 41–3, 49–50, 67, 75, 83,
  89, 92, 100, 107–16, 124, 126–8, 130,
  136, 146, 180, 185, 208, 244, 274,
  290, 307, 360–2

  and Zionists 46–54, 256
  see also Jewish people
Russian language 44, 137
Russkiya Vedomosti 143
Russo-Japanese War 117 n., 140
Rutenberg, Pinhas 137, 139–141, 147,
  148, 160

Sabaheddin, Prince 16
Sacher, Harry 175–8, 188, 237, 307
Safed 22, 65
St Jean de Maurienne conference 255
St Petersburg 15, 23, 47, 49, 140
  see also Petrograd
Salonika 15, 26, 75
Samaria 305
Samuel, Herbert 92–8, 148, 171, 177, 189,
  191–2, 203, 224, 228–9, 232–3, 237,
  239–40, 252, 281, 283, 286, 289, 331,
  347
Samuel, Stuart 286, 290
San Remo conference 326, 367
Sazonov, S. D. 111, 192
Schiff, Jacob 115, 117, 190, 342
Scholem, Gershom 123 n.
Scott, C. P. 155, 214, 232–5, 250, 252
Second *'Aliya* 67, 139
Sèvres, Treaty of 325, 367
Shazar, Zalman 66–7
Shcherbatov, Prince N. B. 110
Sheinkin, Menahem 11
Shereef of Mecca 202
  see also Feisal, Emir
Simon, Julius 336
Sinai 210
Smuts, General Jan 207
Sokolov, Nahum 21, 22, 25, 28, 29, 34, 57,
  68, 80–1, 83, 120, 131, 148, 165, 178,
  189, 223–7, 237, 240–62, 268, 275–7,
  284, 286, 290, 304–8, 311–12, 320,
  328–41, 349–56, 360–1, 363
Sonnino, Baron G. S. 247, 351
Spire, André 348–9, 351, 353–5
Spring Rice, Cecil 115–16, 185, 206, 219,
  264
Stamm, Captain Herz 138 n.
Stand, Adolf 11, 28
Stanley, Venetia 95
State Department, United States 266,
  313
Steed, Henry Wickham 104, 279
Stolypin, P. A. 38–9, 41–2, 48–50, 308
Swaythling, Lord 278, 282

Sykes, Sir Mark 98, 104, 161, 198–9, 202–6, 211–14, 217, 219–24, 227–8, 231, 234–5, 237–51, 260, 269, 281, 292, 300, 302, 304, 324–5, 318, 320, 340, 371
Sykes–Picot Agreement *see* Anglo-French Agreement
Syria 19, 78, 79, 80, 83, 93, 94, 100, 194, 201, 250, 253, 319, 320, 343, 351, 357, 367, 368
Syrkin, Nachman 13, 120

Tahsin Bey 18
Tardieu, André 341, 351, 356–7
Tarschis, Moritz 131 n.
Tchlenov, Yehiel 25, 28, 52, 130–1, 133, 148–9, 165, 178, 191, 226, 251, 257–9, 303, 305–8, 311, 336
Thon, Ya 'akov 314
Tiberias 65
Tiempo, El 24
Times, The 116, 155, 276–9
Tolkowsky, Shemu'el 351, 356
Toynbee, Arnold, J. 328
Transjordania 305
Transylvania 351
Tribune, Di 151–3
Tripoli 83
Trumpeldor, Yosef 137–9, 141–3, 146
Turkey:
    and the Powers 82–5, 89–92, 98–102, 143, 178, 199–214, 262–3, 266–7, 325, 343, 367
    regime and politics 6–8, 13, 15–16, 23, 63, 70–82, 104, 125, 136, 145–6
    and the Zionists 6–8, 13–14, 16–20, 23–34, 54, 56, 59, 75–85, 126, 154, 158, 162, 250, 298, 374–5
    see also 'Abd al-Hamid; Allied Powers; Anglo-French Agreement; Arabs; Erez-Israel/Palestine; Jewish people; Syria

Ukraine 61, 139, 142, 358–9
United States:
    Government and opinion 18, 112–19, 182–6, 218–19, 262–67, 284–5, 313, 338–9, 342, 367–8; *see also* House; Lansing; Morgenthau; Wilson
    Zionists in 132, 261, 264, 311, 328, 334; *see also* Brandeis; Frankfurter; de Haas; Provisional Committee for General Zionist Affairs

Ussishkin, Menahem 14, 21–2, 25, 27–8, 68, 78, 120, 133, 135, 148–9, 153, 257, 259, 310, 336, 338, 340, 352–3

Vámbéry, Arminius 18
Vatican 192, 244, 246–9, 289, 301
Versailles, Treaty of 367
Vilna 15, 23, 27–8, 44, 48, 50, 51, 53
    see also Zionist movement: in Russia

War Cabinet and Cabinet Office 209, 211, 231, 244, 268, 280–2, 284–93, 340
War Office 148, 155, 231, 371
Warburg, Otto 29, 54, 55, 58–9, 68, 70, 116, 120, 126, 131–3, 137, 148, 165, 191, 303–4, 307, 314, 333–5
Warsaw *see* Jewish People
Washington 115–16, 311, 335
    see also Morgenthau; State Department; Wilson
Weil, Colonel 267
Weizmann, Chaim:
    and anti-Zionists 175–8, 188, 225–6, 277–8
    and Arabs 315–20
    and British 189, 192, 232–5, 237–41, 250–3, 261–8, 286–7, 290, 313–23, 365–6
    career, character, and purposes 156–66, 223–7, 233–4, 266 and n., 333 n., 353, 360–1, 363–6
    at Peace Conference 351–3, 355–7
    and Zionists 27–9, 164–6, 304–7, 311–12, 332–8
Wilson, President Woodrow 218–19, 262, 281, 285, 287–9, 300, 324–5, 328, 338–9, 342
    see also House; Lansing
Wiseman, Sir William 288
Wolf, Lucien 108–9, 118, 172–6, 179, 181, 183–90, 204–5, 225–8, 236, 259–61, 271, 274–6, 279, 281–2
Wolffsohn, David 15, 17–19, 20, 22–9, 34, 50–2, 54–8, 68
Woolf, Virginia 103

Yahuda, A. S. 266 and n.
Yanushkevich, General 110–11
Yiddish 44, 137, 154, 361
yishuv 61–7, 75–85, 125–6, 132, 134–6, 145, 147, 151, 154, 160

Young Turks *see* Turkey: regime and politics

Zangwill, Israel 8, 25, 67, 97, 120, 150, 155, 159, 224
Zion Mule Corps 146–7, 149, 229
  see also Jewish Legion
Zionism and the Jewish Future 276
Zionist Commission 310–20, 339, 345, 347, 366
Zionist Conference *see* London: Zionist conference in
Zionist movement and organization:
  Actions Committee (EAC and GAC) and Central Office 13, 15, 21–9, 49, 55–9, 72, 78, 89–90, 120–4, 129–36, 151–6, 164–5, 177–9, 196, 227, 237, 251, 257, 303–4; 'activist' opposition to 136–56; Copenhagen meetings and liaison office 129–36, 148–50, 152–3, 303–4, 310–12, 333–6, 338–60
  aims and major tendencies: before

Great War 4–6, 8–9, 13, 17–18, 20–5, 26–8, 33–4, 43–8, 50–4, 57–8, 63–4, 78–9, 84–5; in wartime 120–9; after 1917: 303–4, 333–5, 360–4, 369, 372–6; 'cultural' 14, 33–4, 59–61, 176 (*see also* Ahad Ha- 'Am); 'political' 8–13, 372–4 (*see also* Herzl); 'practical' 10–13, 23, 85 (*see also* Ruppin; Warburg)
  Charter for 12, 27, 32, 85, 306, 311, 372
  Congresses: First 31; Fourth 9 n.; Seventh 17; Eighth 9–13; Ninth 26–34; Tenth 54–61; Eleventh 69–70, 72, 176
  in Germany 57, 84, 123–4, 131–5, 158
  in Great Britain 155, 224–6, 306, 312
  in Russia 25–8, 43–54, 57, 133, 253, 256–60, 304–11, 334–6, 354, (*see also* Petrograd; Vilna)
  see also London: Zionist Conference in; Zionist Commission; *under* France; Germany; Great Britain; Russia; Turkey

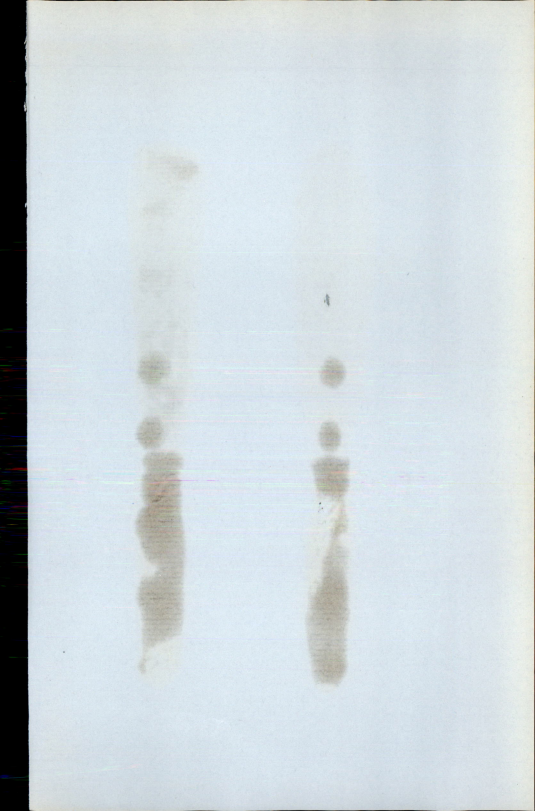